Black Business in the New South

BLACKS IN THE NEW WORLD
August Meier, Series Editor

WALTER B. WEARE

Black Business in the New South

A SOCIAL HISTORY OF THE NORTH CAROLINA MUTUAL LIFE INSURANCE COMPANY

University of Illinois Press
Urbana Chicago London

© 1973 by The Board of Trustees of the University of Illinois
Manufactured in the United States of America
Library of Congress Catalog Card No. 72–92690
ISBN 0–252–00285–7

For Juanita and my sister Jean

Preface

While casting about for a dissertation topic at the University of North Carolina, I once made a long list of neglected subjects in U.S. history which I thought held some promise for research. Far down the list in order of preference was the North Carolina Mutual Life Insurance Company, a topic that would not have appeared on my list at all had it not been a part of the local geography. I knew of course that the North Carolina Mutual, founded at Durham in 1898, was the largest and one of the oldest black businesses in the United States, yet it did not impress me at first as a favorable topic. I could not dissociate the institution from business history, an alien field for me; moreover, I presumed that a standard business narrative of a relatively small life insurance company would be of small importance. But as my list narrowed, my view of the North Carolina Mutual expanded. Each time I saw its new office building guarding the horizon of Durham and each time I contemplated the historical significance of the firm, I increasingly realized that I was looking at an important piece of the New South, that I was dealing with an important black institution, and that here perhaps was a window to Afro-American history.

I have tried to remain faithful to this conceptual outlook, although freely admitting that business history must necessarily form the chronological core of the study, and that greater attention to business history, more particularly to entrepreneurial history, might have enriched my insights. Nonetheless, the disclaimer stands: this study is less a business history than it is a social and intellectual history of a black business, the thesis being that the significance of the enterprise rests in its ethnic identity rather than in its economic identity, and that its history speaks less to the financial progress of a single black business than to the ideology of racial progress inherent to all black institutions. The history of the Company further speaks to the long-standing encounter between cultures, to the Afro-American search for a *modus vivendi* with a hostile environment, to Afro-American religion, politics, community organization, and social stratification, to the meaning of the New South, to the absorbing power of the American business ethos, and to the shame of American race relations. One other disclaimer: I do not pretend that this is a study of the black community of Durham. Sociologists have done that at least twice and it needs to be done again. One hopes, however, that through the eyes of a single institution, even with a distorted one-dimensional view, there can emerge useful insights on the larger black community that otherwise might not appear. The test of this assertion depends on the findings of future institutional studies and, of course, their ultimate synthesis.

The assumption throughout is that there is an inseparable relationship between ideas and institutions, and that the history of the North Carolina Mutual cannot be separated from the history of other Afro-American institutions, particularly the church and the mutual benefit society. Nor can the origins of the firm be seen apart from an aggressive Negro business movement born out of the deteriorating race relations of the New South, which for many black leaders stimulated a flight from politics and protest into religion, education, and business. Indeed, apart from Tuskegee Institute itself, the North Carolina Mutual stands as the most conspicuous institutional legacy of the ideas of racial self-help and economic solidarity—ascendant elements in Afro-American thought exalted by Booker T. Washington at the turn of the century when the Company was founded.

Quite by accident, my conception of the study as social history coincided with the kind of sources available to me. Key records which business historians might have found indispensable —minutes of meetings of the board of directors and its executive committee, for example—were for the most part unavailable. What was available, aside from vital sources of oral history and a vast array of fugitive materials, were tens of thousands of items in the personal papers of two of the Company's presidents, Charles Clinton Spaulding and William Jesse Kennedy, Jr., whose respective administrations ran from 1923 to 1952 and 1952 to 1958, and whose overall association with the Company dates from 1900 to the present. After several weeks of rummaging and crude efforts at cataloging, I perceived that although the bulk of these unexplored collections contained perfunctory business correspondence, a surprising volume of material—letters from the humblest sharecropper, from W E. B. Du Bois, or from Franklin D. Roosevelt—dealt with a rich variety of issues far removed from the life insurance industry. Fortunately the files contain carbon copies of out-going correspondence as well, but such good fortune is offset by an absence of papers from the period before 1923. Fire and ill-fated housecleaning account for this tragic loss.

It was ex-President W. J. Kennedy, Jr., an octogenarian of extraordinary mental and physical fitness, who led me to a storage area where, amidst a mountain of pasteboard boxes, we sorted out the extant papers and very likely cheated the incinerator. It is to the kind cooperation of Mr. Kennedy, among other officers and the staff of the North Carolina Mutual, that my research owes its existence. Mr. Kennedy deserves the gratitude of all those who value the past for his preservation of the Company's history through his own research, writing, and archival efforts. Moreover, for events of the past seventy years he stands as an invaluable primary source in his own right—a prominent reminder of the urgent need to preserve oral history. Another ex-president of the North Carolina Mutual, Asa T. Spaulding, was more than helpful, as was his successor, Joseph W. Goodloe. I am especially grateful to Murray J. Marvin, vice-president–

director of corporate planning and public relations, and to Mrs. Viola G. Turner, retired treasurer and member of the board of directors, both of whom graciously eased my official entry to the Company records and gave me support and guidance thereafter.

One hopes that serving as mentor supplied its own reward, for certainly there is no way to thank adequately George Brown Tindall, who gave himself to that task and who has nurtured my progress since graduate school. Professors Joel Williamson, Elisha P. Douglass, Isaac Copeland, and Blyden T. Jackson gave close and thoughtful readings to the dissertation. A post-doctoral fellowship from the National Endowment for the Humanities and a supplementary stipend from the University of Wisconsin-Milwaukee enabled me to spend an academic year writing and revising at Stanford University, where it was my good fortune to encounter the intellect of St. Clair Drake. Thomas P. Govan kindly consented to read most of the revised manuscript; unfortunately, my talents do not always measure up to the demands of his penetrating criticism. The same could be said for John H. Wheeler, a black statesman of Durham and the New South, whose vast knowledge and judicious sense of history corrected at least some of my errors of fact and interpretation. From start to finish, August Meier has been a central figure in sustaining my work. The counsel, criticism, and encouragement he has given me is but a small example of what he has given to countless young scholars and to the field of Afro-American history in general. Hazel Kay and Kathryn Poplawski typed the final draft of the manuscript with care and concern. To these persons and to all those whose assistance goes unnoticed here, I express my gratitude. Finally, I owe the most to Juanita Rae Weare, who provided bountiful love and I am afraid all too much thankless labor.

Contents

Tables

Black Business in the New South

1

The
Evolution
of Uplift

For more than a week during the harvest season of
1910 Booker Taliaferro Washington toured the cities and towns
of North Carolina, paying tribute to the industrial progress of his
race. In Greensboro a crowd of eight thousand listened to the
"wizard" from Tuskegee. Churches and halls strained to hold
his audiences. Nearly everywhere tobacco warehouses were
pressed into service as blacks and whites competed to hear the
South's most popular figure. The black children of Reidsville
scattered roses in his path while the band played "Hail to the
Chief." And at the Negro college in Salisbury he shared the
speaker's rostrum with the vice-president of the United States,
James Schoolcraft Sherman. Yet Washington's hosts held out
the promise of a climax. "Wait until you get to Durham, Dr.
Washington. Wait until you get to Durham," they chanted.[1]

The attraction in Durham was the North Carolina Mutual and
Provident Association, a burgeoning black enterprise which
seemed to vindicate the essence of Washington's self-help philosophy. Founded only a dozen years earlier, the Association
could already boast of being the "World's Largest Negro Life
Insurance Company," and in addition it could lay claim to hav-

---

1. Undated typescript report of the North Carolina tour, in the Booker T.
Washington Papers, Manuscript Division, Library of Congress; Booker T. Wash-
ington, "Durham, North Carolina: A City of Negro Enterprise," *Independent,*
LXX (March 30, 1911), 642–650; clippings, *Boston Transcript,* December 12;
Indianapolis Star, October 31, 1910, Washington Papers.

ing spawned a multitude of lesser black businesses, including a
bank and a cotton mill. This nascent Negro economy so impressed Washington that he ordered the Tuskegee researcher
Monroe Work to study the Durham business community. Washington published the findings in an article for a popular white
periodical which praised Durham as "The City of Negro
Enterprise."[2]

In the years to follow, Durham and the North Carolina Mutual
garnered fame from all sides. In 1912 William Edward Burghardt Du Bois, by this time strongly attracted to socialism, visited Durham and, like Washington, came away singing its
praises, although emphasizing its cooperation over its capitalism.[3] The North Carolina Mutual formed the hub of what the
Negro press extolled as a veritable financial empire, as the "Capital of the Black Middle Class," "The Magic City," "The Black
Wall Street of America." The Negro newspaper of Atlanta,
speaking for a proud economic elite that persistently challenged
Durham's leadership, conceded that "Atlanta yielded only to
Durham in economic and industrial progress." The Negroes
of Durham, the editor wrote, "are an example for the race. . . .
There is more grace, grit, and greenback among the Negroes in
Durham and more harmony between the races than in any city
in America."[4] And in Richmond, Virginia, another pioneering
city in Negro life insurance, a Negro weekly urged its bourgeois
readers to visit Durham rather than tour Europe. With all the
style of a circus barker, the writer admonished Virginia's black
citizens:

> Go to Durham . . . you need the inspiration. Go to Durham and
> see the industrious Negro at his best. Go to Durham and see the

2. Washington, "Durham: A City of Negro Enterprise," pp. 642–650; C. C.
Spaulding to Booker T. Washington, November 18, 1910, Washington Papers.
In 1919 the name of the Association was changed to the North Carolina Mutual
Life Insurance Company (hereafter generally referred to as the North Carolina
Mutual or the Mutual). The Company continues to be the largest black business
in the United States, with assets totaling nearly $123,000,000 and insurance in
force in excess of $1,000,000,000 as of January 1, 1972.

3. W. E. B. Du Bois, "The Upbuilding of Black Durham," *World's Work*,
XXIII (January, 1912), 334–338.

4. *Atlanta Independent*, December 22, 1921.

cooperative spirit among Negroes at its best. Go to Durham
and see Negro business with an aggregate capital of millions.
Go to Durham and see twenty-two Negro men whose honesty
and business sagacity are making modern history. Among your
New Year's resolves, resolve to go to Durham![5]

The story of black Durham and the North Carolina Mutual
belong to the New South, to the age of Booker T. Washington
and his gospel of self-help. But the institutional roots of the
Company, like the origins of Washington's thought, belong to
an earlier age. More than a century before the famous Atlanta
Compromise in 1895 or the founding of the North Carolina Mutual in 1898, free Negro leaders organized separate ethnic aid
societies and issued a call for self-help, moral improvement, and
an elementary plan of sickness and burial insurance. The North
Carolina Mutual is a direct, although distant, descendant of
what began in 1787 under the leadership of two black Philadelphia ministers, Richard Allen and Absolom Jones, who, distressed by the squalor of their incipient ghetto and by their
recent ejection from the white Methodist Church for refusing to
sit in the designated "nigger pew," called upon Philadelphia's
African community to organize itself into "a society . . . without
regard to religious tenets . . . in order to support one another in
sickness and for the benefit of widows and fatherless children."
Thus was formed the Free African Society, in W. E. B. Du Bois's
words, "a curious sort of ethical and beneficial brotherhood"
which constituted "the first wavering step of a people toward
organized social life."[6] The Free African Society itself was short-
lived but proved to be of lasting significance for Afro-American
institutions. The African Methodist Episcopal Church, the first
autonomous Negro church in America, evolved out of the Free
African Society; opposition to the colonization of Negroes in
Africa first arose in the meetings of the Free African Society;
and black abolitionism had ties with the Free African Society.[7]

5. Clipping, *St. Luke Herald*, January 7, 1928, in John Moses Avery Scrapbook in possession of William Jesse Kennedy, Jr., Durham, N.C.
6. W. E. B. Du Bois, *The Philadelphia Negro: A Social Study* (Philadelphia:
University of Pennsylvania, 1899), pp. 19–21, 23.
7. In addition to Du Bois cited above, the origins and significance of the

For the history of Negro life insurance, the vital contribution of the Free African Society was the tradition of the mutual benefit association, which became the common denominator in the evolution of insurance societies into secular business institutions.[8] The Free African Society through its committee on correspondence urged other free Negroes to organize for mutual assistance. By the early 1800's Negro leaders in Newport, New York, Boston, and Baltimore could boast of several such mutual aid programs. The typical organizational pattern of these early societies required members to pay monthly dues, forming a pool from which widows would receive a death benefit, and, in the case of the more affluent societies, from which dependent children would receive assistance in education and vocational training. Particularly in New England, the societies worked to apprentice the sons of members into a craft; others established private schools or founded literary societies, and a few extended credit to their members.[9]

The mutual benefit society can best be described as a rudimentary instrument of social welfare that was both secular and sectarian in origin. Education and religious training usually coincided in these organizations; more often than not, ministers had a hand in the organizing and imposed moral and religious restric-

Free African Society are detailed in a number of studies, most notably Charles Harris Wesley, *Richard Allen, Apostle of Freedom* (Washington D.C.: Associated Publishers, 1935), pp. 58–68, 254; Richard Robert Wright, Jr., *The Negro in Pennsylvania: A Study in Economic History* (Philadelphia: A.M.E. Book Concern Printers, 1912), pp. 30–37; Leon F. Litwack, *North of Slavery: The Negro in the Free States, 1790–1860* (Chicago: University of Chicago Press, 1961), pp. 192–193; and William Douglass, *Annals of the First Church in the United States of America, Now Styled the African Episcopal Church of St. Thomas, Philadelphia* (Philadelphia: King and Baird, 1862), pp. 15–25, 32–47.

8. While the Free African Society was not organized for profit, it was operated in businesslike fashion and in 1790 deposited a surplus of 42 pounds to earn interest in the Bank of North America (Wesley, *Richard Allen, Apostle of Freedom*, p. 68). From the beginning, then, one can detect a dual practice of organizing for uplift and organizing for business.

9. W. E. B. Du Bois, *Economic Cooperation among Negroes*, Atlanta University Publications no. 12 (Atlanta: Atlanta University Press, 1907), p. 96; Dorothy Porter, "The Organized Educational Activities of Negro Literary Societies, 1828–1846," *Journal of Negro Education*, V (October, 1936), 556–576. Also see August Meier and Elliott Rudwick, *From Plantation to Ghetto: An Interpretive History of American Negroes* (New York: Hill and Wang, 1966), pp. 75, 80, 81, which goes well beyond the textbook treatment of these societies.

tions on the members.[10] And just as the church and the benefit society blended into one another, so there was a hazy distinction between the secret fraternal lodge and the benefit society. Secret orders concerned themselves more with recreation and recognition—scarce commodities in the free Negro community. But they often provided insurance benefits for their members, thus overlapping the mutual benefit society, which in turn occasionally copied the fraternal order by adopting ritual and regalia to attract more members.[11]

Apparently there was at least one effort to rush the evolution of Negro life insurance beyond its fraternal and beneficial stages. In 1810 business-minded blacks in Philadelphia founded the African Insurance Company. Almost a century premature, the enterprise died during incubation in 1813. However, its significance lived on as an early illustration of the entrepreneurial impulse to merge business with benevolence, a persistent dualism in the history of Afro-American business thought.[12]

These insurance societies were by no means uniquely Afro-

10. The constitution of the Free African Society, for example, outlawed any "drunkard or disorderly person" from its ranks, and the needy were ineligible for welfare benefits if their plight stemmed from "their own imprudence." See Wright, *The Negro in Pennsylvania*, pp. 31–34, for a reprint of the original constitution and the stringent moral code of the Society. For the secular-sectarian relationship, see in particular William Johnston Trent, Jr., "Development of Negro Life Insurance Enterprises" (Master's thesis, University of Pennsylvania, 1932), pp. 10–11; Abram Lincoln Harris, *The Negro as Capitalist: A Study of Banking and Business among American Negroes* (Philadelphia: American Academy of Political and Social Science, 1936), p. 20; August Meier, *Negro Thought in America, 1880–1915* (Ann Arbor: University of Michigan Press, 1963), pp. 136–137.

11. Du Bois, *Economic Cooperation*, pp. 92–96, 109, 115, 117, 119, 122, 125–127; W. E. B. Du Bois, *Some Efforts of Negroes for Their Own Social Betterment*, Atlanta University Publications no. 3 (Atlanta: Atlanta University Press, 1898), pp. 17–19; Edward Nelson Palmer, "Negro Secret Societies," *Social Forces*, XXIII (October, 1944), 207–212; Meier, *Negro Thought*, pp. 136–137; Daniel Webster Davis, *The Life and Public Services of Reverend William Washington Browne* (Richmond: Mrs. M. A. Browne Smith, 1910), p. 103. The best early examples of these secret fraternal orders were the Negro Masons and Oddfellows. The Masons were founded in 1787 as a response to rejection by the white organization; the same is true of the Oddfellows, founded in 1843. Of the two, the Oddfellows claimed more members and were more insurance-minded, beginning an official mutual benefit program in 1850. The Masons, along with a host of new fraternals, began such insurance programs after the Civil War.

12. Very little is known about this company. See Du Bois, *Economic Cooperation*, p. 98.

American in character, despite Du Bois's strenuous argument
for the African origins of all Negro American institutions.[13] Existing evidence is stronger to support the thesis that, with the
exception of African-like associations among the Gullah people
of the South Carolina sea islands, the societies in North America
began as a pragmatic response to social and economic needs.[14]
In many cases autonomous Negro societies were organized only
after black leaders were rebuffed when they sought to join existing white groups. Allen and Jones, like Washington a century later, were reacting in part to the pressure of an expanding
racism when they urged black people to withdraw strategically
from the crush of white society and to embrace self-help, racial
solidarity, and moral improvement as the solution to the problem of being black in a hostile white environment.[15] Although

13. *Ibid.*, pp. 54–55. Here on an elaborate diagram Du Bois charts the evolution of Afro-American institutions from the African Obeah worship.

14. Du Bois himself was ambivalent on the question of African survivals, and
at one point he compared Negro benevolent societies to the tradition of burial
societies among European serfs during the Middle Ages (*Efforts for Social Betterment*, p. 5). He also conceded that many of the groups were but black "imita-
tions of pernicious, white, petty insurance societies" (*Economic Cooperation*,
p. 96). Melville Jean Herskovits, who carried on the most persuasive argument
for African survivals, admitted that he could not account directly for "the deri-
vation of such organizations, but he was nonetheless convinced by the pioneering fieldwork that he and his students conducted both in the New World and
in Africa that in the case of the beneficial society he was "face to face with one
of the deep-seated drives in Negro life; drives so strong, indeed, that it is difficult if not impossible, to account for them satisfactorily except in terms of a tradition which reaches further than merely to the period of slavery" (*Myth of the
Negro Past* [New York: Harper and Brothers, 1941], pp. 162, 164). Edward
Franklin Frazier, *The Negro in the United States* (New York: Macmillan, 1949),
pp. 19, 370, doubted even an indirect tie between African and American mutual
aid societies. For the Sea Island societies see William R. Bascom, "Acculturation
among the Gullah Negroes," *American Anthropologist*, XLIII, no. 1 (1941),
43–50. The question of African survivals, considered moot by some scholars since
Herskovits, may yet yield to intensified research utilizing the concepts of comparative history and ethnology. What seems most plausible is that the question
of institutional origins will remain obscure, but an analysis of ethnic "style"
within the societies would suggest at least a subtle reinterpretation of African
institutions in a new cultural setting.

15. Allen and Jones in their preamble to the constitution of the Free African
Society viewed their organization as having a rather bourgeois, paternalistic
mission, declaring that they were motivated "from a love to the people of their
own complexion whom they beheld with sorrow, because of their irreligious and
uncivilized state." As for the spiritual quality of the Free African Society, Du
Bois agreed that it "leaned toward Quakerism" (Du Bois, *The Philadelphia
Negro*, pp. 19–20).

negative in its origins, this strategy soon took on a positive life
of its own as a mainstay of Afro-American thought. Afro-Americans, unlike other ethnic groups, have been obligated to link
their institutions, no matter how pragmatic in origin, to an overriding ideology—often utopian in tone—that proposed to solve
the "race problem" for all time. Even the middle-class Negro
business movement of the early twentieth century had a mille-
narian character.

Thus for a variety of reasons the benefit societies proliferated
among free Negroes in northern urban communities, and they
even extended into Canada, where fugitive slaves survived
through mutual assistance.[16] Records from the Society of Friends
reveal that 106 such associations existed in Philadelphia in 1849.
Many families belonged to two or more societies, with a view to
increasing their sick benefits. Premiums or dues ranged from
$.25 to $.37 per month, and benefits were from $1.50 to $3.00
per week for sickness and from $10.00 to $20.00 for death
claims.[17]

Less is known about mutual aid societies in the antebellum
South, unless the South includes Baltimore, where Du Bois found
records of at least twenty-five groups offering insurance benefits
in the period before the Civil War.[18] Despite laws in slave states
inhibiting the assembly of free Negroes, there is evidence that
the free Negro populations of Richmond, New Orleans, and
Charleston openly organized several benefit societies.[19] The old-

16. Du Bois, *Economic Cooperation*, p. 97. The most famous of these societies in Canada was the True Band, founded in 1854.
17. *Ibid.*, p. 95; also see Trent, "Development of Negro Life Insurance," p. 5.
18. Du Bois, *Economic Cooperation*, p. 92.
19. In 1815 free Negroes in Richmond organized the Burying Ground Society of the Free People of Color. See James Blackwell Browning, "The Beginning of Insurance Enterprise among Negroes," *Journal of Negro History*, XXII
(October, 1937), 429–430; Elijah Horace Fitchett, "The Traditions of the Free
Negro in Charleston, South Carolina," *Journal of Negro History*, XXV (April,
1940), 139–152; Harry J. Walker, "Negro Benevolent Societies in New Orleans"
(Manuscript available at Fisk University, 1936). The burial society may have
infiltrated the slave world as well, particularly in the Upper South, according to
William Patrick Burrell, "The Negro in Insurance," Hampton Negro Conference
no. 8 (Hampton Institute, 1904), p. 13. Or, to view it the other way around, the
more important but unverifiable point would be that burial and secret societies

est of these, the Brown Fellowship Society, was organized in 1790 by Charleston mulattoes, who limited their membership to light-skinned Negroes. In reaction to this exclusion, the darker Negroes of Charleston founded a counter group, the Free Dark Men of Color, and permitted only the darkest of persons to join. The invidious distinctions extended even to the burial ground, where the two organizations maintained segregated plots within an already segregated cemetery.[20]

As long as slavery ruled the South, Negro insurance societies could make little headway. Yet their ultimate destiny was bound up with that section, where 90 percent of the black population lived. The heyday of the mutual benefit society and the fraternal lodge waited for emancipation and a New South. After slavery these institutions, along with the Negro church, constituted virtually the only community organizations to which freedmen could turn, outside the white community.

During Reconstruction the emphasis within the Negro leadership centered more on politics, civil rights, and integration than on self-help and the development of ethnic institutions. But for the black masses the economic promises of the Radical Republicans far outweighed the political, and the "missionaries" from the North who preached the Yankee gospel of enterprise, thrift, and property reinforced the ruling American economic myth. Thus, as the political promises of Reconstruction faded and race relations retrogressed, self-help gathered momentum once again among the elite.[21] The leading Negro intellectual of the nineteenth century, Alexander Crummell, told a convention

---

permeated the slave experience, and that the associations among free Negroes were a reflection of the more basic folk movement. Certainly the prime importance of funerals to slaves suggests the possibility of formal organization. See Herskovits, *Myth of the Negro Past*, pp. 201–205.

20. Theodore Dehon Jervey, *Robert Y. Hanye and His Times* (New York: Macmillan, 1909), pp. 6, 68, 69, 434; Browning, "The Beginning of Insurance Enterprise among Negroes," pp. 423–426; Trent, "Development of Negro Life Insurance," p. 7.

21. The best analysis of this shift is in Meier, *Negro Thought*, Ch. 3, "Economics, Self-Help and Racial Solidarity," pp. 42–58. See also Harris, *The Negro as Capitalist*, pp. 46–47, and Monroe Nathan Work, "The Negro in Business and the Professions," *Annals of the American Academy of Political and Social Science*, CXL (November, 1928), 138–144.

of his colleagues as early as 1875 to forget about assimilation and to organize economically and morally, which would "settle all the problems of caste . . . though you were ten times blacker than midnight."[22] With pressing social needs and the shift once again in Afro-American thought, it was inevitable that separate black institutions would mushroom after Reconstruction. Every southern city found itself filled with a myriad of groups with enchanting names such as the Galilaean Fishermen, the Samaritans, or the Knights of I Will Rise Again. Petersburg, Virginia, alone accounted for twenty-two benefit societies in 1898, excluding numerous purely secret societies. The black residents of Warsaw, Georgia, could choose from more than a half-dozen associations in their tiny village.[23]

The function of the fraternal order and the mutual benefit society increasingly overlapped in this period when the desire for social organization rivaled economic needs. In Du Bois's estimation, "a chance for parade," along with "ambition and intrigue," were motives nearly as important as "insurance against misfortune."[24] Another black historian viewed the multitude of post–Civil War societies as "embryonic industrial insurance companies of social tendencies."[25] Railroads happily served the "social tendencies," arranging excursions at "group rates" for the members of the black friendly societies whose conventions and ceremonies offered relief to monotony and oppression.[26] Of the antebellum Negro fraternals, the Oddfellows remained the largest and enjoyed phenomenal growth, building membership from 4,000 in 1868 to 300,000 at the turn of the century. The Masons,

22. Quoted in Meier, *Negro Thought,* p. 44.
23. Du Bois, *Economic Cooperation,* pp. 94–95; Trent, "Development of Negro Life Insurance," pp. 13–14. For examples in other parts of the South, see George Brown Tindall, *South Carolina Negroes 1877–1900* (Columbia: University of South Carolina Press, 1952), p. 284; Vernon Lane Wharton, *The Negro in Mississippi, 1865–1890* (Chapel Hill: University of North Carolina Press, 1947), p. 271; Howard Washington Odum, *Social and Mental Traits of the Negro* (New York: Columbia University Press, 1910), pp. 98–148.
24. Du Bois, *Economic Cooperation,* p. 96.
25. Alrutheus Ambush Taylor, *The Negro in the Reconstruction of Virginia* (Washington: Association for the Study of Negro Life and History, 1926), p. 65.
26. *Ibid.*; Trent, "Development of Negro Life Insurance," pp. 13–14; Tindall, *South Carolina Negroes,* pp. 284–290.

while less than one-fourth the size of the Oddfellows, commanded prestige and economic strength—particularly in Mississippi, where success alongside Negrophobia inspired them to challenge "Governor Vardaman and all other devils this side of Hades" to obstruct "this kind of prosperity."[27] Along with the older orders, new societies like the Colored Knights of Pythias (organized in 1880), the Mosaic Templars of America (1882), and the Elks (1898) attracted thousands.[28] These and other groups prospered in the North as well. Du Bois in his study, *The Philadelphia Negro* (1899), found so many societies that he considered it "impractical to catalogue them."[29]

But easily the most significant step in the evolution of Negro insurance up to the formation of the North Carolina Mutual took place in Richmond, Virginia, where William Washington Browne founded the Grand United Order of the True Reformers in 1881. Browne, an ex-slave who escaped to Wisconsin during the Civil War and served in the Union Army, returned to the South during Reconstruction as a preacher and a politician. The Colored Methodist Episcopal Church sent him to Richmond in 1881, and there in the traditional pattern he combined his preaching with organizing a mutual benefit society, promising that the True Reformers would "break down crime, licentiousness, poverty, and wretchedness" and at the same time promote "happiness, peace, plenty, thrift and protection."[30] Browne was a fascinating man shrouded in an aura of mystery which doubtless added to the attractiveness of his semi-secret fraternal order. Dark-skinned, with a full white beard, a flowing black cape, and a huge flat-brimmed hat which shielded his piercing eyes, he captivated the masses and added an air of the supernatural to the order. To many he appeared as a black John Brown. He took good advantage of this image and imposed a solemn ritual along

27. Meier, *Negro Thought*, p. 137; Du Bois, *Economic Cooperation*, pp. 109–111.
28. Meier, *Negro Thought*, p. 137; Du Bois, *Economic Cooperation*, pp. 115, 117, 119, 122, 125–127.
29. Du Bois, *The Philadelphia Negro*, p. 222.
30. William Patrick Burrell, *Twenty-five Years History of the United Order of True Reformers* (Richmond: n.p., 1909), pp. 36–38.

with lavish regalia upon the members, and he added to that an annual convention which provided Richmond with its largest and most colorful annual parade.[31]

Beneath Browne's occult idealism lay a good measure of self-interest and entrepreneurial acumen. He and his lieutenants admitted that the ceremonial fanfare was a ruse simply to attract members. "Candor compels us, to acknowledge that the ritual is no part of the organization and perhaps . . . as great a good could be accomplished without it. . . ."[32] In the meantime, however, Browne's wife had launched a profitable regalia factory on the first floor of the True Reformers' three-story building; thus more than sentiment was involved in retaining the satin costumes.[33]

Browne had a boundless vision for building his business and uplifting the race—the two ideals are inseparable in assessing his motivation. By the turn of the twentieth century, with "Napoleonic financial moves,"[34] he had clearly drawn the outlines of his empire. In 1888, as an adjunct to the insurance business and a depository for its funds, he established the first all-Negro bank. In the following years he added a special children's department (The Rosebuds), a printing establishment which published a weekly newspaper, a real estate department, a cooperative department store, an undertaking business, Richmond's Negro hotel (the Reformer), an old folks' home, and a 640-acre cooperative farm which he held up as a model for the establishment of black utopian communities.[35] By the time Browne died

31. Davis, *William Washington Browne*, pp. 13, 17, 18, 20–26, 29, 35, 37, 39–40, 47, 50–60; Burrell, *True Reformers*, pp. 36–38.

32. Davis, *William Washington Browne*, p. 103.

33. *Ibid.*, p. 91; interview, Miles Mark Fisher, Richmond, Va., March 10, 1968.

34. This is the language of one of his competitors in Richmond, who saw the True Reformers under Browne as an "Octopus" in the world of Negro business. See Wendell Phillips Dabney, *Maggie Lena Walker and the Independent Order of St. Luke* (Cincinnati: Dabney Publishing Company, 1927), pp. 38–40.

35. Burrell, *True Reformers*, pp. 125, 317; Davis, *William Washington Browne*, pp. 142–147; William Taylor Thom, *The True Reformers*, U.S. Department of Labor Bulletin no. 41 (Washington: Government Printing Office, 1902), pp. 807–814; Harris, *The Negro as Capitalist*, p. 63; Trent, "Development of Negro Life Insurance," pp. 18–21; Carter Godwin Woodson, "Insurance Business among Negroes," *Journal of Negro History*, XIV (April, 1929), 210; Booker T. Washington, *The Story of the Negro* (New York: Doubleday Page and Company, 1909), II, 162–168; Howard H. Harlan, *Zion Town: A Study in Human*

in 1900, the True Reformers claimed 100,000 members and had spread their operations to eighteen states. A decade later, debilitated by his absence and victimized by the overexpansion he fostered, the True Reformers collapsed.[36]

Their legacy for the history of Negro life insurance is vastly important. In a technical sense the True Reformers marked a milestone in the development of Negro insurance enterprises in that they were the first group to take cognizance of life contingencies in their effort to set rates that were based on crude estimates of mortality.[37]

As new insurance societies arose on the heels of the True Reformers, many of them took the next step in the evolutionary pattern, dropping the fraternal and secret features and offering industrial insurance on a more scientific basis, largely copying and refining the system of the True Reformers. In many cases the link between the True Reformers and those who drew inspiration from them was even more direct. What evidence there is suggests that virtually every insurance association founded in the Upper South during the late nineteenth and early twentieth centuries can be traced to ex–True Reformer agents who organized their own societies, each aspiring to become another William Washington Browne.[38]

Indeed, this is precisely what happened in the case of the North Carolina Mutual. In 1883 the future founder of the Company, John Merrick, who had been an agent for the True Reformers, combined with other leaders in Durham to launch a new fraternal insurance society, the Royal Knights of King David.[39]

Ecology, University of Virginia Phelps-Stokes Fellowship Papers, no. 13 (Charlottesville: University of Virginia, 1935), pp. 37–38.

36. Thom, *True Reformers*, pp. 807–814; Dabney, *The Independent Order of St. Luke*, pp. 38–40; Harris, *Negro as Capitalist*, p. 73.

37. Trent, "Development of Negro Life Insurance," p. 21.

38. *Ibid.*, pp. 21, 27–29, 37–38.

39. *Ibid.*, pp. 31, 32, 34, 48; Robert McCants Andrews, *John Merrick: A Biographical Sketch* (Durham: Seeman Printery, 1920), pp. 44–46; Albon L. Holsey, "Pearson: The Brown Duke of Durham," *Opportunity*, VI (April, 1923), 116–117.

William Gaston Pearson, an outstanding Durham Negro businessman and educator who co-founded with Merrick both the Royal Knights of King David and the North Carolina Mutual, looked back from the perspective of the 1920's to assess the transition provided by the fraternals: "These societies were the trail blazers of Negro business. They charted the unknown seas. They furnished the laboratories. They were the business schools in which our leading businessmen have been trained. The Royal Knights of King David trained John Merrick. . . . It pioneered the way for the North Carolina Mutual. . . ."[40]

But for every successful transformation in the evolutionary process literally thousands of benefit societies died during the metamorphosis. In Du Bois's words, "The woods are full of the graves of these earlier companies."[41] In addition to suffering from inexperience and peculation, the small black insurance society unwittingly manufactured its own destruction. Without reliable data on Negro mortality and thus no actuarial tables, most groups simply guessed at what adequate rates should be. Moreover, they generally made no effort to control their mortality experience by selecting risks according to age or health. Inevitably the group found itself forced to assess each member an extra amount to meet the death claims. These assessments on top of the regular dues compelled many members, especially the young and the fit, to leave the society; thus the membership grew increasingly older and the death rate mounted proportionately, requiring even larger assessments, in turn causing another exodus of the fittest members, and so on, until the society collapsed.[42]

As the fraternals failed, those surviving came under scrutiny from an older middle-class elite, who saw the principle of mu-

40. Undated pamphlet published by the Durham Branch of the National Negro Business League, William Gaston Pearson Scrapbook in possession of Conrad Odelle Pearson, Durham, N.C.; also see clipping, *Raleigh Times*, January 11, 1929, in North Carolina Mutual clipping file.
41. Du Bois, *Economic Cooperation*, p. 98. This observation was not original with Du Bois; see Burrell, "The Negro in Insurance," p. 15.
42. Trent, "Development of Negro Life Insurance," p. 22; Du Bois, *Economic Cooperation*, p. 109.

tual aid being abused by black flimflam men and their ephemeral organizations.[43] These critics demanded bona fide black insurance companies, and at the very time when prominent white companies, following the lead of Prudential, were refusing to insure Negroes.[44] White firms that did solicit black policyholders were often fraudulent operations run by white adventurers who, like their black counterparts, saw the promise of a quick dollar in a captive market. One such would-be entrepreneur from Georgia wrote Booker T. Washington in 1900 promoting "The Southern Protective Brotherhood," which proposed to unite "colored men of good moral character for . . . fraternity and insurance." In an ingenuous plea for assistance he announced to Washington: "We are now addressing all prominent darkies in the various Southern States, with a view of securing agents. . . ." Washington penciled an emphatic "do not answer" across the offensive proposal.[45]

By 1898, then, the development of Afro-American institutions along with the rising need for legitimate black insurance enterprises had prepared the way for industrial insurance companies like the North Carolina Mutual, offering reliable health, accident, and life policies on a more scientific basis.

Equally important in explaining the rise of Negro insurance in the age of Booker T. Washington were powerful social and intellectual forces which centered around the American business ethos and the dynamics of race relations. Afro-American

43. Du Bois, *Economic Cooperation,* pp. 4, 96; Du Bois, *Efforts for Social Betterment,* pp. 17, 19, 21; Trent, "Development of Negro Life Insurance," pp. 11, 37–38.

44. During Reconstruction white companies insured blacks on an equal basis with whites, but following a study by the Prudential in 1881 which showed mortality rates for blacks significantly higher than those for whites, most companies reduced by one-third the benefits paid to blacks, or raised the premium rates for blacks, or refused to insure them at all. This trend intensified in the 1890's, particularly after another study by the Prudential in 1896. Lawrence N. Brown, "Insurance on American Negro Lives" (Master's thesis, University of Pennsylvania, 1930), pp. 9–10; Winfred Octavus Bryson, Jr., "Negro Life Insurance Companies" (Ph.D. dissertation, University of Pennsylvania, 1948), pp. 7–10; Trent, "Development of Negro Life Insurance," pp. 15, 16, 18.

45. Ben A. Neal to Booker T. Washington, April 24, 25, 1900, Washington Papers.

thought could not escape the impact of *laissez faire* economics and materialism in the late nineteenth century. Du Bois, in his attitude toward the decline of the mutual benefit societies and the rise of the more businesslike industrial insurance company, best illustrates the crosscurrents conditioning Negro business thought. He admitted that the older societies "represent much extravagance and waste in expenditure, an outlay for regalia and tinsel, which too often lack the excuse of being beautiful, and . . . divert the savings of Negroes from more useful channels."[46] But at the same time he spoke with nostalgia of the "wholesome" benefit societies which he believed in large part to be a cultural expression traceable to West Africa. He was "sorry to see their decline," and while the change from aid to enterprise indicated "higher economic development," he feared "disastrous results" from these new companies, because they corroded the spirit of cooperation with the ethic of capitalism, which "opened wide the door for cheating on both sides."[47] Du Bois recognized a fusion of the economic and the social in the history of Negro life insurance, and he fervently hoped that the American zeal to profiteer would not overtake the African impulse to cooperate. At the turn of the century it appeared to Du Bois that the incipient Negro insurance industry possessed an uneasy combination of the two motives. In fact, in his Atlanta University Publications Du Bois had difficulty classifying insurance organizations. In 1898 he saw insurance as a part of *Efforts of Negroes for Their Own Social Betterment*, and in his volume the following year, *The Negro in Business*, he chose to ignore the insurance societies and look instead at the stream of Negro business involving the lone black entrepreneur as barber, grocer, restaurateur, craftsman, drayman, and so forth. By 1907 he had decided that the "Social Efforts" he studied in 1898 had economic foundations; thus one could think of both insurance and "business" as *Economic Cooperation among Negroes*. In John Merrick, the barber and the fraternal insurance official, Du Bois witnessed the convergence of the two traditions of Negro busi-

46. Du Bois, *Efforts for Social Betterment*, p. 17.
47. *Ibid.*, pp. 19–21.

ness, and he openly applauded the North Carolina Mutual as an exemplary synthesis of the mixed heritage.[48]

Du Bois grew increasingly restive, however, under Booker T. Washington's uncritical "gospel of Work and Money," and in his *Souls of Black Folk* he took the lead in resisting the crassness of the white business-oriented culture that Washington accepted. He idealized, instead, the Christ-like character of the black man as a refreshing counterimage to that of the cunning Caucasian. The soul or spirit of black folks, Du Bois insisted, represented the only reservoir of humanity in the tooth-and-nail struggle, "the sole oasis of simple faith and reverence in a dusty desert of dollars and smartness."[49]

But Washington's gospel carried the day. As Du Bois clearly understood, "the ascendancy of Booker T. Washington" came at a time "when the nation . . . was concentrating its energies on dollars." Washington simply "grasped the spirit of the age"— "triumphant commercialism."[50] Even those who came to oppose Washington were not immune to his commonsense approach, emphasizing material progress. John Hope, college president and later an arch-enemy of the Tuskegee machine, reminded his peers in 1899:

> We are now under the immediate sway of business, more than humanity has ever been before. We are living among the so-called Anglo Saxons and . . . they are a conquering people who turn their conquests into their pockets. . . . Business seems to be not simply the raw material of the Anglo-Saxon civilization, but almost the civilization itself. Living among such a people is it not obvious that we cannot escape its most powerful motive and survive?[51]

48. See all three studies, but particularly *Economic Cooperation among Negroes*, pp. 10–11. It is noteworthy that Alonzo Herndon, founder of the Atlanta Life Insurance Company, was also a barber who in 1905 purchased a mutual benefit society from two Atlanta ministers and turned it into a Negro enterprise second in importance only to the North Carolina Mutual. See Merah Steven Stuart, *An Economic Detour: A History of Insurance in the Lives of American Negroes* (New York: Wendell Malliet and Company, 1940), pp. 117–124.

49. W. E. B. Du Bois, *The Souls of Black Folk: Essays and Sketches* (London: Archibald Constable and Co., 1903), pp. 11–12, 50.

50. Du Bois, *Souls of Black Folk*, pp. 41–43.

51. Quoted in W. E. B. Du Bois, *The Negro in Business*, Atlanta University Publications no. 4 (Atlanta: Atlanta University Press, 1899), pp. 58–59.

Survival amounted to more than a matter of economics. Lynchings in the United States during the last decade of the nineteenth century averaged more than one every other day, the vast majority of the victims being southern Negroes. Politically, for the black man, there was no survival. Following the example of Mississippi the majority of the southern states rewrote their constitutions or enacted legislation to disfranchise Negroes.

North Carolina folklore argues that the state's race relations, in contrast to the rest of the South, have always been amicable, particularly in Durham. Even today one hears a great deal about the "Durham spirit"—a feeling of pride among the town fathers, both black and white, recalling the highlights of interracial cooperation. There is, in fact, a white version of the origins of the North Carolina Mutual which cites friendliness between the races as the explanation for the inception and success of the Company. This benign version perpetuated by the city historian of an earlier generation, William K. Boyd, has become an oral tradition. To embellish the romance of benevolence and interracial euphoria in early Durham, Boyd contrived a dialogue between John Merrick and Washington Duke, founder of American Tobacco. Merrick was Duke's barber, and Boyd imagined the following conversation in Merrick's shop: "John," said Mr. Duke, "you have too much sense to be a mere barber. Why don't you make money among your own people?" "But how, Mr. Duke?" "Well, for instance, why not establish an insurance company?" Boyd also had Duke joining another white industrialist to get the Company on its feet through personal loans. There is simply no documentary evidence to support this claim.[52] To say that the North Carolina Mutual would not have begun without white assistance is to ignore the internal development of Afro-American institutions and the emphasis on business within Afro-American thought. Furthermore, Merrick was not a "mere

---

52. William Kenneth Boyd, *The Story of Durham: The City of the New South* (Durham: Duke University Press, 1927), pp. 280, 281, 286. The Duke Family Papers (Manuscript Division, Duke University Library) reveal loans to other Negro leaders in Durham, but none to Merrick at this time. Nor do the minutes from the North Carolina Mutual Board of Directors meetings account for any loans at this early date.

barber" but by all standards a very successful small businessman, owning six barber shops and a real estate business in Durham, and by the standards of the Negro world an immensely wealthy man. In fact he did not need the loan, and had been engaged in the insurance business since 1883 with the Royal Knights of King David.[53]

This is not to say that Duke and others did not encourage and advise black businessmen. The later history of the North Carolina Mutual affirms their assistance.[54] And long before the emergence of Booker T. Washington, Duke had been instructing Durham's black leaders on the virtues of the Protestant ethic:

> I have no doubt that each of you would like to be a successful man. It is right that you should feel so, for a proper ambition is God's call to a higher life, but how shall that success be gained? Be industrious, do not always be looking for an easy, soft place. And when you have made yourself industrious, you must be frugal. Establish it as a rule to always spend less than you make. . . . Do honest work for an honest dollar, put it in your pocket, and at night when you lie down with it under your pillow the eagle on its face will sing you to sleep. . . .[55]

Sound advice perhaps, but to credit Duke with the creation of the North Carolina Mutual would be to have the tail wagging the dog. And because a white elite smiled on a black elite there is no reason to believe that Durham was a haven for the Negro. The year in which the Company was organized goes down in history as a tragic time in North Carolina's race relations. In the wake of fusion politics which had brought Republicans and Populists into power, some of whom were black, a white su-

53. Andrews, *John Merrick*, pp. 64–77, 134–147; Stuart, *Economic Detour*, pp. 196–203; interview, William Jesse Kennedy, Jr., February 22, 1968. Moreover, Merrick's initial investment in the Company was only $50. See William Jesse Kennedy, Jr., "North Carolina Mutual Life Insurance Company: A Symbol of Progress, 1898–1966" (Manuscript in possession of Kennedy, Durham, N.C.), p. 3.

54. For extensive real estate purchases or building construction, Merrick apparently had no difficulty borrowing several thousand dollars from the Duke-owned Fidelity Bank. See minutes of North Carolina Mutual Board of Directors meetings, June 1, 8, 9, 12, 1905; February 17, 18, 1908.

55. Address by Washington Duke to convention of Negro educators, Durham, N.C., 1890, as quoted in Boyd, *The Story of Durham*, pp. 279–280.

premacy campaign swept the state in the off-year election of 1898. "Red Shirts" rode by the hundreds in an effort to intimidate Negro voters, and as a climax to the bitter campaign a race riot engulfed the city of Wilmington. White newspapers spread hysteria over the state, printing every report of racial unrest, even feeding a rumor that if the Republicans won the election, black brigands planned to besiege North Carolina and form a Negro republic. Throughout the sensationalism ran a ubiquitous thread linking black domination with the fate of the southern white woman.[56]

Indeed, avenging the honor of southern womanhood served as a pretext for the Wilmington riot. The outspoken editor of the city's Negro newspaper asked the white purveyors of the rumor of rape if their disclosure of white women living with black men did not indicate, instead of threatened carnality, simply that some white women ardently volunteered for such liaisons with black men. He had struck a nerve center. A lynch mob sacked and burned his office and then, unable to find the editor, directed its rage to the Negro community, nearly leveling it and murdering eleven black citizens.[57]

Durham was by no means immune from this hysteria. The *Daily Sun* throughout the late summer and up until election time vilified Negroes and Republicans without regard to even the most modest journalistic restraints. Passions became so heated that a black man rumored to have been living with a white woman (allegedly the wife of a Republican) was lynched and his body left hanging along the roadside between Durham and Chapel Hill to serve as a ghastly lesson in white supremacy, a lesson which Durhamites proved they could teach as well as anyone.[58]

The terror of 1898 unquestionably heightened the pervasive mood of withdrawal and racial solidarity essential to the success

56. Josephus Daniels, *Editor in Politics* (Chapel Hill: University of North Carolina Press, 1941), pp. 283–312; Helen Grey Edmonds, *The Negro and Fusion Politics in North Carolina, 1894–1901* (Chapel Hill: University of North Carolina Press, 1951), pp. 136–177; *Durham Daily Sun*, October 20, 29, November 5; *Raleigh News and Observer*, October 25, November 11, 1898.

57. Edmonds, *Fusion Politics*, pp. 159, 168–174.

58. *Durham Daily Sun*, October 29, November 5, 7, 1898.

of Negro business. As a black merchant in Indiana later complained to journalist Ray Stannard Baker, "The trouble here is that there is not enough prejudice against us. You see we are still clinging too much to the skirts of the white man. When you hate us more it will drive us together and make us support colored enterprises."[59] Seen in this light one had to agree with Booker T. Washington that the South was the best place for Negro business.

It is a curious paradox that Negro business thrived on a modicum of racial hostility, yet at the same time its supporters incessantly prescribed it as the surest cure for unhealthy race relations. This message formed the heart of Washington's philosophy. The *New York Age*, a leading Negro newspaper of the period and the mouthpiece of Washington, urged its readers to recognize that "there is plenty of commercial opportunity everywhere. Let us hammer away. The almighty dollar is the magic wand that knocks the bottom out of race prejudice and all the humbugs that fatten on it."[60]

The general response of the Negro leadership, when confronted with the nadir of race relations, was nothing short of a sublimation into the world of business and education as a substitute for politics and protest. Washington in his *Story of the Negro* (1909) entitled one chapter "The Negro Disfranchisement and the Negro in Business," leaving no doubt as to the reciprocal relationship. "They [Negroes] began to see," he affirmed, "that there was still hope for them in economic, if not in political directions."[61] John Merrick, in his only known public

59. Ray Stannard Baker, *Following the Color Line* (New York: Doubleday, Page and Company, 1908), pp. 228–229.

60. Clipping, *New York Age*, March 14, 1901, in "Negro Business," Hampton Institute clipping scrapbooks (hereafter cited as Hampton Clippings).

61. Washington, *Story of the Negro*, II, 191. While there is wide statistical disagreement on Negro business in the twentieth century (the National Negro Business League included homeowners and farmers in its statistics, and the Census Bureau made no clear classification for "businessmen"), there is general agreement that business was more important in Afro-American life in the first two decades of the century than at any time since, with the possible exception of a short-lived boom in the 1920's and the "black capitalism" movement since

speech, lamented shortly after the Wilmington riot that whites
in the New South had

> ... turned their attention to making money and we turned ours
> to holding office and paying debts of gratitude. The Negroes
> have had lots of offices in this state and they have benefited
> themselves but very little . . . nothing comparing with what
> they could have done along business and industrial lines had
> they given it the same time and talent. And I claim they have
> done the masses harm in this way. Had the Negroes of Wil-
> mington owned half of the city . . . there wouldn't anything hap-
> pened to compare with what did. Let us think more of our em-
> ployment and what it takes to keep peace and to build us a
> little house and stop thinking we are the whole Republican
> Party. . . .[62]

Of the six men who joined Merrick in organizing the North
Carolina Mutual, five had been active in politics. But they saw
little reason to continue in the face of the disfranchisement campaign, and all redirected their energies into business and education, into separate black institutions.[63]

Nearly as important as the overt white hostility in reinforcing
ethnocentrism was a massive covert attack by the scientific ra-
cists and their popularizers, many of whom predicted that the
Negro race was destined to die out within fifty years—and all
for the good, because the black man was a parasitic weight on
the progress of the republic. These prophets of doom portrayed
the Negro as childlike and pointed to rising mortality rates as

1968. Gunnar Myrdal, *An American Dilemma* (New York: Harper and Row,
1944), I, 304–318; E. Franklin Frazier, *The Negro in the United States* (New
York: Macmillan, 1957), pp. 392–413; Eugene P. Foley, "The Negro Businessman: In Search of a Tradition," in Talcott Parsons and Kenneth B. Clark, eds.,
The Negro American (Boston: Beacon Press, 1967), pp. 555–592.

62. Quoted in Andrews, *John Merrick*, pp. 158–161.

63. Daniels, *Editor in Politics*, pp. 312, 317; Garrett F. Weaver, "Durham
City Race Relations: Attitudes, Irritations, and Accommodations" (Seminar
paper, Department of History, University of North Carolina, 1968); Kennedy,
"North Carolina Mutual," pp. 1–16. One of the organizers, Edward Austin Johnson, dean of the Law School at Shaw University, left the South and went back
into politics in New York City, where he won election to the State Assembly in
1917.

proof that he could not survive without the parental supervision and care he enjoyed under slavery.[64]

Black leaders closed ranks, and out of their response emerged a gospel of progress which occupied a prominent position in Negro thought until World War I. Black periodicals overflowed with a harvest of statistics verifying the progress of the race since emancipation. Race leaders assembled elaborate fairs and expositions to impress the doubters. Washington's National Negro Business League acted as the administrative center for the progress movement, and its annual conventions resembled camp meetings with businessmen issuing testimonials of racial salvation. Negro schools conducted essay contests on progress and scheduled forums in which whites and blacks debated the question: "Resolved: That the Negro of the South is in worse condition today than before the war."[65]

Self-adulation abounded in black newspapers. One headlined an article with the question, "Is the Negro growing rich?" and then marshaled statistics which answered the question affirmatively.[66] The *New York Age* proclaimed in bold type, "Afro-Americans Own Millions," while the other major New York

64. For a catalog of racist literature in this period, see Idus A. Newby, *Jim Crow's Defense: Anti-Negro Thought in America, 1900–1930* (Baton Rouge: Louisiana State University Press, 1965). Of special significance here because of its connection with discrimination against Negro risks in white life insurance companies is Frederick Ludwig Hoffman's *Race Traits and Tendencies of the American Negro* (New York: Macmillan, 1896), esp. Chs. 2, 6. One black businessman later thanked Hoffman for discouraging the Prudential and other white firms from insuring Negroes: "Without Hoffman's pernicious propaganda there would have been no North Carolina Mutual . . ." (Harry Herbert Pace, "The Attitudes of Life Insurance Companies toward Negroes," *Southern Workman*, LVII [January, 1928], 5).

65. Clipping, *Detroit Informer*, March 28, 1908, Hampton Clippings, "Negro Progress and Prosperity," vol. I. It seems significant that librarians at Hampton Institute chose "progress" as a subject heading, and significant that they found such a wealth of material. The decade leading up to the fiftieth anniversary of the Emancipation Proclamation witnessed an incredible mass of material written on "Negro progress." Typical examples of entire volumes devoted to the topic would include G. F. Richings, *Evidences of Progress among Colored People* (1902); W. H. Crogman, *The Progress of a Race: The Remarkable Advancement of the Afro-American* (1902). See Monroe N. Work, *Bibliography of the Negro in Africa and America* (1928), pp. 583–588, where he sets off an entire section entitled, "The Progress of the Negro."

66. Unidentified clipping in Hampton Clippings, "Progress and Prosperity," vol. I.

Negro paper, the *Amsterdam News*, listed its data under the heading, "Not a Child Race." The *Detroit Informer* reviewed Negro progress and concluded that "BUSINESS IS KING": "Do you know that less than two score years ago, even the most intelligent colored man was content to be a . . . porter. Today we have 'The Negro in Business.'" And Booker T. Washington's book, *The Negro in Business*, according to the *Informer*, was "more interesting than a novel."[67]

Occasionally the white press joined the black in countering the stereotype. With all the trappings of Horatio Alger tales, the *New York Sun* published a piece entitled "Some Rich Colored Men, What They Are Worth, and How They Came by Their Money." And the *Washington Post* agreed with Negro businessmen that there was no need to despair; "Money power will raise the Negro as it has the Jew, who was once as much persecuted as the Negro is now."[68]

One interesting piece of evidence suggests that black spokesmen, in a defensive effort to elevate their status, were not loath to look for an alternative mudsill of society. A National Negro Business League convention in Oklahoma issued a striking description of the local Indians. The Negro editor reported the Indians as

> . . . half nude and gaily painted . . . remaining uncivilized . . . ignorant, idle, and dependent on the United States Government. . . . Unlike the Negro [he continued], they have no banking institutions; neglecting their opportunity, they are fast losing their birth right, while on the other hand, NEGRO INDUSTRY, THRIFT, AND SELF-INITIATIVE have given to our race 10,000 mercantile enterprises, 63 banking institutions, 400 drugstores, 20 million acres of land, and material wealth exceeding $700,000,-000.[69]

67. Clippings, *New York Age*, April 4, 1907, Hampton Clippings, "Progress and Prosperity," vol. I; *Amsterdam News*, June 7, 1916, Hampton Clippings, "Progress and Prosperity," vol. II; *Detroit Informer*, December 28, 1907, Hampton Clippings, "The Negro in Business," vol. I.

68. Undated clipping, *New York Sun*, Hampton Clippings, "Progress and Prosperity," vol. II; clipping, *Washington Post*, August 15, 1900, Hampton Clippings, "The Negro in Business," vol. I.

69. *Proceedings* of the Fifteenth Annual National Negro Business League Meeting, Muskogee, Okla., 1914.

The overweening pride within the Negro business movement suggests that the crusade for black capitalism during the age of Booker T. Washington was in itself a form of protest thought, as was the larger idea of race progress.

Caught between two cultures, Afro-American thought is a synthesis, constantly creating its own mood while assimilating that of the larger society. So it was with the gospel of progress and the gospel of the New South.

Perhaps more than any other city in the South, Durham represented the raw, unabashed materialism characteristic of the New South. During Reconstruction Durham was a village having no pre–Civil War history or strong antebellum traditions. In many ways it resembled a western frontier community with its twenty-one saloons lining Main Street, the promise of quick fortunes, and an air of excitement involved in watching this rough industrial city rise up out of the red piedmont hills. Here a man was judged less by his past than by his ability to survive and win in the struggle for success.[70] In this struggle Durham Negroes witnessed the accumulation of one of the great American fortunes. Washington Duke's son Buck made no idle boast when he pledged "to do for tobacco what John Rockefeller did for oil."[71] Edward Franklin Frazier, in analyzing the phenomenon of Negro enterprise in Durham, observed that Durham's black entrepreneurs "grew up with the exploitation of the New South." These black and white advocates of progress were, in Frazier's words, "brothers under the skin."[72]

Almost as if trying to compensate for her lack of history, Durham expressed a fervent New South nationalism. This industrial

70. *Durham Daily Sun*, September 20, 1898; interview with Conrad Odelle Pearson, Durham, N.C., February 22; Wyatt Dixon, Durham, N.C., February 14, 1968. Pearson, a black attorney, and Dixon, a white newspaperman, are both longtime Durham residents whose memories stretch back to the nineteenth century. Dixon possesses a valuable file of clippings which reveal the temper of early Durham.

71. Quoted in Comer Vann Woodward, *Origins of the New South, 1877–1913*, (Baton Rouge: Louisiana State University Press, 1951), p. 130.

72. Edward Franklin Frazier, "Durham: Capital of the Black Middle Class," in Alain Locke, ed., *The New Negro* (New York: Albert and Charles Boni, 1925), p. 339.

enthusiasm spilled over into the Negro community and, when grafted to the black cult of progress, produced a hybrid of incredible vigor. Durham's first Negro newspaper, the house organ of the North Carolina Mutual, captured the zeal of black Durham's New South creed:

> Everything here is push, everything is on the move, every citizen is looking out for everything that will make Durham great. The Negro in the midst of such life has caught the disease and . . . has awakened to action. We are certainly proud that the Negro is learning to imitate in business as well as a few vices. Durham! The very name has become a synonymous term for energy, pluck and business ability. When you shout Durham! the gloomy and befogged financial atmosphere becomes clear and there is a mad rush and scramble for her bonds. When you say Durham! the wheels begin to turn, the smoke rolls in massive clouds from every stack and the sweet assuring music of busy machinery is heard. Durham! and as if by magic, everything springs into new life, the veins and arteries of business throw off their stagnation and the bright sun of prosperity sends its radiant beams out upon the world. . . .[73]

The historian must always view entrepreneurs as actors in a system; thus the system becomes an object of study no less important than the behavior of the entrepreneurs themselves. From this perspective the North Carolina Mutual was inevitable—not its success, but its origins, as an expression of a century-old evolution in Afro-American institutions, the legacy of a sturdy strand of Negro thought epitomized by Booker T. Washington, the product of race relations, and the values of the New South. Washington and the North Carolina Mutual invented very little, but inherited a full-flowing stream of thought.

That ideology embodied the evolution of uplift as well as the evolution of enterprise. Thus when the company began operat-

73. *Durham Negro Observer*, June 23, August 4, 1906. Technically, the *Observer* was the second Negro paper in Durham, the first being the *North Carolina Mutual*, which grew into the *Observer*. However, the *Observer* continued to serve as the "Company" paper as well as the community paper and was printed by the North Carolina Mutual, as was the third black newspaper in the city, the *Durham Reformer*, which passed into the hands of the Company from the defunct True Reformers in Richmond.

ing in April, 1899, its motto, "The Company with a Soul and a Service," expressed not so much a catchy slogan as it did the ambivalent heritage of Negro business. Not since the Puritan merchants linked economic success with the will of God had there been such an air-tight defense of the virtues of making money. Under the prevailing philosophy of Booker T. Washington Negroes were urged to harness their pecuniary drives and put them to work, enriching the race in the process of enriching themselves. For the North Carolina Mutual the motives of altruism and capitalism were thoroughly fused.

The extraordinary success of the Company, the fascinating careers of the black men who directed it, and the function of the institution in the social history of a biracial community is the larger story to be told, but one which belongs less to the standard sagas of American business than to the history of an oppressed people who improvised their existence in the shadows of American economic opportunity.

2

The Company
with a Soul
and a Service

The occasion for the organization of the North Carolina Mutual and Provident Association came on an October evening in 1898 when seven black men, at the call of John Merrick, gathered in the office of Dr. Aaron McDuffie Moore, Durham's Negro physician. Assembled with Merrick and Dr. Moore were William Gaston Pearson, teacher, principal, and business colleague of Merrick; Edward Austin Johnson, historian, attorney, and dean of the Law School at Shaw University in nearby Raleigh; James Edward Shepard, preacher-politician-pharmacist, and future founder of North Carolina College; Pinckney William Dawkins, Durham schoolteacher; and Dock Watson, a local tinsmith.[1] Merrick presided over the meeting and declared its purpose was to devise a means "to aid Negro families in distress"; thus "an insurance association similar to the two organized by Negroes in Richmond in 1893 and 1894 should be organized in Durham."[2]

1. W. J. Kennedy, Jr., "North Carolina Mutual Life Insurance Company: A Symbol of Progress, 1898–1966" (Manuscript in possession of W. J. Kennedy, Jr., Durham, N.C.), pp. 2–3; *Whetstone* (North Carolina Mutual monthly publication founded in 1924), October, 1936; Robert M. Andrews, *John Merrick: A Biographical Sketch* (Durham: Seeman Printery, 1920), p. 64. Biographical information also can be found in the personal files of W. J. Kennedy, Jr., Durham, N.C.

2. Minutes of the first organizational meeting, October 20, 1898, in possession of W. J. Kennedy, Jr. Merrick had in mind the Southern Aid Society of Virginia and the Richmond Beneficial Life Insurance Company, neither of which were

A few months earlier Negro leaders could have been holding a political caucus here, but the "Red Shirts" had done their work well, and organizing activities that had become frustrating and dangerous in politics emerged as popular and safe when directed to business. For some the meeting signified the end of political aspirations; they turned from the impossible to the practical, goaded by white supremacy campaigns and the pervasive spirit of Booker T. Washington. In Afro-American history, organizing the North Carolina Mutual stands out as one of the "little events" symbolic of the "great event"—a microcosm of the racial flight from politics and protest to white-approved alternatives. A North Carolina Mutual manager later reflected that the "turn of the century marked the time when the Negro of North Carolina turned his attention to . . . education, business and industrial progress . . . realizing that the economic must precede the political," and that the compulsory strategy was "to keep quiet and saw wood."[3]

Before the men left Dr. Moore's office that evening, each pledged fifty dollars to the cause of a Negro insurance association, and they agreed that Johnson should draw up a charter to be presented as a bill before the State Assembly when it convened in January, 1899.[4] Johnson passed on to Thomas Oscar Fuller, North Carolina's last Negro state senator, the political task of making the North Carolina Mutual a legitimate industrial insurance association sanctioned by the laws of the state, rather than just another "coffin club."[5] There is a fitting sym-

---

fraternals or mutual aid societies, but chartered industrial insurance corporations. Both organizations have survived as small industrial companies, and the Southern Aid Society is generally considered the oldest Negro life insurance company in the United States. See Merah S. Stuart, *An Economic Detour: A History of Insurance in the Lives of American Negroes* (New York: Wendell Mallient and Company, 1940), pp. 229–238.

3. Charles N. Hunter, untitled, unpublished manuscript dated July 24, 1928, in the Charles N. Hunter Papers, Manuscript Division, Duke University Library (hereafter cited as Hunter Papers).

4. Kennedy, "North Carolina Mutual," p. 3.

5. Thomas Oscar Fuller, *Twenty Years in Public Life* (Memphis: T. O. Fuller, 1913), p. 69; Helen G. Edmonds, *The Negro and Fusion Politics in North Carolina, 1894–1901* (Chapel Hill: University of North Carolina Press, 1951), p. 110; interview, W. J. Kennedy, Jr., January 29, 1968; clipping, *Tri-State Defender*, September 11, 1954, in North Carolina Mutual clipping file.

bolism in Fuller's spending the dying days of his political career as anxious midwife to a black business. Fuller himself retreated into business and the ministry in Tennessee after white supremacy ended his political life in North Carolina.

A black by-product of North Carolina's "fusion politics" between Republicans and Populists during the 1890's, Fuller recalled that chartering the North Carolina Mutual proved to be the hardest fight of his short legislative career. The bill was delayed and shuttled from chamber to chamber, tactics which Fuller thought were designed "to force me to withdraw my opposition to certain measures in the Senate." It is unlikely that the lone black senator in a body of fifty possessed a power to reckon with; the assessment of North Carolina historian Helen Edmonds—that the bill met scattered opposition on racial grounds—seems a more likely explanation.[6] Fuller worked diligently indeed to keep the bill alive, tracking it through an amazingly circuitous journey in the two houses, reintroducing the bill at one point, and finally arranging the compromise between Senate and House that gave the Company its charter on February 29, 1899.[7]

The charter specified that the North Carolina Mutual and Provident Association shall be known by the motto "Merciful to All,"[8] having "the object of . . . relief of widows and orphans, of the sick and of those injured by accident, and the burial of the dead, and . . . a certain per centum of the proceeds to be fixed by the board of directors, shall be turned over to the Colored Asylum at Oxford, North Carolina."[9] That the founders thought of their new enterprise as partly philanthropic is clear from the charter; that they wished to put their charitable foot forward as

6. Fuller, *Twenty Years*, p. 69; Edmonds, *The Negro and Fusion Politics*, p. 110.

7. *North Carolina House Journal* (1899), pp. 391, 674, 804, 853, 1011; *North Carolina Senate Journal* (1899), pp. 137, 145, 152, 155, 406, 459, 478, 639, 735; Fuller, *Twenty Years*, p. 69.

8. Some time during 1899 the Company began to substitute the more alliterative "The Company with a Soul and a Service" for the chartered motto, and it was the new motto that lasted and appeared on the Company letterhead for a number of years. See North Carolina Insurance Department manuscript report on the North Carolina Mutual, 1929, in the North Carolina Mutual files.

9. *Private Laws of North Carolina* (1899), Ch. 156, pp. 375–376.

a matter of political tact is also possible. Certainly no fixed Company allowance for the Oxford Orphanage was forthcoming, although private philanthropy among the founders became legendary.

It is far easier to identify large and impersonal forces in Afro-American history which compel black men to embrace the idea of capitalism (and particularly the institution of life insurance) than it is to assess the immediate motives and local forces contributing directly to the beginning of the North Carolina Mutual. Interpreting the oral traditions that surround Merrick's decision to launch the Company constitutes a historiographic problem compounded by race relations, stratification and envy within the black community, and a half-century of myth-making; indeed, such an analysis is perhaps more instructive on these points than on the origins of the enterprise.

Essentially there are two major traditions, one white, the other black. As a rule the white version repeats the notion that Merrick, the contented barber, had reached the limits of his entrepreneurial imagination until Washington Duke kindly advised him to establish an insurance company. Indeed, a prominent white attorney in Durham found it necessary to repeat and further debase William K. Boyd's imaginary dialogue between Duke and Merrick:

'John, . . . why don't you hunt up a better job?'

'Lor', Mr. Duke, what can a po' nigger like me git?'

'Why organize an insurance company and make every dinged nigger in the United States pay you twenty-five dollars a year.'

"John danced with delight and thought it over. . . ."[10]

Whatever the embellishments of the folklore, white Durham took it for granted that "the white man's push" launched the Mutual.[11] This interpretation would become an article of faith,

10. Robert Watson Winston, *It's a Far Cry* (New York: Henry Holt and Company, 1937), p. 249.
11. Interview, Wyatt Dixon, February 13, 1968. Dixon is but one of many white spokesmen for early Durham who hold this view. The author found only one variation within the white version—that Benjamin N. Duke, rather than

possibly a mechanism of defense, as whites looked at one of the largest businesses in their city and sought to explain it in the context of white supremacy. Black economic success presented a striking contradiction to conventional expectations; such success was rationalized, and not without a measure of truth, as evidence of white training, white assistance, or white blood. Booker T. Washington fulfilled the stereotype and fastened the image onto other successful blacks. Southern moderates and liberals saw Negroes as backward, but not inherently so, and with high-minded whites tutoring them blacks could succeed and whites should applaud.

There is greater diversity within the black oral history, although one black version adheres closely to the white and even reconstructs Boyd's barbershop scene, but with an added element of credibility. Lower-class blacks, so the story goes, often interrupted Merrick and his patrons to "pass the hat" for a Negro funeral. One day, "Mr. Duke watched the proceeding with quiet interest and after the beggar had left . . . he suggested to Mr. Merrick that the colored people should organize an insurance company. . . ."[12]

Similarly Durham blacks outside the Mutual circle have traditionally believed that Merrick received not only advice but a vast amount of money from Duke and other white leaders. Class conflict, in part, explains this view. The lower-class blacks often identified the "big niggers" with the white community; they found it difficult from their station in life to understand how a black man could, on his own, achieve such success, a success

his father, counseled Merrick. Also see William K. Boyd, *The Story of Durham: The City of the New South* (Durham: Duke University Press, 1927), pp. 280–281, 286. Generally the black oral tradition refuses to give this much credit to the white man, denying the implication that the North Carolina Mutual owes its existence to the advice of the Dukes. The black version acknowledges white counsel and the benefits of white sympathy to the development of Negro business in Durham, but it gives the black man major credit for beginning the Company and the white man partial credit for advising the black man on what he was going to do anyway. Interviews with black citizens in Durham: Conrad O. Pearson, February 22; Mrs. Viola G. Turner, June 13; Charles Watts, June 6; W. J. Kennedy, Jr., January 29; Mrs. E. R. Merrick, June 20; Louis Austin, January 15, 1968.

12. Albon Holsey, "Pearson: The Brown Duke of Durham," *Opportunity*, VI (April, 1923), 116; interview, Clyde Donnell, June 10, 1968.

which they constantly overestimated. A black sociologist studying Durham during the 1930's found this typical view expressed
by an elderly black worker: "I don't suppose there is a man living who got as much money from white people as Merrick got.
Old man Duke gave him plenty."[13] Despite class feelings, the
masses always exhibited an ambivalent sense of pride in the
Mutual, and it may have been satisfying to think that Merrick,
notoriously clever with whites, had maneuvered them out of
their money.

Even among Durham's middle-class blacks there is controversy as to the proper history of the founding. Is it plausible
that Merrick, the uneducated ex-slave, could have conceived
of such a plan and could have taken command over college-
trained professionals? Perhaps, instead, the physician, the phar-
macist, the principal, or the lawyer among them had planted the
idea. Most likely, say these dissenters, W. G. Pearson, the entre-
preneur-educator and president of the Royal Knights of King
David, sparked the movement for an industrial insurance company. True, Merrick needed advice, they say; but rather than
coming from whites, it came from Durham's black "talented
tenth." Merrick was simply the entrenched Negro capitalist to
whom new ideas were supplied for the financial support and
good will he could secure from whites.[14]

Pearson, however, never claimed such credit. Instead, he acknowledged that the "Royal Knights of King David was the
forerunner of the North Carolina Mutual and both organizations
sprang from the vision of the late John Merrick."[15] While Merrick's biographer engaged in a good deal of filiopietism, his treatment of the origins of the Company withstood the scrutiny of
meticulous Dr. Moore, who read the manuscript for accuracy on
this very point. He confirmed that throughout the organizing
stages the initiative belonged to Merrick.[16]

13. Harry J. Walker, "Changes in Race Accommodation in a Southern Community" (Ph.D. dissertation, University of Chicago, 1945), p. 83.
14. Interviews, anonymity requested, Durham, N.C., 1968.
15. Clipping, *Raleigh Times,* January 11, 1929, in North Carolina Mutual
clipping file.
16. Interviews, Mrs. Viola G. Turner, June 13; Mrs. E. R. Merrick, June 20,
1968.

Finally, in assessing individual responsibility for the founding of the North Carolina Mutual one has to look to the personal, rather than the ideological, influence of Booker T. Washington. Washington's great power and influence throughout the black South maintained itself through direct advice and assistance, letters of support, and the largesse of white philanthropy to those who adhered to his principles in business and education. "Easily the most striking thing in the history of the American Negro since 1876," wrote Du Bois, "is the ascendancy of Mr. Booker T. Washington."[17]

In analyzing the origins of the Mutual it is tempting to magnify Washington's influence, vast as it was, in order to establish a neat and direct relationship between him and the economic institution which has given such dramatic testimony to his ideology. One rather questionable piece of evidence suggests that there was such a relationship. In the fall of 1896 Washington came to Durham on a speaking tour and thrilled a tremendous crowd with his famous fingers-fist simile, in the context of which he decried politics, praised business, and advised his black listeners, "When it comes to business, pure and simple, the black man is put on the same footing with the white man and here it seems to me is our great opportunity."[18] Nearly twenty years later Charles Clinton Spaulding, general manager and the driving force of the North Carolina Mutual, declared that it had been this speech by Washington which had inspired the Company: "Some years ago, Dr. Booker T. Washington visited our city and made a stirring address.... Dr. Washington emphasized the ... value of business ... and during that speech there were some good seed sown in our town, the result of which can be seen today in the North Carolina Mutual and Provident Association."[19]

Spaulding's tribute to Washington, delivered on the platform

17. W. E. B. Du Bois, *The Souls of Black Folk: Essays and Sketches* (London: Archibald Constable and Company, 1903), p. 41.

18. *Durham Recorder*, October 15; *Durham Daily Sun*, October 14, 1896.

19. National Negro Business League, *Proceedings* of the Eleventh Annual Meeting, New York, 1910, p. 101; Sixteenth Annual Meeting, Boston, 1915, p. 118; and *Lodge Journal and Guide*, August 20, 1910, clipping in John Moses Avery Scrapbook in possession of W. J. Kennedy, Jr.

of the National Negro Business League with Washington present, would seem in large part to have been a public salute to the king. To suggest that Merrick and others were in 1898 acting out a two-year-old suggestion from Washington once again denies Merrick's business experience. Washington received no mention at the time the Company was founded, and he is not remembered in the oral tradition—black or white. That Washington and the Mutual provided vindication for one another there can be no doubt, but that Washington had a hand in creating the North Carolina Mutual is more dubious than the credit given to Duke.[20]

Assuming that Merrick deserves to be remembered as the founder of the "world's largest Negro business," there remains the question of his personal motivation. Conventional wisdom among those of lengthy association with the Mutual asserts that Merrick acted less for profit and more for uplift. As a man who had already won social and economic status by 1898, he had become something of an elder statesman in the community and a devotee to humanitarian causes. Such a description easily fits Dr. Moore, who spent most of his life in philanthropy. Merrick, on the other hand, was doubtless attracted to the prospect of establishing a financial empire; his previous successes, rather than dampening his entrepreneurial spirit, could have fired such motives. Too, he may have been negatively inspired to remove from his shop the bothersome beggars who expected the richest black man in town and his white customers to assume the burden of Negro welfare. Why not begin a responsible Negro insurance company, end the harassment, make a profit, and uplift the unfortunate at the same time?[21]

20. W. J. Kennedy, Jr., past president of the North Carolina Mutual and an invaluable primary source, says that Washington played no personal role in the founding or early growth of the Company, but that his "spirit" has had a sustaining influence. Surely this was the case with C. C. Spaulding, who modeled much of his life after Washington's. My research in the Washington Papers uncovered little contact between Tuskegee and the Mutual—in fact, comparatively little contact with North Carolina at all. These findings are supported by Louis Harlan, who has worked in the voluminous Washington collection for years.

21. Interviews, Clyde Donnell, June 10; Mrs. Viola G. Turner, June 13; Charles Watts, June 6; Asa T. Spaulding, July 18, 1968.

In 1936 the Company itself evaluated the motives of Merrick in its official monthly publication. The judgment has a completeness that suggests reliability. According to the *Whetstone* Merrick, "possessing a desire . . . to reach out and to prosper by his own work, skill, judgment, and initiative," called the October meeting "to encourage members of his race to save a part of their earnings as a preliminary step to future independence." And within his character there was a "confidence" which came from the "contacts with the Dukes and other successful white capitalists [who] convinced him that the Negro could create wealth, provided he exercised the same thought and thrift these men employed."[22]

Forces in the black world alone are adequate to explain the origins of the Mutual and much of Merrick's motivation. The quest for survival as a young ex-slave, pushing his way from bootblack to barber, constitutes the formative experience of Merrick the black businessman. But outside white influence undoubtedly accounts for his "confidence"—his entrepreneurial outlook after survival. The spirit of capitalism, so profoundly imbedded in the white American ethos and so largely absent in the Afro-American subculture, had to transfer at some point in the lives of successful black businessmen.[23]

For Merrick the barbershop provided the means of transfer. In the words of his biographer: "Merrick's college course was taken in his barber shop, largely by the Socratic method . . . with the leading white businessmen of Durham. The barber shop was the original chamber of commerce, men's club and civic forum. . . . The industrious barber appropriated . . . information and business methods through such contact."[24] At the peak of his barbering career, Merrick owned six barbershops— three for whites, three for blacks. Managing this small empire

22. *Whetstone*, October, 1936, p. 3.
23. Du Bois, *Efforts for Social Betterment*, p. 21; John Henry Harmon, "The Negro as a Local Business Man," *Journal of Negro History*, XIV (April, 1929), 122. The absence of a capitalist spirit has been seen as a cultural blessing—a part of the "gift of black folks"—see Ch. 1.
24. Andrews, *John Merrick*, pp. 39–40.

was no simple task, and his success indicates that he had learned well the principles of business. As head barber at his Main Street shop, where he attended only to special white customers, Merrick spent a good part of his life in the company of the South's leading capitalists. Only a deaf man could have escaped the profound influence of this indirect tutelage.

The process was not always indirect or limited to the whimsy of barbershop talk. As Washington Duke's personal barber and occasional traveling companion, Merrick rode Pullman cars, listened to the talk of money being made, toured New York City in the company of "robber barons," and generally found himself exposed to a world infinitely beyond the black man's South. Duke at his paternalistic best even saw Merrick as a boyish business partner, whom he contracted to dismantle old barns belonging to the American Tobacco Company. Out of this arrangement Merrick formed a small black construction company and a real estate business. With used lumber he built rentals in the Negro community to house the waves of black workers who came to labor for American Tobacco.[25]

Behind Merrick and the Mutual stood an impressive show of white support. Always paternalistic, the support sometimes amounted to direct assistance; more often it counseled a protective, salutary neglect. "If the Negro is going down," wrote the editor of the *Durham Morning Herald*, "for God's sake let it be because of his own fault, and not because of our pushing him."[26] Booker T. Washington found Durham, perhaps like most southern cities he visited, to have "the greatest amount of friendly feeling between the races," and "the sanest attitude of the white people toward the black."[27] Du Bois, certainly more skeptical than Washington, nonetheless agreed that a kind of gentle Darwinism operated in Durham, which revealed itself in the "dis-

25. *Ibid.*, p. 40; interviews, Conrad O. Pearson, February 13; W. J. Kennedy, Jr., February 29; Mrs. Viola G. Turner, June 13; Miles Mark Fisher, March 10, 1968.

26. *Durham Morning Herald*, as quoted in Boyd, *Story of Durham*, p. 279. Boyd does not give the exact date.

27. Booker T. Washington, "Durham: A City of Negro Enterprise," *Independent*, LXX (March 30, 1911), 642, 647.

position of the . . . white citizens . . . to say: 'Hands off—give them a chance—don't interfere.' " "A notable few" of the whites, in Du Bois's mind, had been more than neutral; they had been "sincerely sympathetic and helpful."[28]

The point is that, while oppression may stimulate Negro business as it breeds racial solidarity, diminishing returns set in when hostility stifles entrepreneurial initiative. In Durham, unlike many places in the South, "whitecapping" of "well-behaved" black businessmen would not have been tolerated by the white power structure.[29] Du Bois speculated, undoubtedly with error, that the "high ideals" of Trinity College (now Duke University) with its "professors who have dared to speak out for justice toward black men . . . made white Durham willing to see black Durham rise without organizing mobs or secret societies to 'keep the niggers down.' "[30] "It is precisely the opposite spirit in places like Atlanta," lamented Du Bois, "which makes the way of the black man . . . so hard. . . ."[31]

The ideals of Trinity College had less to do with the "Durham spirit" than did the ideals of Tuskegee Institute. In the pressing search for the place of the black man in southern society, the white leaders of Durham were certain that Booker T. Washington had found the answer. Removing Negroes from politics and putting them into industry seemed a practical and a humanitarian reform which would put the section at ease and at the same time arouse her economy.

Nobody captured this spirit more completely than Durham's Julian Shakespeare Carr, cotton mill mogul and financier, who

28. W. E. B. Du Bois, "The Upbuilding of Black Durham," *World's Work*, XXIII (January, 1912), 336.

29. "Whitecapping"—attacks on the property and person of successful black farmers and businessmen "to let them know their place"—occurred throughout the South. See especially Hampton Clippings, "Whitecapping, 1900–1920," 2 volumes; also Arna Bontemps, *They Seek a City* (Garden City, N.Y.: Doubleday and Company, 1945), p. 78; William F. Holmes, "Whitecapping: Agrarian Violence in Mississippi, 1902–1906," *Journal of Southern History*, XXXV (May, 1969), 165–185.

30. Du Bois, "The Upbuilding of Black Durham," p. 338.

31. *Ibid.* Du Bois could understandably rejoice over what he found in Durham, in contrast to his disillusioning experience with the 1906 Atlanta "race riot" in which black businessmen were lynched.

personified the "divided mind" of the South and the interlocking
relationship between paternalism and white supremacy. Carr
possessed a pathological fixation on the Old South and persistently invoked the "lost cause." Carr believed that "next to sending His only Son to die . . . the wisest providence of a . . . just
God . . . was the enslaving of the Negro. . . ."[32] He spoke of a
"country south of the shimmering waters of the Potomac, where
the mocking birds sing so sweetly and where the fragrant mag-
nolia perfumes every passing breeze, a Paradise fit for the Gods
. . . but for the Ku Klux Klan would have been a Black Republic."
And with such redemption, the South's "best asset . . . Ah,
Woman—lovely Woman . . . had been spared her."[33] "The future
of the Negro," he warned, "must be deferred for settlement until
we have restored . . . a feeling of security to the humblest [white]
woman in the poorest cabin in the remotest corner of the
South."[34] In the meantime, he told a Negro audience, "If we
can but succeed in weaning the negro from believing that politics is their calling by nature . . . and turn the bent of his mind
into the development of manufacturing industries, what will the
end be?" But, he threatened, "if the negro is to continue to make
politics his chief aim . . . there can be but one ending." What
gave him hope was the "rise of such respectable men as . . .
John Merrick."[35] The Durham experience proved to Carr that
the "black race" only need "go forth like Booker T. Washington
from Hampton, with the gospel of faith and work."[36]

What drove Carr to his rhetoric—the New South vision of an
industrial economy and a biracial society—drove him to action
as well. Inviting Negroes to help the South overtake the economy
of the North, he established a "Jim Crow" cotton mill to provide
employment for blacks outside the established lily-white mills.
Carr's Negro mill could be seen entirely as a tactic to exploit

32. Julian S. Carr, speech at Concord, N.C., February 8, 1898, in Julian S.
Carr Papers, Southern Historical Collection, University of North Carolina, Chapel
Hill (hereafter cited as Carr Papers).
33. Julian S. Carr, undated speech, Carr Papers.
34. Clipping, *Raleigh News and Observer*, May 26, 1899, Carr Papers.
35. Carr, speech at Concord, N.C., February 8, 1898, Carr Papers.
36. Clipping, *Raleigh News and Observer*, May 26, 1899, Carr Papers.

cheap Negro labor, but he just as eagerly lent his support to a Negro-owned cotton mill begun in 1898 by W. C. Coleman, a black businessman in Concord, North Carolina; and later he sent his white technicians to assist a similar mill begun by Merrick and others in Durham.[37] Carr engaged in ostentatious philanthropy in the black community, distributing wagonloads of provisions during tough times, and serving "cake and buttermilk" at the Colored Fair. During the Spanish-American War he insisted on supporting the family of every black soldier.[38] The result of such friendliness, thought Carr, "was a colored population . . . well behaved, prosperous, contented and happy. . . ."[39]

But Nat Turner lurked in Carr's mind to counter the ubiquitous Uncle Tom; and so there was within him a vindictive redeemer to counter his paternalism. Recalling his Reconstruction days spent in Chapel Hill, he bragged that "less than ninety days after my return from Appomattox, I horse whipped a negro wench until her skirts hung in shreds, because upon the streets of this quiet village she had insulted and maligned a Southern lady. . . ."[40]

Unquestionably John Merrick was one of Carr's favorite Negroes. He boasted of knowing him "since his [Merrick's] boyhood days in Raleigh," and when Merrick fell ill in 1919, Carr visited him "regularly."[41] It was in this context of race relations, in this accord between capitalism and caste, that the North Carolina Mutual was born and sustained. White leaders in Durham had fashioned their understanding with blacks, and the Mutual served as an instrument of that accommodation. It could not have prospered for a day without adjusting to this setting.

37. Boyd, *Story of Durham*, p. 125; interview, Conrad O. Pearson, February 13, 1968; Washington, "Durham: A City of Negro Enterprise," p. 648; G. F. Richings, *Evidences of Progress among Colored People* (Philadelphia: G. S. Ferguson Company, 1902), pp. 481–484; Du Bois, *Efforts for Social Betterment*, p. 27; Du Bois, *Negro in Business*, p. 19; National Negro Business League, *Proceedings*, First Annual Meeting, Boston, 1900, pp. 206–209.

38. Interview, Conrad O. Pearson, February 13, 1968; *Durham Daily Sun*, October 14, 1896; clipping, *Boston Traveler*, September 21, 1898, Carr Papers.

39. Carr, speech at Columbus, Ohio, July 2, 1919, Carr Papers.

40. Carr, speech at Chapel Hill, N.C., June 2, 1913, Carr Papers.

41. Carr to Charles Clinton Spaulding, August 7, 1919; Carr speech, Columbus, Ohio, July 2, 1919, Carr Papers.

If white Durham provided the golden mean of paternalism and hostility to sponsor a bonanza of black business, the nature of black Durham was a positive factor as well. As a raw city of the New South, Durham possessed neither a white aristocracy nor a "cream of colored society" which one would find in older cities like New Orleans or Charleston. Without age or lineage it had to be a city of social upstarts who would grow their own aristocracy, and what time and breeding had not given them they could buy with money, as was the case with Carr. Without a white aristocracy there could be no black aristocracy that derived its status from its symbiotic attachment. In the shifting strata of black society in Durham at this time, the self-made Negro businessman and professional commanded high status and did not suffer condescension from an older, white-oriented servant class that in other cities felt its status threatened by a rising *petite bourgeoisie* that had its economic base in the black world.[42]

The invidious distinctions between "new issue" and "old issue," house servant and fieldhand, light and dark, had given Negro society internal restraints to entrepreneurial activity based on racial solidarity. At the turn of the century increasing segregation, discrimination, and urbanization encouraged the rise of a black business class which threatened to reorder the Negro status system that had been determined by antebellum forces. Obviously the conflict would be less in cities without an entrenched antebellum social order.[43] Durham thus escaped a part of this institutional drag on its black economy. Here apparently there was no "status revolution." Merrick was both upper class and *nouveau riche*. He served whites as a barber and sensed no conflict in promoting an all-black enterprise at the same time. Merrick helped create whatever upper-class criteria there were

42. This ideological and class conflict within the Negro community has been best analyzed by August Meier, *Negro Thought in America, 1880–1915* (Ann Arbor: University of Michigan Press, 1963), pp. 151–155; also see Meier, "Negro Class Structure and Ideology in the Age of Booker T. Washington," *Phylon*, XXIII (Fall, 1962), 258–266; Meier and David Lewis, "History of the Negro Upper Class in Atlanta, Georgia, 1890–1958," *Journal of Negro Education*, XXVIII (Spring, 1959), 128–139.

43. Meier, *Negro Thought*, pp. 151–155.

in the open, youthful, Durham Negro community; he encouraged whatever business activity arose out of the concept of racial solidarity. The kind of ideological conflict that found the colored gentry resisting the black capitalist had little meaning in Durham, where wealth and status coincided.[44]

Status anxieties aside, it is perhaps no accident that the large black insurance companies first arose in Durham, Washington, D.C., and Atlanta—in or near the South in rapidly expanding urban areas that offered industrial opportunity for a peasant class and occupational opportunity for the formation of a black middle class. No longer tied to the land, these new city-dwellers could not predict (as had been predicted for them) what their offspring would do upon the death of the head of the family. A sharecropper's widow could remain attached to the land and, with the labor of her children, continue to survive. In the city, where the job replaced the land as the economic base, no vestige of security remained after the death of the breadwinner; thus urbanization and occupational changes sponsored the rise of Negro life insurance on a more businesslike pattern, in place of the folk-oriented burial society.[45]

The tendency toward black capitalism in Durham and the success it achieved must be explained in a broad conceptual framework, but basic to the success of a segregated economic institution was the practical matter of consumer support. Many Negro communities never attained a sufficient level of employment or wealth to build a business sector on the foundation of

44. *Ibid.*; interviews, Conrad O. Pearson, February 22; W. J. Kennedy, Jr., January 29, 1968. If Durham had a traditional aristocratic element, it would have been the Fitzgerald family, which came to Durham from Pennsylvania during Reconstruction. The Fitzgerald brothers, highly educated mulatto artisans with a long heritage of freedom, manufactured bricks in Durham. Richard Fitzgerald became wealthy in his brick business, and until the rise of the North Carolina Mutual he enjoyed the highest status in the Negro community. For a fascinating semi-fictional history of the Fitzgerald family, see Pauli Murray, *Proud Shoes: The Story of an American Family* (New York: Harper and Brothers, 1956), esp. pp. 16, 33, 55, 56, 60, 61.

45. For a good discussion of the beginnings of life insurance in general, and its relationship to the rise of capitalism, occupational changes, and urbanization, see Shepard B. Clough, *A Century of American Life Insurance: A History of the Mutual Life Insurance Company of New York 1843–1943* (New York: Columbia University Press, 1946), pp. 4–16.

black patronage. Durham at the turn of the twentieth century, however, approached something of a "takeoff" period. During the 1890's Durham suffered from the depression of 1893 and passed through a comparatively static period in its economic history. Population and employment increased very little. It remained a town of struggling young factories, bringing into its limits only the minimum number of workers to keep the wheels turning. The total population in 1890 was 5,485, and a scant increase brought it to 6,679 in 1900;[46] the black population grew proportionately from 1,859 in 1890 to 2,241 in 1900.[47] But boom times returned to Durham during the next decade. The total population more than tripled to 18,241 by 1910; likewise, the black population increased threefold to 6,869.[48]

Booker T. Washington reported in 1910 (and one should allow for his optimism) that "W. Duke Sons and Company" alone employed 1,548 Negroes with an annual payroll of $440,000.[49] Washington and Du Bois were equally impressed by the black business community at this time. In 1912 Du Bois counted "fifteen grocery stores, eight barber shops, seven meat and fish dealers, two drugstores, a shoe store, a haberdashery, and an undertaking establishment." Du Bois acknowledged, "This differs only in degree from a number of towns, but black Durham in addition to this developed five manufacturing establishments which turn out mattresses, hosiery, brick, iron articles, and dressed lumber. Beyond this the colored people have a building and loan association, a real estate company, a bank, and three industrial insurance companies."[50]

Durham obviously provided relative economic opportunity for blacks, and they migrated to the city in great numbers. The primary attraction was the tobacco factories, which during the 1898–1900 period hired Negroes in unprecedented numbers, not to be equaled again until the World War I years. Apparently

46. Boyd, *The Story of Durham*, p. 128.
47. *Ibid.*, p. 283; U.S. Bureau of the Census, *Negro Population in the United States, 1790–1915* (Washington: Government Printing Office, 1918), p. 101.
48. Bureau of the Census, *Negro Population, 1790–1915*, p. 101; Boyd, *The Story of Durham*, p. 128.
49. Washington, "Durham: A City of Negro Enterprise," p. 648.
50. Du Bois, "The Upbuilding of Black Durham," pp. 334, 335.

there was a temporary white displacement of black tobacco workers after 1900; the Durham city directories reveal a sharp decline in the number of such workers, as well as domestic servants, and a corresponding increase in the number of white workers in those fields.[51]

Despite displacement, the demand for labor of any color went unrelieved, and Julian S. Carr's novel creation of a cotton mill for blacks more than offset the declining opportunities in the tobacco industry. Founded in 1902, the Durham Hosiery Mill "Number 2" employed over 250 blacks by 1910 and continued to expand into the 1920's. Carr's son recalled, "There was a distinct shortage of white workers. . . .We decided to try them [Negroes] out in a mill . . . established to knit cheap socks out of cotton that had formerly been sold as waste. Opposition was instant; advisory spirits told us that the rhythm of the machines would put the darkies to sleep . . . and the white workers . . . threatened to blow up the factory."[52] The mill prospered, nonetheless.

With a labor shortage coinciding with the formative years of the North Carolina Mutual, a time when any small economic reverse or hostile white action could have scuttled the tiny operation, the Company enjoyed a good base of consumer support and at the same time a relatively secure atmosphere in race relations. Black and white workers were fully employed to promote racial harmony, and purposely divided to prevent class unity; those who paid their wages had the city under control.

In the meantime all the positive institutional forces combined could not make a popular idea into a practical reality. The detailed planning taking place in Dr. Moore's office was for the moment more important. Between the time of the first organiza-

51. See Durham city directories 1897–1920 for a good picture of what appears to be an interesting cyclical pattern of Negro employment, displacement, and re-employment in various occupations. Also see Emerson E. Waite, Jr., "Social Factors in Negro Business Enterprise" (Master's thesis, Duke University, 1942), pp. 39, 50, 68, 76, 78, 81, 113–114, 124, 129.

52. Julian S. Carr, Jr., speaking in 1919 as quoted in Boyd, *Story of Durham*, pp. 125–126; for figures on employment also see Waite, "Social Factors in Negro Business," p. 96.

tional meeting in October, 1898, and the passage of the bill chartering the Company, the organizers met several times, always on the assumption that Senator Fuller would be successful. Thus looking ahead to launching the business, officers were chosen: Merrick, the obvious president; Fuller, while not among the original seven, had shown sufficient dedication in the state assembly to earn himself the vice-presidency; Dr. Moore, the penny-wise physician, seemed a natural choice as treasurer–medical director; Dock Watson, the multi-talented craftsman, and the only founder able to give his full time to the Association, became secretary–general manager largely by default; and E. A. Johnson, fully occupied in Raleigh, agreed to look after legal affairs as the Company's absentee attorney.[53]

During this interregnum Watson, who had a bent for bookkeeping, began calculating rates, collecting office supplies, and recruiting part-time agents. Within a week after the Company received its charter, Watson and the other officers had recruited agents in Durham, Chapel Hill, Hillsboro, Raleigh, and Greensboro. Dr. Moore agreed to share his office with the Company for $2 per month; a local black carpenter built a desk for $4; and for $3 more Watson bought six chairs to complete the furnishing of the first home office. The North Carolina Mutual and Provident Association declared itself officially in business on April 1, 1899.[54]

But there was not a customer in sight. Watson's task, as general manager and the only full-time employee, was to put down the roots of an agency system, quickly build up a clientele, and have the Company on a paying basis in time to meet what could

53. Minutes of organizational meetings of the North Carolina Mutual and Provident Association, November 17, December 15, 1898; January 19, February 15, 1899. Other members on the original board of directors included Merrick, Moore and Johnson. Pinckney W. Dawkins, perhaps because he lacked the $50, disappeared from the ranks of the officials; he later became a part-time agent. Nathaniel C. Bruce, a classics professor from Shaw University, filled his place, but apparently in no official capacity. James E. Shepard and William G. Pearson, both deeply involved in other ventures, retained an official identity with the Company as members of the board of directors.

54. *Ibid.*; Minutes of North Carolina Mutual Board of Directors meeting, March 9, 1899 (hereafter cited as Minutes); Kennedy, "North Carolina Mutual," pp. 3–4; Andrews, *John Merrick*, p. 64.

be embarrassing claims for an infant enterprise without a reserve of capital. Watson's incentive was a substantial one, sell or go hungry, for he had no set salary and depended entirely on the 40 percent commission from the policies he sold and the smaller percentage he received from the sales of agents he recruited. The other officers were at most part-time members of the Company; none received any salary, but each was urged to act as an agent. For all the men the Company was something of a sideline in their lives; all but Watson were established professionals who could spend little time with this venture. Merrick and Moore found time to assist Watson, however, and the three of them along with part-time agent P. W. Dawkins sold most of the policies during the early months of the Company's history.[55]

The first month's business was anything but heartening. Only the Durham agency reported, and the total collections after commissions amounted to only $1.12. At the end of another month, the Company had sold a total of 300 policies, but the vast majority of these were the nickel-a-week variety against which the Company was betting $1.60 per week that the policyholder would remain healthy, and $20.00 that he would not die. A few cases of the mumps or an epidemic of the measles could have destroyed the Mutual during these first few months. As it turned out, good fortune delayed the first sick claim until May, and the first death waited until August.[56]

But throughout the summer and fall Watson found little else to rejoice about. Premium income increased slightly but still averaged scarcely $50 per month. Watson had worked to establish agencies in fifteen towns in the piedmont area, but keeping them intact proved nearly impossible. His men, usually inexperienced, often became immediately dissatisfied with the difficult work of part-time selling, and the Company could offer no salary to encourage more qualified men to come into the business on a full-time basis. Reports were difficult to obtain from the agents; Watson could not build and supervise an agency system and

55. Kennedy, "North Carolina Mutual," p. 24.
56. Minutes, April 27, May 25, June 22, August 17, 1899.

sell insurance, too. He spent most of his time doing the latter in order to make a living wage. In view of this, the directors agreed to give Watson 50 percent of the agency income (after commissions) and instructed him to spend less time acting as an agent himself. Still, progress was hardly measurable. In February, 1900, the fifteen agencies remitted only $63.59; after deducting Watson's 50 percent commission and $10.00 monthly for a clerk, little remained to pay claims. Miraculously, the claims remained small. At the end of a full year's operation, premium income amounted to $595.79, and expenses somehow came to only $335.85, of which $79.01 went for sick claims and $40.00 for death claims.[57]

Despite the fact that Watson had not gone hungry, the possibility threatened, and it appears that only an element of luck preserved funds for him which normally might have been consumed by claims. And while the Company had not failed, it could scarcely be called a success, or a business at all, considering that the founders had planned to serve a large segment of the black population and to stand as a significant example of black capitalism. Thus far it had done neither, and seemed to hold out no promise that it could even survive. Moreover, good luck changed to bad as summer approached in 1900; claims mounted, and Merrick and Moore had to dip into personal funds to meet them. The other officers were not prepared to do this, nor was Watson, who became disillusioned and left Durham, resigning his position in June. By July the other members of the Company withdrew as well, leaving only Merrick and Moore, who persisted and reorganized the Association on July 1, 1900. Merrick remained as president, and Moore assumed a portion of Watson's position as secretary. A new figure, Charles Clinton Spaulding, was promoted from part-time agent to general manager.[58]

It is difficult to explain the actions of Merrick and Moore in terms of predictable business behavior. Neither man had much more than $50 in the Company; thus it seems unlikely that they

57. *Ibid.*, August 17, October 19, 1899; January 18, March 15, April 19, 1900.
58. *Ibid.*, June 21, July 2, 1900; Andrews, *John Merrick*, p. 65.

pushed on in an effort to recover their investment, and surely the chances appeared at least as certain that they would enlarge rather than recoup their losses. Nor was either man given to a gambling spirit in business affairs. Moore was conservative to a fault in such matters, and Merrick's caution and his eye for the good deal had earned him lavish praise from the white business community. Perhaps the two men really believed that the North Carolina Mutual was a company with a "Soul and a Service"— that to desert their policyholders was to discredit their people. For socially conscious black businessmen more was at stake than organizing an enterprise; they saw themselves organizing a people. Surely the goal was worth pursuing one more time. But in July, 1900, no one—perhaps not even Merrick and Moore themselves—would have bet very much on the outcome.

3

Survival
and Success

Charles Clinton Spaulding is often remembered as a one-man staff who "came to work early in the morning, rolled up his sleeves and did janitor's work. Then . . . rolled down his sleeves and worked as an agent. And a little later in the day he put on his coat and was general manager."[1] Thus, in a success story of epic proportions, he appeared as the savior of a flagging enterprise and transformed it into the unparalleled pride of black capitalism.

There is more truth than myth to this story, but successful entrepreneurs seldom succeed alone. Spaulding's energy and optimism served as a catalyst in the reorganization of the Company, and the Merrick-Moore-Spaulding "triumvirate" possessed important complementary qualities which together provided the strength to lift the Company out of defeat.[2]

Merrick, the only ex-slave of the three, had developed, in part because of his background, an astuteness in dealing with

1. Spaulding often spoke of his early experience with the Company in this way; see W. J. Kennedy, Jr., "North Carolina Mutual Life Insurance Company: A Symbol of Progress, 1898–1966" (Manuscript in possession of W. J. Kennedy, Jr., Durham, N.C.), p. 26. Upon Spaulding's death, John Cameron Swayze in an NBC News program eulogized him in the above words, as quoted in *Whetstone*, XXIX (third quarter, 1952), 7.

2. Triumvirate is a term often used by the Company to describe the relationship among the three leaders. Andrews spoke of them as the "triangle" which a "kindly fate brought together and cast . . . into one frame" (Robert M. Andrews, *John Merrick: A Biographical Sketch* [Durham: Seeman Printery, 1920], p. 17).

white men that was of incalculable value to the success of the Company. Born in 1859 on the edge of eastern North Carolina's black belt, Merrick was the son of a dark-skinned slave woman and a white man. In 1871 his mother left the plantation in Sampson County and went to Chapel Hill, where she worked as a domestic while John labored in the local brickyard and learned to read and write in one of the Reconstruction schools. After six years in Chapel Hill his mother married and went north to Washington, D.C. Young Merrick stayed behind and became a hod carrier and brick mason in Raleigh, where he helped build Shaw University. During a lull in his construction trade he worked as a bootblack in a Raleigh barbershop and quickly advanced to cutting hair. Merrick and his senior colleague, John Wright, became the favorite barbers of the Dukes and Julian S. Carr, who came to Raleigh because of the unsatisfactory service they encountered in frontier Durham. Carr finally persuaded Wright and Merrick to come to Durham and grace the New South city with the kind of tonsorial parlor that wealthy white men deserved. They opened their Durham shop in 1880; Merrick worked as Wright's assistant for six months, then bought a half interest, and the two men continued as partners until 1892, when Wright sold out to Merrick and went North. Merrick expanded the business, soon owning five shops, and for a brief time as many as nine. In the meantime he had become involved in a real estate business and the Royal Knights of King David.[3]

While Merrick's business sense can be counted as an indispensable contribution to the triumvirate, his shrewdness was necessarily balanced with an "affability" that had helped him succeed as a servant of white men. He knew perfectly how to play the role, how to wear the mask. Laughing at darkey stories

3. *Ibid.*, pp. 31–35; Booker T. Washington, *The Story of the Negro* (New York: Doubleday Page & Company, 1909), II, 37–38; interviews, Clyde Donnell, June 10; Charles Watts, June 6; W. J. Kennedy, Jr., February 26, 1968. Merrick had a constant eye for opportunity: in 1890 he sought to market his own hair tonic and dandruff cure, making a public appeal in the white newspaper to "treat your head at once with Merrick's Dandruff Cure. We don't claim to bring hair back on a bald head . . . [but] no dandruff cure has ever been put upon the market that has found such favor with the Tonsorial Profession." Quoted in Andrews, *John Merrick*, p. 36; *Whetstone*, first quarter, 1942.

and telling his own, Merrick pleased his white patrons; yet he knew how to navigate between affability and buffoonery. The white leaders thought of him more as the competent Negro businessman than as "John, the white man's barber." His greatest gift was creating consensus, and even blacks who saw him as a "white man's Negro" respected him for his accomplishments and his benevolence. His physical appearance added to his prestige. Very handsome, impeccably dressed, and with polished manners, he was seen by Julian S. Carr as a "Chesterfieldian Gentleman." But blacks knew that he could with "great poise, tip his hat to the white man and at the same time call him a son-of-a-bitch under his breath."[4]

While Merrick shared many of the puritan virtues for which the black middle class of Durham became famous, he was not loath to flaunt his wealth now and then, buying expensive cars, sporting a pool table in his spacious Victorian home, and generally earning a reputation as a man "who liked to have a good time," being "as unstinted in his enjoyment of the material things as he was in his charities."[5]

Dr. Moore, on the other hand, was the studied example of the frugal, serious-minded philanthropist who sought material gain only as an incidental necessity and quietly gave away what he did accumulate. Deeply religious, perhaps a bit inscrutable, and reputed as a philosopher whose "intellect completely dominates impulse,"[6] he brought a steadying influence to the group. He was born in 1863, not far from Merrick, in Columbus County, North Carolina, where he grew up as the son of a yeoman farmer who belonged to the third generation of a proud Negro-Indian-Caucasian family that had owned land in this area as free farmers since the early nineteenth century. Moore, like his nine brothers and sisters, worked on the family farm and at-

4. Interviews, anonymous, Durham, N.C., 1968. Andrews, *John Merrick*, pp. 168–202; Julian S. Carr, speech, Columbus, Ohio, July 2, 1919, Carr Papers.
5. Andrews, *John Merrick*, p. 146; interviews, Asa T. Spaulding, July 18; Mrs. Viola G. Turner, June 13; Clyde Donnell, June 10; Charles Watts, June 6, 1968.
6. Andrews, *John Merrick*, p. 18.

tended the county school during the four or five months it remained in session. After completing the eighth grade he attended normal schools in Lumberton and Fayetteville, returning from time to time to teach in his county school and work on his father's farm. In 1885 he enrolled in the newly built Shaw University and planned to become a professor. His teachers steered him instead into the University's Leonard Medical School, where he completed the four-year program in three years and placed second in the North Carolina medical board examinations. In 1888 he became Durham's first Negro physician.[7]

He settled into his practice, married the daughter of John C. Dancy, one of North Carolina's leading black political figures, and became involved in politics himself while it was still possible to do so. But even in 1888 he found whites so antagonistic to his campaign for county coroner that he withdrew and generally agreed with W. G. Pearson that for the moment they would have to settle for "the quiet exercise of the franchise" and throw their support to whichever party would best serve the interests of the "whole people."[8]

In 1895 Moore helped launch a pharmacy for Negroes, and from that time on he participated in virtually every business venture begun in Durham. For him the "Negro business movement" represented one part of an overall program of self-help involving equal parts of education and religion. Indeed, he is better remembered for his philanthropy than for his business efforts, a distinction that lost its meaning in terms of the racial self-fulfillment that Dr. Moore had in mind. With Merrick's help in raising money from the white community Dr. Moore founded Lincoln Hospital in 1901 and the Colored Library in 1913. Between 1914 and his death in 1923 he became absorbed in the rural school movement for Negroes. He personally paid the salary of North Carolina's first rural school inspector as

7. *Ibid.*, p. 24; interviews, Asa T. Spaulding, July 18; W. J. Kennedy, Jr., February 26, 1968.

8. *Durham Tobacco Plant,* October 15, 1888; John Campbell Dancy, *Sands against the Wind: Memoirs of John C. Dancy* (Detroit: Wayne State University Press, 1966), p. 70.

the initial step in demonstrating the need for such a program. Then, working closely with Tuskegee, he successfully campaigned for the funds necessary to qualify for the matching Rosenwald grant.[9]

Moore spent another part of his life working for the Baptist Church. Locally, in the White Rock Church, he was chairman of the board of deacons, a member of the board of trustees, and superintendent of the Sunday school for twenty-five years. Beyond Durham he served as president of the Baptist State Sunday School Convention. His work for the Lott Cary Foreign Missionary Convention carried him to Haiti at his own expense; there, with the funds he had raised in the United States, he founded the Haitian White Rock Baptist Church. Moore also insisted that the Durham congregation send a monthly allotment to Liberia. He served as chairman of the board of trustees of Shaw University and left in his will $5,000 to that Baptist institution.[10]

An aura of reverence clings to the memory of Dr. Moore. He is remembered as a man who transcended his times, who defied labels within the political spectrum. He "spoke straight from the shoulder"[11] and played no roles for favors. "He could tell white folks things that they wouldn't take from others," and he approached white leaders from a position of equality, assisted perhaps because he could nearly pass for white.[12] He is eulogized as the philosopher-physician who worked himself to death at the hospital he founded, but who still saved time to teach himself Spanish and to write and meditate far into the night.[13] He

9. *Whetstone*, October, 1935; interviews, W. J. Kennedy, Jr., January 26; Asa T. Spaulding, July 18, 1968. See Washington Papers, box no. 12, for information on the rural school program and Moore's participation in it.

10. Clipping, *Standard Advertiser*, May 1, 1923, in W. J. Kennedy, Jr., Scrapbook; interviews, Mrs. Viola G. Turner, June 13; Charles Watts, June 6; Clyde Donnell, June 10; Asa T. Spaulding, July 18; Mrs. E. R. Merrick, June 29, 1968; letters from A. M. Moore to Emmett J. Scott, April 12, 16, May 11, 1920; Scott to Moore, April 14, 23, May 6, 1920; Emmett J. Scott Papers, series I, box 19, Morgan State College.

11. Interview, Mrs. E. R. Merrick, June 20, 1968.

12. Interview, Asa T. Spaulding, July 18, 1968. Spaulding claims that the "weight of Dr. Moore's words couldn't help but impress everyone who met him."

13. *Ibid.*; interview, Mrs. E. R. Merrick, June 20, 1968; *Whetstone*, first quarter, 1942.

emerges from the history of black Durham as a Messiah moving quietly among his people, giving aid and comfort—"helping people was his whole life."[14] "No trumpeters proclaimed . . . the service he gave to the poor. Very few know of the poor children he educated."[15] If he made a house call and found the family destitute, he not only gave free treatment, but free medicine, food, and fuel. And he unfailingly queried the children about their Sunday school attendance. He accepted no excuses; if it was a matter of shoes or coats, he arranged for that, too. On Sunday mornings he stood in front of White Rock Church, collaring errant black youths; no matter what their dress, he ushered them into Sunday school. With praise and lament those who venerate Dr. Moore point out that, despite a several-fold increase in Durham's black population, the Sunday school enrollment of White Rock has declined in the half-century since his death.

Among the triumvirate Moore was chiefly responsible for fastening the North Carolina Mutual to a philosophic base. The ideas were already there, of course, but he reinforced them within the structure of the Company. In the mosaic of his thought one can see much of Booker T. Washington and the preeminence of Christ. His sense of a racial mission tempered by an intellect that looked to universalism is reminiscent of W. E. B. Du Bois. In many ways he resembled an American progressive who believed in social justice, the extension of public services, the unlimited powers of education, the social gospel, and (as an exacting administrator) the gospel of efficiency. But his missionary dedication was bound up in race and Christianity, and it militated against the secularization of the North Carolina Mutual. Just as Du Bois feared the power of Mammon over the souls of black folk and could mourn the passing of the authentic mutual benefit societies, so Moore hoped that the Mutual would not lose its soul in an effort to

14. Interview, Asa T. Spaulding, July 18, 1968. Spaulding thinks of Moore as one of the "forgotten figures of Negro history."

15. Clipping, *Standard Advertiser*, May 1, 1923. His daughter, Mrs. E. R. Merrick, recalls that he brought "at least a dozen Negro children up from Columbus County to be educated in Durham."

provide Washington with his "captains of industry." After Merrick's death Moore, as the new president, admonished the employees that the Company did not exist just "for the sake of getting business." There was a larger truth, he asserted, and "if the Company cannot live on truth, then let her go."[16] Moore's training, character, and intellect gave ballast to the purpose and direction of the Company, and on a more practical level inspired professional competence. It was he, for example, who taught C. C. Spaulding to write a formal business letter.

But if the new general manager had a lot to learn from Dr. Moore and lacked Merrick's influence with the white leaders, he had what the others did not: youth, time, and a restless energy. He, too, was born in Columbus County, almost next door to Dr. Moore, his uncle. In fact, three of the first five presidents of the North Carolina Mutual came from this area, which is in itself an intriguing fragment of Afro-American history. Located in southeastern North Carolina, Columbus County was the home of a small Negro population of decidedly mixed ancestry. The settlement felt a sense of community in a special ethnic and chromatic sense that set it apart from its surrounding racial matrix—white, black, and Indian—and it possessed a community tradition based not only on ethnic characteristics, but on its heritage of freedom, land ownership, religion, legends, and a maze of kinship ties formed from generations of marriage inside the community, often between first cousins. While very proud and even exclusive, the community chose not to isolate itself. In fact, much of its pride rested on a remarkable history of sending out into the world young men who achieved notable success. George White, the last Negro congressman from the South (1897–1901), came from Columbus County. A persistent legend links George White with the English colonizer of Roanoke Island, John White. According to the legend, settlers from the mysterious "lost colony" made their way to the mainland, inter-

16. Speech of Dr. Moore in 1920, as quoted in *Whetstone*, April, 1935; clipping, *Standard Advertiser*, May 17, 1923, in Kennedy Scrapbook; interviews, Asa T. Spaulding, July 18; Mrs. Viola G. Turner, June 13; Charles Watts, June 6; W. J. Kennedy, Jr., February 26, 1968.

married with Indians and later Negroes, and thus established this insular colony of free mulattoes.[17]

The Spauldings and the Moores make no claim to such ancestry. Another oral tradition explains that Spaulding's great-grandfather (Dr. Moore's grandfather) was a mulatto house servant emancipated from a plantation near Wilmington at the end of the eighteenth century. He married and settled in Columbus County as a free Negro farmer in the 1820's. His nine children married other free Negroes in the community, and in turn they produced large families, all of which rendered a hopelessly confused genealogy. One can decipher that Spaulding's father, Benjamin McIver Spaulding, married his first cousin, Dr. Moore's sister, and that of their ten children Charles was the second-oldest son.[18]

Spaulding, like his uncle, attended the local school and worked on his father's farm in a puritanical environment of early risers who took immense pride in their crops and land, their homes and families, and who looked to religion and work as the mainstay of life. Spaulding's father was not only a successful farmer, but also a blacksmith and an artisan who forged his own plows and implements, built his own furniture, and did custom work for his neighbors, black and white. During Reconstruction he served as the county sheriff. He was a proud patriarch who assigned family responsibilities to his children at an early age. Spaulding remembered that, when he was not working with his father in the field, he was mending harness, and that all the children helped his mother preserve food, scrub the board floors of the cabin with "soap and sand," plant flowers in the spring, and manicure the farmyard throughout the summer.[19]

17. Interview, Asa T. Spaulding, July 18, 1968; U.S. Bureau of the Census, *Sixth Census of the United States: 1850,* manuscript reports, schedule 1, Columbus County, N.C., pp. 235–236; Hamilton McMillan, *The Lost Colony: An Historical Sketch of the Discovery of the Croatan Indians* (Lumberton, N.C.: Robesonian Job Print, n.d.), pp. 1–35.

18. Interviews, W. J. Kennedy, Jr., February 26; Asa T. Spaulding, July 18, 1968; pamphlet entitled "Noble Ancestry" with family trees of Spaulding and Moore families, in possession of W. J. Kennedy, Jr.

19. Manuscript copy of an incomplete autobiography of C. C. Spaulding, in C. C. Spaulding Papers, North Carolina Mutual Life Insurance Company, Durham, N.C. (hereafter cited as Spaulding Papers); interviews, Asa T. Spauld-

Thus, long before Moore and Spaulding encountered white Durham, they had lived under the influence of the Protestant ethic, an influence that continued to be imported from the home community and imposed on all those who joined the Mutual and the black middle class of Durham in general. Recognizing the force of these "Puritan values" in Durham, E. Franklin Frazier wrote in the 1920's: "Durham offers none of the color and creative life we find among Negroes in New York City. It is not a place where men write and dream; but a place where black men calculate and work."[20] In contrast to what he would later castigate as a pathological "black bourgeoisie," Frazier saw the black capitalists of Durham "practising the old-fashioned virtues of the old middle class, their lives . . . as free from the Negro's native love of leisure and enjoyment . . . as Franklin's life. Hard work was their rule."[21] But far from identifying these traditional virtues as simply vestiges of a fading asceticism, Frazier characterized the stern entrepreneurial outlook of a man like Spaulding as representative of the "New Negro" in the New South. A white observer in Durham agreed, citing the contrast between Merrick and Spaulding as "the difference between the old-fashioned, contented Southern darkey and the new, restless, ambitious, college-bred Negro. John [Merrick] would say, 'Thank you, sir,' for every fifty-cent tip that came his way." But not Spaulding. "Lean, Cassius-like, and copper-colored, he

ing, July 18; W. J. Kennedy, Jr., January 21; Mrs. E. R. Merrick, July 20, 1968. E. Franklin Frazier in his *Negro Family in the United States*, rev. ed. (Chicago: University of Chicago Press, 1966), pp. 191–200, describes a community of "rural black puritans" which bears a striking resemblance to Columbus County.

20. E. Franklin Frazier, "Durham: Capital of the Black Middle Class," *The New Negro*, ed. Alain Locke (New York: Albert and Charles Boni, 1925), pp. 333–334.

21. *Ibid.*; Asa T. Spaulding, president of the North Carolina Mutual, 1959–67, and perhaps the most famous product of Columbus County, traces the style of the older Durham Negro middle class to this family heritage and the formative influence of his cousin C. C. Spaulding and, more importantly, Dr. Moore. He presents these men as secure and self-confident, firmly in possession of their identities, and without psychic compulsion to exaggerate their own importance. As a consequence, he argues, they were able to look beyond personal gain and to share prestige and power in order to make the necessary cooperative entrepreneurial decisions.

seldom smiled. He sought no tips. All he asked of life was an open field and a fair chance. He was strictly business."[22]

In 1894 Spaulding left the farm for Durham, where he finished what was then considered high school. He remained in the city working at a succession of jobs: dishwasher, bellhop, waiter, and office boy for a white attorney. Then in 1898 he became manager of a cooperative Negro grocery store. His extraordinary zeal in this effort so impressed Merrick and Moore that they turned to him as the pivotal figure in reorganizing the Mutual. This "go-getter," a "natural-born salesman," brought life to the dying North Carolina Mutual. He was bold, almost rash, and could hawk insurance without the slightest diffidence on street corners, in Jim Crow cars, or wherever he found a listener. When the Company paid its first death claims under his management, he "hit the streets" waving the receipts and buttonholing black folks with his evidence that the North Carolina Mutual "paid off," and that only a foolish Negro could not afford a policy.[23]

Spaulding immediately began to develop the market and inspire a new group of agents. The Company responded. By the end of 1900 the premium income doubled what it had averaged under Watson, but still the operation remained in the most precarious condition. It would take nearly three years before the triumvirate could look beyond a month-to-month existence.[24]

At the end of his first six months Spaulding had placed agents in twenty-eight towns and cities of North Carolina. This expansion increased his premium income 100 percent, but he soon encountered diminishing returns as his agency expenses more than doubled. More crucial was the mortality experience: sick claims by January, 1901, had tripled since the preceding July,

22. *Ibid.*; Robert Watson Winston, *It's a Far Cry* (New York: Henry Holt and Company, 1937), p. 249.

23. Interviews, Asa T. Spaulding, July 18; Clyde Donnell, June 10; W. J. Kennedy, Jr., January 21; Arthur E. Spears, Sr., May 15, 1968; John H. Wheeler, August 4, 1970.

24. Minutes, August 17, 1900, through January 15, 1905; Kennedy, "North Carolina Mutual," p. 31.

and death claims quadrupled.[25] Nor could Spaulding yet begin
to count on consistency from his agents; fewer than half both-
ered to report during some months. And the costs of quick expansion contined to mount, particularly expenses for Spaulding's
travel and wages for clerical assistance at the home office. In
the fall of 1901 Merrick and Moore loaned the Company $300
to meet past-due accounts, pay death claims, and buy out the
$50 interests of W. G. Pearson, Dock Watson, and James E.
Shepard.[26]

There are dozens of turning points in the history of the North
Carolina Mutual, but in its early survival 1902 stands as the
critical year. Losses continued to outrun profits into 1902. In
March the board discovered that the February sick and death
claims totaled approximately $400—nearly $300 more than the
premium income for the same month.[27] The decision before
Merrick and Moore was more difficult than when they chose to
reorganize the Association two years earlier. That decision had
involved no immediate risk or sacrifice. Now, twice in the space
of ninety days, they had to advance the Company over $300.
Even for Merrick this was a sizable amount of money, and the
financial commitment approached the point where neither man
could extricate himself in the future without a significant loss.
This was a true entrepreneurial decision involving risk, and, with
more at stake now, it would make each succeeding decision that
much more difficult. Nor was there any assurance that the next
month would not curse the Company with an equally disastrous
number of claims. Two years with Spaulding had hardened the
faith of Merrick and Moore; still, it is difficult to know the limits
of their faith, as it is difficult to know the limits of their liquid
resources. Would another month like February, 1902, have

25. Minutes, December 20, 1900; January 17, 1901.
26. *Ibid.*, June 20, October 18, 1901. Other than the original $50, this was
apparently the first personal advance to the Company. The widely told story that
Merrick and Moore had been sustaining the Mutual from the beginning is not
borne out in the record, particularly the dramatic story of digging into their
pockets to pay the first death claim.
27. *Ibid.*, March 19, 1902. The premium income for February, 1902, was
$129.

finished the enterprise? Perhaps, but once again good fortune averted the crisis. No policyholders died during March and the sick claims slackened.[28] One thing is certain—had Merrick and Moore not possessed a personal fund, or not been willing to use it, the Company would have gone under.

Entrepreneurial historian Arthur Harrison Cole has written, ". . . enterprises which escape 'infant mortality' may well acquire a zest for survival . . . a drive for success, which has but loose correlation with profit conditions."[29] Perhaps after three years of survival the men saw themselves past the infancy stage. Relative success had reinforced the *raison d'être* of the Company, and Spaulding had provided a powerful, relentless momentum. Perhaps they understood, too, that with expansion and initial success they should expect greater expenses, that initial deficits were often a sign of growth, and that they could not retreat before the risk at such a pivotal point.

Apparently Spaulding thought this way, for he kept on with unflagging optimism, and favorable events during the summer of 1902 vindicated his conviction. Claims diminished and premium collections doubled. By December Spaulding had agents working in fifty towns, and he had raised the premium income to $600 per month—more than the total income of the entire first year.[30] The triumvirate had turned a corner.

Even though they carried a small deficit going into 1903, their monthly collections grew with a new consistency that permitted prediction and planning. The Mutual operated only in the periphery of the strict scientific principles of life insurance and would not really advance to actuarial soundness until the 1930's, when the young mathematical genius Asa Timothy Spaulding became the Company actuary. Yet the directors could determine rates based on rough averages of monthly business and a much rougher prediction of the average mortality and morbidity experience. The process represented something like predicting

28. *Ibid.*, April 17, 1902.
29. Arthur Harrison Cole, *Business Enterprise in Its Social Setting* (Cambridge: Harvard University Press, 1959), p. 39.
30. Minutes, August 21, December 18, 1902.

the weather in an unstable climate based on several years experience.[31]

After 1902 survival, while still the Company's preoccupation, no longer posed quite the same monthly perils as it had before. With an established agency base in over fifty cities and towns by the end of 1903, and with income running well ahead of expenses, the Mutual could turn to consolidating that base. Spaulding had spent nearly all his effort selling and recruiting, and while those efforts had kept the Company afloat and had turned it toward success, it was now clear that he would have to stand back and give more attention to the administration of what he had built. He could not supervise agencies, manage the home office, sell, recruit, and mop floors. In 1903, then, he hired the first full-time agents and converted some of his men into traveling agents who would supervise in addition to selling. He expanded the office staff to include three full-time clerks, rented more office space, bought a typewriter and a safe. He read whatever he could find on the principles of life insurance and business management. Increasingly he saw himself as a "scientific" businessman, intent on removing the Mutual from the class of Negro burial societies. Early in 1903 the board realized that he could not manage more and sell less without a guaranteed salary. At $15 a week Spaulding became the first of the triumvirate to receive a set salary.[32]

The prosperity of 1903 encouraged the Company to increase its advertising, and it did so in dramatic fashion by beginning its own newspaper, the *North Carolina Mutual*. During the summer Spaulding advised that the Company publish a monthly newspaper "which will serve as an advertising and motivation medium for agents . . . [provide] news about Durham people and institutions and a list of sick and death claims. . . ."[33] Irwin H. Buchanan, a local music teacher and flamboyant phrase-maker, agreed to edit the paper; the Duke family allegedly gave

31. *Ibid.*, February 19, March 20, 1903.
32. Kennedy, "North Carolina Mutual," pp. 29, 31–35; Minutes, January 5, May 12, June 18, July 16, 1903; interview, Asa T. Spaulding, July 18, 1968.
33. Minutes, July 16, 1903.

the printing press.[34] Unfortunately, there are only a few extant copies of the *North Carolina Mutual.* (Buchanan's widow burned a truck full of the papers in the 1950's.) It is not only the best source for the early history of the Company, but as an organ of the Durham Negro community, the New South, and the economic philosophy of Booker T. Washington it is an extremely valuable source of Negro history in general. Moreover, with the exception of the original charter, nothing else in the early history of the Company so clearly illustrates the ambivalence of Negro business thought. Spaulding looked to the advertising function of the paper, but he also sensed that it had a community function. The motives again are elusive, but the burden of race would not allow the paper to be just a Company paper, any more than it would allow the Mutual to be just an insurance enterprise. Business historian Thomas C. Cochran has noted that company magazines did not begin in earnest until after World War I, and then only among the large businesses. That such an economically insignificant enterprise as the Mutual, having fewer than a half-dozen full-time employees in 1903, would begin a professionally printed newspaper which compared in technical quality and size with many small-town weeklies is a striking demonstration of the influence of culture on business thought and behavior.[35]

Merrick, before Spaulding, keenly appreciated advertising and public relations, and for a number of years had been writing ads in the white press for his barber shops. But when Spaulding became manager of the Mutual he was given almost no budget for such publicity. As a substitute he read Negro newspapers, particularly the *Raleigh Blade,* and then wrote the businessmen who advertised, appealing to them on the strength of racial cooperation to spread the word about the North Carolina Mutual.[36] With singular temerity Spaulding passed out leaflets

34. *Ibid.*; also minutes of August 20, 1903; interview, W. J. Kennedy, Jr., January 26, 1968.

35. Thomas Childs Cochran, *The American Business System* (Cambridge: Harvard University Press, 1957), p. 75.

36. Kennedy, "North Carolina Mutual," pp. 29–30, 36.

wherever he went, and he sent Company calendars to strategic persons, including President Theodore Roosevelt.[37] Given Spaulding's spirit and Buchanan's style, the *North Carolina Mutual* had to be a distinctive publication.

Buchanan, whether advertising or editorializing (often indistinguishable), prized the epigram in a setting of hyperbole. His argument for insurance was arduous and direct—so direct, in fact, that his serious pitch seems humorous in retrospect. "Get an accident policy," he urged, "someone may break your skull or you may lose one of your limbs."[38] To persuade the doubters, Buchanan often printed testimonials or recounted cases of tragedy that brought the Company to the rescue. In one such instance he told of a farmer who tripped and took a fatal plunge into his well. Buchanan drew the lesson: "Just such a sudden transition may befall any of us. Who knows?"[39] The high-pressure message was the Spaulding-Buchanan forte. They warned black fathers, ". . . death is pursuing you this moment. Don't let your departing words be: 'Good-bye darling. I bequeath you my troubles and debts. Give me a decent burial.' "[40] At the same time, they raised the dubious charge that "people who do not carry insurance do not help the churches,"[41] or that "the man who dies expecting to go to heaven and leaves his sorrowing wife and hungry children to face the cold charities of the world . . . will deserve a seat away back behind the thief."[42]

These admonitions reveal the ingenuity of Buchanan and co-editor Spaulding, but beneath these tactics lay a desperate and frustrating effort to convince the black masses that the North Carolina Mutual, as a Negro enterprise, could be trusted and was not destined to fail. Unquestionably one of the major problems confronting the Mutual agents at least up through the 1930's was countering Negro suspicion of a Negro company. If given a choice between a policy from a white company and one

37. *Ibid.*, p. 80; Andrews, *John Merrick*, p. 84.
38. *North Carolina Mutual*, May, 1906.
39. *Ibid.*
40. *Ibid.*, January, 1906.
41. *Ibid.*
42. *Ibid.*

from a black company, the Negro customer would very often choose the white. "It is past our understanding," complained Buchanan, "why there are yet some colored people who still think 50 cents from a white company is as much as $1.00 from a colored. . . ."[43] Spaulding sardonically quipped throughout his career that "colored folks think the white man's ice is colder." The irony is less striking when the numerous failures among small Negro insurance societies are taken into account. In part the suspicion was well founded; moreover, white companies like the Metropolitan, when they consented to insure Negroes, could afford to offer a more attractive policy than the Mutual and other leading black firms. The psychological element of "self-hatred" cannot be discounted; neither can it be confidently analyzed.

Most distressing was the unscrupulous white agent who preyed on the doubts of blacks. Merrick, writing in the columns of the *North Carolina Mutual*, instructed his agents: "Some of our people are easily made to believe that because you represent a negro enterprise it must be weak and unreliable, but you must . . . offset such impressions."[44] "Negroes," demanded Buchanan, "must stop letting white agents 'juggle' their reasoning."[45] A white company in Winston-Salem distributed a pamphlet in Negro communities, warning the residents that black insurance companies were "little concerns . . . of no account and soon bust. They call and call, and collect very promptly while you are well, but when you get sick they never come near your house. They tell you to uphold your color . . . but you will have a hard time getting your money out of them."[46]

Spaulding described such tactics as "satanic" and regretted that it took "years building up confidence and nailing falsehoods to the earth,"[47] but at the same time he acknowledged the damage done to the Mutual by the small, unreliable Negro societies. He implored his readers to be reasonable and to remember that

43. *Ibid.*, May, 1906.
44. *Ibid.*, September, 1904.
45. *Ibid.*, May, 1906.
46. Quoted in the *North Carolina Mutual*, June, 1904.
47. *Ibid.*, May, 1906.

"Negro companies are not all alike, even as white companies are not all alike."[48] Rival Negro agents were less than ethical in circulating the rumor that, while it was true that the North Carolina Mutual was the largest company, it was about to collapse because the officers embezzled funds and bought big homes for themselves.[49] The rumors proved so troublesome that the triumvirate offered a $500 reward to anyone who could substantiate charges that the Mutual lacked legitimacy or failed to pay its claims.[50] Buchanan commonly printed notices, testifying, for example, "We paid to Emanuel Thompson, who recently died of consumption, the sum of $24.00. We publish this to condemn the false statement . . . that we did not pay him anything."[51] Other enterprising Negroes tried to use the growing positive image of the North Carolina Mutual to their advantage. Some posed dishonestly as Mutual agents; a competing firm in Durham named itself the Carolina Mutual Life Insurance Company; another, the North Carolina Mutual Benefit Company. To prevent imitation, the Company adopted as its exclusive trademark a photograph of the triumvirate.[52]

The Association waged a persistent battle to keep its image clean, a struggle in which it encountered the dilemma of dissociating itself from other Negro businesses at the same time it fervently preached the cause of business cooperation among Negroes.[53] "The Mutual has no time for fighting other [Negro] companies if they are treating our people right," Spaulding announced, but "remember, we are here to see that the people are protected."[54]

Obsessively the Company newspaper sought to reassure the public of its integrity. "This is no 'Get Rich Quick' scheme," Buchanan told his readers. "The directors of this institution are

48. *Ibid.*, October, 1904.
49. *Ibid.*, January, 1906.
50. *Ibid.*, November, 1903.
51. *Ibid.*, October, 1904.
52. *Ibid.*, March, 1904; May, 1906.
53. See *North Carolina Mutual*, January, 1906, for example.
54. *Ibid.*

. . . willing to lose rather than take a penny from those whom they invite to invest."[55] Nearly contradicting himself, the editor continued, "We are no side show with a great long array of gold gilded adjectives to lure you into our ranks."[56] And when the general manager did uncover dishonesty among his agents, he was quick and sensational in presenting the matter to public view: "We offer a reward of $25.00 for the arrest of M. S. F. Lee, a former agent . . . who deducted money from his reports. . . . His presence is wanted on the public roads of Wayne County. We warn all agents to be careful. See that your record is clean."[57] In a similar notice concerning an agent who "collected $40.00 in Hillsboro and ran off to Norfolk," Spaulding pointed out to policyholders, "Of course the members will not lose a cent. . . ."[58]

The vigorous efforts to build a strong agency force and a favorable public image were rewarded with a tremendous business increase in 1904. During the first nine months of that year more policies were sold than in the entire history of the Company to that time.[59] Much of the rapid growth also came as a result of the Company's expansion into South Carolina, a move which was coupled with important innovations in policies. Industrial "straight life" policies were offered without the attendant sick and accident provisions. Thus for five or ten cents a week one could buy either life insurance or sickness and accident insurance at cheaper rates than the old combination policies.[60] Offering the policyholder a choice in the type of insurance he bought represented an important step in the North Carolina Mutual's continuing evolution from the mutual benefit concept of minimum social welfare measures for the indigent to a more businesslike approach which recognized the growth of a black middle class. In 1904 the Company introduced some-

55. *Ibid.*, March, 1904.
56. *Ibid.*
57. *Ibid.*, January, 1906; see also May, 1906.
58. *Ibid.*, January, 1907.
59. *Ibid.*, January, September, October, 1904.
60. *Ibid.*, March, 1904; Kennedy, "North Carolina Mutual," p. 46.

thing beyond industrial insurance, offering ordinary whole life, twenty-pay life, and twenty-year endowment plans.[61]

Not a great deal is known about Company rates and their calculation at this time. Unfortunately a fire in 1914 destroyed most of the early records, but it appears that in the beginning rates were largely a result of guesswork without regard to actuarial principles. The True Reformers had, by the 1890's, adopted a step-rate system which advanced the rates in proportion to the age of the policyholder, but in 1899 the North Carolina Mutual and Provident Association insured any "healthy man woman or child" at the same rate regardless of age.[62] (See Table 1.)

The Association insisted that these rates were the "cheapest" and the benefits the "greatest." Perhaps they were too favorable to policyholders, for by 1904 rates were classified according to age—and in general policyholders paid higher premiums for less protection.[63] (See Table 2.)

Determining rates continued to be a trial-and-error affair; when experience showed the Company it would have trouble

61. Kennedy, "North Carolina Mutual," p. 46; *North Carolina Mutual*, June, October, 1904, January, 1905; Andrews, *John Merrick*, p. 86. Industrial insurance is generally defined as minimum protection for people of the working class on limited budgets who pay their small premiums on a weekly basis, usually to an agent who makes weekly rounds. In contrast, ordinary insurance offers larger amounts of protection with premiums mailed in by the policyholder, usually on a quarterly basis. Industrial insurance is more expensive for both the policyholder and the insuror than ordinary insurance because of the greater expense in servicing the policies, but this nickel-and-dime-a-week plan was often the most attractive and practical insurance for the masses. Other differences would include fewer benefits for the industrial policyholder, such as loan and surrender values and rate of dividend, if any; on the other hand, no stringent medical examinations were required to qualify for these small policies. "Whole life" simply means that the policyholder pays his premium for the whole of his life, and the policy presents full payment only at the time of death. Limited-payment life, however, requires higher premium payments during a specified number of years—say twenty, as in the case of the Mutual policy mentioned above—after which time the policy is considered "paid up" and the protection continues. This has been an attractive plan for those whose smaller income during retirement would make continuing premium payments a burden. Endowment insurance combines investment with protection. The face amount of the policy is paid upon the person's death, if it comes before the end of the endowment period, or if the policyholder survives the endowment period—twenty years, for example—he receives the face amount. An endowment policy is a form of retirement insurance in the sense that one does not have to die to collect.

62. Andrews, *John Merrick*, p. 78.

63. *North Carolina Mutual*, August, 1903; September, 1904.

TABLE 1. NORTH CAROLINA MUTUAL AND PROVIDENT ASSOCIATION:
RATES AND BENEFITS, 1899

Weekly payment	Sick benefit	Death benefit
5¢	$ 1.60	$ 20.00
10	3.25	40.00
15	3.75	50.00
20	4.50	60.00
25	5.50	70.00
30	6.50	80.00
35	7.50	90.00
40	8.50	100.00
45	9.50	115.00
50	10.00	120.00

TABLE 2. NORTH CAROLINA MUTUAL AND PROVIDENT ASSOCIATION:
RATES AND BENEFITS, 1904

Ages	Weekly payment	Sick benefit	Death benefit
3–12	5¢	$ 1.00	$ 18.00
	10	2.00	35.00
	15	2.75	45.00
	20	3.50	55.00
	25	4.00	65.00
12–40	5¢	$ 1.25	$ 20.00
	10	2.50	40.00
	15	3.25	50.00
	20	4.00	65.00
	25	5.00	75.00
40–45	5¢	$ 1.25	$ 20.00
	10	2.00	35.00
	15	2.50	40.00
	20	3.00	45.00
	25	3.50	50.00

meeting claims, rates were increased, or benefits reduced, to a point projected sufficient to meet operating expenses. While the Association had the power to assess its members until its legal status changed from an assessment organization to a legal reserve company in 1913, it apparently preferred to change the rates rather than to assess each member directly, just the opposite from the older societies. The Company simply felt its way along, hoping that the volume would increase enough to take care of the death claims and that the rates would be adequate.

With only three men involved in the management of the Company (and only one on a full-time basis), decision-making, in general, was a simple and pragmatic process. Within broad limits Spaulding had full rein. Merrick and Moore dropped in on their lunch hours to advise and consent, and in this informal setting they worked out the difficult problems. The monthly board meeting provided the formal occasion to codify their decisions and review the manager's report. The Company by-laws, adopted in 1900, provided that the board of directors should be elected annually, but no electorate was specified. For several years the triumvirate simply succeeded itself as both directors and officers of the Company.[64] State regulations of mutual insurance companies called for something quite different; namely, that the policyholders, in an advertised annual meeting, elect the board of directors.[65]

The triumvirate was unaware of these regulations and did not fully comprehend the nature of a mutual insurance company, particularly the legal distinction from a stock corporation. There is reason to believe that the directors regarded themselves as stockholders and considered their original $50 investment a purchase of ownership.[66]

Regulation of insurance companies was a novelty for North Carolina, which established its Insurance Department in 1898, the same year the Mutual was organized. Apparently the two institutions knew very little about one another until 1906. The Insurance Department concerned itself with regulating large northern firms doing business in the state and had little interest in watching over another Negro "coffin club." In the institu-

64. See Minutes, 1899–1911.
65. A mutual insurance company, unlike a stock company, is owned by the policyholders. Officers and directors are technically salaried employees of the policyholders.
66. Interview, W. J. Kennedy, Jr., June 5, 1968; Minutes, January 15, 1905.

tionalized biracial society of the South, the Mutual belonged to another world. Completely out of touch with the white insurance industry, the black directors knew no more about the celebrated Armstrong Investigation than they did about the Portsmouth Conference. And as long as the Company attracted no attention or presented no threat, it could continued to be ignored and isolated as an extension of a Jim Crow world that merited no formal supervision.[67]

This neglect probably served the interest of the Company during its early survival years, at a time when any additional barrier could have forced the men to abandon their efforts. The regulation that came after 1906, however, unquestionably assisted the Mutual's efficiency and expansion.[68] Scholars have debated the benefits of state regulation of insurance companies. W. O. Bryson, in analyzing the failure of the True Reformers, laid the blame on a lack of regulation that allowed the firm to fall into unsound business practices.[69] Du Bois, on the other hand, claimed that the True Reformers and a multitude of other Negro insurance societies failed because of a white conspiracy within "Southern legislatures [which] only began to awaken to this need [regulation] when Negro societies began driving the whites out of business."[70] Certainly the legislatures were not above such behavior, but Du Bois overestimated the political influence of the tiny white organizations which sporadically pursued Negro business. In fact, it was the larger black com-

67. The North Carolina Mutual is not listed in the Insurance Department *Reports* until 1906, and Winfred Octavus Bryson, "Negro Life Insurance Companies" (Ph.D. dissertation, University of Pennsylvania, 1948), p. 10, asserted, "The North Carolina Mutual was engaged in the insurance business for several years before the insurance commissioner was aware of . . . its existence." The Armstrong Investigation conducted in New York in 1905 and presided over by Charles Evans Hughes revealed that insurance companies had become a part of the "frenzied finance" of the period. The findings and recommendations of the Investigation brought about much tighter regulation of insurance companies and a general demand for greater public responsibility. (The Portsmouth Conference in 1905 negotiated the peace settlement of the Russo-Japanese War.)

68. See pp. 74–75, 92–94.

69. Bryson, "Negro Life Insurance Companies," p. 10.

70. Du Bois, *Economic Cooperation among Negroes*, Atlanta University Publications no. 12 (Atlanta: Atlanta University Press, 1907), p. 100.

panies like the Mutual who lobbied for greater restrictions on the small black societies that plagued the reputation and good will of the established Negro companies.[71]

It is a credit to Merrick, Moore, and Spaulding, who thought and acted as if they possessed more power over the Company than was legally theirs, that they managed the enterprise much as if they were being supervised all the time. They even exceeded the legal requirements of the state for a mutual assessment association when they voluntarily set money aside in an informal reserve fund. They could have pocketed this occasional surplus by voting themselves higher salaries, and then (without the reserve) assessed members or raised premiums during a lean period.[72]

Despite initial skepticism, one is persuaded that an overriding sense of trusteeship governed the triumvirate. Entrepreneurial historian Harold F. Williamson, in his business history of the Northwestern Mutual Life Insurance Company, discovered such a characteristic among its early leaders, a quality of leadership undoubtedly determined by what Arthur H. Cole labeled "internal entrepreneurial forces." "External forces" (societal norms) promoting such public responsibility were not sufficiently strong to explain the behavior of white entrepreneurs at this time.[73] For the North Carolina Mutual, however, in addition to similar internal forces best exemplified in Dr. Moore, powerful external forces from the Negro subculture compelled the leaders to acknowledge public responsibility. Not all black businessmen accepted the responsibility of racial uplift, but none escaped at least the psychic burden of these external forces, which demanded something more than that asked of the white business world.

71. See, for example, an importuning speech of John Merrick before the North Carolina General Assembly in 1910 requesting a $10,000 bond requirement for any insurance association beginning business in the state. Typescript of the speech is in C. C. Spaulding Papers.

72. Kennedy, "North Carolina Mutual," pp. 75–76; Andrews, *John Merrick*, p. 91.

73. Harold F. Williamson and Orange A. Smalley, *Northwestern Mutual Life: A Century of Trusteeship* (Evanston, Ill.: Northwestern University Press, 1957), p. 4; Arthur H. Cole, *Business Enterprise in Its Social Setting*, pp. 17–22.

Whatever praise belongs to the triumvirate, it is a mistake to think, as many do, that these men were so supremely selfless that they gave their money and time with no thought of repayment. On the contrary: when the Company became prosperous enough to sustain salaries and withdrawals from the treasury, they sought to compensate themselves rather handsomely for their past sacrifices. At the beginning of 1905 Spaulding was receiving a monthly salary of $75; Merrick and Moore were still without salaries. During the year the directors voted Dr. Moore $25 per month for his part-time work, and Merrick began selling ordinary policies at a lucrative 50 percent commission, plus a $100 per month salary when he left the barber shop and turned his full attention to the Company.[74] Early in 1906 the officers decided that hard work and success justified payment for past services and they voted themselves $5,000 each as a kind of deferred "dividend." The State Insurance Department, now acquainted with the Company, declared such a payment illegal under the rules regulating mutual life insurance companies. The men were told that they could legally claim no more than the actual money they loaned the Company. Thus Merrick and Moore recovered $1,713 at 6 percent interest, the total amount of money they put into the Company during the years 1899–1903. The Insurance Department also disallowed Merrick's 50 percent commission and informed the directors that they could no longer succeed themselves without an annual policyholders' meeting advertised in several newspapers throughout the state.[75]

That Merrick and Moore would consider not only reimbursement but a bonus during 1905–6 is an indication of the Company's progress. The expansion into South Carolina brought an abundance of new business, prompting editor Buchanan to generalize that black South Carolinians "have a good deal of race pride and like to encourage negro enterprise."[76] The total number of policyholders doubled during 1904, from 20,000 to 40,000,

74. Minutes, January 2, December 24, 1905.
75. *Ibid.*, January 6, November 8, November 23, December 12, 1906; January 14, 1907; interview with W. J. Kennedy, Jr., June 5, 1968.
76. *North Carolina Mutual*, March, 1904.

and by the spring of 1906 the number had doubled again.[77] Adding to its variety of insurance the Company introduced a popular policy in 1906 designed for "the protection of those of our people who are especially exposed to accidents."[78] For an annual premium of $1.25 the black worker could insure himself for $100 in the case of accidental death, $50 for loss of a limb, down to $5 for a broken rib.[79]

The rapid advance of business greatly encouraged Merrick and increasingly weaned him away from his barbering. "I know I am the proudest negro that lives today," he declared in 1904, "because the North Carolina Mutual and Provident Association is planted on a firm basis. It looks like the Company has at last scaled the mount. . . ."[80] Buchanan outdid himself when Merrick announced in January, 1905, that he intended to take charge of the ordinary insurance and give his full time to the Company: "Hurrah! Hurrah! Port Arthur falls again," the editor exclaimed, as he presented a parable of the underdog prevailing through strategy and perseverance.[81] Four months later the newspaper reported, "Merrick has been hustling since the first of January and has written several thousand dollars worth of endowment insurance in Durham and Chapel Hill. . . ."[82]

Beginning in 1906 the Company initiated what was to become commonplace in the history of its growth—the reinsurance of small, financially distressed societies on the verge of collapse. Unless these companies were heavily encumbered with debts, the Mutual knew it was better to buy them out than to watch them fail and further erode public confidence in black business. In many instances the officials of the failing enterprises welcomed the escape from impending failure because reinsurance meant jobs for them and no loss of security for the policyholders. For example, in 1906 the Mutual paid $1,000 for the

77. *Ibid.*, October, 1904; May, 1906.
78. Minutes, February 15, 1906.
79. *Ibid.*; *North Carolina Mutual*, May, 1906.
80. *North Carolina Mutual*, September, 1904.
81. *Ibid.*, January, 1905. "Port Arthur" referred to the unexpected 1904 defeat of Russia by the much smaller Japan.
82. *Ibid.*, April, 1905.

People's Benevolent and Relief Association in Charlotte, North Carolina. In turn the Mutual gained 10,000 members and two life-long employees of executive caliber.[83] In a very pragmatic sense the small insurance society could be a positive and necessary cog in the development of Negro insurance; the large grew at the expense of the small, which served as sacrificial instruments of recruitment and training. Stricter state regulation of mutual assessment organizations greatly aided this process, particularly in South Carolina, where in 1908 the state legislature demanded a $10,000 bond from all such associations. For most the demand meant doom, and the North Carolina Mutual absorbed them in wholesale lots, often just transferring the policyholders and paying little or nothing for their dubious assets.[84]

When the number of policyholders exceeded 100,000 in January, 1907, the Mutual boldly printed on its letterhead, "North Carolina Mutual and Provident Association Greatest Negro Insurance Company in the South."[85] Soon the letterhead was revised to read: "Greatest Negro Insurance Company in the World."[86] In support of this claim the Company newspaper relentlessly imposed on its readers a profusion of numbers and dollar signs. The figures were insignificantly small in the context of the larger life insurance industry, but Buchanan assumed that statistics would overcome Negro incredulity; thus he invited all those who doubted that the Association possessed in 1907 "assets worth $28,413.47 or that it had paid out over $40,000 in claims" during 1906, to write the North Carolina Insurance Department for corroboration.[87]

83. Kennedy, "North Carolina Mutual," pp. 62–64; Minutes, November 20, 1906; January 14, 1907; *North Carolina Mutual*, January, 1907.

84. Minutes, April 1, 18, 29, 1908; August 23, 25, September 15, 1909; Kennedy, "North Carolina Mutual," p. 67. Du Bois's argument that southern legislatures demanded these bonds to force Negroes out of business might have some validity in South Carolina, where there were a tremendous number of these organizations. The amount of the bond was increased to $15,000 in 1910. Spaulding often noted that South Carolina dealt severely with the Mutual in court cases, and perhaps as a form of harassment demanded a reserve even before the Company achieved legal reserve status.

85. See letter from agent Charles N. Hunter to C. C. Spaulding, May 25, 1907, Hunter Papers, Duke University.

86. C. C. Spaulding to Charles N. Hunter, December 13, 1909, Hunter Papers.

87. *North Carolina Mutual*, January, 1907.

Those who visited Durham in 1906 saw tangible proof of the Company's success. In January the Mutual occupied its handsome new brick office building on Parrish Street. The directors had considered moving to Hayti (the commercial area of the Negro community), but white businessmen advised Merrick that property values would appreciate much faster on Parrish Street, contiguous to the heart of the white business district.[88] The *Durham Sun* found the new office building "a very imposing structure . . . beautifully carpeted and furnished." The Mutual occupied only a part of the upper floor of the two-story office building, renting the remaining space to the Royal Knights of King David, the Oddfellows, two Negro lawyers, and Dr. Moore. The lower floor and an adjoining one-story ell had been built to provide room for expansion and housing other black businesses.[89] Within two years the Company purchased additional lots and added to its offices, forming a black business complex that included two clothing stores, a barber shop, a large drugstore, a tailoring shop, offices of the Negro newspaper, and the Mechanics and Farmers Bank. Durham's other white newspaper, the *Morning Herald,* celebrated the North Carolina Mutual business center as the "Colony of the Colored" with its "Beautiful Business Block" being managed by "these thrifty people . . . who have not only an eye for business but one for beauty. . . . Not a street in this town would object to having an outside or an interior as attractive as these stores that front Parrish Street."[90]

Once installed in its new offices, the Company took on an increasingly businesslike posture. The directors hired a trained stenographer, Susan Gille, from Wilberforce University; she brought to the Mutual not only her valuable skills, but also a surprising amount of publicity. She represented the colored gen-

88. Minutes, June 1, 2, 8, 9, 1905; *North Carolina Mutual*, January, 1906.

89. *North Carolina Mutual*, January, 1906, quoting the *Durham Sun*, n.d.

90. Clipping, *Durham Morning Herald*, July 29, 1908, in Avery Scrapbook; Andrews, *John Merrick*, pp. 92–93; also see clipping, *Greensboro Daily News*, August 20, 1910, in Avery Scrapbook. White real estate dealers offered the Company property on Main Street for the new building, but the founders circumspectly chose Parrish Street out of concern that such boldness "would tend to create a race problem" (*Whetstone*, first quarter, 1940).

tility of Ohio, and created something of a sensation in undignified Durham as she stepped from the train impeccably dressed in multiple black skirts, white puffed sleeves, and whale-bone collar; round-topped trunk in tow, she made her way across the unpaved streets with an aristocratic bearing, speaking a brand of English that betrayed her classical background. In her person the Mutual added "culture and class" to black Durham; moreover, a Negro stenographer was indeed a novelty in the city. Black schoolchildren descended on the home office to watch "the flying fingers of the colored girl from the North who typed without even looking at the keys."[91] Sensing the potential for training others, the Company encouraged Miss Gille to offer lessons in typing and shorthand to the interested townspeople, thus inaugurating a rudimentary Negro business school to supply the needs of Durham's black enterprises and perpetuating an interesting version of the "Yankee school marm."[92] As another indication of the expanded business outlook, the Company hired on a retainer basis Durham's prominent white law firm, Winston and Bryant. Ironically, Spaulding had once worked as an office boy and personal servant for Winston.[93]

Relatively secure and prosperous, with office space on its hands, the Mutual, like nearly every large Negro business, began to act as a mother institution within the black community. To a large extent it resisted crossing so many institutional boundaries and dangerously overexpanding as did the True Reformers and later the Standard Life Insurance Company of Atlanta, but the need for investment areas and the ideal of racial self-fulfillment made it virtually impossible to avoid overlapping the various sectors of the Negro community. In the summer of 1906 the Company officially put itself into the newspaper business.[94]

91. Interview, W. J. Kennedy, Jr., January 29, 1968; *Whetstone*, fourth quarter, 1940.
92. Kennedy, "North Carolina Mutual," p. 58; *North Carolina Mutual*, May, 1906.
93. Minutes, August 15, 1906; Andrews, *John Merrick*, p. 66.
94. Minutes, April 15, 1906.

The *North Carolina Mutual* had served for three years as a monthly community paper, but Buchanan and the Mutual officers believed that a new weekly, the *Durham Negro Observer*, was in order. "We scan papers of other races," announced Buchanan, "and find we hardly get honorable mention unless we play leading roles as 'chicken thief,' 'rapist,' 'murderer,' 'bad nigger.' We have read too much about the dark side. . . . We have come to let you know that there is yet hope."[95]

The *Observer* resembled a weekly version of the *North Carolina Mutual*. Buchanan edited both papers under the watchful eye of assistant editor C. C. Spaulding, who, along with Merrick and Moore, was also a director of the newly formed subsidiary, the Durham Negro Publishing Company.[96] Apparently the enterprise failed to prosper, and Dr. Moore, afraid that the Mutual would be dragged down by a parasitic venture, advised the Board in October, 1906, to dissolve the publishing company before a substantial amount of money was lost. Buchanan may have continued a few issues on his own, but certainly by 1907 the *North Carolina Mutual* was once again the only Negro newspaper in Durham.[97] The compulsion to publish a weekly community newspaper persisted, however, and in less than three years the Mutual had purchased the defunct *Reformer* from the failing True Reformers. In this case the Company apparently hoped to steer clear of direct management of the paper; instead it transferred to Durham not only the entire Reformer Publishing Company with all of its equipment, but imported the Richmond editor, W. S. Young, as well. Young managed the paper for a year and then bought it from the Mutual and continued to operate it until about 1918. Unfortunately, there is only a single known extant copy.[98]

95. *Durham Negro Observer*, June 23, 1906.

96. *Ibid.*, July 21, 1906.

97. Minutes, October 15, 1906; interview, W. J. Kennedy, Jr., January 29, 1968.

98. Minutes, August 9, 1909; May 20, 1910. I found only one disintegrating issue of the *Reformer*—July 27, 1911—in the possession of C. C. Spaulding, Jr. W. S. Young was a member of the family that has published the *Norfolk Journal and Guide*; correspondence with the Young family uncovered no copies of the *Reformer*.

It is difficult to disentangle the motives behind the Mutual's persistent efforts to publish a newspaper. Perhaps such a decision involved a built-in racial responsibility to serve the community, to build a duplicate black society and fill in all the institutional gaps—as well as a pragmatic search for investment opportunities and publicity. Certainly the Mutual felt the need to pick up the pieces of broken enterprises like the True Reformers, thus vindicating the cause of Negro business and preventing the stain of failure from extending further into the black consciousness. In any event, between 1903 and 1911 the Company launched, in addition to its newspapers, a variety of subordinate business efforts, including a drugstore, a bank, a real estate company, and a hosiery mill.

As early as 1903 the Company began an investment program in real estate, largely as an outgrowth of Merrick's efforts, which by this time had made him the owner of more than sixty houses in Durham. Following his example, the Company, with loans from Merrick and Moore, purchased several old buildings and from the salvaged lumber built rentals on its lots in the black community.[99] In this process Merrick acted as an informal building contractor for the Company. Such an arrangement might have invited peculation reminiscent of the railroad scandals in microcosm, but clearly in this case the Company chose to work through Merrick because he could "buy the material and hire the labor and erect the building so as to save the Company the cost of the contractor."[100]

Not only was Merrick the "Company builder" but in general he also served as the firm's realtor, with authority from the board to "act as agent for the Company to invest the surplus in staple real estate and loans on first mortgages on real estate."[101] He was most adept at buying cheap land and obtaining cheap materials. He bought land for taxes and once purchased an entire house for nine dollars; moreover, it is reasonable to assume that

99. Minutes, March 20, June 18, 1903; Kennedy, "North Carolina Mutual," p. 35.
100. Minutes, September 19, 1909; March 1, 1910.
101. *Ibid.*, March 15, 1905.

he still acquired old buildings from the Dukes in exchange for the labor to wreck them.[102]

Without Merrick's contacts with white bankers many vital investment opportunities would have been lost, and the general expansion of the Company would have been retarded. The several lots purchased on Parrish Street and the business complex constructed there were financed in large part with money from the Fidelity Bank, owned by the Duke family, and from the Home Savings Bank of Durham, owned by another white business pioneer, George W. Watts.[103] In 1908 the Association, plagued by excessive claims and caught with much of its money tied up in real estate, could not meet a large mortgage payment or complete a construction project. Merrick borrowed $6,000 from the Fidelity Bank and presented his personal holdings as collateral.[104] This transaction reveals two important points: first, that the Company through Merrick had immediate access to capital when it needed it—an indispensable requirement for an infant business; second, that the triumvirate often acted as if the Mutual was in fact their personal property, which obligated them to loan it money in time of need; and the reverse was true as well. Indeed, Merrick and Spaulding in their private real estate dealings did not hesitate to borrow money from the Company.[105]

With little supervision the triumvirate managed the Company instinctively, and the instincts fortunately balanced themselves between the public and the private interest. The sense of trusteeship proved always to be at least as strong as self-interest. The men could have milked the Company without ever consciously overstepping the law, but "race man" and businessman confronted one another to create an extralegal burden of public responsibility.

Merrick's influence and the absence of alternative investment opportunities produced a portfolio dangerously top-heavy in

102. *Ibid.*, April 20, 1906; November 18, 1907; January 4, 1908; interview with C. O. Pearson, February 22, 1968.
103. Minutes, June 1, 8, 9, 12, 1905.
104. *Ibid.*, February 17, 18, 1908.
105. *Ibid.*, January 25, 1909.

real estate. At the end of 1907 real estate holdings accounted for three-fourths of the Mutual's total assets.[106] Had it not been for the boom conditions in Durham and easy credit from white bankers, the Company could have foundered on such a surfeit of nonliquid and relatively insecure assets. With this danger in mind the insurance commissioner advised the directors to unload much of their real estate and replace it with secure bonds and mortgage loans. The Company complied, and in the process gave birth to the inevitable offspring—a real estate company—the Merrick-Moore-Spaulding Land Company.[107]

Of larger significance for the future of black business in Durham was the Mutual's investment and organizing effort in the Mechanics and Farmers Bank. The origins of the bank in 1907-8 are obscured by a controversy over who first suggested the enterprise, but there is no doubt that the triumvirate played a leading role. As early as 1906 Merrick, Moore, and Spaulding, along with several other black professionals, formed a temporary organizing committee to begin a Negro bank in Durham.[108]

Regardless of who carried the initiative—Merrick, W. G. Pearson, or Robert Fitzgerald—the Mechanics and Farmers Bank received its charter in 1907 and opened its offices on the first floor of the North Carolina Mutual Building in 1908.[109] The triumvirate served on the board of directors and owned a controlling interest in the bank, an interest buttressed by a separate $1,000 purchase of stock by the Mutual. Technically the Mechanics and Farmers Bank, like the Land Company, possessed a separate corporate identity, but the Mutual gave it life and sustained it; the directors of the two institutions usually coincided, and the president of one has often been the president of the

106. Statement of investments attached to Minutes, January 1, 1909.
107. Minutes, February 28, May 15, June 15, 1911; Andrews, *John Merrick,* p. 58. The Land Company was incorporated December 8, 1910.
108. Printed notice announcing this organizational meeting February 15, 1906, in Hunter Papers. In part the notice read: "Everywhere there is a tendency for the colored people to get together and organize along business lines for mutual help, protection, and . . . as legitimate avenues for investments. For this reason the progressive colored citizens of Durham . . . have organized themselves . . . for the purpose of forming a bank."
109. Andrews, *John Merrick,* pp. 51–55; Minutes, April 15, 1907.

other. A Negro bank obviously complemented the insurance company as a depository for its funds and an outlet for its investments; moreover, it filled a strategic vacancy in the imaginary mosaic of a black economy.[110]

More visionary than the bank and a striking example of the Mutual's racial motivation was the founding of the Durham Textile Mill in 1910. The triumvirate had learned the lesson of the True Reformers and generally resisted the grandiose and the utopian. Yet the compulsion to prove a point to the white man lay near the heart of Negro entrepreneurial behavior and could seldom be contained. It is significant that Dr. Moore, the antithesis of the business speculator (but the most race-conscious of the directors), took charge of boosting the Company's least practical project. In doing so he did not step out of character; rather, he sought to vindicate the race. After the failure of Warren C. Coleman's cotton mill in Concord, North Carolina, white critics drew the moral that Negroes could never operate such complicated enterprises. Moore took up the challenge, presented his cause to the annual convention of the National Negro Business League, and asked the race to rally behind an "idea that had evolved from the ruins of the Coleman Cotton Mills."[111]

The Mutual raised $5,000 to launch the mill, which never wanted for funds. Instead, the weakness of the venture centered on a scarcity of trained black labor and the difficulty of establishing a market. The Company found a graduate of the North Carolina Agricultural and Technical College to manage the firm, and Julian S. Carr loaned a few experienced hands in the beginning. Like Carr's Negro mill, the firm planned to manufacture socks,

110. *Ibid.* Also in 1908 the men of the Mutual began the Bull City Drug Store and thus added another business to the "Mutual Block" of black enterprises on Parrish Street. The drug store prospered and even opened a branch in the Hayti section of the Negro community. The North Carolina Mutual ran the store for five or six years and then sold it to the managing pharmacists. See Andrews, *John Merrick*, pp. 56–57.

111. National Negro Business League, *Proceedings*, Eleventh Annual Meeting, New York, pp. 59–62. Andrews gives 1914 as the beginning date of the Durham Textile Mill (*John Merrick*, pp. 58–59). Apparently this is an error, for Moore in his 1910 report indicated that the mill was already in operation.

although not solely the cheapest grades. Unfortunately, the Negro company did not share Carr's market, nor could it build one of its own. Moreover, there developed a surplus of hosiery (or so it seemed to Moore), and none of the triumvirate could afford the time and effort that the cotton mill demanded. Tragically, in view of its didactic purpose, the mill struggled for six years in direct competition with the giant white enterprises and then collapsed.[112]

As eager as Moore and his colleagues might have been to display before the world an impressive array of black industries, they never lost sight of their home base, the Mutual. Spaulding spread his agencies throughout the Carolinas. The two states produced a solid base of business and inspired the Company to look for new fields to conquer. In 1910 the directors toured the southern states and even sailed to Cuba, ostensibly to survey the market there, but more likely to excite publicity. As a result of the trip the triumvirate marked Georgia for expansion, and in the spring of 1911, after depositing a $5,000 state bond, the Mutual invaded the territory of its rival, the Atlanta Life Insurance Company.[113]

Obviously, expansion cost money and created other difficulties for the developing firm. Since 1903 the steady expansion of the Company had brought on problems that were sometimes more than proportionate to its growth. Sick claims often climbed beyond reason. Mortality experience remained largely unpredictable and on occasion threatened to wipe out an entire year's premium income.[114]

112. *Ibid.*; clipping, *Urbana (Ohio) Informer*, March, 1910, Hampton Clippings, "Negro Business," vol. I; Thomas W. Holland, "Negro Capitalists," *Southern Workman*, LV (December, 1926), 536–540.

113. Georgia, like South Carolina, immediately increased its bond to $20,000, more than enough to invite suspicion within the ranks of the Company (Andrews, *John Merrick*, pp. 84, 146; Minutes, January 15, 1910; March 25, April 18, November 8, 1911; clipping, *American Citizen* [Atlanta, Ga.], May 6, 1911, in Avery Scrapbook). Andrews dated the southern tour and Cuban trip 1909—the Company minutes indicate the trip took place in 1910.

114. A smallpox epidemic in 1904, for example, threatened disaster for the Company (Minutes, September 15, 1904). Death claims during the first year, 1899, had totaled four; by 1907 they averaged nearly two per day. See *North Carolina Mutual*, January, 1907; and Minutes, February 18, 1907.

At least 90 percent of the premium income came from industrial policies sold by poorly trained agents to poorly selected risks whose small and unsteady earnings meant a tremendous lapse rate. In addition, the collection system itself often broke down during the spring rains. For a variety of reasons policyholders missed their payments and allowed their policies to lapse. It is doubtful that such turnover could have been controlled effectively in the early years; moreover, one could question whether the Company would have gained much from pursuing permanency. Industrial policies carried little or no surrender value; thus with so many poor risks among the insured, the Company might have profited by permitting a policy to lapse *after* it had paid for its processing, but *before* the inevitable claim. There is no evidence that the Mutual contrived such a strategy, but, faced with overwhelming attrition, its first response seemed to place more emphasis on finding new policyholders than on retaining old ones.

Spaulding lived on the hope that his agents during any given year could sell enough new business to make up for the losses. This did not always happen. For example, in 1909 more insurance lapsed than was sold. The Association began the year with over $2,000,000 insurance in force and ended with $1,500,000, despite issuing $500,000 of new insurance. In 1911, a better year, the lapse rate remained a frightful $2,500,000, but Spaulding pushed his agents to offset the losses with new policies worth $3,500,000.[115] Despite increased holdings in real estate, over 80 percent of the Company's income came from premiums;[116] had policies lapsed faster than they could be replaced for a sustained period of time, the firm would have met disaster. Given the lack of a trained agency force, an unpredictable mortality experience, and a tenuous balance between lapses and sales, the Company was indeed fortunate that economic disaster did not strike before 1929.

In discussing his problems before the National Negro Busi-

---

115. North Carolina Insurance Department *Report* 1909, pp. 222–224; 1910, p. 245; 1912, p. 249.
116. North Carolina Insurance Department *Report* 1912, p. 249.

ness League in 1910, Spaulding complained first of a high Negro mortality rate and the accompanying lack of actuarial tables, and, second, of the black man's inexperience in business. He further complained of the "many failures among Negro insurance companies" as "one of the greatest and most deplorable evils. . . . The novice imagines that there are millions in it and all one needs to do is . . . to count the gold by the thousands."[117]

If Spaulding agonized over incapable agents from other companies, he had trouble with his own as well. The Company paper constantly reminded agents that too many dubious sick claims were being honored (in part because the agents lacked training) and issued persistent warnings that those who forged physicians' signatures and fraudulently collected the sick claim, sometimes in collusion with the policyholder, would be vigorously prosecuted.[118]

Fraud constituted but a small part of a larger problem. Selecting, training, and supervising agents severely taxed Spaulding's energy—not until after World War I did the Company form a separate agency department with its own director and staff. In the meantime Spaulding found himself seeking assistance to manage an agency force that grew to 200 by 1904 and 700 by 1915.[119] Pragmatically he developed a system of supervision. Each agent filed a weekly report with the home office. From these reports Spaulding could direct his "traveling agents," who, as proven salesmen, supervised other agents while they drummed up business of their own. In the cities and larger towns salaried district managers or supervisors replaced the traveling inspector, and a chain of command emerged linking Spaulding to the manager and in turn to the agent who reported regularly to the district office. Still, throughout the thousands of small

117. National Negro Business League, *Proceedings*, Eleventh Annual Meeting, New York, 1910, pp. 103–104; also see *Proceedings*, Sixteenth Annual Meeting, Boston, 1915, p. 115.

118. *North Carolina Mutual*, May, 1906; January, 1907. For specific examples of fraud, see Charles N. Hunter to C. C. Spaulding, May 6, and Hunter to B. B. Steptoe, July 7, 1907, Hunter Papers.

119. *North Carolina Mutual*, March, 1904; Minutes, June 2, 1904; National Negro Business League, *Proceedings*, Sixteenth Annual Meeting, Boston, 1915, p. 118.

towns in the rural South, supervision and training remained woefully inadequate. In an effort to substitute motivation for supervision and to aid in recruitment, the Company paid its agents an attractive commission of 40 percent.[120] But Spaulding hoped to build among the agents an *élan* independent of material reward, something he later called "that good old Mutual spirit."

In 1904, in an effort to foster a sense of Company identity and mission, Spaulding invited all Mutual employees to attend the Colored State Fair in Raleigh. This "first annual agency meeting" resembled in many ways the conventions of Negro fraternal societies, complete with railroad excursions to bring the "Mutual Family" to the fair. Publicity may have been a strong ulterior motive, and, not unlike conventions of the National Negro Business League, a camp meeting atmosphere prevailed. Agents testified to the powers of racial cooperation and served up resolutions for the coming year in sessions purposely opened to the public. The Mutual put every well-dressed agent and prosperous manager on display and preached Washington's message of racial solidarity at every opportunity. These agency meetings stand as perhaps the most unusual in the annals of American business history, and they clearly reveal the influence of the Afro-American experience on entrepreneurial thought and behavior.[121]

The Company did not begin formal management schools and agency training until the 1930's, but it did begin as early as 1908 to hold "superintendents' conferences" at the home office.[122] While more businesslike than the meetings at the fair, these "management symposiums" became more important as summer social events. Durham had no Negro hotel, and the Company housed the managers in the homes of the black middle class. Word spread rapidly that important men were in town and that

120. See Company file of the *North Carolina Mutual*, 1903–1905; Kennedy, "North Carolina Mutual," p. 31.

121. Minutes, December 15, 1904. For descriptions of subsequent meetings like this at the fair grounds, which apparently continued for several years, see the *North Carolina Mutual*, January, 1905; January, 1906; Kennedy, "North Carolina Mutual," pp. 50–51.

122. Kennedy, "North Carolina Mutual," p. 71.

public gatherings were scheduled at the St. Joseph's African Methodist Episcopal and White Rock Baptist Churches. Spaulding acknowledged that the purpose of the conventions was to "publicize our aim and what we are doing for the people."[123] The public meetings combined equal parts of singing and speaking, punctuated by prayer. Church suppers divided the daytime activities from the evening entertainment, and at times it would have been difficult to distinguish between these "business conventions" and a church encampment.[124]

Much of this institutional overlap was, of course, unconscious and natural. The church and the Mutual formed the matrix of community organization in Durham. The Company's leadership and history gave it a close kinship with the church; indeed, the institutional demarcation between the Negro church and insurance society was never so clear that the two could not share an identity under the aegis of uplift. The alliance between church and business has been all-important to the success of the North Carolina Mutual. The church served as recruitment center for agents, and the lists of employees in the Company newspaper reveal a profusion of "Reverends." Preachers often used the power of the pulpit to sell a little insurance, and every superintendent knew he must above all else win over the ministers in his district.[125]

If "Reverends" made up a significant proportion of the agency force, so did "Professors."[126] So many teachers became Mutual agents that in 1904 editor Buchanan observed, with pardonable exaggeration, "The Association is causing a drain upon the supply of teachers in eastern North Carolina."[127] Rosters of early agents also reveal a striking number of women working for the Association. In pointing out that nearly one-fourth of all Mutual agents were women, according to a Company count in 1912, Spaulding boasted that the Association hired "anyone who can

123. *Ibid.*, p. 73.
124. For a detailed account of this meeting, see Minutes, August 15, September 21, 1908.
125. See Company file of *North Carolina Mutual*, 1903–12, particularly May, 1906.
126. *Ibid.*
127. *North Carolina Mutual*, January, 1904.

deliver the goods."[128] Spaulding also reported to his colleagues that out of 700 employees in 1915, 4 were white. On this point he did not boast. When queried from the floor of the National Negro Business League Convention about the whites, he answered apologetically and explained that "they are agents in a few communities where we could not get competent colored agents."[129]

The home office staff of the early years possessed an interesting background. Of twenty full-time staff members in 1912, eleven were women, the majority of whom had college experience, most notably the official stenographer and Spaulding's secretary, Susie Gille, with her degree from Wilberforce. Three-fourths of the employees came from North Carolina and about half from Durham. Most of the men had been "professors." The bookkeeper, a West Indian, held a degree from the London College of Music and had written "prize winning essays in the modern history of the Leeward Islands."[130] Even though the Company preached the philosophy of Booker T. Washington, its employees came from the "talented tenth."

Despite the exceptional individuals that the Company attracted, it was the rare person who came to the Mutual with any business experience or knowledge of life insurance. While Spaulding constantly deplored the hardship of inexperience, particularly among his agents, he was at the same time very proud that the Company had overcome weaknesses through "diligence." Betraying his affinity for Booker T. Washington, he sometimes questioned the utility of higher education. "We put more stress upon the practical . . . than upon the theoretical," he announced at a Business League meeting. "Our training not only includes technical knowledge . . . but also lessons in promptness, neatness and honesty."[131]

128. National Negro Business League, *Proceedings*, Sixteenth Annual Meeting, Boston, 1915, p. 119.
129. *Ibid.*, p. 118.
130. *Durham Reformer*, July 27, 1911; *North Carolina Mutual*, July, 1912; Kennedy, "North Carolina Mutual," p. 97.
131. National Negro Business League, *Proceedings*, Sixteenth Annual Meeting, Boston, 1915, p. 116; also see National Negro Business League, *Proceedings*, Seventeenth Annual Meeting, Kansas City, 1916, p. 114.

And Spaulding might have added that every agent had to master the lessons of accommodation. Managing the home office in Durham was one thing; being an agent in the backwoods of Georgia was another. It is axiomatic that the Negro in the South constantly had to test the white temper and calculate his move accordingly, for he could advance only as fast as the most liberal white leaders would permit. Thus while wearing a high white collar and walking the streets of the white business district as a black executive became permissible—even functional, in the race etiquette of Durham—appearing ultra-respectable in other settings could backfire. When the Mutual expanded into Georgia, Merrick's oldest son, Edward, began organizing agencies throughout the state. At least twice he found himself in jail because "he dressed too well and received too much mail."[132] On one occasion the sheriff of Macon, Georgia, arrested young Merrick on "suspicion of stolen baggage" when he showed up in town carrying two handsome leather bags. Not until a well-known Negro leader carefully explained Merrick's identity did the constable believe that a young black man could own such luggage.[133]

Despite the dominance of C. C. Spaulding, the administration of the Mutual had never been a one-man show; this became increasingly true after 1907, when John Moses Avery joined the home office staff. Avery came from the Blue Ridge country of North Carolina, where he had worked as an agent for Merrick's Royal Knights of King David during the 1890's. In 1899 he enrolled in Kittrell College, an A.M.E. school near Durham, and after graduation he returned to the mountains of Carolina as a "professor." In 1905, after an unsuccessful attempt to establish his own academy, he abandoned teaching and became a traveling agent for the North Carolina Mutual. Within two years he convinced the directors that they needed his talents in Durham, and they appointed him Spaulding's assistant. It would be diffi-

132. Clipping, *East Tennessee News* (Knoxville), June 5, 1941, Kennedy Scrapbook; *Whetstone*, second quarter, 1941.
133. Interview, Mrs. Viola G. Turner, June 13, 1968. Also see Stuart, *Economic Detour*, p. 214; *Whetstone*, second quarter, 1941.

cult to overestimate Avery's influence on Spaulding and the management of the Company. He perfected Spaulding's innovations, schooled the manager in the art of public speaking, improved his business correspondence, and generally provided the polish that enabled Spaulding to become a respected national figure. More important, as the first agency director he laid the groundwork for the permanent organization of all field personnel. As secretary and vice-president of the Company he gave the Mutual mature guidance, not unlike that of Dr. Moore. His national prominence in the A.M.E. Church brought the Company added publicity; indeed, until his untimely death in 1931 he was probably the most widely known Mutual executive. "Few [A.M.E.] Bishops were elected," a Negro editor observed, "who had Avery as an opposing factor." After Avery took his place on the board of directors of the North Carolina Mutual in 1911, it would be difficult to think any longer of a triumvirate.[134]

While none of the early staff matched the influence of Avery, Spaulding counted on able support from a number of others. Joseph Garner emerged in South Carolina as "a sterling young man" who took charge as state agent and managed the South Carolina office in Columbia.[135] In 1908 Arthur John Clement joined Garner in South Carolina as superintendent of the Charleston district. The Mutual inherited both Clement and Bessie Alberta Johnson (Mrs. B. A. J. Whitted) as important executives when in 1906 it reinsured the Peoples Benevolent Relief Association. Clement remained in Charleston as district manager until his retirement in 1949. Mrs. Whitted, "a whiz at mathematics and English," became an indispensable person in clerical matters, eventually becoming chief bookkeeper and cashier for the Company. She worked fifty-one years for the Mutual before she retired in 1957.[136]

134. Kennedy, "North Carolina Mutual," p. 60; Stuart, *Economic Detour*, pp. 207–208; clippings, *Carolina Times* (Durham), July 16, 1924; January 22, 1926; March 7, 1931, in Kennedy Scrapbook; interviews, Dr. Clyde Donnell, June 10; Mrs. Viola G. Turner, June 13, 1968.

135. Andrews, *John Merrick*, pp. 89–90; Kennedy, "North Carolina Mutual," p. 53.

136. Kennedy, "North Carolina Mutual," pp. 62–64; interview, W. J. Kennedy, Jr., January 29, 1968.

Edward Richard Merrick was ten years old when his father organized the Mutual, and almost from the beginning he ran errands and helped around the office. After graduating from Greensboro Agricultural and Technical College in 1907 he worked as a clerk in the home office, and then in 1909 he went into the field as a traveling agent. Under the guidance of Avery and Spaulding he later took responsibility for opening Georgia. Merrick returned to the home office in 1913 and spent most of his career as treasurer of the Company until he retired in 1957.[137]

If E. R. Merrick pioneered the expansion of the Mutual into Georgia, it was John Leonidas Wheeler who kept the state intact. Wheeler, educated at Wilberforce and the University of Chicago, gave up an established academic career as president of Kittrell College to come to work for the North Carolina Mutual in 1908. After managing the Raleigh district and serving in the home office, Wheeler moved to Atlanta in 1912; there he remained, passing through a series of promotions to vice-presidency and keeping the Mutual prosperous in the face of a powerful challenge from a large black middle class that founded two major Negro life insurance companies in Atlanta.[138] In 1911 three of these new executives, Avery, Garner, and E. R. Merrick, were elected to the board of directors.[139]

The additional executive personnel and the resulting administrative changes reflected the general growth and prosperity of the Company. At the time of these changes in 1911 the Insurance Department conducted an audit, and the Association had a premium income of roughly $250,000, assets of nearly $120,000, insurance in force of over $2,000,000, and close to 500 employees.[140] Represented by these figures the Mutual made up an infinitesimally small percentage of the total life insurance industry.

137. Kennedy, "North Carolina Mutual," p. 70; Stuart, *Economic Detour*, pp. 213–215.

138. Kennedy, "North Carolina Mutual," pp. 68–69; Stuart, *Economic Detour*, pp. 226–227; interview, John H. Wheeler, August 4, 1970.

139. Kennedy, "North Carolina Mutual," p. 90; Minutes, January 9, 1911.

140. North Carolina Insurance Department *Report* 1912, p. 249; Kennedy, "North Carolina Mutual," pp. 93, 98–102; Andrews, *John Merrick*, pp. 92–99.

John Hancock, for example, the smallest of the large white companies, then had assets totaling over $90,000,000 and insurance in force exceeding $500,000,000. The largest company in the United States, New York Life, had assets of $735,000,000 and over $2,000,000,000 insurance in force. But of course the comparison is absurd. The Mutual lived in another world and never pretended to have economic significance in the total life insurance industry. Still, the Association had done well by any standards; heroically, in the context of black economic development, for it could not be classified as a "small business" in the category of shops and taverns. One can extrapolate that the annual payroll of the Company in 1912 was approximately $100,000, the bulk of that going to the agents and an increasing amount to the directors, who had begun to draw significant salaries. In 1907 the triumvirate had voted Merrick and Spaulding $300 each as monthly salaries, and Dr. Moore, $225. By 1910 all three received $400, and in 1913, as directors of a legal reserve company, Merrick commanded $600 per month, Spaulding and Moore, $500 each.[141]

With this kind of relative progress the Mutual no longer saw itself as a struggling assessment association. In a technical sense it had surely outgrown its charter, which legally defined it as essentially a fraternal insurance association. It had never thought of itself in those terms and had eschewed the "tinsel and regalia." Nor, as already noted, had it ever operated as an assessment organization. By introducing a variety of policies including ordinary insurance, the Company had consciously spurred its own evolution toward an "old line legal reserve company."[142] In 1913 the directors raised $100,000 to meet the legal

141. Minutes, April 15, 1907; January 15, 1910; January 13, 1913.
142. "Old line" generally refers to companies which sell ordinary insurance on a level premium plan—"level premium" meaning that the premium is leveled out over the policyholder's mathematically projected lifespan. Thus a man in his youth pays more than the actual cost of his insurance in order to compensate for what would otherwise be prohibitive premium rates during his old age. This excess that policyholders pay during their youth must be set aside as a reserve fund to pay current and future claims. Theoretically this is a foolproof system, as long as mortality can be accurately predicted. Indeed, if the actual mortality experience can be improved over what is statistically expected, and the firm's overhead and investment returns are favorable, a surplus beyond the legal reserve

reserve requirements of North Carolina, and the state rechartered the Association, giving it official legal reserve status.[143]

In practice the Mutual had operated as a legal reserve company since 1909, when South Carolina demanded an "extra-legal reserve," and even before 1909 it had been accumulating an informal reserve. For a number of years before 1913 the Company thought of itself as having reserve status and increasingly viewed the small nonreserve organizations as a public nuisance and a potential threat to the reputation of the Mutual. The directors welcomed tighter state restrictions on insurance associations and advocated a $10,000 bond requirement. In 1910 Merrick went before the state legislature with such a proposal, and in a classic display of his political art he told the white legislators:

> I am a Negro and I don't want to appear smart, but . . . half the companies in the State . . . have no assets save the weekly collection of the people. These companies are a God's blessing . . . as it stopped the begging list. . . . But the whole thing has been imposed on. A half dozen politicians and Wise Men from the East get together and raise $50; take $25 for a charter, and $25 for literature and then take a book and start collecting from the people . . . with not a dollar to protect their contract.[144]

The Assembly did not promptly act on Merrick's recommendation, but attrition took its toll all the same. In 1909 the North Carolina Insurance Department listed thirteen Negro and twelve

---

results, and the policyholders receive dividends. Negro companies seeking legal reserve status began with a nearly insurmountable disadvantage—the high rate of Negro mortality, and no actuarial tables to adequately predict the average death rate. Not until 1944 could the Mutual afford to pay a dividend. In the meantime, had large white firms chosen to solicit Negro risks consistently, the Mutual and other black companies could not have hoped to compete.

143. Kennedy, "North Carolina Mutual," p. 103. In an old dispute over which Negro insurance company first received legal reserve status, the truth seems to be that the Mississippi Life Insurance Company in 1909 was the first to be *chartered* as a legal reserve company, and the North Carolina Mutual was first to *operate* as a legal reserve company. See Trent, "Development of Negro Life Insurance," p. 39; Stuart, *Economic Detour*, p. 284; National Negro Business League, *Proceedings*, Fourteenth Annual Meeting, Philadelphia, 1913, p. 161.

144. Typescript of Merrick's speech dated 1910 in Spaulding Papers.

white assessment associations in the state. The combined assets
of the twenty-five organizations amounted to $92,000, of which
the North Carolina Mutual accounted for $82,000. By 1916 only
five of these companies had survived, two Negro and three
white.[145] As a curious sidelight of the history of the South, the
Mutual was until World War I the largest "home-owned" insurance company in North Carolina. Several larger companies
operated in the state, but they were northern imports domiciled
in New York City and New England.[146]

Within the local economy of Durham the Mutual had become
a factor of some significance, even if measured only by its demand for credit. Between 1909 and 1913, in order to meet the
increasing bond requirements of South Carolina and Georgia
and to qualify as a legal reserve company in North Carolina,
the Company borrowed over $135,000. Much of this money came
from the Duke-owned Fidelity Bank; thus, if there was a white
conspiracy to drive black companies out of business, it certainly
did not extend to the bankers of Durham.[147] Experience taught
whites that loaning the North Carolina Mutual large sums of
money involved no risk. Paternalism aside, well-secured money
at 6 percent interest tended to be color-blind.

In attaining legal reserve status the Company marked a significant milestone in its business history, and such objective economic achievement perhaps aroused the "scientific" side of
Negro business thought. Spaulding began to point out that if
black businessmen were to succeed they must overcome "Negro
familiarity" and carry on business with the proper calculation.
"Insurance is business," he told an audience in 1915. "It was this
realization which caused our Company to build upward from

145. See North Carolina State Insurance Department *Report* 1909, pp. 206–
232; 1916, p. 150 and *passim*; also Kennedy, "North Carolina Mutual," pp. 78–80.
146. Clipping, *Norfolk Journal and Guide*, February 3, 1917, in Hampton
Clippings, "Negroes in Business, Insurance and Real Estate, 1900–1922"; North
Carolina State Insurance Department *Reports*, 1906–17.
147. Minutes, August 23, 25, September 15, 1909; April 20, 1910; March
25, April 18, 1911; April 6, November 8, 1912; March 15, 1913; Kennedy, "North
Carolina Mutual," pp. 67, 75–76, 103; Andrews, *John Merrick*, pp. 89–91; Jesse
Edward Gloster, "North Carolina Mutual Life Insurance Company: Its Histori-
cal Development and Current Operations" (Ph.D. dissertation, University of
Pittsburgh, 1955), p. 60.

a small beginning until the present proportions have been reached."[148] More than once during his career would Spaulding temporarily think of himself as just a businessman, but he, like the Mutual, possessed a dual identity, and it was more ethnic than economic.

Every success and failure of the Company would be seen inevitably, by blacks and whites alike, as a racial success, a racial failure. Becoming a legal reserve company meant more than changing a charter or upgrading a business. In the summer of 1912, shortly after the Company had applied for its new charter, the *North Carolina Mutual* captured the other side of the dualism when it recapitulated the success story of the Mutual and analyzed its "larger significance." "All are aware," the editor presumed, "that the North Carolina Mutual and Provident Association has placed itself in the category of national reputation. . . ." But he wondered if everyone recognized the profound parable the history of the Association taught. The Mutual "as a small acorn" had grown into a "mighty oak . . . a mighty tree whose branches afford shelter and protection to thousands. . . ." And the allegory had yet a more vital message: "The substantial growth of this Association affords an interesting study in the history of the darker races."[149]

What the Company could do, the race could do. And what might have been a lesson for business success became a lesson for racial success. Far from being just an economic institution, the Mutual stood as an expression of Afro-American thought centering on the doctrine of self-help and racial solidarity. But now the idea had dramatic substance, and the substance became symbolic. The Mutual became the servant of myth; it became both the lesson and the teacher in a ceaseless search for a *modus vivendi* within a hostile environment. Thus the Company could address the masses, asking them "to redouble your efforts and cooperate with us for a generation yet unborn."[150]

148. National Negro Business League, *Proceedings*, Sixteenth Annual Meeting, Boston, 1915, p. 116.
149. *North Carolina Mutual*, July, 1912.
150. *Ibid.*

From the first hint of lasting success the Company leaders began to forecast their legacy and espouse a racial ideology. Anticipating the slogan of black capitalism during the 1930's— "double-duty dollars"—Merrick reminded Negroes in 1903 that a policy from the North Carolina Mutual bought "double protection": life insurance and Negro employment. The prospect of such employment provided by a black economy moved Merrick to add, "I hope that my children and yours will be in better condition and will have this company to point to with pride." [151] From a firm economic foundation based on racial solidarity, an institution like the Mutual could cure economic and social ills, enhance racial pride, improve race relations; in short, it could solve the "Negro problem."

As an object lesson in self-help the Company reminded the people, "We as a race have reached the point where we must try to turn up something for ourselves. . . . Our every departure into business is a sign that we are . . . eager to go from infancy to manhood." [152] And perhaps the Mutual could supply the inspiration to make that departure. "A great cloud, a dark night of lost confidence," lamented Buchanan, "has hovered over our people for years. The name negro has suggested fallibility. . . . The North Carolina Mutual shows that the race is gradually emerging from under that cloud." [153] The Mutual was teaching, and "Negroes all over the country" were "learning the secret of successful accumulation." [154] The lesson was basic and left no doubt that it came from the primer of the Tuskegeean. "We have turned from pursuing the phantom of political spoils," the editor wrote, "and are settling down to development along safe lines. With such a wise determination we may safely say we are gliding out among the shoals and our view opens to a clearer, deeper sea." [155]

151. *Ibid.*, November, 1903; for the notion of a duplicate black economy, see *ibid.*, September, 1903.
152. *Ibid.*, September, 1904.
153. *Ibid.*, January, 1904.
154. *Ibid.*, January, 1906.
155. *Ibid.* While none of the triumvirate was intimately associated with Washington, Merrick and Spaulding visited Tuskegee and in 1908 accompanied Washington on a trip to Florida. In 1905 Spaulding gave effusive praise to Wash-

Certainly Washington could have written much of what appeared in the two newspapers. "Be reliable," advised the *Observer*. "Strive for excellence and you will be in demand. Make the community dependent upon you. Live within your means. . . ."[156] "Don't work half the time and go fishing the other half."[157] In the interest of uplift the paper passed out directions on child-rearing that would have equally warmed the hearts of Booker T. Washington and John D. Rockefeller.

> Our people should see to it that their boys are put to work. There is no excuse for anyone being idle in Durham. Begin upon your boys when they are young. . . . You need not expect them to be anything when you spare the rod. Keep your boys off the streets . . . from such a class who hang around pool rooms . . . keeping out of the way of jobs . . . chain gangs are supplied.[158]

The New South message, as noted earlier, ran throughout the Company newspapers. Buchanan in one of his striking similes declared, "Industry is like smallpox. . . . It is contagious."[159] And he insisted that economic success bode well for racial amity: "With such prosperity facing the country the 'spell binder' . . . will have to get a new theme. Shouting 'nigger' has become a little threadbare. When it comes to the vital issues of progress . . . cheap politicians who can only appeal to passion dwindle away like mist before the sun. . . ."[160] Buchanan was certain that there existed "no other community in which the harmony between the races is quite so perfect as here," and could have been even better were it not for "outsiders" and "hotheaded speakers" who failed to understand the "spirit of Durham."[161] Clearly the Mutual saw itself paving the road to better race relations. In

ington in a public speech, saying, "Long may this Hero live and continue to lead our race" (*North Carolina Mutual*, April, 1905; also interview, W. J. Kennedy, Jr., July 8, 1968).

156. *Durham Negro Observer*, June 23, 1906.
157. *Ibid.*, June 30, 1906.
158. *Ibid.*, July 7, 1906.
159. *Ibid.*, August 4, 1906.
160. *Ibid.*
161. *Ibid.*, September 29, 1906.

celebrating its legal reserve status, the Company advertised its many qualifications and capped the list by claiming to have "A Key to the Solution of the Race Problem."[162]

In the entente between racial elites, black and white rhetoric sometimes became indistiguishable. As Durham's black businessmen convinced the editor of the *Morning Herald*:

> It is a good day to live and work in. Durham presents the pleasing spectacle of all men at labor in the . . . spirit of "work is worship." It shows the colored people striving, and the white man willing. The African asking only for hope, and room for effort; the Caucasian bidding him to his work and assuring him that if he fall, it must be by the weight of his own demerits and not by the tyranny of the great white race.[163]

Unquestionably the success of the Negro in Durham had a therapeutic value for white Southerners. An editor in Greensboro complained that "people of the north . . . have been so effected [*sic*] by yellow journalism until they are certain that the negro is not given the opportunity by whites in the South." But Merrick, Moore, and Spaulding, the "trio that is a synonym for success," clearly illustrated that "racial antipathy in North Carolina is a mere shadow and that this state offers the energetic negro with character an opportunity to make himself a man of affairs."[164]

While accommodation certainly occupied a place in North Carolina Mutual rhetoric, its more basic proposal was racial solidarity which in turn depended on an element of nationalism. The Company could scarcely conceal its pleasure when white companies discriminated against Negroes, thus proving the point that Negroes should support their own enterprises. In 1907 Metropolitan Life, recurrently accepting and rejecting Negro risks, decided once again to suspend Negro business. The *North Carolina Mutual* claimed to feel "indignant" over the decision, but quickly added, "God moves in mysterious ways."[165]

162. Advertisement from 1913 quoted in Andrews, *John Merrick*, p. 96.
163. Clipping, *Durham Morning Herald*, July 29, 1908, Avery Scrapbook.
164. Clipping, *Greensboro Daily News*, August 20, 1910, Avery Scrapbook.
165. *North Carolina Mutual*, January, 1907.

The paper occasionally denounced white agents who refused to respect Negro women or Negro homes, a grievance which Spaulding felt free to emphasize in an all-black setting: "In my part of the country it has frequently happened that white agents . . . have walked right into a Negro home without even knocking . . . or taking off his hat. It is up to us to put a stop to such discourteous practice . . . and the best way we can do it is to . . . patronize some colored insurance company of standing. . . ."[166]

The accusation that Negro businessmen championed racial pride only to line their own pockets was one that became increasingly vocal during the twentieth century. As early as 1905 the Mutual found it necessary to avow, "We have never appealed to the support of the people under the cry of color. We came out like men, faced the world and conquered because we offered better advantages."[167] But the truth is that the Mutual, like the entire Negro business community, with assistance from the National Negro Business League, constantly appealed for patronage based on color. After all, racial solidarity was the lifeblood of Negro business. When quizzed about his rates in contrast to those of old-line white companies accepting Negro risks, Spaulding admitted, "We are just a little bit higher . . . but there are many advantages which accrue to our race to more than offset this slight difference in rates."[168] Earlier, in a more direct demand for racial consciousness, the Company asked Negroes to "stop trying to bleach themselves," and instead to couple "racial pride with the Christian spirit. . . ."[169]

While the Mutual generally adhered to the Tuskegee line, its public statements were not a blind copy of the Washington creed. The leadership was well aware of the Washington-Du

166. National Negro Business League, *Proceedings*, Sixteenth Annual Meeting, Boston, 1915, p. 116.

167. *North Carolina Mutual*, September, 1905.

168. National Negro Business League, *Proceedings*, Sixteenth Annual Meeting, Boston, 1915, p. 118.

169. *Durham Negro Observer*, July 7, 1906. Penetrating the motives of the triumvirate and those around them is a formidable and perhaps impossible task. One can only reiterate that these men, led by Dr. Moore, were a breed wholly different from the pathological image of Negro businessmen conjured up in E. Franklin Frazier's *Black Bourgeoisie* (Glencoe, Ill.: The Free Press, 1957).

Bois controversy, and on certain issues it stood with a foot in each camp. An obvious theme in Du Bois's *Souls of Black Folk* (1903) was anti-materialism and the dread fear that the materialism of Washington and the white world would corrupt the humanity, the souls, of Negroes.[170] Certainly the Mutual shared this tradition of anti-materialism in its philosophy, so for every exhortation to pursue the dollar, there was a countermand to resist Mammon. "Prosperity, though apparently harmless," warned the Company paper, "often turns to a dangerous disease which destroys the soul. The appendages of wealth and such are not the sole standards of measurement to manhood by all people, though this be the age of money getting."[171] Du Bois rather than Buchanan could have written this, and it bears the stamp of Dr. Moore, who undoubtedly influenced an article in a later issue of the *Observer* entitled "Christianity in Our Business Relations." "Can anyone believe," asked the author, "that Christianity is in the business methods of today? We want less selfishness and more brotherly love, less taking advantage of a brother's misfortune. . . ." This piece attacked not only materialism, but took on imperialism and the trusts, sided with organized labor, and called for the social gospel among Negro ministers. The entire article stands as a black testimony to the precepts of the progressive movement.[172] And the paper left some doubt as to whose educational philosophy it supported. "Straight out muscle work without that great power, *brain force,*" warned the editor, "can amount to but little. . . ."[173]

If the Company seemed to meet some of the qualifications for progressivism, it was not because its leaders were keenly attuned to the intellectual ferment that inspired the northern-based reform movement. The men were neither progressives nor enlightened capitalists in the usual sense of these terms; rather,

170. See Ch. 1, pp. 17–18.
171. *North Carolina Mutual,* September, 1904.
172. *Durham Negro Observer,* August 25, 1906. As early as 1903 the Company paper had endorsed the work of labor unions in Durham (*North Carolina Mutual,* October, 1903).
173. *North Carolina Mutual,* October, 1904.

the explanation for their views rests with the burden of race, which meant they began business with a different set of predilections than the white man.

The influence of race on business built a direct relationship between the Company and the community. By 1910 the North Carolina Mutual had helped to found the Negro hospital, library, college, and three newspapers. Moreover, it had lent valuable support to the town's churches. With the exception of its public "business meetings," the most interesting social function of the Mutual during the early years was its sponsorship of an accomplished Negro baseball team which challenged clubs from other cities and provided the black community with a full season of entertainment.[174] Like the newspapers, the baseball team was not a part of the company unionism that would flourish in the 1920's; it was, instead, largely a matter of race. That part of Negro thought which necessarily emphasized the community over the individual placed the Mutual a step ahead of American business in the area of public relations. And in retrospect, an *economically* backward institution appears *socially* advanced.

The Mutual also indirectly conditioned the character of the Durham Negro community. Aided by its offspring, it attracted to Durham an inordinate number of the "talented tenth," who became a resource of leadership in the social, economic, and later the political life of Durham. As early as 1903 the town could support a literary society. No mere social circle, the Volkamenia Club conducted rigid reading programs, entertained lecturers, held debates, and engaged in self-evaluation. The Schubert-Shakespeare Club soon appeared and began a similar program. Like the earlier literary societies among free Negroes, these clubs imitated the white intelligentsia at the same time they sought to organize the race for "social betterment."[175]

The North Carolina Mutual and Provident Association from 1900 to 1913 had struggled, survived, and succeeded, evolving

174. *Ibid.*, August 18, 1906.
175. William K. Boyd, *The Story of Durham: The City of the New South* (Durham: Duke University Press, 1927), p. 296; interview, W. J. Kennedy, Jr., January 29, 1968. The clubs sponsored Negro health campaigns and generally encouraged education and home ownership.

from an assessment insurance society to a legal reserve company. For Negroes, and perhaps more for whites, the North Carolina Mutual had become the Cinderella story of black business in the New South. A combination of factors explain its survival and success: a potentially captive, though reluctant, Negro market; a complex cultural setting engendered by forces of the New South which gave black business an amicable reception in Durham; a reservoir of black capital adequate to sustain the struggle until white bankers decided to assist; a fortuitous blend of personal qualities among the gifted leaders; plus a blessing of good fortune at critical moments in the history of the Company.

Evaluating its own success at that time, the Mutual discounted the notion of "chance or luck" and with basic accuracy assigned the victory to "honest and faithful effort."[176] Yet intangible elements had to be acknowledged. No one could overlook C. C. Spaulding's entrepreneurial spirit, which acted as the catalyst. It happened that he was "the right man in the right place," observed Buchanan.[177] And what might be attributed to luck was credited to "Providence" by the Company leaders. "The North Carolina Mutual is one of God's ways through which He is reaching our people," an agent testified; and mixing his deities, he added as an immediate afterthought, " 'Lower your buckets where you are.' "[178]

Armed with a new charter, economic momentum, effective leadership, ideological legitimation, and respect across the color line, the Company began a new wave of expansion that would extend into the 1920's.

176. *North Carolina Mutual*, April, 1905; also see National Negro Business League, *Proceedings*, Sixteenth Annual Meeting, Boston, 1915, p. 116.
177. *North Carolina Mutual*, January 1904; also see May, 1906.
178. *Ibid.*, April, 1905.

4

Expansion
and Retreat

When Booker T. Washington died in 1915 he left as part of his legacy an enthusiastic Negro business movement. Of the institutions that survived him, the National Negro Business League ranked second in importance only to Tuskegee itself, and at the head of the business movement stood a growing Negro life insurance industry. The period circumscribed roughly by Washington's death and the end of the 1920's marked a time of rampant expansion in the industry. And, just as for American business at large, expansion meant consolidation as the larger firms sought to bring order to the chaos of competition. Racial cooperation provided an added motive for organizing the industry. But the economic inclination to compete eroded the inherent racial need to cooperate, and these opposing forces, while not unique to Negro business, created a dualism of singular intensity in Afro-American economic thought. A unanimous and urgent plea for brotherhood and racial solidarity was matched with a tendency toward internecine financial warfare, a struggle which saw the survivors of consolidation "flying at one another's throats."[1]

The struggle in the South took place chiefly among the "big four": the North Carolina Mutual, Atlanta Life, Standard Life (also in Atlanta), and National Benefit Life in Washington,

1. William J. Trent, Jr., "Development of Negro Life Insurance Enterprises" (Master's thesis, University of Pennsylvania, 1932), pp. 48–49.

D.C. The Standard Life, founded in 1913 by Heman Perry, had a short and sensational history. Perry, the dean of black promoters, "the busiest and brainiest Negro in the South," performed the almost impossible task of raising $100,000 in order to charter the Standard not as an assessment association, but as a legal reserve company at the outset. "A slave to caprice and novelty, impatient of routine, prone to shun the drudgery of details," Perry turned quickly from one scheme to another in an effort to build a black-owned empire and "command the narrows." No sooner did the Standard seem to succeed than he turned his attention to a cadre of affiliated enterprises, including a holding company.[2] By the early 1920's the Standard challenged the North Carolina Mutual as the "World's Largest Negro Business." But Perry's buccaneering tactics, along with insurmountable financial difficulties and an alleged white conspiracy guided by the Georgia Ku Klux Klan, led inexorably to his downfall in 1924. After that the Standard passed into the hands of a white company, and finally, in 1927, "back home to Negroes only to die in the arms of another expiring Negro company"—the National Benefit Life Insurance Company.[3]

The National Benefit Life was founded in 1898 by Samuel Rutherford, a sewing machine salesman and ex-agent of the True Reformers who organized the firm as an assessment association on the model of the Reformers. Rutherford, like Perry, succumbed to the dream of "big business" and unwisely expanded into a total of twenty-eight states, ten in one year. Unsound management practices and a good deal of financial chicanery characterized both companies, which as proprietary rather than mutual enterprises lent themselves to manipulation. On the eve of the Depression the National Benefit had nearly twice as much insurance in force as had the North Carolina Mutual, but the former was perilously overextended and doubly burdened with the inherited mistakes of the Standard, as well as

2. Merah S. Stuart, *Economic Detour: A History of Insurance in the Lives of American Negroes* (New York: Wendell Malliet and Company, 1940), pp. 307–310.

3. *Ibid.*, p. 310; interview, John H. Wheeler, August 4, 1970.

its own. In what became a *cause célèbre* for the Negro press, the
National Benefit crashed in 1931. In the meantime Atlanta Life
had steered a steady, conservative course, and the Mutual had
begun an all-out retrenchment program.[4]

The cause for retrenchment in the late 1920's indicates that
the Mutual had not altogether resisted the rush of headlong expansion during and after World War I. As early as 1910 the
directors had committed the Company "to spread the insurance
business throughout the Southern states."[5] But the leadership
wisely delayed such expansion and concentrated its energies on
the Carolinas and Georgia until 1916. In that year the Company
began a program of wholesale expansion; significantly, it made
its first move not further into the southern states, but to Washington, D.C.

Between 1914 and 1916 it seemed to southern Negroes that
the boll weevil, disastrous floods, and a severe depression had
conspired to drive them north. Embittered race relations
strengthened the push, but the pull from the North was at least
as forceful. The European war reduced foreign immigration to
the United States by more than two-thirds, and a war-stimulated
northern economy found itself starved for labor. White employment agents scoured the South, and black newspapers, the *Chicago Defender* in particular, portrayed the northern city as the
promised land. Estimates of black migration for the decade
1910–20 run from 300,000 to over 1,000,000. Even before the
great migration the Census Bureau in 1910 reported that Washington, D.C., had the largest Negro population of any city in
the United States. By 1916 over 100,000 Negroes lived in Wash-

4. James B. Mitchell, *The Collapse of the National Benefit Life Insurance Company: A Study of High Finance among Negroes* (Washington, D.C.: How-ard University, 1939), pp. 1–21, 35–47; Stuart, *Economic Detour*, pp. 310, 315–316. Atlanta Life, like the Mutual, tended to be more conservative and stable in its administration, also more willing to cooperate with its rivals. See Stuart, *Economic Detour*, pp. 117–132, 323, 324, 329.

5. William J. Kennedy, Jr., "North Carolina Mutual Life Insurance Com-pany: A Symbol of Progress, 1898–1966" (Manuscript in possession of W. J. Kennedy, Jr., Durham, N.C.), p. 86.

ington, making up roughly 30 percent of the city's population.[6] As blacks fled the South, the Mutual, like the black church, followed the flock.

From its established base in Washington the Company extended itself to Baltimore in 1917 and at the same time opened agencies throughout Virginia. The North continued to tempt the directors, but the stringent entrance requirements of New York and Pennsylvania discouraged further expansion there, and Chicago and Detroit seemed beyond the logic of contiguity. Moreover, the directors remained philosophically and emotionally tied to the South, to that part of the Booker T. Washington philosophy which counseled them to "cast down their buckets" where they were. Not until 1938 would the Company expand north of Maryland.[7]

In part, the attention given to the North during 1916–17 came as a response to the nearly disastrous experience of the Company in the South during 1915. In the midst of the cotton depression which gripped the South in that year, the Mutual lost nearly one-third of its business. Between 1911, when the Company had expanded into Georgia, and the end of 1914, when legal reserve status had provided a new momentum, the Company more than doubled its insurance in force from roughly $2,000,000 to $5,-000,000.[8] But during 1915 low sales and a high lapse rate reduced the volume to $3,500,000.[9] If the North prospered while the South languished, it seemed common sense to follow the black masses and to open new markets in Washington and Baltimore.

But the new territory alone could not account for the Company's remarkable recovery during 1916. At the close of the year the Mutual had a record $8,000,000 insurance in force, and it

6. U.S. Bureau of the Census, *Negro Population in the United States, 1790–1915* (Washington: Government Printing Office, 1918), pp. 87–93.

7. Kennedy, "North Carolina Mutual," p. 87; Robert M. Andrews, *John Merrick: A Biographical Sketch* (Durham: Seeman Printery, 1920), pp. 100–101, 107.

8. North Carolina Insurance Department *Report* 1912, pp. 247–249; 1915, pp. 149–151.

9. *Ibid.*, 1916, pp. 150–152.

seemed that prosperity had returned to the South as quickly as it had departed.[10] Cotton, which sold for five cents a pound in 1914–15, brought twenty-five cents by 1916–17, and in 1919 peaked at thirty-five cents to produce the most valuable crop in history.[11] A journalist traveling through Georgia reported that black sharecroppers were "rolling in wealth."[12]

However exaggerated the benefits of the boom to the black man, the Mutual's southern market did recover. Sales in North Carolina more than doubled, and the pattern repeated itself in Georgia and South Carolina.[13] The directors, comforted by the renewed opportunity in their familiar home section, eagerly returned their attention to "spreading insurance throughout the South." Thus within two years the Company expanded into six new states: Tennessee in 1918; Florida, Mississippi, and Arkansas in 1919; and Alabama and Oklahoma in 1920.[14]

Statistics clearly document the dramatic expansion of the Company during the war years. Between 1914 and 1919 premium income increased from $404,766 to $1,224,541; insurance in force, despite the temporary setback in 1915, rose spectacularly from less than $5,000,000 to $26,000,000; and assets grew from $153,000 to nearly $1,000,000.[15] Over one-fourth of these assets, or $258,000, was invested in war bonds, an investment which paid an interesting extra dividend in public relations. Subscribing to the Liberty and Victory Loans earned any organization popular favor, but for the Mutual the act carried a special sig-

10. *Ibid.*, 1917, pp. 165–167; clipping, *Norfolk Journal and Guide*, February 13, 1917, in Hampton Clippings, "Negroes in Business, Insurance and Real Estate."

11. George Brown Tindall, *The Emergence of the New South, 1913–1945* (Baton Rouge: Louisiana State University Press, 1968), pp. 33, 60.

12. Charles Lewis, "Thirty Cent Cotton and the Negro," *Illustrated World* (May, 1918), 470; quoted in Rupert B. Vance, *Human Factors in Cotton Culture: A Study in the Social Geography of the American South* (Chapel Hill: University of North Carolina Press, 1929), p. 138.

13. North Carolina Insurance *Report* 1917, pp. 165–167.

14. Kennedy, "North Carolina Mutual," p. 87; Andrews, *John Merrick*, pp. 100–101, 107.

15. North Carolina Insurance *Report* 1915, pp. 149–151; Andrews, *John Merrick*, pp. 108–109.

nificance; it illustrated once again, observed southern-born Secretary of the Treasury William Gibbs McAdoo, "the patriotism of the Negro race in the South. . . ."[16]

In a more practical vein, wartime prosperity enabled the Company to survive the influenza epidemic of 1918, which cost an unexpected $100,000 in claims. Not only did the Mutual meet this crisis without breaking its stride, but during the halcyon year 1919 it felt confident enough to raise the limit of risk on any individual policyholder from $1,000 to $5,000. Symbolizing the progress and optimism of 1919, the directors officially changed the name of the Association to the North Carolina Mutual Life Insurance Company, thus removing the remaining trace of an assessment society.[17]

If 1919 brought success, it also brought sadness. For months John Merrick had hobbled about on an ulcerated foot which failed to respond to radium treatments at Johns Hopkins Hospital. Amputation came too late to halt the spreading malignancy, and after long days of intolerable agony, heightened by the humid heat of Durham in August, the president died. His death evoked hundreds of public eulogies in which the white press, more than the black, hastened to present the life of Merrick as "a lesson" recalling the teachings of Booker T. Washington. "Instead of bewailing any actual or supposed handicap," moralized Josephus Daniels in the *Raleigh News and Observer*, Merrick "devoted his energy to making the best of the wide opportunities that this country gives all men, black or white. . . ."[18]

16. Andrews, *John Merrick*, p. 103; also see Kennedy, "North Carolina Mutual," pp. 114–115. The bond purchase also reflects the conservative investment policy characteristic of the North Carolina Mutual. The Company regularly invested over half of its assets in federal, state, and municipal bonds. The conservatism was partly a matter of necessity. State insurance departments demanded safe investments, and the Mutual, like other Negro companies, found itself closed out of the larger world of finance where there existed sound and attractive investment alternatives—mortgage loans, for example. Also the Company remained overloaded with real estate—which constituted nearly 25 percent of its assets, when less than 10 percent was recommended. See North Carolina Insurance *Report 1917*, p. 165; Andrews, *John Merrick*, pp. 102, 109, 113; Joseph B. Maclean, *Life Insurance*, 9th ed. (New York: McGraw Hill, 1962), pp. 292–293.

17. Kennedy, "North Carolina Mutual," p. 103.

18. Quoted in Andrews, *John Merrick*, pp. 201–202, also see pp. 147, 170–

Dr. Moore immediately succeeded Merrick, and scarcely a ripple appeared in the smoothness of the administration. C. C. Spaulding, with Avery and others behind him, provided a depth of executive talent and experience that had been guiding the Company for years. Merrick's death constituted a great spiritual loss, but he had long since ceased to be an indispensable cog in the machinery of the Mutual.[19]

In surviving Merrick's death the Company had overcome an endemic weakness of Negro business—the inability of an enterprise to outlive its founder. This unusual strength stood out again with the death of Dr. Moore in 1923 and the transfer of the presidency to Spaulding. The leadership had changed hands three times, and the Company was still intact and growing. Negro sociologist E. Franklin Frazier, impressed with the meaning of this succession, remarked in the 1920's, "We have in Durham today the outstanding group of colored capitalists who have entered the second generation of business. This is significant, as few Negro enterprises have survived the personal direction of the founders."[20]

The Mutual did not have to be told that its achievement was significant, for since 1906 it had been reinsuring firms which expired along with their founders. In 1924, for example, an otherwise stable Negro company in Reidsville, North Carolina, lost its leader and simply had no one to pick up the reins. The remaining officers asked Spaulding to reinsure their company. That such a crisis in leadership never plagued the Mutual can in part be attributed to the administrative accident of the trium-

200; clipping, *Insurance Leader*, August 6, 1919, p. 178, in Avery Scrapbook; Kennedy, "North Carolina Mutual," pp. 128–129.

19. Kennedy, "North Carolina Mutual," p. 129.

20. E. Franklin Frazier, "Durham: Capital of the Black Middle Class," *The New Negro: An Interpretation*, ed. Alain Locke (New York: Albert and Charles Boni, 1925), p. 334. E. A. Shils, "The Bases of Social Stratification in Negro Society" (Memoranda from the Carnegie-Myrdal Study, 1940), p. 30, lists this "intergenerational continuity" as one of the most important contributions of the North Carolina Mutual. Passing a business from generation to generation without loss of efficiency and business knowledge was a rarity, Shils suggested, particularly among Negroes. In observing the one-generation syndrome, Hylan Lewis in his *Blackways of Kent* (Chapel Hill: University of North Carolina Press, 1955), p. 126, quipped that "Negroes bury their business."

virate, which established a tradition of cooperative decision-making and consciously built a strong second line of managers. As president, Dr. Moore relied on Spaulding, of course, and behind him he could see Avery. Moreover, by 1920, when the Company had completed its sweep into the Deep South and Southwest, it had also recruited an impressive group of new executives.[21]

Arthur Eugene Spears came to the Mutual in 1915 with a degree from A & T College at Greensboro and several years' experience as a traveling salesman in the South. Assigned to an agency in South Carolina, he immediately established himself as district manager but refused to stay behind a desk. He possessed remarkable sales ability and was thus appointed "special ordinary agent." In 1919 he sold nearly a quarter-million dollars of insurance. Finally in 1927 he settled down to a key administrative post as manager of the Charlotte district, a district second in importance only to Atlanta.[22]

The year 1916 produced a bonus in executive talent for the Mutual. All on the same day, September 1, the board hired Martin Arthur Goins, Dr. Clyde Donnell, and William Jesse Kennedy, Jr., three men destined to become directors, and one of them president of the Company. Goins went to the South after taking a degree from Earlham College in his native Indiana and studying business administration in graduate school at Northwestern University. He taught accounting and business courses at the Agricultural and Technical College in Greensboro before he was hired away by the Mutual to develop a statistical department in the home office. Over the years he served in a variety of positions, including assistant manager and director of public relations. He enhanced his business skills with literary-

21. Clipping, *Carolina Times*, June 1, 1926, in Kennedy Scrapbook; *Whetstone*, May, 1926. The company in Reidsville was the International Mutual Life, founded in 1907. The Mutual also reinsured four other companies during the 1920's: Toilers Mutual Life in Tarboro, N.C., 1921; Afro-American Mutual Life in Rock Hill, S.C., 1922; Afro-American Life in Charlotte, N.C., 1923; Provident Relief Association in Danville, Va., 1925. See *Whetstone*, fourth quarter, 1938.

22. Kennedy, "North Carolina Mutual," p. 119.

philosophic interests, and unofficially he served as Company ideologue and speechwriter for C. C. Spaulding.[23]

Dr. Donnell, born and reared in Greensboro, took a degree from A & T College and then traveled North to Howard University, from there to Harvard Medical School, and finally to a Boston hospital for internship before returning to North Carolina as assistant to Dr. Moore. As the Company's first full-time medical director, Dr. Donnell established a separate medical department and a special Life Extension Bureau. Through his efforts, along with those of actuary Asa T. Spaulding, the Company eventually gained control of its unfavorable mortality experience.[24]

Kennedy, who had an intriguing family background, was born in 1889 at Andersonville, Georgia. His grandfather, a giant 6'8" slave-craftsman who specialized in bridge-building, continued his craft after emancipation and put together a family farm of nearly 400 acres. Interestingly, part of the land he purchased had been the site of Andersonville Prison. Grandfather Kennedy made sure that his grandson inherited the carpentry trade, and the youth also acquired a keen sense of business from tending his father's prosperous meat market in Andersonville. After graduating from a Baptist academy in Americus, Georgia, young Kennedy worked several years as a carpenter, traveling salesman, and insurance agent for a Negro firm in Savannah before the triumvirate convinced him to come with the Mutual. The directors made Kennedy manager of the Savannah district, which under his direction experienced 500 percent growth and became one of the Company's leading districts by 1919. Following Merrick's death the home office summoned him to manage the Ordinary Department. In 1920 he advanced to the board of directors, and by 1923, after the death of Dr. Moore, he emerged as the third man in a loose hierarchy of leadership behind Spaulding and Avery. As assistant secretary–office manager under Avery he studied every function of the home office until he understood

23. *Ibid.*, p. 120; *Whetstone*, February, 1934.
24. Kennedy, "North Carolina Mutual," pp. 122–123; Stuart, *Economic Detour*, p. 218.

the operation whole. With a dogged tenacity and thoroughness he worked his way through a mountain of deferred difficulties arising out of the Company's quick expansion. He handled the correspondence, attended to all personnel problems, provided communication between departments, and generally attracted unresolved and knotty problems from all directions. Unquestionably he stands as the strong, silent figure who bolstered the Company at a crucial time during the 1920's when all appeared prosperous and secure but when the pains of rapid growth threatened a loss of control. Dr. Moore praised Kennedy as "a Moses sent to the North Carolina Mutual." Asa T. Spaulding, while a student at the University of Michigan, wrote Kennedy from the perspective of the ivory tower in Ann Arbor: "I often wonder what would have been the history of the company for the last decade without your stabilizing influence and foresight."[25]

Through much of his career Kennedy counted on the valuable assistance of William Daniel Hill, brother of the Urban League executive T. Arnold Hill. A native of Richmond, Virginia, and a graduate of Virginia Union College, Hill had been an agent for both the True Reformers and the Richmond Beneficial Life Insurance Company before going to work for the Mutual in 1917. After several years in the field he came to the home office in 1922 as an assistant to Avery in the Agency Department and later as assistant secretary to Kennedy.[26]

However, for the future of the Agency Department the most significant find of the period was George Wayne Cox, a "super salesman" hired in 1919. Cox came from a noted family in In-

25. Interviews, W. J. Kennedy, Jr., January 21, 29, 1968; Asa T. Spaulding to W. J. Kennedy, Jr., March 22, 1931, in W. J. Kennedy, Jr., Papers, North Carolina Mutual Life Insurance Company, Durham, N.C. (hereafter cited as Kennedy Papers). For other biographical information on Kennedy and his role in the Company as secretary-manager, see *Whetstone*, May, 1931; Stuart, *Economic Detour*, pp. 216–217. Kennedy became president of the Mutual on C. C. Spaulding's death in 1952, serving until retirement in 1959. He continues to serve on the board of directors and is remarkably active in Company and community affairs.

26. Kennedy, "North Carolina Mutual," pp. 123–124; Stuart, *Economic Detour*, pp. 219–220.

dianola, Mississippi, where his aunt gained national fame as the Republican-appointed postmistress who endured the wrath of the champion "red neck" politician James K. Vardaman.[27] George's uncle, Wayne W. Cox, owned a successful Negro bank in Indianola and was the founder of the first Negro legal reserve life insurance company, Mississippi Life. While working as an agent for his uncle's company, Cox met John Merrick at Hot Springs, Arkansas, where Merrick was taking treatments for his ailing foot. Deeply impressed with Merrick and the "Durham story," Cox left the family enterprise for the Mutual and assumed the responsibility for organizing five of the six southern states in the Company's new territory: Alabama, Arkansas, Florida, Mississippi, and Oklahoma. "Little George" made up for his slight stature with a powerful personality. His irresistible enthusiasm made him a natural leader, and he lost little time in organizing operations for the new states. By 1923 he had produced $13,000,000 worth of business in his territory. Because of his obvious ability and the mounting problems in the home office, Avery and Kennedy requested that Cox be called to Durham. As associate agency director he absorbed the brunt of the work required to oversee the sprawling agency system. He thrived on activity and became a nearly indispensable force, traveling throughout the field motivating managers and boosting morale.[28]

The Company continued to attract career officials during the 1920's. David Crocket Deans, Jr., an agent for the Southern Aid Life Insurance Company, switched firms in 1920 to manage the Richmond district for the Mutual. His success in Richmond moved the directors to appoint him regional supervisor of the

27. White folks refused to have their mail "forked out to them from the paws of a Negress," declared Vardaman, and he invited a showdown with President Theodore Roosevelt, who suspended postal service to Indianola rather than submit to Vardaman's demand for a white postmaster. Willard B. Gatewood, "Theodore Roosevelt and the Indianola Affair," *Journal of Negro History*, LIII (January, 1968), 48–69.

28. Stuart, *Economic Detour*, pp. 224–225; Kennedy, "North Carolina Mutual," pp. 124–125; *Whetstone*, April, 1932; interviews, George Wayne Cox, Jr., March 13, 1968; John H. Wheeler, August 4, 1970.

northern agencies in Virginia, Washington, D.C., and Maryland.[29] When Cox recruited Viola Gwendolyn Thompson (Mrs. V. G. Turner) in 1920, he bargained for no more than a keenly intelligent secretary. For a number of years she fulfilled that role as the woman behind John Avery and E. R. Merrick, but in the meantime she mastered the Finance Department so thoroughly that she succeeded Merrick as vice-president–treasurer and became the only woman elected to the board of directors.[30] Richard Lewis McDougald, in the tradition of Dr. Moore and C. C. Spaulding, came out of Columbus County to earn a place in black Durham. He attended North Carolina College, worked as a bookkeeper in the Mechanics and Farmers Bank, and in 1922 transferred to the Finance Department of the North Carolina Mutual, where he became an expert on investment. He was elected to the board in 1923, and until his premature death in 1944 he served a dual role as an officer and director of both the Mutual and the Mechanics and Farmers Bank.[31] Joseph Waverly Goodloe, like E. R. Merrick, literally represented a second generation of executives. His father, the Durham district manager, joined the Mutual in 1904, two years before Joseph was born. At the age of twelve young Goodloe, while "barefoot and playing in the street," encountered Dr. Moore, who reproved his summer idleness. "Boy, go in the house," the doctor told him, "and tell your mother to put some shoes on you; I'm taking you uptown to work." Goodloe spent a long succession of summers working for the Company and prepared himself for a full-time post in 1927 with a business degree from Hampton Institute. He rose steadily from clerk to a succession of key positions, ultimately in 1968 to the presidency.[32]

Understandably the Mutual would continue to search in vain for employees who combined business training with insurance

29. Kennedy, "North Carolina Mutual," pp. 129–130; Stuart, *Economic Detour*, pp. 227–228; *Whetstone*, February, 1934.

30. Kennedy, "North Carolina Mutual," pp. 130–131. While Mrs. Turner has been the only female member of the board, several women have been officers in the Company.

31. *Ibid.*, pp. 146–148.

32. *Ibid.*, pp. 150–151; *Whetstone*, first quarter, 1942.

experience, but by the 1920's the Company had little trouble commanding the attention of a growing body of underemployed black intellectuals and professionals. The first black woman to earn the Ph.D. degree in the United States, Sadie T. Mossell, brought her doctorate in economics from the University of Pennsylvania to the Mutual in 1921 and worked as the Company's unofficial actuary. Dr. Mossell compiled statistics on the Company's mortality experience and edited a Company magazine, *The Mutual,* along with the official journal of the National Negro Insurance Association, a trade association organized at Durham in 1921. Unfortunately for the Company, Dr. Mossell returned to the University of Pennsylvania for a law degree and a subsequent career as a practicing attorney.[33] In retrospect the largest prize to slip through the fingers of the directors was Robert C. Weaver, who worked briefly for the Mutual before achieving fame as a member of Franklin Delano Roosevelt's "black cabinet" and later as secretary of housing and urban development in Lyndon Baines Johnson's cabinet.[34]

As one of the ironic "advantages of disadvantages," the Mutual had access to a relatively untapped reservoir of college-trained men. The paucity of respectable occupations for black graduates made the Mutual stand out as a beacon of opportunity; therefore the Company enjoyed a buyer's market in recruiting new personnel. In 1926, when the home office staff numbered eighty, seventy-five (female clerks included) had attended college. A. E. Spears boasted that his Charlotte agency alone had seventeen "college men," and that this wealth of college graduates enabled the Company to build its enviable administrative depth through an effective "understudy program."[35]

Moreover, the background of the Mutual leaders shows that

33. Kennedy, "North Carolina Mutual," pp. 153–154.
34. Interview, W. J. Kennedy, Jr., January 29, 1968; North Carolina Mutual Founders Day ceremony in honor of Robert Weaver, October 20, 1967, Durham, N.C.
35. *Whetstone,* March, 1926; December, 1933; Kennedy, "North Carolina Mutual," pp. 124, 144. J. Owen Stalson in his *Marketing Life Insurance: Its History in America* (Cambridge: Harvard University Press, 1942), p. 620, has pointed out that white college graduates were often repulsed at the idea of being life insurance agents.

the compelling American myth of rags to riches applied no more to black than to white businessmen. Like the white subjects of William Miller's "American business elite,"[36] the black executives of the Mutual ascended the ladder of success from a starting point well above the bottom rung. Available information on fifty men serving the Mutual as officers from 1898 to 1968 would paint a composite portrait of a light-brown man born, reared, and schooled in the urban Southeast, who tended to be an active Methodist (A.M.E.), Baptist, or Episcopalian, and who almost without exception possessed a college degree, generally from a southern black institution. Mutual men were well traveled, both inside and outside the South. As a rule they came to the Company either fresh from college or comparatively late in life on the rebound from another profession, most likely teaching, business, or government service. Their parents were predominantly upper-class professionals or middle-class craftsmen, and almost always property-owners. Nearly half of the fathers and a majority of the mothers had attended college.[37]

The rising number of recruits, agents as well as administrators, indicated that the Company was growing into its vast new territory, which by 1920 included eleven states and the District of Columbia, requiring the services of nearly 1,100 employees.[38] In the process of expansion the home office force, now numbering over sixty, had long since outgrown its original quarters and had moved into space vacated by black tenants on Parrish Street. In 1914 a fire destroyed a large part of the Mutual Block; although the area was rebuilt, the directors since that time had considered constructing a new home office in the black community. In fact, land was purchased in 1917 for the new building in the Hayti section. But the board, for reasons not entirely clear,

36. William Miller, ed., *Men in Business: Essays on the Historical Role of the Entrepreneur* (New York: Harper and Row, 1962), pp. 309–337.
37. Biographical data were compiled through questionnaires and interviews. About half of the fifty cases represent younger men who have joined the Mutual since the 1930's, and whose backgrounds tend to add a disproportionate positive weight to the amount of travel and the status of parents.
38. Kennedy, "North Carolina Mutual," pp. 124, 144.

deferred and finally abandoned the construction plans. Kennedy suggests that the railroad tracks ran too near the proposed site on Pettigrew Street, and it is reasonable to assume that Merrick, still very much in contact with white businessmen, once again saw the logic of improving the more valuable property in the white business district.[39]

In 1920 the Company contracted, at $250,000, the construction of an ultramodern six-floor office building on Parrish Street.[40] The home office staff occupied the building in the late summer of 1921, and in December Negro leaders descended on Durham to attend the official dedication ceremony. Obviously the significance of the new building far exceeded the importance it held for housing an expanding business. Rather, it stood dressed in its marble trim and metallic doors as a great depository of racial pride, a literal monument to "Negro progress." The ceremony attracted over a thousand guests, almost a third of them from "out of town." Benjamin J. Davis, newspaper editor, devotee of Booker T. Washington, and general manager of the Negro Oddfellows in Atlanta delivered the keynote address.[41] For Davis the new building symbolized the "industrial prowess of our group . . . our potentialities as a race." Moreover, the Mutual impressed him as "a striking example of racial consciousness . . ." and he took the occasion to expound a bourgeois black nationalism: "Let us point out . . . that the white man does not read Negro newspapers, trade in Negro stores, patronize Negro doctors, employ Negro lawyers, carry life insurance with Negro companies . . . that he is seeking . . . white supremacy . . . in every . . . phase of our national life." Thus it seemed to Davis that if there was white nationalism, why not a little black nationalism: "The white man builds businesses for the employment of white boys and girls; we must build businesses for the employment of black boys and girls." More than that, Davis insisted, "Let us

39. Minutes, August 15, 1915; May 15, 1916; January 8, 1917, as cited in Kennedy, "North Carolina Mutual," pp. 105–106; interview, W. J. Kennedy, Jr., January 29, 1968.

40. Kennedy, "North Carolina Mutual," p. 137.

41. Clipping, *Durham Morning Herald*, December 18, 1921, in Kennedy Scrapbook.

put our money in Negro banks . . . insure in Negro insurance companies . . . and do nothing with the white man that we can do with the Negro, except . . . buy his land and sell him our produce . . . for he does nothing with us that he can do with a white man." Echoing Booker T. Washington, Davis made it clear to the mixed crowd that he preached an economic doctrine which shunned the "political agitators among us," looking instead to the "captains of industry." "We want more North Carolina Mutuals," he concluded, "more producers of wealth."[42]

The white response to the new building equaled the black in its exuberance, and, similarly, left no doubt as to the ideological significance the black achievement held for the white community. The *Morning Herald* described the building as an "architectural gem . . . of white brick rising above all other buildings on Parrish Street."[43] In fact, the new structure rose above all other buildings in Durham except one. The directors had carefully checked the measurement of the tallest building in town and then had made sure that theirs did not exceed it. The "Durham spirit" encouraged Negro business, but that, too, had its place, and the black businessman was obliged to command an extra skill, indeed an extra consciousness, in his public relations.[44]

If the white leadership sensed any threat from the imposing new edifice on Durham's undistinguished skyline, such an attitude never showed. On the contrary, "The building and the company are things that every citizen of Durham . . . can justly be proud of," claimed a white editor. "Durham *boasts* of being the home of the largest negro insurance company in the world."[45] The same editor clarified his boast when he asserted that the new building "is an example of what can be done by the negro if he goes about it in the right way."[46] Another white source, even before the building was completed, felt moved to acclaim

42. Typescript of Davis's speech delivered December 17, 1921, in Spaulding Papers; also see *Atlanta Independent*, December 22, 1921.
43. Clipping, *Durham Morning Herald*, December 18, 1921, in Kennedy Scrapbook.
44. Interview, W. J. Kennedy, Jr., January 29, 1968.
45. Clipping, *Durham Morning Herald*, December 18, 1921, in Kennedy Scrapbook. Italics mine.
46. *Ibid.*

the Mutual as the "wonder insurance company of this century, lifting its race from the quagmires of careless spendthrifts," and removing the fear of "the bogie man they themselves have created in their own minds."[47]

The impressive new headquarters managed by impressive black executives clearly represented more than buildings and businessmen. They represented an ideology, a movement, and could not be separated from the principle of racial solidarity and the philosophy of Booker T. Washington. Amidst the euphoria of black progress and white praise, the Mutual once again thought seriously about the prospects of a Negro economy. Since the failure of the Durham Textile Mill, the directors had abstained from subsidiary efforts, but the rationale was always present. Each black business stood as a stepping stone to another in an ethnic theory of economic development. And without regard to theory, one institution often grew naturally out of another; Negro banks, for example, sprang almost involuntarily from Negro insurance companies.

Between 1915 and 1920, while the Mutual was absorbed in its own expansion, the most substantial effort to diversify and extend black business in Durham came from John Merrick's former insurance partner, W. G. Pearson. Pearson continued to operate the Royal Knights of King David into the 1920's with remarkable success, and, having moved his office from the Mutual building to Hayti, he thought of developing financial services to parallel and perhaps exceed those on Parrish Street. In 1915 he organized the Peoples Savings and Loan Association, a short-lived enterprise succeeded in 1920 by his Fraternal Bank and Trust Company, also unsuccessful. Pearson's activities were both competitive and cooperative with the Mutual, which suffered occasional criticism for being located in the white community. The two financial camps shared directors, however, and it was understood that Pearson's bank provided services for those who were reluctant to go up to the white district, or who

47. Unidentified clipping, February 17, 1921, in the North Carolina Mutual clipping file.

resented the "whiteness" of the Mechanics and Farmers Bank. A surprising number of whites patronized the Mechanics and Farmers Bank because they thought it the surest way to keep their financial affairs confidential in a southern town. Paradoxically, blacks might withdraw support from an institution because it allowed white intrusion and at the same time question the strength of an institution because it was all black.[48]

Parrish Street absorbed the faltering Fraternal Bank and Trust Company in 1922, and in the meantime Mutual leaders, partly in collaboration with Pearson, chartered two enterprises destined for greater success: the Bankers Fire Insurance Company and the Mutual Building and Loan Association. As a unique Negro institution Bankers Fire gained considerable notoriety, much of it attracted by the dramatic appeal of its founder, Wanti W. Gomez.

Gomez, the mystery man, appeared in Durham out of nowhere early in 1920 and asked the Mutual to grant him a special agency. He refused to become a regular agent and convinced the directors to allow him to operate independently with his own crew of agents and examining physician. With such a traveling team he cut wide sales swaths through the South and sold a fantastic amount of life insurance. Hoping to capture his magic, the directors called Gomez to the home office and created a position for him as director of the Educational Department. But he would not be bound to an administrative post, and he immediately turnéd to bolder schemes—the first being Bankers Fire, which he organized in the summer of 1920. The black business leaders of Durham fell before his charm, and by utilizing their contacts throughout the South he sold $100,000 of stock in a few weeks. He skillfully sensed the need for consensus between Pearson and

48. Undated pamphlet on the Peoples Savings and Loan Association in W. G. Pearson Scrapbook, which also contains an undated typescript outlining Pearson's business career; Hugh P. Brinton, "The Negro in Durham: A Study of Adjustment to Town Life" (Ph.D. dissertation, University of North Carolina, 1930), p. 180; clipping, *Norfolk Journal and Guide*, August 7, 1920; and clipping, *Carolina Times*, August 6, 1927, both in the Pearson Scrapbook; clipping, *New York Age*, August 28, 1920, in Hampton Clippings, "Negro Business, Banks, Banking," vol. 2; interviews, Conrad O. Pearson, February 22; and Clyde Donnell, June 10, 1968.

the Mutual, and he installed Pearson as president of Bankers Fire, Spaulding and Moore as vice-presidents, and Avery as treasurer. Gomez chose to direct from backstage as secretary.[49]

His first effort a success, Gomez moved on to the grandiose, organizing an investment banking service to black businesses throughout the country—the Durham Commercial Security Company. But this enterprise was only preliminary to his boldest idea—the National Negro Finance Corporation—a national Negro bank which Gomez founded in Durham in 1924 to provide capital and counsel for prospective black businessmen.[50]

In the winter of 1926 Gomez disappeared from his Durham office, never to be seen again. Negro leaders throughout the country were shocked to learn that Gomez (Louis Jones) was a fugitive from Kentucky, where he was wanted for arson. He absconded with the funds from his Durham Commercial Security Company but left the other institutions (if not the serenity of black Durham) intact. There is more than a little irony in this brief foray of a confidence man and alleged arsonist, who left an impeccably sound fire insurance company in the conservative stewardship of Durham's unsuspecting black puritans.[51]

Less sensational than the Bankers Fire, but no less significant, was the founding of the Mutual Building and Loan Association in 1921. Organized principally by R. L. McDougald "for the purpose of teaching our group the importance of owning their own homes," the Loan Association aimed for the masses, selling

49. Interview, W. J. Kennedy, Jr., July 18, 1968; undated typescript on the Bankers Fire Insurance Company, Spaulding Papers; list of officers, 1921–26, Rencher Harris Papers, Manuscript Division, Duke University; clipping, *Norfolk Journal and Guide*, July 13, 1920, in Hampton Clippings, "Negro in Business, Insurance and Real Estate," vol. 1; clipping, *Norfolk Journal and Guide*, July 23, 1921, in Hampton Clippings, "Negro in Business, Banks and Banking," vol. 2. Before 1920 Negroes made several unsuccessful attempts to organize mutual fire insurance associations in Arkansas and Texas. Also in 1920 the Great Southern Fire Insurance Company, a Negro firm in Atlanta, was founded, but in 1922 it merged with Bankers Fire.

50. Thomas W. Holland, "Negro Capitalists," *Southern Workman*, LV (December, 1926), 536–540; clipping, *Philadelphia Tribune*, January 5, 1927, in Kennedy Scrapbook. See Ch. 5 for additional information on the National Negro Finance Corporation.

51. Interview, W. J. Kennedy, Jr., July 18, 1968; clipping, *Norfolk Journal and Guide*, June 8, 1935, in Kennedy Scrapbook.

its "shares" at twenty-five cents each. These shares were converted into saving certificates akin to bonds which matured in 333 weeks. McDougald calculated that such a program would enable the black worker to accumulate a down payment on a home and then, of course, borrow the balance from the Association. North Carolina Mutual leaders have always pointed to the number of Negro-owned homes in Durham, which they attribute to the influence of their Company and its associated banking institutions. The Mutual Building and Loan Association seldom strained to employ its social philosophy. It sold "self-help"—thrift and property—and thus provided an unaffected relationship between enterprise and uplift. Spaulding best expressed the straightforward rationale, "The company [MB&LA] has built several hundred homes on the easy payment plan and . . . we feel that home ownership makes better citizens."[52]

The uninhibited vertical development of Negro business centering on the Mutual continued in Durham throughout the 1920's. After John Merrick's death the real estate firm, Merrick-Moore-Spaulding, lingered momentarily as the Moore-Spaulding Company. In 1922 it became the (E. R.) Merrick-McDougald-Wilson Company, and that enterprise, which bought and sold real estate, managed the rental properties of the Mutual, and sold liability insurance, evolved into the Union Insurance and Realty Company at the end of the decade.[53] In 1926 W. G. Pearson, with the support of the Mutual, began the Southern Fidelity and Surety Company. At this time Durham Negro businesses, particularly the Mutual and the Royal Knights of King David,

52. Typescript materials on the Mutual Building and Loan Association, Spaulding Papers; see, in particular, "Facts about the Mutual Building and Loan Association," dated 1931. Unquestionably, black capitalism in Durham made it possible for many Negroes to buy homes, but by 1930 the benefits had not yet seeped down to the masses, a great many of whom were transient and followed the seasonal opportunities of tobacco work. Among twenty-one cities in North Carolina having 10,000 or more inhabitants in 1930, Durham ranked nineteenth in Negro homeownership. See U.S. Bureau of the Census, *Negroes in the United States, 1920–1932* (Washington, D.C.: Government Printing Office, 1935), p. 279.

53. A small amount of correspondence bearing letterheads of the above companies is in Spaulding Papers, along with a greater volume of receipts and financial statements. Interviews, W. J. Kennedy, Jr., January 29; Miles Mark Fisher, March 10, 1968; Brinton, "The Negro in Durham," pp. 182–183.

were spending $8,000 per year with white companies for bonding purposes. Pearson chartered the new company in order to keep as much money as possible in the black community and to avoid the racism of white firms which saw blacks as inherently poor risks. Pearson, Merrick, and McDougald were the key officers, and the company, while small, became important and prosperous, supplementing its income by selling automobile insurance.[54] Perhaps in an effort to vindicate the ideas (if not the practices) of Wanti Gomez, in 1929 Spaulding, Merrick, and McDougald organized the Mortgage Company of Durham. It refinanced mortgages, granted long-term loans, dealt in stocks and bonds, and attempted to serve as a financial clearinghouse for the Durham black business community.[55] In the proliferation of enterprises the Mechanics and Farmers Bank did not neglect its opportunities; in 1922 it opened an immediately successful branch in Raleigh.[56]

Technically every black business created in Durham in the 1920's had an independent corporate identity, but each held a dependent relationship to the Mutual. Just as "the Wachovia Bank relies on the R. J. Reynolds Tobacco Company," asserted Spaulding, "likewise the Mechanics and Farmers Bank can always turn for support to . . . the Race's financial bulwark, the North Carolina Mutual."[57] The various enterprises shared a common source of capital, personnel, patrons, and, most important, a common ethnic identity. The Mutual and the Mechanics and Farmers Bank formed the vital sections of the organism, and the rest of the parts lived in symbiotic relationship to the two. On occasion the leaders, often for personal reasons or to pre-

54. Undated clipping, *Durham Morning Herald*, in W. G. Pearson Scrapbook; clipping, *Carolina Times*, August 18, 1928, in Kennedy Scrapbook; Brinton, "The Negro in Durham," pp. 182–183; C. C. Spaulding, untitled manuscript on Negro business in Durham dated October 2, 1930, Spaulding Papers.

55. Brinton, "The Negro in Durham," p. 183. The Mortgage Company, while apparently not an official brokerage firm itself, did spawn such a business, T. D. Parham and Associates, Incorporated, also founded in 1929.

56. C. C. Spaulding to Charles N. Hunter, October 13; Spaulding to Hunter, December 13, 1921, Hunter Papers; *Carolina Times*, July 31, 1948, "Fortieth Anniversary History of the Mechanics and Farmers Bank."

57. C. C. Spaulding to the depositors of the Mechanics and Farmers Bank, December 30, 1930, Spaulding Papers.

clude public criticism, insisted that the firms were rigidly independent. But everyone knew otherwise. As legal entities, for example, the North Carolina Mutual and the Mortgage Company of Durham stood completely separate, but the distinction dissolved in practice. C. C. Spaulding reproved the graphic artist on the payroll of the North Carolina Mutual who submitted a bill for work done at the Mortgage Company. Spaulding expressed surprise that the man would expect pay beyond his regular salary, because "after all the Mortgage Company and the North Carolina Mutual are practically the same."[58]

But the Mutual never allowed itself to become an overextended confederacy of corporations like its Atlanta rival, the Standard Life Insurance Company, which eventually drowned in a swamp of heavily watered stock enterprises. If the North Carolina Mutual did make a mistake during the 1920s, it was more in its horizontal than in its vertical expansion. This expansion across the South, while better grounded and more conservative than the blind proliferation of the National Benefit Life Insurance Company, was nonetheless ill-advised. On paper the growth of the Company seemed more than impressive. Insurance in force during the decade 1914–24 soared from $4,986,-344 to $42,779,641, a percent of gain never equaled in the history of the Company.[59] But other statistics would reveal the undesirable side effects of expansion. The mortality experience, always bad, worsened as the emphasis on volume undercut the caution of risk selection. The vastness of the territory created a burdensome overhead and almost insuperable problems in service and supervision. With difficulty in selecting and servicing risks, an adverse lapse rate was inevitable.

While the Company could improve its mortality experience with more exclusive risk selection, much of the risk was, of course, predetermined by social conditions. Among the many disfavors dealt out by American racial injustice was the statis-

58. C. C. Spaulding to W. W. Micheaux, June 30, 1934, Spaulding Papers.
59. North Carolina Insurance *Report* 1915, pp. 148–151; Kennedy, "North Carolina Mutual," pp. 116–117.

tical certainty that Negroes would die earlier and proportionately in greater numbers than whites. In 1920 whites died at the rate of 12.4 per 1,000 of population; blacks, at 18.7 per 1,000. The 1930 census revealed some improvement, but the relative gain was scarcely perceptible: 10.6 whites per 1,000; 16.5 blacks per 1,000.[60] According to data compiled for the Metropolitan Life Insurance Company by the eminent statistician Louis Dublin, Negroes during the 1920's had a life expectancy of 47 years, while whites could count statistically on living until age 59.[61]

In the eleven states and the District of Columbia where the North Carolina Mutual operated during most of the 1920's, the Negro death rate differed very little from the national Negro rate.[62] But for reasons of efficiency the North Carolina Mutual operated as much as possible in cities. Urbanization eased the agent's task but threatened the Company's mortality experience. In 1930 the death rate for all Negroes averaged 14.2 in rural areas, but 19.8 in cities.[63] And in fifteen selected cities within the Mutual's territory the rates ran somewhat higher, 22.3 per 1,000 population, a rate nearly twice that for whites.[64]

In 1920 the U.S. Public Health Service studied Negro mortality in seventeen states, North and South, urban and rural, and concluded that the southern rural Negro had the longest life

60. Bureau of the Census, *Negroes in the United States, 1920–1932*, p. 445. All mortality rates cited here are exclusive of still births (which averaged two and one-half times higher for blacks than for whites).

61. These data, based on the experience of the Metropolitan Life Insurance Company with insurance on Negro lives and Census Bureau information, are probably more reliable than the census figures themselves because of the statistical skill of Dublin and his assistants at Metropolitan. By 1927 Metropolitan had insured over 2,000,000 Negroes. Jesse Edward Gloster, "The North Carolina Mutual Life Insurance Company: Its History, Development and Current Operation" (Ph.D. dissertation, University of Pittsburgh, 1955), p. 54, has a breakdown of the Metropolitan findings; Louis Dublin, "Life, Death, and the Negro," *American Mercury*, XII (September, 1927), 42–43.

62. In 1930 the Mutual territory had a 16.4 per 1,000 population death rate; the national Negro death rate was 16.5 per 1,000. The Mutual withdrew from four of the eleven states in 1926, but the 1920 census did not include all of the Mutual territory in its registration area for measuring Negro mortality. Thus, the 1930 census is used as an approximation of the mortality problems the Mutual faced during most of the 1920's in most of its districts.

63. Bureau of the Census, *Negroes in the United States, 1920–1932*, p. 443.

64. *Ibid.*, p. 452.

TABLE 3. NEGRO AND WHITE DEATH RATES PER 1,000 POPULATION (EXCLUSIVE OF STILL BIRTHS) IN SELECTED NORTH CAROLINA MUTUAL CITIES, 1920 AND 1930

Cities	1920		1930	
	Negro	White	Negro	White
Atlanta	22.8	14.6	23.2	11.6
Baltimore	23.3	14.0	19.6	12.7
Birmingham	22.6	12.3	19.3	10.0
Charleston	31.6	16.7	33.0	14.6
Charlotte	19.0	14.0	19.1	10.1
Durham	29.9	10.0	22.4	11.8
Jackson	48.5	22.2	21.1	13.1
Jacksonville	20.3	14.1	21.0	11.8
Memphis	26.8	15.6	23.5	13.5
Montgomery	27.0	14.3	22.1	13.1
Nashville	24.0	15.5	23.1	13.7
Richmond	23.3	13.4	21.4	12.3
Savannah	31.4	16.7	26.5	13.6
Washington, D.C.	20.6	12.7	21.0	12.9
Winston-Salem	20.9	11.4	18.9	10.4
Averages	26.1	14.5	22.3	12.3

expectancy and the southern urban Negro the shortest. Urban South Carolina experienced the highest average death rate with 37.4 per 1,000 population, and rural Louisiana the lowest with 13.5 per 1,000. There is no question that whatever advantages might accrue to the urban Negro, the ghetto shortened his life. It served as the perfect incubator for the terrible scourge, tuberculosis, along with other diseases.[65]

Tuberculosis, while less devastating in 1930 than a decade earlier,[66] remained the black man's nemesis, accounting for 11 percent of Negro mortality in 1930. In all North Carolina Mutual districts tuberculosis killed three times as many blacks as whites,

65. U.S. Bureau of the Census, *Mortality among Negroes in the United States*, Public Health Bulletin no. 174 (Washington, D.C.: Government Printing Office, 1938), p. 30, as cited in Brinton, "The Negro in Durham," p. 257; also see Gloster, "North Carolina Mutual," p. 30.
66. Dublin, "Life, Death, and the Negro," p. 42, claimed a 40 percent decline in tuberculosis death rates among Metropolitan's Negro policyholders during the 1920's.

and in the Company's ten largest cities the ratio was four to one.[67] A Mutual agent in Savannah, Georgia, kept a comparative death count during March, 1924, and found that 107 Negroes died from all causes, in contrast to only 52 whites. Referring to his death claims, he reported, "They have come in like sheep."[68] The Mutual's medical director, Dr. Donnell, lamented, "We die three or four times faster than the white folks from almost any kind of disease."[69]

Year after year during the 1920's the North Carolina Mutual paid more in death benefits than it had anticipated. In only one year of the decade, 1922, did the mortality rate conform to the expected. (See Table 4.)[70] No wonder C. C. Spaulding looked

TABLE 4. NORTH CAROLINA MUTUAL LIFE INSURANCE COMPANY MORTALITY RATIOS, ACTUAL TO EXPECTED (100 = EXPECTED)

Year	Ratio	Year	Ratio
1917	123.9	1924	120.8
1918	181.2	1925	123.4
1919	114.7	1926	121.9
1920	109.2	1927	125.9
1921	105.8	1928	142.5
1922	98.5	1929	120.5
1923	117.9	1930	129.0

with nostalgia to his agrarian roots in Columbus County, where octogenarians were commonplace. In fact, throughout rural North Carolina the Negro death rate ran only about half that of Durham.[71] Thus the Mutual leaders could see at their very doorstep the nature of the problem, and they increasingly com-

67. Bureau of the Census, *Negroes in the United States*, pp. 445, 454–455.
68. I. R. Spaulding, district manager in Savannah, to W. J. Kennedy, Jr., April 24, 1924, Kennedy Papers. Negroes constituted 45.8 percent of the Savannah population in 1930.
69. Clipping, *Durham Morning Herald*, April 12, 1925, Kennedy Scrapbook.
70. Figures are from 1952 typescript compiled by N. H. Bennett, Jr., associate actuary of the North Carolina Mutual, Spaulding Papers; also see Winfred O. Bryson, Jr., "Negro Life Insurance Companies: A Comparative Analysis of the Operating and Financial Experience of Negro Legal Reserve Life Insurance Companies" (Ph.D. dissertation, University of Pennsylvania, 1948), p. 34.
71. Brinton, "The Negro in Durham," p. 260.

mitted the Company not only to selecting healthier risks but to improving Negro health in general.

In 1925 Dr. Donnell launched the Life Extension Department. Dr. Moore, while president in 1921, had begun a Health Department, and Donnell simply expanded his idea. To assist Donnell the directors hired Dr. Roscoe Brown, a Negro physician and former employee of the U.S. Public Health Service. He and Donnell turned the entire second floor of the home office into a virtual hospital, complete with an operating room. Within a few weeks they were treating 60 persons a day, over two-thirds of whom were tuberculosis patients. The two doctors also kept a much closer watch on the 600 physicians who conducted field examinations, offering them advice and suggesting that they send questionable cases to the home office. The Company employed a white physician to teach a physiotherapy course to employees and patients, and the Life Extension Department conducted lecture tours, showed films, and distributed huge numbers of bulletins from the U.S. Public Health Service along with pamphlets of its own—nearly 300,000 in 1925 alone.[72] Through its new monthly magazine, the *Whetstone*, the Company waged war on mortality with health tips to policyholders, medical information for agents, and a veritable correspondence course for physicians in the field.[73] Even the North Carolina Mutual Glee Club joined the campaign, "singing out for better health" on extraordinary tours that combined public relations, entrepreneurial adroitness, and racial uplift.[74]

A multitude of variables makes it impossible to measure precisely the salutary effect of the public health program. But it seems significant that in the 1920's Durham, almost alone among United States cities, achieved a notable reduction in Negro mortality, while at the same time experiencing an actual increase

72. Clippings, *Durham Morning Herald*, April 12; *Afro-American*, April 25, 1925, Kennedy Scrapbook; Kennedy, "North Carolina Mutual," pp. 170, 175; North Carolina Mutual broadside from 1926 Philadelphia International Exposition, where the Life Extension Department (also referred to as Life Extension Bureau) won a golden award for its display on improving Negro health.

73. See *Whetstone*, 1927, all issues.

74. Interview, W. J. Kennedy, Jr., January 29, 1968; clippings, *Durham Morning Herald*, April 12; *Afro-American*, April 25, 1925, Kennedy Scrapbook.

in white mortality.[75] Perhaps the combined efforts of the Mutual and Lincoln Hospital[76] improved the chances for Negro survival in what was apparently an unhealthy city for either race.

Whatever the success of the Company's direct attack on Negro mortality, it still groped in darkness for actuarial precision. President Spaulding took pride in pointing out that his policyholders had a lower death rate than Negroes insured by the Metropolitan—a fact easily explained, thought Spaulding, by the "Negro agent's familiarity with colored risks . . . an understanding of distinctions among Negroes to which white men, through racial prejudice have blinded themselves."[77] But this cultural familiarity did not solve the actuarial problem; that solution, acknowledged Spaulding, would come only with experience and a scientific familiarity. "Your company has long since realized," he wrote in the *Whetstone*, "that the only way it can continue . . . is to adhere to a program formulated out of its own experience. No company insuring Negro risks exclusively has been operating long enough to give us any information on which we could absolutely rely, and . . . it would be folly to formulate a program . . . on the same plan followed by white companies."[78] Despite the scientific nature of life insurance, cultural differences meant that black companies could founder on white assumptions. It would eventually take a black actuary, Asa T. Spaulding, to link the science with the culture.

If urbanization posed problems for the Company, so did the overwhelming ruralness of its southern territory. Obviously an agent would spend more time and money contacting customers in the country than he would in the city. Not only did distances reduce efficiency, but in isolated rural areas the insurance agent

75. See Table 3, p. 126. The only other city in the United States to experience such a striking relative improvement in Negro mortality was Vicksburg, Miss., but the extraordinarily high death rates among both races in 1920 at Vicksburg as well as at Jackson would suggest an epidemic in the area, thus accounting for the tremendous relative improvement during the decade. Also see Bureau of the Census, *Negroes in the United States, 1920–1932*, pp. 445–453.

76. The hospital was administered in large part by Mutual officials.

77. Clipping, *Standard Advertiser*, November 1, 1923, Kennedy Scrapbook.

78. *Whetstone*, May, 1927.

came to the dreary world of the sharecropper as a welcome visitor who might sit a while. The agent knew the latest jokes, brought news from the city as well as from the neighboring farms, and generally complimented the husband on his animals and crops, the wife on her garden and children. With his business suit, briefcase, and Model T, he stood in psychological terms as a "significant other" who countered the syndrome of white success. Therapy for the farmer, however, meant increased costs for the Mutual.[79]

By the mid-1920's the North Carolina Mutual had extended its operations to an area much too wide to be adequately serviced, considering its rural nature. The expense of collecting premiums produced more overhead than profits, and in 1924 the directors discontinued the expense allowance for agents traveling in rural areas. Most agents quit collecting, and the entire burden of keeping up the premiums fell to the insured. Industrial policies lapsed by the hundreds, and complaints were legion. In response to an inquiry from the North Carolina Insurance Department, Kennedy replied, "Recent examination . . . [showed] that our work was scattered too much in rural communities and . . . that we must discontinue the traveling expense allowance . . . to agents for going to rural territories and advise the policyholders to mail their premiums to the nearest district office."[80] The complaints continued and occasionally revealed the troublesome tradition of intraracial distrust. One policyholder wrote Kennedy praising the Metropolitan while criticizing the Mutual for its service and an alleged underpayment on his claim: "I knowed when you all was so long paying it that you all was going to steal some of it Nigger like."[81]

If the Company hoped to compete with the Metropolitan, which often avoided Negro risks but nonetheless in 1928 had

79. Interviews, W. J. Kennedy, Jr., February 26; A. E. Spears, Sr., May 15, 1968.
80. W. J. Kennedy, Jr., to Stacey W. Wade, North Carolina Insurance Commissioner, May 21; also see Kennedy to Mrs. Cora C. Smith, Vernon, Okla., March 21; Kennedy to Joseph Alexander, Camden, S.C., May 14, 1924, Kennedy Papers.
81. Ransom Smith to W. J. Kennedy, Jr., January 7, 1925, Kennedy Papers.

twenty times more insurance on Negro lives than did the Mutual,[82] it would have to make immediate corrections. Underestimated mortality, quick lapsing, and a spiraling overhead inevitably increased the cost of a Mutual policy. The Company could not immediately make Negroes live longer, nor could it radically change its rate of return on investments; these were relatively fixed matters. It could turn only to the third basic ingredient in the cost of life insurance: the "loading," or operating expenses.

As early as 1922 some of the directors worried that the Company sustained too many agents for too little increase in volume, an inefficiency which reflected an unwieldy triangular territory stretching from Baltimore to Oklahoma City to Jacksonville. And the decision for retrenchment was foreshadowed by the virtual withdrawal from scattered rural communities in 1924. Thus early in 1926 the North Carolina Mutual sold its business in Oklahoma, Arkansas, and Mississippi to the Century Life Insurance Company, a black enterprise in Little Rock. The Florida business went to a smaller but well-established Negro firm in Jacksonville, the Afro-American Life Insurance Company.[83] Agents in the four vacated states simply transferred their employment as a part of the reinsurance agreement. At the home office the Mutual found it possible to reduce its staff by 18 percent. The curtailment meant an immediate 15 percent reduction in premium income, but operating expenses declined more than 20 percent.[84]

The decision to cut back, while an obvious one, was marked with ambivalence. It admitted a mistake, readily construed as a racial mistake, and it threatened a loss in prestige. Temporarily the Mutual relinquished the title of "World's Largest Negro Business" to the National Benefit Life. President Spaulding, who counseled retrenchment, presented the decision as con-

82. Harry Pace, "The Attitude of Life Insurance Companies toward Negroes," *Southern Workman*, LVII (January, 1928), 3.

83. Kennedy, "North Carolina Mutual," pp. 167–168; clippings, *Jacksonville Journal*, February 8, 1927; *Carolina Times*, December 31, 1926, Kennedy Scrapbook.

84. Kennedy, "North Carolina Mutual," p. 169.

sistent with the sound business philosophy of Merrick and Moore. And he felt constrained to cover the retreat with the rhetoric of Booker T. Washington and the Bible. Far from a retreat, the strategic return to the South Atlantic region was only preliminary to an impending advance on the Middle Atlantic states. "We will let down our buckets where we are," said Spaulding, before we "go up and possess the land."[85] It is unlikely that the Company planned any sudden expansion to the North. Rather, such an announcement was intended to allay the Negro suspicion that the Mutual's retrenchment was a precursor to failure. Indeed, during the Depression Spaulding would argue that the withdrawal of 1926 was part of a prescient vision to *avoid* expansion before the oncoming disaster.[86]

Retreat, like expansion a decade earlier, amounted to more than a business decision. The North Carolina Mutual was preeminently a racial institution, and the Afro-American subculture guided its every move and largely determined its character and style. Despite its constant pursuit of objective business performance and its bourgeois economic position, the Mutual could not, indeed would not, slough off the folkways of race.

85. *Whetstone*, January, 1927; also see clipping, *Pittsburgh Courier*, January 1, 1927, Avery Scrapbook.
86. *Whetstone*, June, 1932; Gloster, "North Carolina Mutual," p. 65.

5

That Good Ol'
Mutual Spirit

Every Saturday morning the custodians pushed back the tables in the Company cafeteria, lined up the folding chairs, and transformed the dining hall into the "auditorium." At eleven o'clock the employees descended from their offices; Mrs. Bessie Whitted took her place at the piano, and to the tune of "Old-Time Religion" "the Mutual family" broke into a chorus of the Company song:

> Give me that good ol' Mutual Spirit,
>
> . . . .
>
> It was good enough for Merrick,
> It was good enough for Moore,
>
> . . . .
>
> And it's good enough for me.

The "Forum" was in session, and on Company time.[1]

Entrepreneurial historians have observed that enterprises of any size and duration acquire a "social personality."[2] The Mutual had more than its share of personality, much of it a given part of its racial heritage, and much of it developed in concert

---

1. Interviews, W. J. Kennedy, Jr., February 29; Mrs. Viola G. Turner, June 13, 1968. Miscellaneous materials concerning the Forum are scattered throughout the Spaulding and Kennedy Papers as well as in the Company magazine, the *Whetstone*.

2. See Thomas C. Cochran, *The American Business System* (Cambridge: Harvard University Press, 1957), p. 194.

between countless external and internal forces ranging from race relations to personal characteristics of its leaders. It lived always in three worlds: a black world, a white world, and a business world, a mutually inclusive mélange out of which the Mutual sought its own identity. Its style of management, the primacy of religion, reverence for the founders, a sense of mission and family, and a firm commitment to racial cooperation and uplift combined to form the salient features of its character.

The Forum, which expressed much of the Company's personality, began in 1921 under the hand of C. C. Spaulding, who fashioned it after a devotional ceremony he had witnessed in an Arkansas Negro fraternal society. Religion, ideology, and ritual made the Forum much more than just a pep rally. Spirituals and the Negro national anthem, "Lift Every Voice and Sing," mingled with the improvised Company songs, and sufficient prayer was offered to qualify each session as a church service. Nobody could escape the conclusion that the Mutual saw its cause as a holy one. Religion and business were indivisible, and the secular ideas of self-help supplied but another inextricable part of the whole.[3]

Self-improvement invariably occupied a place in the program of the Forum. Organized "spelling matches" offering a $2.50 gold piece to the winner whipped up considerable enthusiasm and underscored the Company's concern for the rudiments of education.[4] Young officers in particular were encouraged to test their oratory at the Forum and thus improve their public speaking. Forensics, in fact, often dominated the meetings, and informal debate flourished in special sessions reserved by the employees to air their grievances. In this capacity the Forum served as an ingenious device to provide a sense of communal participation and a healthy catharsis at the end of the week. Spaulding insisted that no officer could be president of the

3. *Whetstone*, August, 1924; May, 1925; interviews, W. J. Kennedy, Jr., February 29; Mrs. Viola G. Turner, June 13, 1968; Emerson E. Waite, "Social Factors in Negro Business Enterprise" (Master's thesis, Duke University, 1940), p. 127.
4. *Whetstone*, February, 1926.

Forum, and that the leadership come from the lower ranks as much as possible. In this way he strengthened the feeling of family that he considered vital. Everyone felt Spaulding's presence, nonetheless, for he kept a watchful eye on the meetings and occasionally used them as a platform to give his corporate family a fatherly lecture.[5]

With great success the Forum committee sought the services of prominent outside speakers. Negro leaders constantly passed through Durham, sometimes specifically to visit the North Carolina Mutual. The middle-class Negro world was a small one which possessed a very practical sense of solidarity born out of the rigors of travel without adequate public accommodations; thus it was natural that dignitaries should stop in Durham and spend the night with "friends." Race transcended ideology; a black socialist might very well room with a black capitalist, and in effect the large upper-class Negro homes on Fayetteville Street served as hotels. Professors from Tuskegee and Hampton, the self-help centers of the South, often spoke at the Forum. Traveling glee clubs and even college athletic teams included Durham and the Forum on their itineraries. The fame of Durham as the "capital of the black middle class" made the city a favorite oasis for Negro travelers, indeed a tourist attraction. In an obvious play on the Forum as one of the attractions, the *Whetstone* declared, "All roads lead to Rome and the North Carolina Mutual."[6] From the standpoint of self-improvement and intellectual stimulation the Mutual staff profited immensely from this flow of travelers. For weeks on end the Forum might be nothing less than a black Chautauqua. As one of his fringe benefits, each employee stood the chance of meeting a race leader every Saturday. W. E. B. Du Bois, Asa Philip Randolph, Robert Russa Moton, James Weldon Johnson, and Adam Clayton Powell, Jr., numbered among an impressive list of Forum visitors during the 1920's and early 1930's. Foreign guests, particularly from Africa, and even an Italian count from Rome took

5. Interviews, W. J. Kennedy, Jr., February 29; Mrs. Viola G. Turner, June 13, 1968; Waite, "Social Factors in Negro Business," p. 127.
6. *Whetstone*, February, 1928.

the road to Durham, as did American whites, including Norman Thomas, Mary White Ovington, and Eleanor Roosevelt, all of whom spoke at the Forum.[7]

The management encouraged the employees to develop their literary and musical talents; thus, when the Forum did not serve as a lyceum, it provided light entertainment—a series of skits or a talent show. Out of the Forum grew the North Carolina Mutual Glee Club, the smaller Treble Clef Club, and the Company Quartette, all of which not only entertained the Mutual family, but also performed for black and white audiences throughout the state as "singing ambassadors of good will."[8] President Spaulding sometimes traveled with the singers and lectured on racial solidarity or interracial cooperation, depending on the audience. The troupe was highly accomplished (under the direction of Mrs. Whitted) and served as an astute instrument of public relations with its equal appeal to blacks and whites. The role of the Glee Club plainly illustrates that successful advertising for a black enterprise encompassed dimensions of public opinion never contemplated by white businessmen. The Club sang mostly in Negro churches, where, along with Spaulding, it could easily link the cause of the Mutual with the cause of the church, and at the same time make a musical plea for better health. Spirituals were the mainstay of the repertoire, and the enthusiastic white response encouraged the group to think that it could temper race relations. In addition to singing in white churches, particularly in Chapel Hill, the Glee Club sang at the Duke University annual spring music festival—on one occasion "to a hall nearly filled with white people who could scarcely get enough . . . of the spirituals," which, according to

7. *Whetstone,* May, June, 1924; May, 1925; March, 1933; March, June, 1934; clipping, *Durham Morning Herald,* June 12, 1934, Kennedy Scrapbook; William J. Kennedy, Jr., "North Carolina Mutual Life Insurance Company: A Symbol of Progress, 1898–1966" (Manuscript in possession of W. J. Kennedy, Jr., Durham, N.C.), pp. 194–196; Asa Philip Randolph to C. C. Spaulding, December 16, 1927, Kennedy Papers; *South African Outlook,* LXIV (December 1, 1934), 273–274.

8. Kennedy, "North Carolina Mutual," pp. 161–162; interview, Mrs. Viola G. Turner, June 13, 1968; *Whetstone,* May, 1925; December, 1932.

an unconsciously insightful white reporter, "only the Southern negro can sing to a haunting melody."[9]

The Forum, like the Company newspaper, baseball team, and Life Extension Bureau, became a social agency that extended beyond the Mutual and into the black community to offset a lack of established institutions. In 1928 the Company organized the "Forum Chest," an obvious response to the deficiency of the Community Chest. Like its white counterpart the "Chest" provided for voluntary payroll deductions, but the money went to Negro charities.[10]

Because of race the Mutual had always been a quasi-public organization, operating well in advance of what Frederick Lewis Allen called the "big change" in American business, which saw capitalism forced into a position of greater social responsibility during and after the Depression.[11] The Mutual did not grow into its social conscience under the political pressure of American reform; rather, it inherited the quest for social justice as an implied part of its reason for being. It was this larger outlook, this tempering of rugged individualism by the requirement for racial cooperation—group economic development—and the tradition of a socially conscious leadership that gave the Mutual its sense of mission and family. Men and women alive today who worked for the Company as early as the 1920's recall the

9. Clippings, *Durham Morning Herald*, May, 1925 (no exact date); *Carolina Times*, May 1, 1925, Kennedy Scrapbook; *Whetstone*, May, 1925; December, 1934; interviews, W. J. Kennedy, Jr., February 29; Mrs. Viola G. Turner, June 13, 1968; Kennedy, "North Carolina Mutual," p. 161; W. J. Kennedy, Jr., to R. M. Hardee, June 22, 1930, Kennedy Papers.

10. *Whetstone*, January, 1933; W. J. Kennedy, Jr., to C. S. Hicks, December 20, 1930, Kennedy Papers.

11. Frederick Lewis Allen, *The Big Change: America Transforms Itself, 1900–1950* (New York: Harpers, 1952), pp. 155–157, 234–258; Cochran, *The American Business System*, pp. 11, 154–155, 190–204. As an internal example of social concern, the Mutual provided group insurance for its agents as early as 1925, at a time when only a half dozen American life insurance companies like the Metropolitan and the Prudential, felt they could afford this service. Indeed, by 1939 only twenty companies were providing such a benefit. See J. Owen Stalson, *Marketing Life Insurance: Its History in America* (Cambridge: Harvard University Press, 1942), p. 623; *Whetstone*, February, 1925.

poignant feeling that they were sitting atop a movement, a racial cause, that transcended business and inspired a loyalty to the Company out of all proportion to salary reward. Nor could the officers be motivated by ownership and stock profits, since the firm was organized as a mutual. The Mutual spirit, while racial at base, apparently did not repeat itself exactly in other Negro companies. Witnesses with wide contacts in black business testified to this difference.[12] By 1930 Durham and the North Carolina Mutual had become so much a part of the racial folklore that each new employee came to the Company with a vested interest in its image. The Mutual stood as the black middle-class Zion in the wilderness of white America, and acceptance into its ranks provided a distinctive security, a coziness wrapped in racial pride and the bittersweet satisfaction of succeeding in spite of handicaps. Contacts with whites inside the black environment only added to the sense of satisfaction. White salesmen who asked for "Charlie" or "John" confronted proud secretaries responding: "Charlie? We don't have a Charlie here, do we ladies? Oh, you must mean Mr. Spaulding. May I take your hat while you wait?" And for sheer compensation the white men often waited longer than necessary. One person who insisted on calling Avery "John" became so irritated with Mrs. Viola Turner's countertactics that he threatened to "report her to the Ku Klux Klan."[13]

While the outside world did much to sustain the spirit, internally the tradition perpetuated itself through the easy transmission of values from one generation to another and a network of marriages within the Company. Success and status in black families are uncommonly precious commodities, often retained within a tightly restricted orbit governed by racial-family solidarity. Surely it made sense, for example, that E. R. Merrick should tread in his father's footsteps with so few alternatives available. Who would leave Zion for uncertainty, and why not

12. Agency Director George W. Cox, for example, knew other firms intimately and turned down attractive offers to work for them because he recognized the special quality of the Mutual.

13. Interviews, Mrs. Viola G. Turner, June 13; W. J. Kennedy, Jr., February 29, June 4, 8; Asa T. Spaulding, July 18; Charles Watts, June 6, 1968.

marry in it? It seemed more than logical for young Merrick to wed one of Dr. Moore's two daughters. Richard McDougald married the other, and C. C. Spaulding had long since taken John Merrick's half-sister as his wife. W. J. Kennedy, in turn, would marry Spaulding's sister; Dr. Donnell, the daughter of John Merrick; and Donnell's successor, Dr. Charles Watts, the daughter of E. R. Merrick. The maze of kinship connections at the officer level gave rise to the charge of nepotism. Critics can cite, for example, that six of the Company's first seven presidents have been related either by ancestry or marriage. The Mutual family became a family in both blood and spirit. Where kinship was not real, the Company fostered at least a *feeling* of kinship involving solemn obligations and a spiritual commitment to the institutional family and hence to the ethnic family. The Mutual functioned as an instrument of socialization, creating a cultural niche within the substance of the larger Afro-American culture.[14]

President Spaulding generally viewed the extended family as an asset which buttressed the heritage and guaranteed a supply of "Mutualized" managers. But he often criticized Negro business in general for its "familiarity," for being too casual, and by the end of the 1930's, when the dimensions of kinship were clearly drawn and the spirit of "closeness" deeply entrenched, he wondered if it had been "unfortunate that we are so closely allied in a social way . . . be it as it may, it is our duty . . . to exercise due precaution and diligence in seeing that our actions are in keeping with those of directors of all well-regulated organizations."[15]

Whatever his reservations, Spaulding's administrative style was a very personal one. Virtually all of the employees, with the possible exception of the officers, referred to him as "Papa," quite in keeping with his role as father figure in the family. The relationship among the directors was unusually democratic, as Spaulding relied heavily on the advice and expertise of others,

14. *Ibid.*; Booker T. Kennedy to W. J. Kennedy, Jr., November 22, 1930, Kennedy Papers; Thomas W. Holland, "Negro Capitalists," *Southern Workman*, LV (December, 1926), 539; *Whetstone*, second quarter, 1941.

15. C. C. Spaulding Report to Executive Committee, 1938, Spaulding Papers.

but only at the Forum was there the illusion of democracy for
the rank and file. For most of the employees President Spaulding
was the patriarch, a moral overlord, and something of a mother
hen. While of a different breed than the petty tyrants who sometimes commanded the small Negro colleges in the South, he took
more than a passing interest in the public behavior of his employees, and in this small patrimonial world he possessed considerable power. Traditionally Spaulding took new employees
to the court house and registered them to vote, usually an im-
possibility without his sanction.[16] In the 1930's his political role
would greatly expand, including even a small say in political
patronage at the national level, but until the onset of the New
Deal he generally eschewed politics and instead preached moral
and economic improvement.[17]

Spaulding bore a heavy burden in assuming that he could
change white attitudes through moral instruction to his people;
moreover, the weight of responsibility grew heavier as he fell
under the illusion that the tactic was working. White opinion,
he observed in 1926, was "breaking in the Negro's favor and . . .
the black man must go forward carefully, for the slightest mistake may cause a reaction . . . detrimental to the generations that
are to come."[18]

So it was that Spaulding felt a special obligation to look after
his charges. An oral legend holds that one not only had to attend church, but the correct church, in order to work for the
Mutual. Such a notion embellishes the truth, but there is no

16. Interviews, Mrs. Viola G. Turner, June 13; Conrad O. Pearson, February
22, 1968.
17. The activities of the Mutual leaders in politics and race relations warrant
a separate study. In part this has been done in sociological studies of the Durham
Negro community. See esp. Margaret Elaine Burgess, *Crescent City: Negro
Leadership in a Southern City* (Chapel Hill: University of North Carolina Press,
1960) and Harry J. Walker, "Changes in Race Accommodation in a Southern
Community" (Ph.D. dissertation, University of Chicago, 1945); and in part I
deal with these topics in Ch. 8. In general, Mutual leaders avoided overt politics
until 1935 with the organization of the renowned Negro political pressure group,
the Durham Committee on Negro Affairs. Spaulding became a conspicuous leader
in the Commission on Interracial Cooperation, and after 1933 he gave increasing
amounts of his time to race relations, national affairs concerning race, and *sub
rosa* politics in Durham.
18. Clipping, *Carolina Times*, April 23, 1926, Kennedy Scrapbook.

question that Spaulding catechized his employees. His office door, along with his Bible, was always open, and he customarily read an appropriate verse as prologue to his advice. Seldom would the directors present a problem for which the president did not in some way prescribe the scriptures; and to officers on vacation, he often made the Bible assigned reading.[19]

He boasted that "no poker players worked for the Mutual," and whiskey-drinking was similarly taboo. But perhaps the surest way to fall out of favor with Papa was to persist at tardiness or to default on a debt. The *Whetstone* published a monthly honor roll for punctuality, reflecting what amounted to an obsession with Spaulding.[20] Businessmen in Durham, black and white, knew his distaste for delinquent debts, and they skillfully used him as a powerful collection agent. Men of the Mutual, he acknowledged to creditors, must be "above board and . . . live within their income."[21] "It is not our policy to have men . . . who neglect their obligations."[22] He wished to run a tight ship, but more than that, it was the example that counted. The Mutual, he thought, could represent the race to the white world and thus alter the stereotypes of indolence and irresponsibility.

Spaulding best expressed what E. Franklin Frazier described as "old middle-class values"[23] when he established next door to his own residence on Fayetteville Street the North Carolina Mutual Clerks Home, a dormitory for all single female employees without a family or guardian in Durham. The home,

19. Interview, Mrs. Viola G. Turner, June 13, 1968; clipping, *Carolina Times*, April 9, 1926, Kennedy Scrapbook; C. C. Spaulding to W. J. Kennedy, Jr., December 24, 1929, Kennedy Papers. Spaulding might exercise his moral authority on other business leaders in Durham as well. To an undertaker he wrote, "Your refusal to pay any money for the support of the church is not breeding the best spirit . . . for you and your business. I have never seen money withheld from the church bring any dividends." Spaulding to J. F. Williams, July 21, 1931, Spaulding Papers.

20. Interview, Mrs. Viola G. Turner, June 13, 1968; *Whetstone*, January, 1932.

21. C. C. Spaulding to A. Sam Williams, October 17, 1931, Spaulding Papers.

22. C. C. Spaulding to Roger Cheek, October 26, 1931, Spaulding Papers.

23. E. Franklin Frazier, *Black Bourgeoisie* (New York: The Free Press, 1957), p. 125, uses Durham and the leaders of the North Carolina Mutual to distinguish between the puritanical "old middle class" and the pathological "new middle class"—his infamous Black Bourgeoisie.

complete with cafeteria and housemother, practiced *in loco parentis* to a fault. Spaulding saw the city as evil and was deeply distressed by the social malaise of Negro migration, particularly by the manifold reports from Harlem that nefarious urban forces were ruining country girls. He reminded the Mutual house-mother that under no circumstances were the women to have gentlemen in their rooms: "We want to safeguard the good name of our home and of our young women."[24]

Aside from the Forum, the best index of the Company's personality was its monthly periodical, the *Whetstone*, founded in 1924. Unlike earlier publications, the *Whetstone* served only as the house organ. Each issue greeted new employees with a "Welcome to the Mutual Family." It was a witty little paper filled with epigrams, aphorisms, and Horatio Alger stories—usually from within the Company. Admonitions and homilies abounded, along with a good many tales repeating the moral of Elbert Hubbard's "Message to Garcia." The editor listed health tips, and danger signs along the various paths to perdition. Spaulding warned his agents of the slight difference between "recreation and dissipation."[25] He asked them to shun "fancy clothes" and to remember that Merrick and Moore "bought Ford cars . . . until they were able to buy a Dodge."[26]

Much of the time the *Whetstone* devoted its pages to a boost-erism scarcely distinguishable from that of any other sales organization. It provoked a great competitive drive for "agent of the month" and publicized the ubiquitous contests the Company

24. C. C. Spaulding to Mrs. M. F. Carr, August 7, 1934, Spaulding Papers; interviews, Mrs. Viola G. Turner, June 13; W. J. Kennedy, Jr., February 29, 1968. For information on Clerks Home see W. J. Kennedy, Jr., to Miss Dorothy M. Johnston, May 21, 1925, Kennedy Papers.

25. *Whetstone*, July, 1926. The first number of the *Whetstone* dedicated itself to improving the mind and spirit of the employees: "As tools are sharpened with the whetstone, so this publication is designed to be a whetstone for the minds of the employees of the North Carolina Mutual Life Insurance Company" (*ibid.*, February, 1924).

26. *Ibid.*, July, May, 1926; August, November, 1928. Mrs. Viola G. Turner remembers that it was this asceticism that first struck her about the Durham community. She had heard so much about Durham that she expected a great display of wealth and night life; instead, she found the city relatively dull.

sponsored among the agencies.[27] Agency Director George Cox, very skillful at arousing a sense of urgency, used the *Whetstone* to mobilize his men as "Cox's Army." He extended the analogue to commissioning a hierarchy of honorary officers, one's rank depending upon his sales.[28]

If the Mutual exhorted its agents in much the same manner as all insurance companies, it could and often did appeal to racial pride, a heritage, and a mission. Spaulding reminded the agents that they were competing not just with one another, but with a white world, and specifically with white insurance agents who, if unchallenged, would "beat us in a game among our own."[29] "No, you cannot afford to acknowledge," declared the president, "that the 'other agent' has more influence over your own flesh and blood."[30] Cox informed his agents that of the $1.4 billion of insurance on Negro lives in the United States, over $1 billion was carried by white companies, a sad fact in Cox's mind, which meant a loss to the race of over $72 million in annual premium income and some 13,000 jobs. "Take this message to the people," instructed Cox. "We must have this great reservoir under the control of 'race men.' "[31]

Each member of the Mutual family had inherited through Merrick and Moore a special obligation to serve the race. "Our fallen leaders" made sure the Company would have a "soul in it," affirmed Spaulding. "The best thing we can do," he added, "is to perpetuate the company in their memory . . . and hope that each one will catch the spirit."[32] After Dr. Moore's death in 1923 the Mutual strengthened its mystique. Merrick and Moore emerged in the *Whetstone* as icons for inspiration, their photographs inscribed, "Lest We Forget."[33] Every employee could feel that he too might make race history by drinking deep from the well of the Mutual and its venerated leaders, who during

27. *Ibid.*, February, 1924; June, 1925.
28. *Ibid.*, December, 1928.
29. *Ibid.*, August, 1927.
30. *Ibid.*, August, 1925.
31. *Ibid.*, December, 1926.
32. *Ibid.*, May, 1924.
33. *Ibid.*

Negro History Week were portrayed as next to Douglass and Lincoln, and deserving of worship, thought Spaulding, behind only Christ Himself: "We shall think first of Thee and then of them."[34]

And to "think of them" obliged one to "carry on" the dream of racial self-fulfillment, "the unselfish spirit of cooperation . . . they so earnestly practiced. . . ."[35] The dream, not unlike that of Harlem or Chicago, where Negro leaders in the 1920's envisioned the utopian "black metropolis," was to extend the idyllic business kingdom beyond Durham, to embrace all Negroes in a compact of racial cooperation and self-sufficiency. There is no question that Spaulding was deeply imbued with the concept of racial cooperation on a theoretical plane beyond the experience of the Mutual.

Since 1900 economic cooperation among Negroes had been tied to the National Negro Business League, as had a good many other movements within the progress and self-help crusade. Apparently the North Carolina Mutual found itself fully absorbed in its own survival and played no prominent role in the early history of the League. Merrick and Moore attended the 1900 founding convention in Boston, and Merrick later accompanied Washington on Negro business tours of the South, but as of 1905 none of the triumvirate was listed as a dues-paying member.[36] In 1914, the year before Washington's death, Spaulding enrolled as a life member in the League and began instructing Mutual agents to organize chapters in their local communities.[37] After Washington's death Spaulding ascended

34. *Ibid.*, February, June, 1927.
35. *Ibid.*, June, 1926.
36. Booker T. Washington, *Story of the Negro* (New York: Doubleday, Page and Co., 1909), II, 37–38; National Negro Business League, *Proceedings* of the First Annual Meeting, Boston, 1900, pp. 268, 271; Sixth Annual Meeting, New York, 1905, pp. 208–217. The leaders of the early Business League in North Carolina were an educator and an A.M.E. Bishop, John R. Hawkins and Bishop George W. Clinton. See list of NNBL life membership in 1910, Booker T. Washington Papers, box no. 859, Manuscript Division, Library of Congress, Washington, D.C.; also see John R. Hawkins to Booker T. Washington, October 22, 1904, box no. 847, Washington Papers.
37. F. W. Littlejohn to Emmett J. Scott, April 10, 1914, box no. 853, C. C.

to the inner circles of the NNBL, serving as secretary-treasurer as well as chairman of the executive committee during the 1920's.[38] R. R. Moton, Washington's successor at Tuskegee, occupied the presidency of the organization, but he depended on Spaulding "to outline a program for the League's future."[39]

Spaulding's leadership in the NNBL enhanced the Mutual spirit and the general image of black Durham. By 1925 the city could boast of having the nation's largest chapter of the League. "All eyes are turned towards Durham," he acknowledged with pleasure. "We never go anywhere but what the people say don't let us down, we are looking to you."[40] The League displayed Durham as its model in a pamphleteering campaign, advertising it as "The City of Complete Protection."[41] With Durham as his base, Spaulding engineered a statewide organizational effort for the NNBL. He, John Avery, and the vibrant George Cox, also important figures in the League, divided North Carolina into districts, and with a displaced political zeal they led more than twenty Durham leaders across the state, giving campaign speeches entitled, "North Carolina: Prophet of the New South," or "The Durham Spirit: A Study in Cooperation."[42] Not until

---

Spaulding to Emmett J. Scott, September 17, 1914, box no. 854, Washington Papers.

38. C. C. Spaulding to Emmett J. Scott, July 14, 1916, box no. 857; National Negro Business League letter head, August, 1922 (no exact date), box no. 858; Spaulding to R. R. Moton, June 6, 1922, box no. 859; Berry O'Kelly to R. R. Moton, June 15, 1922, box no. 859, Washington Papers.

39. Spaulding to Albon Holsey, August 26, 1922, box no. 859, Washington Papers.

40. Clipping, *Carolina Times*, February 26, 1926, Kennedy Scrapbook.

41. National Negro Business League pamphlet, 1927, W. G. Pearson Scrapbook. Negro editor George Schuyler boosted Durham as "a hustling little city" (clipping, *Pittsburgh Courier*, December 4, 1926, Kennedy Scrapbook). Mutual officials reinforced the image at every opportunity; Kennedy wrote to a Wilmington, N.C., resident, "We have often heard that people there seem to have a drowsiness and a care-free disposition, and we are sure that the commercial atmosphere is nothing like it is in Durham" (Kennedy to Helen Wilkerson, April 3, 1925, Kennedy Papers).

42. See programs and literature on the North Carolina Negro Business League, 1926–27, Spaulding Papers. C. C. Spaulding wrote letters to business-men, ministers, and educators around the state, asking that they boost the Business League. See, for example, C. C. Spaulding to J. A. Blume, August 19, 1927, Spaulding Papers: "Every business man in North Carolina should belong to the League, whether he is a bootblack, insurance man, teacher or preacher.

1929 would anyone suggest that "Chicago vies with Durham . . . as the Capital of Negro Business."[43]

In the meantime Spaulding and the North Carolina Mutual took the lead in organizing an all-important affiliate of the NNBL, the National Negro Insurance Association. From the early years of the NNBL each profession had formed its own "trade association." The bankers and undertakers organized early, in contrast to the insurance leaders, although the industry did make an unsuccessful effort to establish a "Federated Insurance League" at Hampton Institute in 1908.[44] In 1915 Spaulding tried to arouse officials at Tuskegee, principally Emmett J. Scott and Albon Holsey, to set up an insurance association that would "put real teeth into the National Negro Business League."[45] At the 1917 NNBL convention he assembled the National Association of Negro Insurance Men, but the leaders admitted, "It is not well perfected."[46] A year passed and the Insurance Men accomplished little more than to change the name of their group to the National Negro Insurance Association, and to elect Spaulding president.[47] The NNIA lay dormant until 1921, when it was reorganized twice: once at the NNBL convention in Atlanta, and finally as a permanent body at the Mutual's new home office building in Durham. Spaulding easily won the presidency again, but his quest for cooperation was far from victorious. Only thirteen of the forty-two major Negro life

---

Men, let's get together and put over this program as we have done before. . . . Our boys and girls are to be inspired . . . by our own enterprises and it is our duty to work and think together in order to do so." Churches were institutional allies of the League, and in Durham Rev. S. L. McDowell at the White Rock Baptist Church gave special Sunday evening sermons on business cooperation. See R. McCants Andrews to W. J. Kennedy, Jr., December 4, 1925, Kennedy Papers.

43. John Henry Harmon, "The Negro as a Local Business Man," *Journal of Negro History*, XIV (April, 1929), 151.

44. Clipping, *Springfield Republican*, August 23, 1908, in Hampton Clippings, "Negroes in Business, Insurance and Real Estate;" Hampton Negro Conference, *Fourteenth Annual Report*, Hampton, Va., 1910, p. 41.

45. C. C. Spaulding to Emmett J. Scott, August 31; Scott to Spaulding, September 3, 1915, box no. 856, Washington Papers.

46. National Negro Business League, *Proceedings* of the Eighteenth Annual Meeting, Chattanooga, Tenn., 1917, p. 154.

47. *Ibid.*, Nineteenth Annual Meeting, Atlantic City, N.J., 1918, p. 318.

insurance companies sent representatives to the Durham meeting. One of the big four, the National Benefit Life, numbered among the absent. The Association circulated a "black list" of unscrupulous agents and an "impairment bulletin" listing names of those who had been refused insurance as bad risks. But a proposed pooling of mortality data and a program of cooperative advertising fell significantly short of the goal. And while the Association did begin a trade journal, the *Radiator*, in which it published useful statistics, it did not construct the actuarial tables that the industry so badly needed.[48] Of the NNIA membership, Kennedy commented: "We do not believe that the National Negro Insurance Association has developed to the point where it . . . is strong enough to do all that an association of this nature should be able to do. We find . . . some of the companies . . . causing statements to be published which are not true."[49] Jealousy and competition were difficult to subdue in a world where success came so dear, and smaller firms continued to vent their envy against the "giants" of Negro enterprise. A black banker in Virginia threatened to drop his policy with the Mutual, alleging to puritanical Kennedy that the Company could pay dividends like the Metropolitan if it did not have so many "Big Niggers squandering the profits on big cars and pleasure trips."[50]

The limited success of the NNIA could not stifle Spaulding's enthusiasm. He continued to dream of racial cooperation and expressed confidence that the Mutual spirit would catch fire. Solidarity would come, he thought, if enough people could see Durham and if the leaders would organize around the Durham experience. Thus he expended an increasing amount of effort in the cooperative movement: helping to organize the National Negro Finance Corporation, arranging national conferences in

48. W. J. Trent, Jr., "Development of Negro Life Insurance Enterprises" (Master's thesis, University of Pennsylvania, 1932), pp. 50–51; Stuart, *An Economic Detour*, pp. 323–328; Kennedy, "North Carolina Mutual," p. 145; clippings, *Chicago Defender*, November 21, 1921, in Hampton Clippings, "The Negro in Business, Insurance, and Real Estate;" *Durham Sun*, October 26, 28, 1921, Avery Scrapbook.
49. W. J. Kennedy, Jr., to Claude A. Barnett, June 1, 1928, Kennedy Papers.
50. Henry Davis to W. J. Kennedy, Jr., September 2, 1929, Kennedy Papers.

Durham, and working with the federal government in an incipient program to aid black capitalism.

As early as 1900, at the first meeting of the NNBL, Booker T. Washington suggested a central source of capital and advice to encourage the development of Negro enterprise.[51] At the 1917 meeting of the NNBL, R. R. Moton called for such a corporation, primarily for granting long-term loans at low interest to aspiring Negro businessmen. Moton reported, however, that he got the idea not from Washington but "from observing the Irish and the Jews."[52]

Whatever the origins of the idea, it took Wanti Gomez to give life to the National Negro Finance Corporation in 1924. Everyone agreed that Durham should be headquarters for the Corporation, and they eagerly accepted Gomez's plan "because of the confidence and respect which the negroes of the country have in the local men who have built such organizations as the North Carolina Mutual, Bankers Fire, and the Mechanics and Farmers Bank. . . ."[53] Capitalized at $1,000,000, the NNFC made a good start with Moton, largely a figurehead, as president; Spaulding, nominal leader of Negro business in America, as vice-president and chairman of the executive committee; and Gomez, the indomitable salesman-organizer, as secretary–general manager. Gomez presented the institution as a "money pool" which would make loans, market securities, and seek investments, all in a black setting. More than a financial organization, the Corporation pledged itself to social uplift, specifically to purchase bond issues for Negro schools and recreation programs. In the meantime it had to sell its own securities. By 1926 over $250,000 of stock had been sold to a thousand investors, and the Corpora-

51. Promotional pamphlet for the National Negro Finance Corporation in the W. G. Pearson Scrapbook (n.d., but from the context appears to be 1926; hereafter cited as NNFC promotional pamphlet, 1926). This pamphlet alleges that Washington proposed something like the NNFC, but the proceedings of the meeting reveal no such formal proposal by Washington.
52. Clipping, *Carolina Times*, May 1, 1925, Kennedy Scrapbook.
53. *Durham Morning Herald*, November 18, 1924; quoted in Thomas H. Houk, "A Newspaper History of Race Relations in Durham, North Carolina, 1910–1940" (Master's thesis, Duke University, 1941), p. 91.

The Triumvirate, John Merrick, C. C. Spaulding, and Dr. A. M. Moore, ca. 1900.

Organizers of the North Carolina Mutual and Provident Association in 1898. From left to right, seated: Dr. A. M. Moore, John Merrick, T. D. Watson; standing: W. G. Pearson, P. W. Dawkins, and James E. Shepard.

1902 office scene: C. C. Spaulding and clerk Dora Whitted in two-room office that served the Association from 1902 to 1905.

Meeting of the Triumvirate, 1906.

First home office building, 1906.

First home office building, 1906.

First agency conference at the North Carolina Colored State Fair, October, 1906. Dr. Moore, John Merrick, and C. C. Spaulding, center second row.

C. C. Spaulding, salesman-manager, about age thirty (ca. 1905). Spaulding printed this photograph on the face of postcards for advertising purposes.

C. C. Spaulding, about age forty.

John Merrick (President, 1899-1919) about age fifty.

Home office clerks, 1909.

Booker T. Washington and entourage visiting North Carolina Mutual, 1910. Washington, center second row, with John Merrick (profile) to his right. C. C. Spaulding, first row center.

John Merrick standing on balcony of his home, 506 Fayetteville Street, ca. 1910.

North Carolina Mutual Glee Club, 1929.

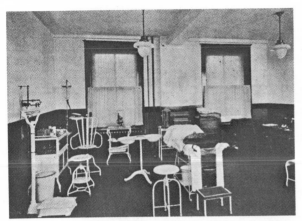

North Carolina Mutual medical facilities in the 1920's for examining and treating policyholders.

Dr. A. M. Moore (President, 1919-23) late in life.

North Carolina Mutual Quintet. Left to right: Hattie Livas, Lyda Merrick, Susan Gille (Norfleet), Martha Merrick, Bessie A. J. Whitted.

Home office building, 1921-66.

The Forum in session, 1920's.

The Forum celebrating President Spaulding's sixty-first birthday, August 10, 1935.

Mechanics and Farmers Bank in the 1930's.

Thrift Club, urban, about 1935.

Thrift Club, rural, about 1935.

Board of Directors, 1929. Left to right: E. R. Merrick, M. A. Goins, John Avery, W. D. Hill, W. J. Kennedy, Jr., C. C. Spaulding, R. L. McDougald, George W. Cox, John L. Wheeler.

Managers Conference posed on roof of home office building, 1935.

Launching the S.S. *John Merrick,* 1943.

An agency in the Deep South, Augusta, Georgia, 1934.

The Philadelphia agency, 1942.

Board of Directors, 1944. Left to right, seated: John L. Wheeler, A. J. Clement, Sr., George W. Cox, C. C. Spaulding, E. R. Merrick, M. A. Goins, W. D. Hill; standing: W. J. Kennedy, Jr., A. E. Spears, Sr., Dr. Clyde Donnell, D. C. Deans, R. L. McDougald, Asa T. Spaulding.

C. C. Spaulding (President, 1923-52) late in life.

W. J. Kennedy, Jr., President, 1952–58.

Asa T. Spaulding, President, 1958-67.

Asa Spaulding introducing Hubert H. Humphrey at dedication of new home office building, April, 1966.

Board of Directors, 1967. Left to right: Dr. Clyde Donnell, Joseph W. Goodloe, Noah H. Bennett, Jr., C. C. Spaulding, Jr., A. W. Williams, Maceo Sloan, A. E. Spears, Sr., W. A. Clement, Dr. Charles D. Watts, W. J. Kennedy III, Thomas W. Young, Dr. J. M. Nabrit, Jr., W. J. Kennedy, Jr., Viola G. Turner, Asa T. Spaulding.

Joseph W. Goodloe, President, 1968-72.

W. J. Kennedy III, President, 1972–.

Scene of new home office building.

New home office building.

tion was in the midst of a $135,000 bond issue. The board of directors declared a 6 percent dividend and reported that the Corporation had loaned $150,000 to black businessmen.[54]

Such a bright beginning caused the *Durham Morning Herald* to wonder "if the forces behind that work are white"; but "if . . . colored," the editor speculated, "they should be praised, even more so, for their handicap is greater. . . . We have a class of negroes here who are DOING MORE FOR THEMSELVES . . . than anywhere in the country."[55] And it seemed to blacks that Gomez was surely correct: "Parrish Street is the Negro Wall Street of America," and Durham, undoubtedly, "The Magic City of Negro Finance."[56]

But the bright prospects faded with the man who had brought them into being. The mysterious disappearance of Gomez in 1926 created a bear situation for NNFC stock, to say the least. Stockholders lost confidence, and a good many buyers whom Gomez had skillfully sold on margin repudiated their contracts when they learned of his ignominious departure. Spaulding and Moton sought to divorce the memory of Gomez from the NNFC, and they came close to restoring confidence. Spaulding told stockholders in 1929 that the Corporation would soon be paying dividends again, but the Depression delivered the death blow. Had Gomez stayed on, the result would have been the same, but a more noble defeat might have spared Spaulding what he feared most: an incident to impugn the integrity of the Mutual and Negro business in general. "The entire situation is rather embarrassing," he wrote to Moton, "as it has always been our ambition that no Durham institution should fail."[57]

The repercussions of the Gomez affair were not so great as to

54. NNFC promotional pamphlet, 1926; William K. Boyd, *The Story of Durham: The City of the New South* (Durham: Duke University Press, 1927), p. 290; Thomas W. Holland, "Negro Capitalists," *Southern Workman*, LV (December, 1926), 536–540; interview, W. J. Kennedy, Jr., February 29, 1968; Wanti Gomez to W. J. Kennedy, Jr., July 15, 1926, Kennedy Papers.
55. Durham *Morning Herald*, n.d., as quoted in NNFC promotional pamphlet, 1926.
56. NNFC promotional pamphlet, 1926.
57. C. C. Spaulding to NNFC stockholders, February 1, 1929; Spaulding to R. R. Moton, October 2, 1931, Spaulding Papers; interview, W. J. Kennedy, Jr., February 29, 1968.

shake the Mutual spirit of race cooperation. Indeed, for a moment Spaulding and other leaders thought the cooperative movement had gathered impressive new strength. Secretary of Commerce Herbert Hoover had officially embraced the cause of black capitalism, and Negro businessmen hoped that a greater NNFC would be the outcome. In 1927, at a time when "the business of America was business," Hoover launched the Small Business Section, "whose concern was . . . to a very large extent the Negro businessman," and appointed James A. Jackson, a black economist, as "Business Specialist."[58] Jackson worked closely with Albon Holsey, NNBL official and assistant to Moton at Tuskegee, along with Spaulding and other Negro leaders "to the end that business enterprise among Negroes may be more efficiently operated . . ." as a means of lifting "the race out of the rut of being wards of philanthropy into self-supporting, useful citizenship."[59]

Essentially Hoover's program for black capitalism amounted to extended trade association activities under the auspices of government coordination and a campaign among black women to encourage greater economy in their consumer habits. Thus, through pooling business information and grasping the fundamentals of thrift, the Negro could become a more efficient producer, a wiser consumer, and contribute to the solution of the "Negro Problem."[60] Jackson traveled some 50,000 miles promoting Hoover's trade association idea, and Holsey, with Commerce Department assistance, compiled and distributed a statistical study of Negro business in the United States. Cooperating black

58. U.S. Department of Commerce, Bureau of Foreign and Domestic Commerce, "Surveys on the Negro, 1927–1929," record group 151, folder 402.10, National Archives, Washington, D.C. (Hereafter cited as Department of Commerce, "Surveys on the Negro.") In particular, see James A. Jackson to C. C. Spaulding, November 25; Jackson to Julius Klein, December 16, 1927; Jackson to Charles N. Welch, August 6, 1928; Julius Rosenwald to Herbert Hoover, December 12, 1929; Julius Klein to Alfred K. Stern, January 2, 1930. Also see Claude A. Barnett to C. C. Spaulding, April 20, 1940, Spaulding Papers.

59. Department of Commerce, "Surveys on the Negro"; Jackson to Spaulding, November 25, 1937; undated form letter to all Negro businessmen on the subject of National Negro Trade Week.

60. *Ibid.*

merchants passed out government coupons to their customers, who collected them for prizes. Black students competed in essay contests touting the benefits of black business, and "monster rallies" occurred around the country.[61] Beyond this there was little substance to Hoover's program. Nonetheless, with Spaulding and the North Carolina Mutual as persuasive exhibits for the cause, Hoover established, for whatever its importance, a precedent in the relationship between the national government and Negro business.

In the meantime Durham, rather than Washington, D.C., continued to serve as the organizing center for race cooperation. In 1927 Spaulding, acting on the premise that "you have to know where you are to know where you are going," initiated the Durham Stock Taking and Fact Finding Conferences. He collaborated with W. G. Pearson and James E. Shepard in conducting the conferences, and the NNBL acted as the general sponsor. These meetings, which convened periodically into the 1940's, had as their heritage the Negro Convention Movement and the Tuskegee Conferences. The problems and prospects of the race remained the theme. The 1927 participants included W. E. B. Du Bois, R. R. Moton, labor leader Asa Philip Randolph, and Howard University President Mordecai Johnson. Business by no means dominated the conference; education, politics, and religion provided spirited exchanges between Du Bois and the disciples of Washington.[62]

The Mutual spirit emanating from the Forum and the cause

61. *Ibid.*; Julius Klein to Alfred K. Stern, January 2, 1930, record group 151, National Archives.

62. A report on the Conference appears in the minutes of the NAACP Board of Directors meeting, December 12, 1937, NAACP Papers, Manuscript Division, Library of Congress; Guy B. Johnson, "A Stock Taking Conference on the Negro," *Social Forces*, VI (March 1928), 445–447; clipping, *Memphis Times*, November 12, 1927, Avery Scrapbook; Asa Philip Randolph to C. C. Spaulding, December 16, 1927, Kennedy Papers—Randolph congratulated Spaulding on the Conference, claiming it was "epochal" and that Durham showed "its long vision and initiative in projecting so constructive and fundamental a race meet." Also see H. C. Dunn to Claude A. Barnett, March 6, 1930, in Department of Commerce, "Surveys on the Negro"; and clipping, *New York Age*, "Golden Jubilee Edition," 1935 (no exact date), in North Carolina Mutual clipping file.

of cooperation helped turn the Company into a veritable convention center, hosting a great diversity of "race meets."[63] That
the Company cafeteria accommodated such a variety of functions is an indication of how far the Mutual spirit ranged beyond
the commercial confines of collecting premiums and paying
claims. Only recently has American business sought responsibility in social action, but the Mutual lived in another world of
responsibility, where the burden of race made the line between
the public interest and the private interest scarcely distinguishable. Nor in the mission for uplift was the business leader distinct
from other race leaders: "We must climb . . . to the heights
marked for us by the illustrious Douglass," counseled the *Whetstone.*[64] Just as race consciousness and mission could link Du
Bois to Washington for a time, so C. C. Spaulding, the leading
black capitalist, could carry on an amicable relationship with
Asa Philip Randolph, the militant black socialist. The Mutual
even advertised in Randolph's "revolutionary" *Messenger*; for
Randolph, like Du Bois, recognized that the Mutual spirit stood
for race cooperation at least as much as individual entrepreneur-
ship. Similarly, Marcus Garvey's *Negro World* lauded the business efforts of black Durham, particularly the formation of the
NNFC.[65]

The interaction between the external heritage of the race and
the internal characteristics of the Company had by the 1920's
created a social personality for the North Carolina Mutual. The
institution drew its identity from outside its walls, from the
black experience, and from its unique place in that experience.
But the identity was marked with ambivalence. The dilemma of
the Company was the dilemma of the individual black man in
corporate form. Clearly the Mutual was both a business and a

63. A.M.E. bishops, YMCA and Boys Club officials, Negro fraternities, educators, in addition to the businessmen and others, used the Mutual as a meeting
place. See minutes of organizational meeting of the Durham Negro YMCA in
Kennedy Papers, October 14, 15, 1924; C. A. Witherspoon to W. J. Kennedy, Jr.,
November 1, 1928, Kennedy Papers; *Whetstone*, January, 1930.
64. *Whetstone*, June, 1928.
65. Asa Philip Randolph to C. C. Spaulding, March 17; Spaulding to Randolph, March 25, 1928, Kennedy Papers; *Negro World*, August 30, 1924.

a black business, and whether or not it consciously made the choice, the blackness came first. Race cut across virtually every facet of the Company's identity. The men of the Mutual knew this and, unlike E. Franklin Frazier's "new middle class," seemed proud of the fact. Moreover, they knew that if they ever tried to forget their identity, white society would always remind them. A Mutual agent in Mississippi advised Kennedy to drop an impending court case in that state: "You know how these courts are concerning a colored insurance company," he wrote.[66] In Birmingham, Alabama, a district manager asked the home office to forego investigation and pay the death claim for a black youth killed by the Birmingham police. "We know," he said, "that these 'cracker officers' are likely to shoot any of us down for no cause in the world."[67] And C. C. Spaulding could give a first-hand account of the racial bond built on white hostility. In 1931 Spaulding, the distinguished business executive, became just another "uppity nigger" in the eyes of a Raleigh soda jerk, who beat him savagely for sipping a Coca Cola across the color line.[68]

Heightened racial tension and economic depression during the 1930's would produce a new level of racial consciousness within the Company personality. Yet at the same time the directors, under the threat of insolvency, would assume the race-less outlook of efficiency experts, retreating to the hard-nosed principles of American business and demanding all the austerity the Mutual spirit could muster. The ambivalence was built in, and both policies, as in the beginning, were necessary for survival.

66. R. J. Garrett to W. J. Kennedy, Jr., December 15, 1924, Kennedy Papers.
67. Z. S. Todd to W. J. Kennedy, Jr., January 7, 1926, Kennedy Papers.
68. See an entire folder of correspondence and clippings in Spaulding Papers on this incident, which took place August 3, 1931. Every major Negro newspaper in the country reported the story, but the fullest coverage appeared in the *Carolina Times*, August 8, 1931.

6

The Second
Survival

The retrenchment program of 1926 did not anticipate the Great Depression, despite the directors' subsequent claim for prophecy. Rather, like most businessmen of the period, they had trouble recognizing the seriousness of the downturn when it did occur. C. C. Spaulding stoically insisted that there was no depression: "All we have to do is 'press on.' "[1] By 1932–33, however, the leaders acknowledged the situation for what it was, and at the same time assumed vindication for their decision of 1926. Cutting off the four most distant states meant a decline in business from approximately $46,000,000 in 1926 to $36,000,000 at the opening of 1927. But the emphasis on economy and efficiency set the mood for the intense austerity drive necessary to meet the crushing demand for policy loans and surrender values in the 1930's, when the Company could not readily convert its assets in real estate and mortgage loans to liquid capital. Policy loans increased from $301,809 in 1928 to $839,154 in 1932, and during the same period surrender values mounted from $23,770 to $512,672. These unexpected demands, along with relentlessly high mortality rates (until 1933), consituted a frightful drain on the treasury at the worst possible time. The surplus quickly vanished, and disaster loomed as the legal reserve fund diminished. Financial advisor R. L. McDougald counseled an

1. C. C. Spaulding to E. W. Fisher, October 28, 1931, Spaulding Papers.

emergency loan from the Reconstruction Finance Corporation. C. C. Spaulding, intrepid as ever, loaded up on gifts, boarded a train for Washington D.C., and proceeded to lobby North Carolina Congressman William B. Umstead. Spaulding gracefully balanced his executive demeanor with down-home politics to win the southern congressman's favor and secure over $500,000 in RFC loans. Government assistance in itself, however, could scarcely account for the Company's survival.[2]

At the time of the Great Crash, the Mutual had begun to recover the volume it had voluntarily lost three years earlier. Insurance in force at the close of 1929 stood at $39,000,000. It decreased negligibly in 1930–31; under the full weight of the Depression it settled downward to an average of $33,000,000 for the years 1932–33, but immediately recovered to over $36,000,-000 during 1934–35. By 1936 the directors knew that they had weathered the storm, as policy surrenders decreased to a third of their 1932 level and premium income surpassed the 1929 mark, never to falter again.[3] (See Table 5.)

The Depression tested the Mutual and found a resiliency already hardened in the fires of economic and racial adversity. The test for the life insurance industry as a whole, however, was not as severe as it was for other businesses. Stringent state regulations since the Armstrong Investigation imposed a conservatism in finance that made the industry partially immune to the disaster of Wall Street. This regulated stability probably accounted for the low number of failures among life insurance companies during the 1930's. In 1932 alone, 32,000 commercial enterprises failed, but for the entire decade only 39 legal reserve

2. William J. Kennedy, Jr., "North Carolina Mutual Life Insurance Company: A Symbol of Progress" (Manuscript in possession of W. J. Kennedy, Jr., Durham, N.C.), pp. 168, 177, 178, 190; Harry H. Pace, "The Possibilities of Negro Insurance," *Opportunity*, VII (September, 1930), 266–267; Alfred M. Best Company, *Best's Life Insurance Reports*, 1930 (New York: Alfred M. Best Company, 1930), p. 830; C. C. Spaulding to T. Arnold Hill, February 17, 1931, Spaulding Papers. North Carolina Mutual Financial Report, April 15, 1933, Kennedy Papers; interview, John H. Wheeler, August 4, 1970.

3. Kennedy, "North Carolina Mutual," pp. 168, 177, 178, 190; *Best's Life Insurance Reports*, 1930, p. 830; 1935, pp. 707–708; 1938, p. 837.

TABLE 5. NORTH CAROLINA MUTUAL LIFE INSURANCE COMPANY PREMIUM INCOME AND LIFE INSURANCE IN FORCE, 1925–39

Year	Premium income	Insurance in force
1925	$ 745,950 (O)*	$19,090,607 (O)*
	1,879,785 (I)*	25,235,676 (I)*
	2,625,735	44,326,283
1927	510,976	13,796,353
	1,291,794	23,166,743
	1,802,770	36,963,096
1929	511,624	14,255,005
	1,399,820	24,622,181
	1,911,444	38,877,186
1931	523,305	14,385,212
	1,275,230	22,543,542
	1,798,535	36,928,754
1933	434,254	12,512,032
	1,131,832	21,785,179
	1,566,086	34,297,211
1935	484,895	13,648,040
	1,340,251	23,035,581
	1,825,146	36,683,621
1937	531,770	15,045,028
	1,609,517	26,476,924
	2,141,287	41,521,952
1939	640,415	17,590,489
	1,875,309	29,990,704
	2,515,724	47,581,193

*O = Ordinary
 I = Industrial

SOURCE: *Best's Life Insurance Reports*, 1930, p. 830; 1935, pp. 707–708; 1936, p. 861; 1938, p. 837; 1940, pp. 741–742; *Dunnes International Insurance Reports*, 1940, p. 975; Jesse Edward Gloster, "North Carolina Mutual Life Insurance Company: Its Historical Development and Current Operations" (Ph.D. dissertation, University of Pittsburgh, 1955), p. 89.

life insurance firms suffered bankruptcy, and these represented less than 2 percent of the total amount of life insurance in force.[4]

4. R. Carlyle Buley, *The American Life Convention 1905–1952: A Study of the History of Life Insurance*, 2 vols. (New York: Appleton-Century-Crofts,

Much the same can be said for Negro legal reserve companies, of which four succumbed during the 1920's, most significantly the Standard Life of Atlanta. But during the Depression only two of the remaining fifteen failed: National Benefit Life (1931) and Victory Life Insurance Company (1932). Black insurance enterprises suffered earlier and proportionately greater losses during the Depression than did white enterprises, but they enjoyed a quicker recovery. The much higher percentage of industrial insurance carried by the Negro firms probably accounts for this difference. Sixty-three percent of all insurance carried by Negro companies in 1930 was industrial, as contrasted to only 17 percent for white companies. Quite apart from the Depression, the black industrial policyholder generally lived a marginal existence and had no choice but to lapse his policy at the slightest increase of financial stress. But the process worked in reverse: the slightest relief of financial stress could encourage the renewal of a small ten-cent policy.[5]

This is not to suggest that the more industrial insurance on the books, the better. The major black firms of the 1930's experienced a lapse rate for industrial insurance nearly 350 percent higher than for ordinary insurance.[6] Nonetheless, the Mutual, like its competitors, witnessed a proportionate rise in industrial income over ordinary income. The higher premium payments of ordinary insurance discouraged both new sales and renewals, whereas the small weekly premiums and the folk tradition of industrial insurance kept up a surprising volume of sales. Durham folklore argues that the Mutual endured the Depression because it held so many ordinary policies on black schoolteach-

---

1953), II, 724–725, 877; Marquis James, *The Metropolitan Life* (New York: Viking Press, 1947), pp. 279–280, 293.

5. David Abner III, "Some Aspects of the Growth of Negro Legal Reserve Life Insurance Companies, 1930–1960" (Ph.D. dissertation, Indiana University, 1962), pp. 50, 51, 62, 64, 65, 78, 163; Thomas J. Gardner, "Problems in the Development of Financial Institutions among Negroes: Historical Development, Current Trends, and the Future in Business" (Ph.D. dissertation, New York University, 1958), pp. 40–41. Victory Life, based in Chicago and New York City, was salvaged in 1933 and reorganized as a mutual company.

6. Abner, "Some Aspects of Negro Legal Reserve Life Insurance Companies," p. 163.

ers, whose incomes remained relatively stable during the panic. While it is true that the Company insured its share of southern black teachers, these steady premiums by no means sustained Parrish Street during hard times or at any other time. The great bulk of the premium income came not from middle-class ordinary policyholders but from lower-class industrial policyholders. Indeed, Victory Life and National Benefit Life, both of which failed, depended heavily on ordinary insurance. Another black firm, Supreme Liberty Life, averted potential disaster in the early 1930's when it shifted from ordinary insurance to pursuing the more accessible nickels and dimes of the masses.[7]

In retrospect, a well-managed legal reserve company with a capacity to cut expenses and to control its mortality ratio should have been able to survive the Depression. The directors of the Mutual exuded confidence in their public statements that their firm faced no crisis, but privately they worried—and not entirely without cause, for the Company continued to bear the burden of unsolved technical problems, actuarial ones in particular.

Of the three areas that the North Carolina Mutual could attack to strengthen its financial position (investment, operating expenses, and mortality), investment seemed the least capable of improvement during the Depression. Even in good times Negro life insurance companies lacked investment opportunities, particularly in high-quality industrial bonds sold through the large investment bankers primarily to the leading white insurance firms. Operating outside this world, the Mutual generally invested in real estate, mortgage loans, and government bonds.

These relatively unattractive investments, coupled with high mortality, prevented the Company from building a large surplus and paying dividends. This shortcoming provoked angry criticism from policyholders who demanded that the Mutual be the black man's Metropolitan. But low-yield conservative invest-

7. *Ibid.*, p. 65; Pace, "The Possibilities of Negro Insurance," pp. 266–267; *Best's Life Insurance Reports*, 1935, pp. 707–708; 1938, p. 837; 1940, pp. 741–742; interview, Conrad O. Pearson, February 22, 1968; Robert C. Puth, "Supreme Life: The History of a Negro Life Insurance Company" (Ph.D. dissertation, Northwestern University, 1967), pp. 97, 117, 121–123.

ments were not an unmitigated evil in depressed times. Harry H. Pace, president of the Supreme Liberty Life in Chicago, summarized the mixed role of large real estate holdings among black insurance companies: "Real estate has acted in a double way. It has not fluctuated as bonds have . . . and caused our assets to run down inordinately . . . on the other hand, it has been a very . . . immovable asset."[8] Most businessmen emphasized Pace's latter point; frozen assets served little purpose in a time of need, and the Mutual for years had steered its investments away from farm real estate, which declined in value throughout the 1920's.[9]

Investment in bonds, usually the most recommended asset for insurance companies, offered sparse returns in the 1930's—sometimes below the minimum 3.5 percent yield required by the North Carolina Insurance Department. Conditions eventually forced the Department to lower the minimum, but of course a lower investment return presented a new dilemma: raising premium rates when policyholders could least afford such an increase. So depressed was the investment market that many companies could find no outlet for their money and had little choice but to let it lie idle. The Mutual, it would appear, turned increasingly to mortgage loans, partly because the interest rate remained relatively high and partly because the directors agreed with Harry Pace that for a Negro enterprise "not to make mortgage loans would be just as wrong . . . as it would be not to employ colored people. . . ."[10] Social concern constantly conditioned the portfolio of the Mutual. Financing a Negro housing development in Wilson, North Carolina, at this time made more sense racially than it did economically, as did investment in the all-

8. Harry H. Pace, "Meeting the Problems of the Depression," National Negro Insurance Association, *Proceedings*, Richmond, Va., 1934, p. 30; quoted in Gardner, "Problems in Financial Institutions among Negroes," p. 42.

9. Clipping, *Norfolk Journal and Guide*, September 19, 1931, in North Carolina Mutual clipping file. During the Depression the Company found itself enlarging its assets in real property through foreclosures.

10. Quoted in Ira DeAugustine Reid, "The Negro in the American Economic System" (Memorandum for the Carnegie-Myrdal Study of the Negro in America, 1940), pp. 58–59. Also see article on the Negro insurance company investment problem in *Whetstone*, September, 1935.

Negro town of Whitesboro, New Jersey, founded by George White, the former congressman from Columbus County.[11]

An intractable economy rendered the investment function of the Company largely a defensive operation. (See Table 6 for

TABLE 6. COMPARATIVE DISTRIBUTION OF ASSETS: THE LIFE INSURANCE INDUSTRY, ALL NEGRO LEGAL RESERVE COMPANIES, AND THE NORTH CAROLINA MUTUAL, 1930–35 (AS PERCENT OF TOTAL ADMITTED ASSETS)

	Real estate	Mortgage loans	Policy loans	Bonds	Stocks	Cash and misc.	Total assets*
(1930)							
Industry	2.9	40.2	14.9	34.1	2.8	3.1	$18.9 b
Negro	26.5	19.9	11.1	26.0	3.9	12.6	18.1 m
NCM	18.0	33.0	19.0	13.0	7.0	4.0	3.8 m
(1931)							
Industry	3.4	38.1	16.7	33.8	2.8	5.2	20.1 b
Negro	30.0	22.2	11.1	20.1	4.2	12.4	14.4 m
NCM	18.0	31.0	21.0	13.0	7.0	3.0	3.9 m
(1932)							
Industry	4.5	35.4	18.3	32.9	2.8	6.1	20.7 b
Negro	27.6	21.6	12.1	22.4	4.3	12.0	11.6 m
NCM	19.0	30.0	21.0	14.0	7.0	3.0	4.0 m
(1933)							
Industry	6.1	32.1	18.0	34.4	2.3	7.1	20.8 b
Negro	28.2	21.0	11.3	24.2	3.2	12.1	12.4 m
NCM	20.0	31.0	20.0	13.0	7.0	3.0	3.9 m
(1934)							
Industry	7.8	26.9	16.7	37.8	2.2	8.6	21.8 b
Negro	25.6	20.2	10.1	21.7	3.1	19.3	12.9 m
NCM	24.0	37.0	18.0	17.0	8.0	4.0	4.1 m
(1935)							
Industry	8.6	23.1	15.2	43.4	2.5	7.2	23.2 b
Negro	28.4	18.4	9.9	25.5	4.3	13.5	14.0 m
NCM	24.0	38.0	19.0	16.0	8.0	4.0	4.3 m

*b = billion
 m = million

11. See L. W. Wilhoite to C. C. Spaulding, December 13, 1933; C. C. Spaulding to H. W. Spaulding, October 19, November 19, 1934, Spaulding Papers.

the pattern of Mutual investments in the context of other Negro legal reserve companies and the life insurance industry as a whole during the most difficult years of the Depression.)[12] At best, the directors could hope to stand off losses and maintain their assets. This they did, as the table indicates. Only in 1933 did the annual statement show an actual loss in assets. But Spaulding and his officers preferred to expend their zeal for survival on other problems which yielded more directly to their efforts. Most of these problems were endemic to Negro life insurance and were only exacerbated by the Depression.

A high lapse rate, for example, constantly plagued the Company and often bore little relationship to the condition of the nation's economy. In 1928, generally a prosperous year, the Mutual sustained a net loss in business that could be explained only by the convergence of forces persistently at work in the Negro industry, principally the precarious incomes of the policyholders and poor risk selection by the agents.[13] The lapse rate peaked in 1931, as did operating expenses, which ran high despite austerity because of the greater service necessary to handle the unprecedented number of surrender claims and policy loans. Table 7

12. *Best's Life Insurance Reports*, 1931, p. 835; 1932, p. 796; 1933, p. 746; 1934, p. 697; 1935, p. 705; 1936, p. 858; and Abner, "Some Aspects of Negro Legal Reserve Life Insurance Companies," pp. 67, 174, 179, 193, 200, 206, 211. The figures for "Industry" include the figure for the "Negro" category, but the influence is slight because Negro legal reserve companies accounted for less than 0.2 percent of the total life insurance in force during this period (see Abner, "Some Aspects of Negro Legal Reserve Life Insurance Companies," p. 67).

13. *Whetstone*, October, 1938; Winfred Octavus Bryson, Jr., "Negro Life Insurance Companies," pp. 76–83. Some companies consciously pursued a program of "mass production" in industrial insurance, paying little attention to the quality of their risks. Such was the case with the National Benefit Life, which after 1926 mounted a frantic drive for business in order to cover its overcapitalization. It sold over $40 million of insurance per year, but in 1930 it had less insurance on its books than in 1926. The Temporary National Economic Committee investigations of life insurance in the 1930's showed that a few large white firms sought Negro business on a similar short-term basis. An agent for the Equitable, famous for his volume of business among Negroes, testified that he "metaphorically" parked a hearse at the front door and frightened the person into believing that unless he took out a policy "death might take place almost momentarily." These policies quickly lapsed, but the agent noted that he would gladly "rehire the hearse," make another commission, and keep the person on the books long enough for the company to make a small amount (see Bryson, "Negro Life Insurance Companies," p. 80).

reflects the lapse and operating expenses of the Company for the critical years of the Depression.[14]

TABLE 7. NORTH CAROLINA MUTUAL LIFE INSURANCE COMPANY
LAPSE RATIO AND OPERATING EXPENSES, 1930–35

	Lapse ratio		
Year	Ordinary	Industrial	Operating expenses *
1930	16%	59%	48%
1931	21	60	52
1932	25	80	50
1933	20	58	42
1934	14	65	43
1935	22	57	43

* includes both ordinary and industrial

The Mutual entered the Depression with no relief in sight for the distressing death and sickness claims which had burgeoned during the previous decade, but by 1935 the unfavorable Company experience and Negro mortality in general showed marked improvement over that of the 1920's. The Negro death rate decreased from 16.5 per 1,000 population in 1930 to 13.9 in 1940, and a black man born in 1940 could expect to live to age 52, in contrast to age 48 had he been born in 1930.[15] But the sociological gain in longevity could scarcely account for the dramatic change in the Company's mortality experience during the 1930's:[16]

14. Bryson, "Negro Life Insurance Companies," pp. 57, 58, 79, 82; *Best's Life Insurance Reports*, 1935, pp. 705–706; 1938, p. 835. The lapse ratio is the percent of life insurance lapsed in relation to the mean amount of life insurance in force that year. Operating expenses are calculated by simply figuring that portion of the premium charged to cover all expenses (other than claims), including commission, salaries, and a margin for contingencies. Thus in 1932 $50 of a $100 premium went for operating expenses. The Mutual enjoyed slightly lower lapse ratios and operating expenses than comparable black firms, yet theirs were more than 200 percent above the average of white firms (Abner, "Some Aspects of Negro Legal Reserve Life Insurance Companies," pp. 158, 163).

15. Gunnar Myrdal, *An American Dilemma*, 2 vols. (New York: Harper and Row, 1944), I, 1222; U.S. Department of Health, Education, and Welfare, *Vital Statistics in the United States*, 1959 (Washington, D.C.: Government Printing Office, 1960), I, sec. 6, pp. 5–7.

16. Typescript of figures compiled by N. H. Bennet, Jr., associate actuary,

TABLE 8. NORTH CAROLINA MUTUAL LIFE INSURANCE COMPANY MORTALITY RATIOS, ACTUAL TO EXPECTED (100 = EXPECTED)

Year	Ratio	Year	Ratio
1930	129.0	1935	102.5
1931	121.0	1936	82.6
1932	116.8	1937	67.7
1933	90.8	1938	66.7
1934	101.2	1939	61.0

This momentous reversal came as an actuarial breakthrough involving a rigid training program for the agencies, the utmost stringency in risk selection, and an exhaustive scientific study of the Company's claims experience. Masterminding the revolution was Asa Timothy Spaulding, the nation's first professionally trained black actuary and enviable prize of the Mutual. Fresh from graduate school at the University of Michigan, he came to the Company in January, 1933, at the depth of the Depression, fully determined to deliver the Mutual as had his distant cousin a generation earlier. It is probably no coincidence that virtually every dimension of the business improved shortly after his arrival.[17]

Asa T. Spaulding was born in 1902 into the same Columbus County environment that produced C. C. Spaulding, his second cousin, and Dr. Moore, his great-uncle. As a schoolboy he heard a great deal about his distinguished relatives, but the notoriety extended both ways, for the youth quickly established his reputation as the brightest student in the county. Precocious in mathematics, he mastered his multiplication tables to twenty while others were learning to count, and he possessed an uncanny ability to "figure in his head." At the call of Dr. Moore young Spaulding came to Durham in 1919, where he enrolled in the National Training School (North Carolina College) and spent his summers working for the Mutual. In 1923 he received his diploma, along with every other award the college offered; remi-

1952, Spaulding Papers; also see *Best's Life Insurance Reports*, 1935, p. 706; 1939, p. 786; interview, W. J. Kennedy, Jr., June 8, 1968.

17. See Tables 5, 6, 7, and 8.

niscent of Dr. Moore, he returned to Columbus County as the teacher-principal of a country school. But he was attracted back to the Mutual the following year and worked as a clerk before taking a leave of absence in 1924 to study business for a semester at Howard University. Still he hungered for education, and in 1927 he left the Mutual once more to begin a new college career in accounting at New York University, where in 1930 he graduated magna cum laude. At NYU his mathematics professor counseled him to become an actuary and got him admitted to the University of Michigan, which specialized in actuarial science. The home office was more than pleased with the prospect of a black actuary, particularly after information surfaced that corrupt white actuaries had played no small part in the demise of both Standard Life and National Benefit Life. In 1932 Spaulding completed the M.A. in actuarial mathematics. Before returning to Durham he served a short apprenticeship with Haight, Davis, and Haight, a consulting actuarial firm in Indianapolis.[18]

His scholarly achievement gathered attention far beyond the Mutual. Word spread within the Negro middle class about a rising black executive setting academic marks at northern white universities, and the black press "wrote him up" to such an extent that a "young lady from Vicksburg" sent him a letter of proposal.[19] He could never think of himself as just a college student or just an actuary. Dr. Moore, his idol, had steeped him in racial awareness and responsibility which were enriched by the various worlds of Columbus County, Durham, Washington, D.C., Harlem, and Ann Arbor.

New York City taught him the subtle difference between North and South. He could attend the white university, but he would have to room with a relative in Harlem, 138 blocks away. Harlem, however, opened up a broad new expanse of racial consciousness for him. There he visited the offices of the NAACP, the Urban League, the *New York Age*, and worshipped with the

18. Kennedy, "North Carolina Mutual," pp. 148–150; *Whetstone*, July, 1932; *Who's Who in America*, XXXVI (Chicago: Marquis-Who's Who, 1970), p. 2151; interviews, Asa T. Spaulding, July 18, W. J. Kennedy, Jr., June 8, 1968; John H. Wheeler, April 3, 1972.

19. Asa T. Spaulding to W. J. Kennedy, Jr., March 22, 1930, Kennedy Papers.

nation's largest congregation at Adam Clayton Powell, Sr.'s, Abyssinian Baptist Church. He acknowledged to Kennedy, his confidant during these years, that the Harlem experience was the best thing that ever happened to him, but still he "preferred Durham."[20] At least in Durham he could have found a job. "I've attempted to get work since being here," he wrote from Harlem, "but on every hand I found my color a distinct disadvantage . . . because I'm black, I must expect to find the road a little rugged."[21] With a spirit that seemed to combine the racial intensity of W. E. B. Du Bois as a young scholar and the dogged commitment to self-help displayed by Booker T. Washington, Spaulding threw himself into his studies with a fierce competitive drive to beat the white world at the Darwinian challenge it presented. Midway through his first semester at NYU he reported to Kennedy, "Some of the white students have already begun to seek me out to help them with their work, and of course you can realize that it is a pleasure for me to manifest my superiority over them (smiles). They are willing to admit their 'inferiority' for the time being. Isn't it strange?"[22] Kennedy sensed that New York would provide a toughening experience for his young charge, and he encouraged him to remain in Harlem during the summer months and take a job "among the rougher element of . . . our group. . . ."[23] Harlem, whose social ills Spaulding deplored, convinced him "that character is a crying need of the race today. . . . I am taking stock of myself," he wrote Kennedy at graduation time, "and I find that I have a burning passion to be of loyal upright service to my group."[24] The New York experience strengthened his allegiance to the North Carolina Mutual, for Harlem, exciting as it was, offered no comparable black institution which promised him such a positive role "in the life of my people."[25]

At Ann Arbor he found still another environment, more pleas-

20. Asa T. Spaulding to Kennedy, October 19, 1927, Kennedy Papers.
21. Asa T. Spaulding to Kennedy, September 30, 1927, Kennedy Papers.
22. Asa T. Spaulding to Kennedy, November 30, 1927, Kennedy Papers.
23. Kennedy to Asa T. Spaulding, May 8, 1928, Kennedy Papers.
24. Asa T. Spaulding to Kennedy, May 30, 1928, Kennedy Papers.
25. Asa T. Spaulding to Kennedy, October 19, 1927, Kennedy Papers. Ap-

ant than New York at first glance, but much less comfortable for
Spaulding because here he was a man without a community,
thrown into a white sea of midwestern racism. "There are only
a few Negro families here," he complained to Kennedy, and "my
experiences are not altogether pleasant. . . . I am encountering
much prejudice—you know Indiana is not far away. The prejudice, however, only makes me work harder."[26] As an isolated
black scholar in Ann Arbor, Spaulding revealed increasing introspection in his letters and he seemingly intensified his commitment, pledging privately to Kennedy, "I know this: all others
may fail, but by the help of God I shall make good."[27] His academic performance supported his resolution. "I am about to hit
my old 'NYU stride,' " he announced, "and I think they are beginning to feel that I am not a 'quitter,' consequently they may as
well resign themselves to the idea of a Negro actuary."[28] And
becoming an actuary meant essentially two things to Spaulding,
both intrinsic to the racial struggle. First, as he saw success approaching, he declared he was "eagerly looking forward to the
time when I shall turn my head toward Durham that I may join
with you in the fight to keep our company in the front ranks . . .
and to make it rank favorably with white life insurance companies."[29] Second, he hoped that he might contribute directly to
racial uplift; "I have long ago concluded that one of the greatest
needs of the race is prepared, honest and conscientious men, and
I have set out to do my bit in meeting that need."[30]

Thus Spaulding came to the Mutual in 1933 carrying a message for the race. Like Jackie Robinson a decade later, he was
one of the celebrated "Negro firsts." More than an actuary coming to the aid of a troubled insurance firm, he was the heroic
black tactician on his way to battle. Perfecting the operations

---

parently the Mutual spirit dissuaded him from accepting a position with the new
Rockefeller bank in Harlem. See Asa T. Spaulding to Kennedy, July 30, 1928,
Kennedy Papers.
    26. Asa T. Spaulding to Kennedy, September 25, November 4, 7, 1930,
Kennedy Papers.
    27. Asa T. Spaulding to Kennedy, October 31, 1930, Kennedy Papers.
    28. Asa T. Spaulding to Kennedy, November 26, 1931, Kennedy Papers.
    29. *Ibid.*
    30. Asa T. Spaulding to C. C. Spaulding, October 16, 1931, Spaulding Papers.

of the North Carolina Mutual, ostensibly a mundane task, was a symbolic act of improving the race and another exemplary lesson for white folks.

For Spaulding the only way to succeed was to excel, and he knew excellence in the insurance business meant a more scientific, impersonal direction for the Company. Success in the long run might, in the short run, require policyholders to pay higher premiums; families who needed protection might be rejected; the sick could not be insured, or at least not on the same basis as the healthy. Spaulding, better than the others, could bifurcate his world. His basic motivation lay in emotion and race, but he was able to function as the calculating technician, keeping in mind that he did so for a black purpose. His task was to square mathematical laws with racial vows, not the typical charge of the actuary.

He began immediately to form a statistical profile of the Company. Great coils of tape spilled from his adding machine, and he constructed an endless array of charts. He compiled statistics on every detail of the claims experience, attempting to identify the variables and to establish meaningful patterns. Interesting correlations emerged. A disproportionate number of death claims listed cousins as beneficiaries, especially on policies in force only a short time. Spaulding hypothesized that an enterprising person might indeed buy an industrial policy on a sick relative. Thus he warned the agents to "beware of cousins." In general, he found that death claims were highest among policies in force less than five years. The agents obviously exercised little discretion in their risk selection. And since it was impossible to conduct medical examinations for the small industrial policies, Spaulding devised a contract which increased in value for the first five years in force, thereby encouraging the policyholder and beneficiary to act as underwriters. He simply proceeded on the assumption that "if a person is speculating with life insurance, it is very easy to make him part underwriter."[31]

31. Interviews, W. J. Kennedy, Jr., July 8; Asa T. Spaulding, July 18, 1968; *Whetstone*, April, May, June, July, 1934.

With similar logic he fashioned policies that rewarded beneficiaries if the insured did not die within the first five years from
diseases which dominated the claims. If the policyholder died
of tuberculosis in the first year, for example, the beneficiary
would receive only one-fourth of the face value of the policy.
Spaulding knew that these were interim measures designed to
bring immediate relief to the mortality experience. His short-
term tactics simply recognized that it was easier to manipulate
policies than to revamp the underwriting system, which might
require years of weeding out agents and perfecting a compre-
hensive training program in risk selection. But Spaulding, with
the help of George Cox and Aaron Day, Jr., initiated that task,
too.[32]

In 1934 the Company hired Day, an economics professor and
ex-Standard Life executive, as sales training supervisor and gave
him the specific responsibility for developing a curriculum for
in-service training. Beginning in 1935 Day's program required
all district managers to complete an intensive three-week, 120-
hour course at the home office. Assistant managers received a
smaller amount of training at regional centers throughout the
territory. All managers in turn became teachers in year-round
instruction for their agents, under the traveling supervision of
Day.[33]

At the same time Spaulding employed the pages of the *Whetstone* to educate field personnel. Shortly after his arrival the
entire character of the *Whetstone* changed. Month after month
he wrote straightforward, scholarly articles on life insurance
that could have stood the scrutiny of leading insurance periodicals. He congratulated the agents on their wiser risk selection and
cheered the general decline in mortality among black Americans. But his statistical vigilance uncovered a new threat in the
Mutual policyholders' alarming death rate from automobile accidents. One of his charts indicated that by mid-1934 deaths

32. *Ibid.*; Kennedy, "North Carolina Mutual," pp. 200–208; *Whetstone*,
January, 1935; interview, Asa T. Spaulding, August 4, 1970.
33. Kennedy, "North Carolina Mutual," pp. 200–208; *Whetstone*, January,
1935; first quarter, 1946; interviews, W. J. Kennedy, Jr., July 8; Asa T. Spaulding, July 18, 1968.

from auto crashes ranked fourth among all claims. Moreover, such claims called for double and sometimes triple indemnity. Disability claims from automobile accidents posed an even greater threat. Eventually the Mutual, like many companies during the 1930's, was forced to discontinue disability coverage.[34]

Spaulding constantly armed agents and managers with hard information about the industry and the Company. The old-style exhortations remained, but they were dressed in a decidedly professional style, supported by scientific findings and actuarial analysis.[35] He could, for instance, tell the field force that death claims in late 1935 still amounted to 23 percent of the total premium income, and that his analysis of the total industry in relation to the Mutual pointed to 17 percent as the realistic figure for the Company.[36]

While the agents mastered their lessons, Spaulding established a risk selection committee to hedge against the possibility that poor risks might accumulate again.[37] He possessed veto power over the committee and demonstrated that in the aggregate he could predict mortality with precision and efficiency. With his actuarial competence and intimate knowledge of the Company's statistical history, he could quickly calculate a reliable probability of risk for any application. This is exactly the skill that the Company so desperately lacked before 1933.

The Mutual would have survived the Depression without Asa T. Spaulding, but with greater pain, and it would have continued a marginal existence operating slightly out of control with high mortality ratios, no prospect of paying dividends, and a comparative absence of innovation. So impressive were recovery and reform in all areas his hand touched that in 1935 he was elected assistant secretary, a position in the organization chart directly beneath Kennedy. And in 1938, at age thirty-

34. *Whetstone*, January, 1932; May, 1934; May, October, 1935; interviews, Asa T. Spaulding, July 18; W. J. Kennedy, Jr., July 8, 1968; Buley, *The American Life Convention*, II, 684–685, 689–690, 698–699, 720–721.
35. For Spaulding's use of the *Whetstone* as an educational device in the finer points of life insurance, see virtually all issues during the years 1933–36.
36. Asa T. Spaulding to Field Committee, January, 1936, Spaulding Papers.
37. Interview, Asa T. Spaulding, July 18, 1968.

five, Spaulding became the youngest officer on the board of directors.[38]

Whatever the impact of Asa T. Spaulding's considerable achievements, he by no means commanded the Company. While he was busy with his slide rule, often working quietly behind the scenes along with Kennedy, Cox, and others, C. C. Spaulding was conspicuously out front. "Nobody ever doubted that 'Papa' was in charge."[39] The Depression and the death of John Avery in 1931 added to the sense of duty on which President Spaulding thrived. As the personification of the Mutual spirit, he was made to order as morale booster and overseer of the Company's austerity drive.

Always alert to the smallest detail, Spaulding became the penurious taskmaster. He told more often now the story of John D. Rockefeller saving thousands of dollars by using fewer drops of solder to seal a can. He parked his Buick and walked to work, carefully counting the lights burning in the Clerks Home as he returned in the evening. He exhorted managers to work on their landlords for a reduction in rent; during deflationary times, "we should not be paying the same as before." Remembering his early career, he informed managers that if their monthly debit fell below $1,000 they could perform their own janitorial service, as he once did. He wondered if the branch offices really needed telephones and large post office boxes. Secretaries learned to save scrap paper and use it for their carbon copies of business letters. He told the Mutual family to tighten its belt, take a 10 percent wage cut and produce more, all in the spirit of mission which took on new poignancy in this critical time.[40]

38. *Whetstone*, May, 1935; January, 1938. By the time of his tenure as president of the Company (1959–67), Spaulding had won international fame in business and civic affairs; see standard biographical reference works.

39. Interview, Mrs. Viola G. Turner, June 13, 1968.

40. *Ibid.*; C. C. Spaulding to Agency Committee, July 9, 1930; C. C. Spaulding to North Carolina Mutual Managers, August 21, 1931; C. C. Spaulding to G. W. Bolden, February 18, 1932; C. C. Spaulding to Mrs. Mary F. Farr, March 14, 1933, Spaulding Papers. W. J. Kennedy, Jr., to Asa T. Spaulding, March 17, 1932, Kennedy Papers; interview, Asa T. Spaulding, July 18, 1968.

"Work is my hobby," Spaulding declared,[41] and he suggested that others find a similar way to enjoy the Depression. He could scarcely conceive of any problem that would not yield to work and faith. When a business colleague in Arkansas wrote for advice on handling the Depression, Spaulding gave him the simple antidote: "Visit all of your branch offices in person and inspire your managers and agents by showing them the importance of working harder. . . . I have just returned from . . . visiting our districts and it has helped wonderfully."[42] When he could not visit, he wrote scores of open letters, always combining threats with promises, naïve idealism with hard-headed business advice. "Wasn't that depression awful?" he scoffed in 1933. "Well it has passed now. Let's go to work and put the job over in a big way."[43] Simultaneously, he might admit to a crisis but insist, "We can master the situation by fighting back with the weapons we all possess—common sense and hard work. God is not dead, and right will always win. With bridges burned behind us . . . we are facing the future . . . with a spirit that just won't be whipped."[44] Often he was less idealistic: "Any agent is to be dismissed if he is caught violating the company's rules . . ." he warned, "and let me again emphasize that . . . SICK CLAIMS AND ARREARS ARE TO BE BROUGHT DOWN."[45] To another manager he gave notice, "It does not take a philosopher to tell just what will happen if we continue operating at a loss in your district. . . ."[46]

He rightly worried about the sick claims, which often averaged over 40 percent of collections on such policies. This excess violated not only an axiom of health insurance but Spaulding's stern moral code as well, for an alarming number of policyholders were feigning illness and collecting the benefits. In some cases the agent seemed to side with his race brother against the Com-

41. Interview, Mrs. Viola G. Turner, June 13, 1968.
42. C. C. Spaulding to John L. Webb, November 17, 1931, Spaulding Papers.
43. C. C. Spaulding to North Carolina Mutual Managers, March 28, 1933, Spaulding Papers.
44. *Whetstone*, March, 1933.
45. C. C. Spaulding to George J. Johnson, November 18, 1931, Spaulding Papers.
46. C. C. Spaulding to J. B. Drake, August 14, 1931, Spaulding Papers.

pany. "There is entirely too much sentiment in our districts," the President complained. "Agents and managers are afraid of hurting someone's feelings if they turn down an illegal claim. . . ."[47] In other cases the cheating was more sinister and involved well-organized conspiracies between policyholders, agents, and physicians.[48] Spaulding began a crusade against the high claims and the dishonesty. The *Whetstone* reserved its greatest praise for the agent reporting the lowest number of sick claims rather than the highest amount of sales.[49] And Spaulding let it be known that a Mutual agent must be more than honest; he must set an example and act as a reformer among the masses. As an agrarian at heart who abhorred the social repercussions of Negro migration, Spaulding grieved over the exodus of sharecroppers to the city. He urged his agents who dealt with farmers during the Depression to encourage families to remain in the country, to raise gardens, diversify their crops, apply for federal assistance, and of course to pay their debts and go to church.[50]

The Company officially combined business with social policy in its "Thrift Clubs." Organized in 1932 for children who held Mutual policies, the Clubs began as an offshoot of George Cox's heralded "Five-Year Plan."[51] The basic motivation for the Clubs was to increase sales and to inculcate thrift, but as they spread throughout the Mutual territory in the 1930's they became community organizations and the agents, with Spaulding's blessing, became community organizers. Not unlike the children's auxiliaries of the nineteenth-century Negro fraternal societies (the "Rosebuds" of the True Reformers, for example), the Clubs

47. C. C. Spaulding to J. L. Wheeler, July 31, 1931, Spaulding Papers.
48. See W. J. Kennedy, Jr., to D. C. Deans, March 5; Dr. Clyde Donnell to all agents, March 20, 1930, Kennedy Papers.
49. *Whetstone*, January, 1932.
50. *Whetstone*, February, 1930; C. C. Spaulding to Joe F. Burch, July 25; C. C. Spaulding to J. M. Jenkins, September 29, 1933, Spaulding Papers; C. C. Spaulding commencement address, Clarkton, N.C., May 7, 1936, Spaulding Papers.
51. With a curious title for a capitalist program, the Five-Year Plan called for $100 million insurance in force by the end of 1936, with each agent responsible for quotas to meet the goal. See *Whetstone*, March, 1932; C. C. Spaulding to G. W. Bolden, February 18, 1932, Spaulding Papers; Kennedy, "North Carolina Mutual," pp. 190–191.

adopted regalia and staged parades. In some communities they seemed to be a surrogate for the Boy Scouts, with the Mutual agent and a "Matron" serving as leaders in recreation programs and activity meetings. Like a Scout, each member took a pledge, in this case: "to save time and money, to obey parents . . . and to attend Sunday School every Sunday." The official Thrift Club song further revealed the element of uplift in the Company's public relations:

> I used to sit around at home, I had no place to play,
> But the NCM came along and opened up the way.
>
> . . . .
>
> Give us a chance, we'll sure advance,
> We're in the Thrift Club now.[52]

The Depression summarized the socioeconomic dualism that had characterized the history of the Company to that time. The economic crisis evoked the traditional tight-fisted doctrine of business administration and gave it new scientific assistance; at the same time, the crisis provided a platform for the bold repetition of the social ideas upon which the Company was founded. Christianity, the stoic idea of progress, and racial solidarity had built an impregnable defense against cynicism. "Happy days are on their way," C. C. Spaulding predicted in 1933.[53] "If we can only see God in history we can smite pessimism a death blow."[54] Nor would he regret the lean days, for they too came from God and had played an essential role in improving black business. "The depression has made all of us better business men," he wrote W. E. B. Du Bois, "it has taught us how to manage more efficiently."[55]

52. *Whetstone*, December, 1932; August, September, 1933; April, 1934; August, 1936; January, December, 1938; clippings, *Cape Fear Journal*, April 7; *Atlanta Daily World*, May 27, 1934, Kennedy Scrapbook; Kennedy, "North Carolina Mutual," pp. 191–192.

53. C. C. Spaulding typescript, "Happy Days Are on Their Way," 1933, no exact date, Spaulding Papers.

54. C. C. Spaulding, untitled typescript, 1935, no exact date, Spaulding Papers.

55. C. C. Spaulding to W. E. B. Du Bois, March 26, 1931. Du Bois continued to applaud the efforts of black business in Durham; see Du Bois to Spaulding, March 24, 1931, Spaulding Papers.

Like most Negro leaders, Spaulding had spent his whole life trying to make the best out of the worst, trying to "take advantage of disadvantages," and the Depression fit neatly into a philosophy grounded in hardship and religion from which he could constantly invoke the lesson of Job and the message from the Sermon on the Mount. Struggle toughens and prepares the "last to become first." "Depressions are great disciplinarians," he told a high school graduating class.[56] God and Darwinism colluded to strengthen the Company and to strengthen the race. "God has simply put His hand on the whole national machinery"; thus the Depression "is best for all concerned," Spaulding reassured, and he asked only that blacks work "harder than ever, and trust the results to Providence."[57] The roughness of the times burnished the essence of the black experience, and the survival of the Company symbolized the epic survival of a people. Adversity—suffering—was redemptive and brought a truer Christianity and a greater humanism to the race. "Too much success all the time is not the best for mortal man," Spaulding sermonized. "He should know the humanizing touch of failure, the pangs of want, the travail of hopes deferred."[58]

In some minds, perhaps in Spaulding's, a literal relationship existed between the future of the Company and the future of the black man. "Durham seems to be the final effort of our race to carry on," an admirer wrote the president, "so I beg you to hold the line."[59] A black editor saw the Mutual as the last reserve

56. C. C. Spaulding commencement address, Oxford, N.C., May 29, 1935, Spaulding Papers.

57. C. C. Spaulding to C. E. Leathers, March 11, 1933, Spaulding Papers.

58. C. C. Spaulding typescript of untitled speech, 1933, no exact date, Spaulding Papers. The theme of the ennobling experience of suffering as the key to the Afro-American experience has been treated extensively in black literature, particularly in the writings of James Baldwin. S. P. Fullenwider in his *Mind and Mood of Black America* (Homewood, Ill.: Dorsey Press, 1969) traces this theme through Afro-American thought in the twentieth century. Also see August Meier, *Negro Thought in America, 1880–1915* (Ann Arbor: University of Michigan Press, 1963), and a provocative essay on defense mechanisms in the face of oppression by Hortense Powermaker, "The Channeling of Negro Aggression by the Cultural Process," *American Journal of Sociology*, XLVIII (May, 1943), 750–758.

59. William E. Doby to C. C. Spaulding, November 30, 1931, Spaulding Papers.

of racial progress: "The only hope for the Negro is to 'Durham-ize' the race."[60] Thus Spaulding could present an unstrained argument that the North Carolina Mutual embraced the legacy of a people. "It is not just a business at stake," he told his managers, "but a Negro institution . . ." which could easily become "one of the brightest spots in Negro history. . . ."[61]

If the Depression could strengthen the race, perhaps it could also unite the race, economically at least. "The depression is the acid test of Negro business," declared Spaulding, and "the soul of every Negro should be fired with a determination to cherish, love and support his own institutions. . . ."[62] Not since the critical days of the first survival had nationalism occupied such a conspicuous place in the Company rhetoric. In fact, the intense plea for racial solidarity and periods of crisis have roughly coincided in the history of the North Carolina Mutual.

The Depression alone, however, did not awaken this latent nationalism; rather, the failure of the National Benefit Life Insurance Company in the summer of 1931 provided the immediate stimulus. A sensational black press reported the collapse with inordinate fanfare. Conspiracy, suicide, and the exposure of high living and corruption among the black bourgeoisie took on the trappings of a good Hollywood scandal.[63] The failure of the National Benefit Life, which had become a "Christmas tree" for plundering black officials and a white actuary, offered vindication for the conservative retrenchment of the Mutual.[64] But President Spaulding lamented the loss of a Negro institution, and of course he knew that a race failure on this scale would

60. Clipping, *Norfolk Journal and Guide*, March 16, 1935, Kennedy Scrapbook.

61. C. C. Spaulding to Managers, 1930, no exact date, Spaulding Papers; *Whetstone*, November, 1931.

62. C. C. Spaulding typescript, "Happy Days Are on Their Way," 1933, no exact date, Spaulding Papers.

63. Clipping, *Afro American*, July 18, 1931, North Carolina Mutual clipping file; James B. Mitchell, *The Collapse of the National Benefit Life Insurance Company: A Study of High Finance among Negroes* (Washington, D.C.: Howard University, 1939), pp. 136–137; Carter G. Woodson, *Miseducation of the Negro* (Washington, D.C.: Associated Publishers, 1933), p. 42.

64. Mitchell, *Collapse of National Benefit*, p. 124; *Whetstone*, fourth quarter, 1941.

unleash within black popular opinion the specter of impending doom for all Negro companies. Moreover, evidence surfaced that the National Benefit in its death throes had lashed out at the Mutual with damaging rumors sent to a "news wild" press.[65]

In response, Spaulding opened a letter-writing campaign to preserve racial support. He wrote not only in the capacity of race leader and president of the North Carolina Mutual, but as president of the Mechanics and Farmers Bank as well. Letters representing the Bank went out to every black man Spaulding suspected of hoarding a little cash. He flooded Columbus County with appeals for deposits, reminding his multitude of cousins that their money would be "as safe in the Mechanics and Farmers as in any bank in America" (not altogether reassuring), and that the Durham leaders were "struggling to build something that the race can point to with pride . . . which should be sufficient reason for asking for a deposit from you."[66]

Letter-writing, however, expressed only a part of the Company's racial consciousness. Advertising, which in the 1920's presented facts and figures declaring that the Company was as "durable as the Sphinx," appeared lackluster in contrast to the racial theme that dominated advertising in the 1930's. Quarter and half-page ads featured portraits of race leaders ranging from Booker T. Washington and Frederick Douglass to Phillis Wheatley and Paul Laurence Dunbar, all of whom represented a heritage that the Mutual would help preserve for "the generations of Negroes yet unborn."[67]

Economic cooperation lay at the very foundation of Afro-American nationalism and has been consistent with both pro-

65. Melvin Chisum to C. C. Spaulding, July 28, September 20; Spaulding to Chisum, November 17; Carl Murphy to Robert R. Moton, October 23; Moton to Murphy, October 27; Spaulding to S. L. McDowell, November 23, 1931, Spaulding Papers.

66. C. C. Spaulding to Mac I. Spaulding, January 5; to L. L. Spaulding, November 19; to R. O. Spaulding, August 7; to O. H. Lennon, July 31, 1931; to Rolland Campbell, n.d., Spaulding Papers. There are countless other examples; in fact, Spaulding and Kennedy seldom wrote a letter in 1931–32 that they did not find some way to allay fears and call for racial support. Kennedy wrote to Asa T. Spaulding (November 13, 1931), "I think the letters have done the trick."

67. For examples, see clippings, *Norfolk Journal and Guide*, April 15, 1932; April 8, 22, June 3, 1933, North Carolina Mutual clipping file.

test and accommodation as an easily invoked variable within a body of stratagems coming forward, almost without premeditation, to meet a given circumstance. It is impossible to dismember this nationalism and correctly label which parts stem from entrepreneurial opportunism, racial pride, or pent-up aggression. Spaulding may have been exploiting solidarity when he used the ubiquitous white agent as his foil to pressure his managers: "I have noticed the agents of white companies going into *our* homes . . . and writing the business *we* should have."[68] And Kennedy may have answered a customer complaint obliquely when he replied, "It is easy enough for Negroes . . . to withdraw support from Negro institutions, but there is one thing certain, the American white man is gradually closing in on every opportunity the Negro has. . . ."[69] But no one who knew the men would doubt their pride, any more than one would doubt the white threat.

For the black businessman success could serve as a means of protest that advanced pride and relieved feelings of aggression, and he might savor the success for what it was—a racial victory. Surely Spaulding felt more than economic satisfaction when a black principal testified: "A white agent came in to write one of our teachers. . . . I told him we didn't do any white business . . . and I wanted to know if he had ever heard of you and your company. I told him if a teacher in this school would take his insurance, I would . . . demand that she withdraw from the institution."[70] Surely something other than profit motivated Spaulding to assist a black man's application for a federal loan in order to save his property and "keep white people out of [from owning] our Negro section."[71] And surely the irony was more than accidental in Spaulding's response to a white applicant seeking employment during the Depression: "From your

68. C. C. Spaulding to A. L. Goodloe, August 25; also see Spaulding to J. B. Deans, August 25, 1931, Spaulding Papers. Italics mine.

69. W. J. Kennedy, Jr. to John W. Rouse, July 11, 1932, Kennedy Papers.

70. Emanuel M. McDuffie to C. C. Spaulding, March 5, 1931, Spaulding Papers.

71. A. L. Long to C. C. Spaulding, August 30; Spaulding to Long, August 31, 1934, Spaulding Papers.

photograph, we assume that you are white and it is not the policy of our company to employ agents of your race."[72] For C. C. Spaulding the Depression years only dramatized what was manifest from the beginning—the primacy of race in the meaning of the Mutual's existence.

Seen in the broader limits of American social and intellectual history, the meaning of the Mutual's survival would seem to rest in its contribution to mythology. Black capitalism, as the outgrowth of two cultures, is doubly laden with mythology. The North Carolina Mutual provided a germ of truth which nurtured the myth of a self-sustaining black economy which would uplift a people and repair race relations. This black myth was based on a white myth—that of rags to riches—for which the Mutual also provided sustenance.

Surviving the Depression strengthened the mythology. The editor of *Opportunity* magazine hailed the survival and asked if there could be "any more rigid test than this." Deciding not, he proclaimed the North Carolina Mutual as "black capitalism triumphant."[73] But it was the *idea* of the Mutual which triumphed. Institutions express culture, and few cultural values in America ran deeper than capitalism and self-help. And no Afro-American institution appeared better qualified to give them expression than the North Carolina Mutual.

Surviving the Depression also strengthened the substance of the Mutual. The technical advances made under the pressure of events and the guidance of Asa T. Spaulding enabled the Company by the close of World War II to pay dividends, to enjoy enviable mortality ratios, and to find attractive investments. Indeed, wartime prosperity, coupled with the illusory prospect of postwar integration, tended to secularize the Mutual spirit. In the meantime, however, history had made the Company preeminently a social institution with plural functions embracing the whole of community life.

72. C. C. Spaulding to R. C. Horton, August 25, 1931, Spaulding Papers.
73. Quoted in *Whetstone*, February, 1936.

7

The Company
and the Community:
The Burden
of Race

Asa and C. C. Spaulding personified the dual identity of the North Carolina Mutual as it struggled during the Depression to build a technically sound business and a culturally proud institution. The two Spauldings, as engineer and statesman, worked in unison to keep the Company engines running and its racial colors flying. In their efforts they may have strained the standard procedures of actuarial science and the credible limits of their bourgeois black nationalism, but they did so within a larger framework of honesty. They were correct in assuming that more was at stake than a life insurance company. By the end of the 1930's the Mutual had taken on a cultural legitimacy that transcended Negro business. Its survival symbolically expressed racial survival, and in the Durham community the Company acquired a higher meaning than its ostensible commercial relationship to the life of the city.

For nearly two generations the Mutual had served as a landmark in the minds of visitors and townspeople, blacks and whites, and in the collective psyche of the community. Its mere presence evoked a compulsory response from everyone who knew its identity. As long as it stood six stories tall as a black institution in a southern town of squat warehouses and dimestores, and in the white rather than in the black business district, it commanded attention. Blacks and whites daily encountered this anomaly that overshadowed Woolworths on one side and the U.S. Post Office on the other, and they oriented themselves and the relationship between them to its existence.

Whites were never sure whether to consider the Mutual a novelty or an institution, whether to call it "nigger heaven" or the "big colored insurance company." Standing apart from black Hayti, up there on Parrish Street, so prominent, so proud, the Mutual violated what ought to be; yet it was so skillfully presented, so in tune with the white ethos, that it came to represent in the white mind a self-delusory promise of what the black community might be. Whites rationalized the success of the North Carolina Mutual as an exception to the rule of racial incapacity and at the same time proclaimed its success as general proof of the inevitable progress in store for the black man under the benign race policy of the white South. The black success was made over into a white success, even a sectional success. Durham offered three glittering examples of southern achievement: Duke University, American Tobacco, and the North Carolina Mutual—three satisfying symbols of the New South.

Like Ralph Ellison's half-fictional Tuskegee, the Mutual made the larger black community invisible. The Company, its institutional offshoots, and the North Carolina College provided the distinctive features of black Durham and kept it from being seen as a dreary, slum-filled industrial settlement of migrant tobacco workers.[1] And as the Mutual diverted white attention from squalor to relative splendor, it likewise diverted black attention. For black Durham the Company loomed from Parrish Street as a salient example of black success in the white man's world. Black people expected their communities to have big preachers and educators, but the "World's Largest Negro Business" and an internationally known Negro executive were beyond expectation. The Mutual gave the black population a certain psychic, if not economic, sustenance—a sense of identity that, despite class feelings, trickled down undiluted from Parrish Street to the

1. For the best description of the pathological side of black Durham see Hugh Penn Brinton, "The Negro in Durham: A Study of Adjustment to Town Life" (Ph.D. dissertation, University of North Carolina, 1930).

masses across the tracks. In fact, the uptown location probably strengthened the Company's psychological impact. When blacks in expensive suits and big cars rolled up to the white community every morning, they may have stirred resentment among their race brothers who watched the pageant along Fayetteville and Pettigrew Streets. But they stirred pride, too, and their dramatic exit upstaged the larger and more somber scene of black domestics going up to work in the white kitchens. Spaulding and his lieutenants, in contradiction to the general rule, did not set out each morning to serve the white man; instead, it appeared that they were intruding a small distance into the impenetrable mainstream, eroding the power structure, playing the white man's game in the white man's territory and winning. This, too, amounted to delusion—but an essential compensatory delusion in a world where economic success came hard, if at all, and where the need for vicarious achievement was compulsory. In this sense the Company may have given negative as well as positive inspiration. It may have served as an earthly opiate. The Mutual laid to rest another white assumption about black ability; thus, in the event of self-doubt, one could look to Parrish Street. The Mutual could not only insulate the black man from doubt, but it could also function as a substitute for personal success and deter him from action of his own. "Your company," a black woman wrote C. C. Spaulding, "is what keeps our heads up when we don't do enough to help ourselves."[2] Anthropologist Hortense Powdermaker, in her classic study of Indianola, Mississippi, home of George Cox's enterprising relatives, observed that "a handful of people who form the upper class . . . exercises an influence out of all proportion to numbers. It is the privileged class; but it is also the class that works to advance the status of all the Negroes, partly by definite activities in behalf of the others, partly by the proof it offers of what the race can do and be." This assumption of the racial burden by the black upper class absolved the rest of the community from responsibility, allowing them to "relax and enjoy life serene in the consciousness

2. Mabel Hawkins to C. C. Spaulding, March 14, 1933, Spaulding Papers.

... that these more industrious members are looking out for the racial reputation."[3]

While the psychic impact of the Company on the community is the most intriguing dimension of the Mutual's broad influence, it is the least measurable. But symbol and myth seldom stand without empirical support, and there was indeed a tangible interplay between the Company and the community which inevitably fed back into the mystique of the Mutual. Since the days of Dr. Moore the rule had been that a Company man must also be a community man. C. C. Spaulding lived that rule and tried to enforce it as a matter of policy. Historically such a policy was implicit in the origins of the Company and later explicit in its relationship with the black community's first newspaper, its hospital, library, churches, schools, and voluntary associations. As power, prestige, and talent grew within the Parrish Street complex, so did the influence of the Mutual within the community. Its activities were sometimes contrived and often inseparable from shrewd public relations, but much of what it did came out of the inertia of its history. Responsibility devolved upon the Company because of its heritage, the character of its leaders, and simply because of its great visibility in a culture of institutional scarcity. It acquired power because it had power, although the source of that power was often white rather than black. Whether it wanted to or not the Mutual leadership frequently found itself in a position to determine who in the black community found employment, who qualified for credit, who received welfare, who paid fines, and who escaped a sentence to the road gang, or maybe even to the gas chamber. It exercised authority over the press, the sermons, the curriculum, the morals, the arts, relations between the races, the appropriation and allocation of public funds, political appointments, and the vote in the black community. From Howard to Tuskegee the internal affairs of black colleges often reflected the influence of C. C. Spaulding. A letter from him, like one from Booker T. Washington a generation earlier, could win a scholarship or

3. Hortense Powdermaker, *After Freedom: A Cultural Study in the Deep South* (New York: Viking Press, 1939), p. 63.

secure an honorary degree, a place on a board of trustees, a position on a faculty, a promotion, even a deanship or a presidency.

All this is to say that the North Carolina Mutual formed the heart of a black political economy in Durham, which could on occasion extend outside the city limits into the southern region and beyond. Capitalism provided part of its ideological foundation; racial cooperation provided another part. This dual legitimacy best expressed itself in the honorific titles alternately bestowed on C. C. Spaulding: "Mr. Negro Business" and "Mr. Cooperation." When coupled with Christianity the parts became an indistinguishable whole, an orderly abstraction in the minds of the Mutual leaders. In actual practice, however, the political economy was often informal and pragmatic, operating in accordance with daily exigencies and black and white opinion, and within the framework of overlapping Afro-American institutions.

Nowhere in this interrelationship among institutions was the connection closer than that between the Mutual and the church. As seen from the bottom up, insurance had a profound relationship with religion. Conceptually, both dealt with death. Lower-class black policyholders seldom conceived of insurance as the middle-class convention of investment and estate-building. Instead, life insurance in the minds of the masses meant burial insurance. Well into the twentieth century the business of black insurance had not divorced itself from the traditions and practices of the early mutual benefit and burial associations, most of which were linked directly to the church. Insurance was more than a profane financial arrangement; it was a folkway. In his sociological study of a black community in piedmont South Carolina, Hylan Lewis ranked "insurance" as one of the cultural staples along with "church going, cotton, whisky, burying, hunting and fishing."[4] Hortense Powdermaker, in looking at the deeper South, found the "insurance envelope" an omnipresent feature on the walls of Negro cabins in the Mississippi Delta.[5]

4. Hylan Lewis, *Blackways of Kent* (Chapel Hill: University of North Carolina Press, 1955), p. 45.
5. Powdermaker, *After Freedom*, p. 134.

Moreover, the industrial insurance agent became a minor folk figure, occupying a consistent place in the lives of the people. He no doubt deserves a place in Afro-American social history, for his weekly rounds, like those of the circuit-riding preacher, became ritualized in the subculture of southern blacks. It would appear that the agent even inspired an occasional piece of folklore.[6]

C. C. Spaulding liked to think that he presided over a church as well as a business, and of course the history of Negro life insurance reveals that black preachers often presided over a business as well as a church. For Spaulding the Company and the church coincided historically and spiritually. Speaking before a convention of black Baptists, he reminded them that "practically all Negro fraternal societies and Negro businesses were organized in Negro churches," and he affirmed that the strength of the Mutual spirit rested largely on the divine origins of the Company and the divine inspiration of its founders.[7] He thought of the Mutual as "a miracle" in which the gospel of God sanctified the gospel of work, and he daily rejoiced in the glory of the combination.[8] "It really makes me feel good," he confided to his close friend, A. E. Spears, "when I remember that the guiding hand of Providence is the head of this institution."[9]

Spaulding took his religion seriously, to say the least. His every activity was couched in Christianity. On his daily calendar, which survives as a fragmentary diary, he frequently carried on conversations with God: a commitment to his race, a prayer, a line of scripture, a thanksgiving for a good annual report—all of

6. One tale has it that an agent came for his collection at a lean time in a particular household, and the mother hid behind the door, instructing her daughter to tell the agent that she was at church. "Mama's gone off to church," the daughter obediently told the agent. The agent looked down, smiled, and replied, "Well, she must have been in a mighty hurry to run off and leave her feet under the door like that" (interview, Bertram Lewis, February 15, 1971).

7. C. C. Spaulding, speech at the Baptist State Convention, Shaw University, Raleigh, N.C., August 5, 1942, Spaulding Papers. Spaulding occasionally served as a lay preacher, and a church in Chicago offered him the pulpit if he ever retired from business (H. M. Spaulding to C. C. Spaulding, May 28, 1943, Spaulding Papers).

8. Clipping, *Carolina Times*, April 9, 1926, Kennedy Scrapbook.

9. C. C. Spaulding to A. E. Spears, July 9, 1931, Spaulding Papers.

that combined with appointment schedules, statistical notes, and quotations from Booker T. Washington and Elbert Hubbard, supplemented with random thoughts of his own which he stored away for speeches. "Business and religion will mix," he wrote to himself one day, "and neither will succeed unless they do."[10] His first act of every working day was to close his office door, open his Bible, and read from Psalm 91. "I believe in this Psalm," he testified, "as I believe in getting up in the morning."[11]

For Spaulding, working at the Mutual was little different from working in the house of the Lord. He built an unassailable theosophy in which God's purpose was his purpose, and the proof of the unity was the success of the Company. He disclaimed any conflict of interest, insisting that he "never believed in using the church to advance his business," but at the same time—indeed, in the same speech—he cited the fifth chapter of 1 Timothy to warn his black audience that "if any provide not for his own and especially for those of his own house, he hath denied the faith and is worse than an infidel."[12] Spaulding never saw the contradiction because, despite his disclaimer, he never admitted to the separation of church and business. In practice, he constantly admonished his agents to use the church as their "most powerful contact."[13]

Spaulding's advice was scarcely necessary, for his men keenly appreciated the influence of the church and within their districts ardently courted the good will of black ministers. An agent in Virginia, for example, wrote Kennedy at the home office and asked him to give four ministers from his territory the "red carpet

10. C. C. Spaulding, day calendar, March 11, 1943.

11. C. C. Spaulding, "The Land of the Free," *Guideposts*, V (March, 1950), 5–6, 19. While Spaulding found solace and strength in the ninety-first Psalm: "I will say of the Lord, He is my refuge and my fortress: my God; in him will I trust," he just as frequently turned to the first Psalm, especially in his speeches, to sanction the union between business and religion: "Blessed is the man that walketh not in the counsel of the ungodly. . . . And he shall be like a tree planted by the rivers of water, that bringeth forth his fruit in his season; his leaf also shall not wither; and whatsoever he doeth shall prosper."

12. C. C. Spaulding, speech at Howard University, April 4, 1943, Spaulding Papers.

13. Jesse Edward Gloster, "North Carolina Mutual Life Insurance Company: Its Historical Development and Current Operations" (Ph.D. dissertation, University of Pittsburgh, 1955), p. 50.

treatment" when they visited Durham. "Show them the North Carolina Mutual, the Mechanics and Farmers Bank, Bankers Fire, North Carolina College and Duke University," he instructed. "I am trying to sell them on the NCM," the Norfolk agent needlessly explained, and he boasted that he had already arranged "Insurance Sundays" at various churches where "the ministers are giving me their Sunday Service to get my program over to the public." "Is there any reason," he asked Kennedy, "why they can't put us in their sermons at times?" Kennedy could think of none and added that Negro preachers at the very least ought to counsel their parishioners to buy insurance from a "company which hires only Negroes in a time when unemployment is so high."[14]

A minister could easily offer a sermon on insurance as a natural part of the church's program, as historically had been the case. Moreover, the larger message of racial cooperation served the interests of both institutions, and exchanging a little time in the pulpit for a five-dollar contribution conspicuously placed in the collection plate could be construed as an act of racial solidarity, with the preacher and the agent exiting arm in arm at the benediction.[15]

As the embodiment of the Company's public relations program, Spaulding did not depend on his managers and agents to negotiate a confederation with the church. He saw to it that photographs of black bishops appeared on Company calendars, that every Negro minister in Durham received a Christmas gift from the Mutual, often including a crisp five-dollar bill from the president himself, and that on one Sunday of every month the

14. F. V. Allison to W. J. Kennedy, Jr., March 18; Kennedy to Allison, March 26, 1930, Kennedy Papers.

15. To what extent uplift and cooperation dissolved selfish motives in such arrangements is a moot question. Apparently black congregations accepted these alliances as culturally legitimate as long as the minister and agent seemed dedicated to racial uplift. Powdermaker described a funeral in Mississippi where a local insurance agent participated in the eulogy, mixing sales talk with sorrow and reminding the congregation that through his company they too could have such a fine funeral. Powdermaker observed, "Nobody would think ill of him for preaching insurance at a time like this, for if he had done his job as . . . race man, they would all agree that he was working for the good of the race." See Powdermaker, *After Freedom*, pp. 250–251.

Durham churches set aside time to discuss "Business Cooperation."[16]

In general, he directed a steady stream of personal letters to churchmen, urging them to cooperate, to build the race, to boost the North Carolina Mutual. His vision, like Booker T. Washington's, called for a consortium of black institutions supported by race-conscious workers, all pulling together to lift themselves "from the mire of poverty, ignorance and oppression." But this could never happen, he warned, "without self-respect." First, "Negroes must be acquainted with their history and potentialities, then there will be no stopping us."[17]

He believed the race consciousness would come from an educated elite, and in this belief he became a life member and generous supporter of the Association for the Study of Negro Life and History.[18] He realized, however, that for his immediate purposes the church could be more influential. "You know how it is with our race," he wrote a Baptist minister in Statesville. "People are naturally doubtful as to anything done by Negroes, but you are in a position to correct that." He suggested that the minister was also "in a position to speak to the company's stability and the service it is rendering the race." A positive word from the pulpit, advised Spaulding, would enable "our agent who is a member of your church to double his debit. . . ."[19]

Even without Spaulding's ambitious cultivation of the black clergy, the Mutual possessed a considerable indirect and unspoken persuasion over the church. The sectarian politics and philanthropy of John Merrick and John Avery in the African Methodist Episcopal Church had established an important legacy of influence. The same could be said of Dr. Moore, C. C.

16. C. C. Spaulding Christmas message to "policyholders and friends," December 24, 1930; H. L. Fisher to C. C. Spaulding, December 30, 1929; J. Lee White to Spaulding, January 2; F. C. Graham to Spaulding, January 4, 1930, Spaulding Papers; Brinton, "The Negro in Durham," pp. 184–185.

17. C. C. Spaulding, open letter to employees and friends in support of a national church movement, "Self-Respect Sunday" (October 25), October 19, 1931, Spaulding Papers.

18. C. C. Spaulding to Carter G. Woodson, December 8, 1937, March 9, 1943, March 10, 1949; Woodson to Spaulding, May 26, 1939, July 30, 1941, March 6, 1943, Spaulding Papers.

19. C. C. Spaulding to J. W. Croom, September 11, 1934, Spaulding Papers.

Spaulding, and W. J. Kennedy in the Baptist Church.[20] Increasingly the home office became a regional funnel for fund-raising requests and church patronage. The clerics knew that they could depend on President Spaulding and the Mutual for contributions, but more important, they knew that Spaulding's endorsement could unlock larger white purses, particularly the Duke and Rosenwald Foundations, as well as the Slater Fund, of which he was a board member. Negro churches naturally solicited the leading Negro enterprise first when they issued bonds or floated loans. Denominational colleges, especially Shaw University, and Virginia Theological Seminary at Lynchburg, consistently turned to Spaulding as their front-line defense against insolvency. Similarly, black ministers seeking new or better opportunities in the South wrote him for leads and letters of support. Seminaries consulted him as an unofficial placement agent; conversely, churches with empty pulpits did the same. The Negro Baptist and Methodist publishing houses were beholden to him for his insistence that individual churches purchase their hymnals and Sunday school materials from their own publishers. While probably not decisive, his opinions carried weight in the election of the Baptist officialdom, and he occasionally intervened in the politics of other denominations—an AME bishopric contest in St. Louis, for example.[21]

Whatever the scope of Spaulding's power, he always projected himself as a cooperative servant of the church. This may explain why the sniping that was rife within the black middle class seldom extended to him or to the Mutual. As a tribute to his commitment to racial cooperation, and as an unconscious

20. Spaulding succeeded Dr. Moore as president of the Baptist state Sunday School Convention and carried on his uncle's work with the Lott Cary Foreign Missionary Convention, not to mention the various administrative posts he held within Durham's White Rock Baptist Church. W. J. Kennedy, in turn, succeeded Spaulding in most of these positions.

21. S. L. McDowell to Boaz A. Harris, July 26; Boaz A. Harris to C. C. Spaulding, August 25, 1928; Frank C. Foster, director of field work, Union Theological Seminary, to Spaulding, March 20; Spaulding to Foster, April 1; L. G. Jordan to Spaulding, February 5; Spaulding to Jordan, June 24, 1931; Spaulding to whom it may concern, August 13, 1938; Rev. W. A. Cooper to Spaulding, October 20; Spaulding to Cooper, October 25, 1936, Spaulding Papers.

assent to his prowess in public relations, the National Baptist Convention hung his portrait among the leading lights of the church at its Nashville headquarters.[22]

If Baptists in Nashville could appreciate the influence of Spaulding and the Company, Baptists in Durham took it for granted that the Mutual would dominate their leading institution, the White Rock Church, as a part of what has been styled here as the political economy of black Durham. As a rule the Negro church acted as an institutional locus in the black community, with its multiple functions reaching out into the superstructure of community life. In Durham the North Carolina Mutual usurped this position. White Rock, the most prestigious church of black Durham, bore a relationship to the Mutual not so different from that of the Mechanics and Farmers Bank. One Baptist commentator described White Rock as

> the home church of Spaulding, Shepard, Kennedy and the town moguls. There is no church like White Rock in the country. I choose my words with deliberation. . . . In this church you meet capitalism undressed and undiluted. In this church capital dominates and I don't mean chicken feed. It is an interlocking directorate. Shepard's father built the church and he came up with the tycoons and is closely related in a business way. When you rise to preach you look into the face of people . . . who are connected either by family or business with Shepard, Kennedy or Spaulding. All of them are officials of the church, Kennedy being the business manager. Now go there and preach a red hot sermon about the proletariat.[23]

Allowing for journalistic color, the description was not far off the mark. Certainly White Rock had money, and those who furnished the money and filled the administrative posts were more often than not connected with the Mutual. Spaulding once boasted that the church collected $4002.77 on a single Sunday—

22. Interview, Miles Mark Fisher, March 10, 1968.

23. Undated clipping, *National Baptist Voice*, Spaulding Papers. The reporter overestimated Shepard's influence and interest in White Rock. Shepard had a single-minded dedication to his own institution, North Carolina College, which had a chapel and provided church services of its own.

"in cash with no lists, no suppers, all given by members individually."[24] Viewed from afar White Rock seemed a haven for the black minister. "Everything in Durham is roseate," thought black Chicagoans. "All a White Rock minister has to do is to preach on Sunday. The expenses of the church and everything just comes."[25] In the midst of the Depression White Rock offered $200 per month as a starting salary, along with a completely furnished five-bedroom parsonage and all expenses save board.[26]

Yet things were far from rosy. If the Mutual financed the church, it also did the hiring and firing. Spaulding recruited ministers for White Rock just as he recruited top executives for the Mutual. But of course, the ministers did not expect to become men of the Mutual, and they constantly chafed under alleged Company control. With Spaulding's contacts and the congregation's wealth, White Rock attracted the nation's finest black clergymen; but recruitment of strong candidates only aggravated the conflict, as few such men were willing to compromise their traditional roles as spiritual and community leaders. To Spaulding's horror, bitter quarreling erupted during the 1920's between the White Rock pastor and Mutual leaders. The frustrated preacher began to bait his uptown adversaries as "big Negroes" and the "Parrish Street Gang" in an effort to displace them as officers of the church. Spaulding lamented to Kennedy, "So he is after the Parrish Street Gang and wants alley folks to run his church because he can handle them easier."[27] Needless to say, the minister soon left White Rock. His replacement lasted less than a year before retreating to his former pastorate in Virginia, where he enjoyed autonomy and identity as undisputed father of his flock. During the Mutual's rise to power few ministers stayed long at White Rock, the average tenure from 1912 to 1933 being only four years.[28]

24. C. C. Spaulding to H. B. Gavin, November 6, 1937, Spaulding Papers.
25. Miles Mark Fisher to C. C. Spaulding, August 7, 1940, Spaulding Papers.
26. C. C. Spaulding to W. L. Ransome, January 2, 1931; W. J. Kennedy, Jr., to Miles Mark Fisher, November 28, 1932, Spaulding and Kennedy Papers.
27. C. C. Spaulding to W. J. Kennedy, Jr., undated letter, but context places it in September, 1925; C. C. Spaulding to Mrs. L. L. Avery, November 6, 1924, Spaulding Papers.
28. Interview, Miles Mark Fisher, March 10, 1968; Miles Mark Fisher,

Another minister who would not have stayed long, had he gotten the call, was Adam Clayton Powell, Jr. In 1932, with the pulpit empty once again, the church, through Kennedy's contacts with Adam Clayton Powell, Sr., summoned the younger Powell to White Rock for a trial sermon and a round of introductions. Powell, Jr., descended on Durham "dressed in cream colored trousers and a flashy jacket." The deacons and officers left it to the older women of the church to declare, "That boy is too sporty for White Rock."[29]

Instead of Powell, the White Rock officers chose Miles Mark Fisher, son of another famous Baptist minister, Elijah Fisher, former pastor of Mt. Olivet Church in Chicago. Fisher proved more than equal to the unusual demands of Durham. He presided over the White Rock congregation for more than thirty years, an experience which he likened to a "game" pitting the "prominence of the pastor versus the prominence of the officers and deacons who represented the North Carolina Mutual."[30] Fisher played the game with self-effacing deftness and indirection, often sacrificing his prominence to larger goals. "I allowed them to believe that they were running the church," he recalled, "when in fact I carefully fed them ideas and a program which they took over and instituted as their own."[31] Fisher's survival at White Rock, while an accomplishment in itself, was not nearly so important as his success in activating the best instincts of the Mutual spirit in sponsoring a brand of religion not entirely consistent with the capitalist spirit. Fisher preached no red-hot proletarian sermons, but he revealed that the Mutual interests were not altogether hostile to at least a lukewarm effort.

His religion, like his father's, was that of the social gospel, for which black Chicago had given him other examples. The Institutional Church and Social Settlement of Reverdy Ransom, the

Friends: Pictorial Report of Ten Years Pastorate of the White Rock Baptist Church (Durham: Service Printing Company, 1943), pp. 9–10.

29. Interviews, W. J. Kennedy, Jr., April 1; Miles Mark Fisher, March 10, 1968; Adam Clayton Powell, Jr., to W. J. Kennedy, Jr., October 6; Kennedy to Powell, October 28, 1932, Kennedy Papers.

30. Interview, Miles Mark Fisher, March 10, 1968.

31. *Ibid.*

Trinity Mission of R. R. Wright, Jr., and the settlement house efforts of Ida Wells-Barnett impressed upon young Fisher the vital role that the church could play in promoting social justice and providing social services. Thus he expected his own church to sponsor relief, recreation, a day nursery, an employment bureau, and adult education courses. "An earth-centered church is my burden," he forewarned the White Rock officers, and he asked them to be prepared for his "social gospel that would be hurled as a thunderbolt against the present day ideas and customs."[32]

This came as no threat to C. C. Spaulding, who also believed in an earth-centered church in much the same sense that Booker T. Washington believed that ministers should not turn the attention of their parishioners from the gospel of self-help in this world. Furthermore, the social aims of Fisher's program reminded Mutual leaders of Dr. Moore. Fisher, too, would round up the waifs and shepherd them into White Rock, the fanciest church in town. And certainly nothing in the Mutual heritage ran counter to the new minister's community center. With assistance from Parrish Street, Fisher organized a summer softball league, put the town toughs on a boxing team, and introduced table tennis to Durham. This latter sport became so popular that Fisher selected a city team which toured as far as Ohio, losing only four matches in ten years. Under his direction White Rock sponsored the Boy Scouts, began a nursery school, established a health clinic, and brought visiting artists and lecturers to the black community.[33]

Given the profound institutional ties between the North Carolina Mutual and White Rock, Fisher's activities reinforced the Company's social tendencies and at the same time boosted its public relations. Moreover, Fisher contributed his own considerable prestige to the Durham scene. He came to White Rock

32. Allen H. Spear, *Black Chicago: The Making of a Negro Ghetto, 1890–1920* (Chicago: University of Chicago Press, 1967), pp. 92–95, 106; Fisher, *Friends*, pp. 27–28.

33. *Ibid.*; interviews, Miles Mark Fisher, March 10; W. J. Kennedy, Jr., January 26, 1968; Frank Hallowell White, "The Economic and Social Development of Negroes in North Carolina since 1900" (Ph.D. dissertation, New York University, 1960), p. 187.

certified not only in divinity, but carrying a master's degree in history from the University of Chicago. With Spaulding's moral and financial support he returned to Chicago each summer until he completed the Ph.D. degree. His dissertation under the church historian William Warren Sweet grew into a prize-winning publication, *Negro Slave Songs in the United States* (Cornell University Press, 1953), and his articles appeared in scholarly journals, including the *Journal of Negro History* and *Church History*. He taught classes in church history and theology at Shaw University in Raleigh and lectured at other Negro colleges and churches around the country.[34] He wrote many of Spaulding's speeches, including one in which he had him chastise the Fraternal Council of Negro Churches for not addressing itself to "low wages, housing, health, unemployment, peace and war," and for overlooking "that . . . the money for our churches comes from the labor of the lowly." "Our churches," read Spaulding, "have not espoused the just cause of labor along with the right claims of capital."[35]

Fisher was a remarkable combination of intellect and emotion, old-time religion and the social gospel, lower-class sympathies with upper-class training and station—all of which seemed quite compatible with White Rock's hierarchy from the North Carolina Mutual. His social gospel and sense of history united the traditions of mutual aid and distinctive worship in Afro-American religion. Under his guidance White Rock became an extraordinary institution, clearly exceptional to the stereotyped church of the black bourgeoisie. To lure the common folk Fisher invited a well-known revivalist to preach at White Rock, and he recalled that he could scarcely determine "who had the better time . . . White Rock or holiness people."[36] Fisher's intense appreciation of Afro-American culture and his eloquent interpretation of slave religion encouraged Spaulding and others to take pride in their

34. Fisher, *Friends*, pp. 34–36; interview, Miles Mark Fisher, March 10, 1968.

35. C. C. Spaulding speeches, "Functions of the Negro Church in the Economic Life of the Negro," June 29, 1939; "The Job of the Church," n.d.; and untitled speech before the Baptist state convention, Shaw University, August 5, 1942, Spaulding Papers.

36. Fisher, *Friends*, p. 16; interview, Miles Mark Fisher, March 10, 1968.

folk origins, while at the same time his scholarly sermons on Buddhism, Hinduism, and Islam introduced them to a wider world.[37] Like his father, he inspired "enthusiastic religion" but did not "countenance pandemonium."[38] He commanded his congregation to cherish "Negro songs and spirituals" without being "narrow to . . . the music of world masters."[39] He glorified the folkways of the country church, but with Spaulding's hearty approval he "trained White Rock worshippers to assemble on time."[40]

The relative peace that settled over White Rock under the tenure of the Reverend Fisher can be attributed in large measure to the shared platform of racial uplift which formed a bridge between Spaulding's fundamentalism and Fisher's social gospel. However, Spaulding could not comfortably endorse his pastor's advocacy of the welfare state or his conspicuous involvement in the labor movement. When Fisher opened White Rock to organizers in the AFL Tobacco Workers International, Spaulding sounded a familiar theme: "'Those who are in authority and giving employment to our people are watching every move we make." He explained that the white power structure held him responsible, and he suggested that "it might be well for the Union to meet elsewhere." But Fisher held fast long enough to give life to the local union, and Spaulding made no move to censure him.[41]

If Fisher's commitment to uplift blunted ideological dissension, the more important reason for his long coexistence with the Mutual was his ability to share power. With absorbing outside interests and the security of his Ph.D., Fisher felt no compulsion to take sides in petty strife, to administer the mundane, to count and handle the money. Unlike those before him, he happily turned over to the professional managers at the Mutual a large

37. Fisher, *Friends*, p. 33.
38. Miles Mark Fisher, *The Master's Slave: Elijah Fisher, a Biography* (Philadelphia: Judson Press, 1922), pp. 87–88.
39. Fisher, *Friends*, p. 33.
40. *Ibid.*, p. 14; interview, Miles Mark Fisher, March 10, 1968.
41. C. C. Spaulding to Miles Mark Fisher, April 24, 1939; interviews, Miles Mark Fisher, March 10; W. J. Kennedy, Jr., January 26, 1968; Fisher, *Friends*, p. 21.

sector of his administrative duties while he attended to larger issues. He sensed no threat to his importance, for example, when Spaulding became critical of the choir and ordered a member of the Mutual Glee Club to improve its harmony.[42]

Yet he remembered how difficult it was to avoid becoming "Spaulding's man." Spaulding, while frugal to a fault in business matters, indulged in personal philanthropy to such an extent "that people had to watch over him to see that he didn't give everything away."[43] Spaulding knew about Andrew Carnegie's "gospel of wealth," and the shadow of Dr. Moore fell across his every act. He saw himself as the Christian steward of the community's wealth and honor, and he practiced an often unconscious but nonetheless domineering paternalism. Whenever Fisher identified a destitute family, Spaulding dispensed the aid. And Fisher himself became the subject of the president's overpowering philanthropy. Whenever Fisher appeared at the Mutual, Spaulding embarrassed him with personal gifts. "Is that your best pair of shoes," he would ask rhetorically as he pushed twenty dollars into the minister's pocket. As if he were Fisher's "papa," too, he sent the scholar-pastor "a little change to use in any way you wish"[44] during his summer studies in Chicago. In 1938 Fisher found himself the owner of a new Oldsmobile, presented by officers of the North Carolina Mutual and the White Rock congregation.[45] Finally, in 1945 Fisher turned restive under the obliging pressures of Parrish Street and charged Spaulding with trying to "Mutualize" the church. The rupture eventually healed—imperfectly however, for Spaulding could never understand in this instance that his style of support led to subtle control, or that cooperation, even among black institutions, had a point of diminishing returns.[46]

42. C. C. Spaulding to Mrs. S. V. Norfleet, March 29, 1935, Spaulding Papers; interview, Miles Mark Fisher, March 10, 1968.

43. Interview, Miles Mark Fisher, March 10, 1968.

44. *Ibid.*; C. C. Spaulding to Miles Mark Fisher, August 13, 1940, Spaulding Papers.

45. Fisher, *Friends*, pp. 34–35.

46. Letters from C. C. Spaulding to Miles Mark Fisher, July 21, 1945; Deacon Board, White Rock Baptist Church, July 29; W. C. Laster, September 19,

But Spaulding saw no reason why the Mutual spirit could not become the Durham spirit. He compared the Company and its sister enterprises to the hub and spokes within a "wheel of racial progress" that ultimately stood to encompass every community institution in a utopian drive for a self-sufficient black metropolis.[47] Such a notion occupied a prominent position in Afro-American thought, and in his wistful moments Spaulding could easily believe that the Company *was* the community and vice versa. It seemed only natural that the Mutual should extend itself into the affairs of other black institutions, that it should have a social gospel of its own. "Our salesmen are also social workers," Spaulding wrote to a Negro nurse in Charleston.[48] "All of us have to do some things aside from our regular jobs," he reminded his district manager, A. E. Spears. He called on Spears to investigate prison camps in the Charlotte area, "where Negroes are not receiving a square deal," and to report his findings to the Commission on Interracial Cooperation.[49]

The social tendencies which had characterized the Company under the leadership of Dr. Moore did not diminish with his death. Avery, Kennedy, and Spaulding, among others, assumed the obligation and pursued a course which led the Mutual further afield. Spaulding and Kennedy, for example, labored during the 1920's to establish black branches of the YWCA and the YMCA in Durham. While partially successful, this movement was less significant than the Company's effort to establish another youth organization, the John Avery Boys Club, initiated largely by the Mutual's W. D. Hill and a white judge, Mamie

1946; Fisher to James E. Shepard, October 24, 1945, Spaulding Papers; interview, Miles Mark Fisher, March 10, 1968.

47. "The Durham Group Wheel of Progress," undated promotional pamphlet on Negro business in Durham; National Negro Business League, "Durham: The City of Progress," 1933, pamphlet announcing 1933 NNBL convention in Durham, also pictured black institutions in Durham as a self-contained wheel of racial cooperation, Spaulding Papers.

48. C. C. Spaulding to Mrs. Margaret Lawrence, December 17, 1943, Spaulding Papers. In order to keep a professional black social worker in Hayti, Parrish Street subsidized the salary, a rather unusual arrangement for the pay of a municipal employee (C. C. Spaulding to Mechanics and Farmers Bank, September 2, 1937, Spaulding Papers).

49. C. C. Spaulding to A. E. Spears, Sr., September 1, 1937, Spaulding Papers.

Dowd Walker, and chartered in 1939 with Kennedy as president.[50] After World War II Parrish Street persuaded the city to purchase the USO building in the black community, which in memory of a Mutual executive became the William D. Hill Community Center. Hill and John H. Wheeler, an officer of the Mechanics and Farmers Bank, had brought the USO to black Durham in the first place, but it took C. C. Spaulding to convince the city council to turn the building into a community center.[51] The Company's interest in youth and philanthropy earned Spaulding a place on the national executive committee of the YMCA; his national speaking and organizing efforts for the Boy Scouts of America brought him similar recognition in that organization, including a dramatic reading of his life story at the Valley Forge National Jamboree in 1950. Kennedy became equally prominent in the Boys Clubs of America through his success with the John Avery Club in Durham.[52]

Given the profound importance of education in Afro-American culture, along with the Company's keenness on public relations, it is not surprising that the Mutual began its own scholarship program. Established in 1932, the Merrick-Moore Scholarship Fund provided one scholarship in every state within the Mutual territory for students with "character, initiative and financial need" who were successfully pursuing a business degree at a black college within that state.[53]

In addition to its private efforts, the Mutual maintained its involvement in youth affairs through the public institutions of North Carolina. After Dr. Moore's death Spaulding became the

50. C. C. Spaulding to J. H. McGrew, July 28, 1931, Spaulding Papers; C. A. Witherspoon to W. J. Kennedy, Jr., November 10, 1927; W. J. Kennedy, Jr., minutes of YMCA organizational meeting, Durham, N.C., October 14–15, 1924; also Report of Durham Committee on Colored Older Boys Conference, November 10, 1927, Kennedy Papers; Historical Report on the John Avery Boys Club, 1961, Rencher Harris Papers, Manuscript Collections, Duke University Library.

51. *Whetstone*, second quarter, 1947; interview, John H. Wheeler, April 3, 1972.

52. Receipts from the YMCA, March 5, November 20, 1931; C. C. Spaulding to R. H. King, December 27, 1935; Weaver M. Marr to Spaulding, January 28, 1948, Spaulding Papers; *Whetstone*, fourth quarter, 1940, third quarter, 1952; clipping, *Durham Sun*, February 22, 1951, North Carolina Mutual clipping files.

53. *Whetstone*, October, 1937, first quarter, 1943. The scholarships amounted to $100 per year for each student.

most influential trustee of the Oxford Orphanage. While he could and did on occasion pick the president of the institution, he preferred to play a less exalted role, raising funds, channeling boys into the orphanage, and finding homes and adoptive parents for those already there.[54]

Spaulding worried more about delinquents than he did about orphans, however. For a number of years he had protested the absence of a reform school for blacks, while the state, using his tax money, supported two such segregated institutions for white youths. In 1927 white leaders agreed that there ought to be at least one parallel institution; thus the legislature created the Morrison Training School for Negro Boys, and the governor appointed Spaulding chairman of its board of trustees.[55]

Spaulding took more than a passing interest in the new school. He saw himself as a social reformer advocating rehabilitation rather than punishment. Through his contacts with the Rosenwald Fund he arranged for Morrison parolees to receive industrial training at Hampton and Tuskegee, but he took greater pride in his personal contacts with the boys, inviting them to visit his office each Saturday, taking them to the Mutual Forum and home for lunch. His belief in original sin gave way before his environmentalism as he argued that the boys were basically good, but had been corrupted by "bad company" and the evils of urban life. Contradicting his own example of success in the city, he counseled black youths to remain in the country. In fact, to head off delinquency he sometimes sent black boys from Durham down to Columbus County for a few weeks. "I am sending you a boy who won't go to school," he wrote to a relative. "He is not a bad boy, but he needs to get away from the city and work with horses and mules for awhile."[56]

Spaulding's naïve belief that he could treat the ills of society

54. See Oxford Orphanage file in Spaulding Papers, box labeled by author as "Community and Institutions."

55. Typescript report on the Morrison Training School, October 19, 1931, Spaulding Papers.

56. Letters from C. C. Spaulding to O. H. Lennon, September 19, 1938; to E. R. Embree, April 13, 1931; to James Blackwell, October 25, 1933, Spaulding Papers.

with personal attention to individual cases probably accounted for his belated discovery that the institution he presided over had become a medieval hell-hole. On an unannounced visit to Morrison in 1935 he found, among other unspeakable conditions, no bathing facilities, no bed linen, no toilet tissue, no telephone, and 215 boys sleeping in 144 single beds. At Spaulding's insistence, the state relieved the worst of the conditions, but two years later he resigned, realizing that he could never reconcile his idealism with a Jim Crow institution so clearly designed to violate the ideal.[57]

However, this realization reinforced his faith in the importance of legitimate black institutions like the Mutual—institutions created and controlled by race men. Thus projecting the Company into the community, always Spaulding's forte, became his preoccupation by the mid-1930's, and in the collective mind of the black public the North Carolina Mutual and C. C. Spaulding became interchangeable conceptions. Letters came to Durham addressed simply, "Mr. Spaulding, Negro Insurance Company."[58] Paradoxically, as the president played a decreasing role in the highly successful administration of the Company, he received an increasing share of the recognition for that success. He personified not only the success on Parrish Street, but also the progress of the race. Surviving the Depression, in contrast to the dramatized collapse of the National Benefit Life, added immeasurably to the prestige of the Mutual and hence of Spaulding. He emerged as the undisputed leader of the black business world, and his much-publicized tour of Europe in 1931, a bold stroke taken to allay fear and to raise morale, enhanced his and the Mutual's image of invincibility.

Spaulding had received nationwide interracial recognition as early as 1926, when he won the prestigious Harmon Foundation Award for achievement in business. By the time of his death in 1952 he had received so many additional awards, honors, and

57. Undated report, "Observations Made at the Morrison Training School"; letters from C. C. Spaulding to Thad L. Tate, October 4; to F. L. Dunlap, October 25, 1935; to L. L. Boyd, July 26, 1937, Spaulding Papers.

58. See, for example, Lee Roy Sweat to C. C. Spaulding, January 21, 1939, Spaulding Papers.

degrees, served on so many boards and committees, and addressed so many conferences and conventions that it would be virtually impossible to list them.[59] His exposure in the black press multiplied with the Company's every annual report, with his every speech. Company news and personal news coincided, and both were construed as racial news, a cultural gift of publicity for the Mutual. As a public figure he could issue press releases at will; moreover, white leaders often gave him access to the radio waves, including a broadcast in 1939 from the New York World's Fair.[60] The Association for the Study of Negro Life and History added his picture to its gallery of black notables. He found his way into J. A. Rogers's *Great Men of Color* and Langston Hughes's *Famous Negroes*. The need for heroes blurred the distinction between him and Frederick Douglass. In the days preceding each Negro History Week, his office was besieged with requests for biographical sketches and photographs. Schoolchildren wrote poems about him; black townspeople

59. Clipping, *Durham Morning Herald*, January 2, 1927, Kennedy Scrapbook. A partial listing of the positions Spaulding held would include: president, North Carolina Mutual Life Insurance Company, Mechanics and Farmers Bank, Mutual Savings and Loan Association; vice-president, Bankers Fire Insurance Company, Southern Fidelity Mutual Insurance Company; trustee, Howard University, North Carolina College, Shaw University, Oxford Colored Orphanage, White Rock Baptist Church, Stanford L. Warren Colored Library, Lincoln Hospital, John F. Slater Fund; president, National Negro Business League; vice-president, American Bible Society; secretary-treasurer, North Carolina Commission on Interracial Cooperation; vice-chairman, United Negro College Fund; vice-president, National Committee of the Urban League; member: Southern Education Foundation, Durham County Selective Service Board, Association for the Study of Negro Life and History, National Committee for the American Celebration of the 100th Anniversary of Liberia, National Planning Association Committee of the South, New York State Chamber of Commerce, North Carolina Council for National Defense, North Carolina War Fund Campaign, National USO Council, State Medical and Hospital Care Commission of North Carolina; board of directors, John Avery Boys Club, 4-H Club Foundation of North Carolina; executive committee, General Baptist State Convention; National Council, Boy Scouts of America; American Aid for Ethiopia Incorporated; National Association of Teachers in Colored Schools. See *Whetstone*, third quarter, 1952.

60. Mrs. S. H. Cleland to W. J. Kennedy, Jr., August 7, 1939, Kennedy Papers; C. C. Spaulding to Lester A. Walton, April 19, 1939; typescript of C. C. Spaulding, radio addresses, WDNC, Durham, N.C., June 10, 1934; August 9, 1943; "The Negro in Business," broadcast on "Wings over Jordan" program, Columbia Broadcasting System, Atlanta, Ga., March 26, 1939, copies in Spaulding Papers; *Whetstone*, April, 1934.

named their schools and streets after him. He spent much of his time answering fan mail. During the 1940's *Ebony, Readers' Digest,* and the *Saturday Evening Post* put his story and that of the Mutual into public view more than ever before. The premium on race leadership, the wartime need to convince blacks of democracy on the home front, and America's traditional Algerism all converged in the useful image of Spaulding and the Mutual.[61]

Spaulding did not retreat before the limelight. After all, had not Booker T. Washington predicted that universal recognition would follow economic achievement? Of course, he understood the business advantages of publicity, but more than that he enjoyed public speaking, loved to pontificate, and had begun to see himself as the self-educated country sage offering practical advice to confused men in difficult times. Piecemeal, he assumed the burden of race leadership. More and more he pondered the fitting epigram for his next speech, the best folklore from the farm, the relevant parable from the Bible, the choice line of Washington's rhetoric which he memorized and catalogued for all occasions.[62]

He had no idea, however, that the burden of race would weigh so heavily. His popular image as the munificent holder of wealth and power cast him in the role of veritable ombudsman

61. Joel Augustus Rogers, *World's Great Men of Color,* 2 vols. (New York: J. A. Rogers, 1947), II, 679–682; Langston Hughes, *Famous American Negroes* (New York: Dodd and Mead, 1954), pp. 105–111; Archibald Rutledge, "They Call Him Co-operation: World's Biggest Negro Business and Its Founder," *Saturday Evening Post,* CXV (March 27, 1943), 215ff.; Charles Clinton Spaulding, "What American Means to Me," *Reader's Digest,* LIV (March, 1949), 22–25; "The Ten Richest Negroes in America," *Ebony,* IV (April, 1949), 10–18; *Whetstone,* March, 1935, first quarter, 1943, third quarter, 1952; letters to C. C. Spaulding from W. T. Andrews, January 17; from Mrs. Carrie N. Pharr, January 29; from Mrs. Jimmie Bugg Middleton, April 12, 1931; from Charles E. Steward, January 11, 1933; from A. S. Scott, March 19, 1934; from Mrs. Lollie B. Hightower, October 8, 1935; from R. R. Wright, Jr., March 3; from Louisa A. Smith, November 30, 1939; from J. W. Eaton, October 5, 1942, Spaulding Papers. Streets, public schools, and business colleges were named after Spaulding in the following North Carolina cities: Durham, Raleigh, Spring Hope, Bladenboro; also in Shreveport and Baton Rouge, Louisiana; Mobile, Alabama; Norfolk, Virginia; and New York City.
62. See C. C. Spaulding personal notes, speeches, daily calendar, and appointment schedules in Spaulding Papers, particularly the 1940's.

for the race. To the black community in Columbus County, for example, he became the leader in absentia, expected to serve as a representative to his constituency. His relatives and their black neighbors counted on him and his staff for assistance in business and legal affairs, and they turned to the Company in times of crisis. When a cousin's house burned down, the call came to Durham asking Spaulding to mobilize the aid. When the black teachers of the county threatened revolt against their white supervisor, it was Spaulding who received their petition and arbitrated their grievance. When he heard about plans for a new hospital in Whiteville, he asked the county commissioners to present evidence that adequate facilities for Negroes would be provided. When told that the county was without a Negro Farm Demonstration Agent, he joined the cause with a letter to the editor in Whiteville and a petition to the state agent in Greensboro. And when he traveled in the community he noted the roads that needed repair, and sent the highway department diplomatic suggestions on a Mutual letterhead.[63]

He went home as often as he could, looking over the crops, checking on taxes, visiting the sick, fishing if he had the time, and usually loading up on country ham, honey, and homemade preserves. His nostalgia added to his burden as community caretaker. When roads to remote farmsteads became impassable, he went visiting by horse and wagon.[64] And when he sensed the deterioration of his once proud community, he tried to intercede as a corrective moral force. "I am deeply interested in my birth-

63. Letters to C. C. Spaulding from Angeline Spaulding, March 10; from Annie E. Spaulding, March 12, 1931; from Willa Easley, June 4, 1941; letters from C. C. Spaulding to Annie Spaulding, March 17, 1931; to Willa Easley, June 10, 1941; to H. G. Avant, chairman, Board of Columbus County Commissioners, n.d.; to Gordon Lewis, July 2; to R. E. Jones, July 2, 1943; to James M. Thompson, July 15, 1939, Spaulding Papers. By virtue of their position in the Mutual, other executives bore a similar burden. When a tornado struck W. J. Kennedy's home town, Americus, Ga., the black community there promptly wired him for assistance (J. D. Anderson to William J. Kennedy, Jr., February 11, 1940, Kennedy Papers).

64. A. T. Spaulding (not Asa) to C. C. Spaulding, October 31, 1930; letters from C. C. Spaulding to Mrs. Aurelia Newell Bellamy, November 7, 1938; to Mrs. Mattie Campbell, September 11, 1944, Spaulding Papers; interview, Asa T. Spaulding, August 4, 1970.

place and have done all I could to guide our people in the right direction," he apologized to a district judge hearing a case against his errant cousin.[65] "It pains me," he added, "that so many of my people are losing the land left them by their parents which is traceable in many instances to drinking and dissipation."[66] On one occasion Spaulding even instructed the county sheriff where to station himself to intercept bootleggers; but when it came time to prosecute one of his cousins, he advised the defense attorney how to deal with white judges "in a personal way in cases involving a Negro" and thus mitigate the sentence. "Also remind the judge," Spaulding suggested, "that while Kern [Spaulding] was the bootlegger, most of the customers were white."[67]

With C. C. Spaulding bearing the "burden of race," the Mutual became all things to all black people: a clearinghouse for Negro business, finance, and law, a bureau of missing persons, an adoption agency, an information center for federal legislation affecting Negroes, a bureau of vital statistics, the Negro equivalent of Dun and Bradstreet, a complaint center, a court of appeal, an employment bureau, and an instrument of philanthropy and political patronage. One could argue that the social demands made on the Mutual suggested an underlying search for community, and that an institution like the Freedmen's Bureau was still very much in order.

A black farmer wrote the Company asking for advice and assistance in patenting his cure for hog cholera.[68] A deserted wife wondered if the firm, with its contacts throughout the South, might know the whereabouts of her delinquent husband.[69] Similarly, a mother in Harlem who suspected her runaway son

65. C. C. Spaulding to W. C. Harris, February 23; Harris to Spaulding, March 4, 1940, Spaulding Papers.

66. C. C. Spaulding to editor, *Whiteville News Reporter*, February 12, 1941, Spaulding Papers.

67. C. C. Spaulding to Homer Lyons, September 19, October 28, 1931, Spaulding Papers.

68. John E. Smith to North Carolina Mutual, January 16; W. J. Kennedy, Jr., to Smith, January 22, 1924, Kennedy Papers.

69. Martha Wilson to North Carolina Mutual, June 26, 1924, Kennedy Papers.

was "alive somewhere down South" wondered if Spaulding would "keep on the lookout."[70] Other distraught mothers and wives, especially during the Depression, wrote the president importuning letters on behalf of their unemployed sons and husbands.[71] Young men themselves wrote by the hundreds, asking not only for employment but also for scholarships to Negro colleges. A black woman in New Jersey told a heartbreaking story of too many children for her meager resources and beseeched Spaulding to find a good home for her son.[72] In other cases Spaulding acted as guardian for country folk whose children migrated North. He asked the younger generation to remember their parents in the South and to send a little something back home, even if just a "few dollars for fertilizer to make a better crop."[73] A white woman on Long Island brought Spaulding her problem, too: could he send her "a reputable colored domestic?"[74] Other whites saw Spaulding as the financial steward of his people and held him accountable for their individual actions. One Tarheel merchant, a complete stranger to Spaulding, complained to him about Negro farmers neglecting their debts. Aside from race, Spaulding had no connection with the indebted sharecroppers from a distant community, yet he acknowledged the burden and pledged "to relieve the condition."[75] In the white department stores of Durham Spaulding served as the supreme credit reference for the black community. Indeed, a new Easter outfit might depend on his approval.[76]

Anybody who wanted to know anything about a black citizen of Durham inquired at the Mutual, and after the passage of the

70. Mrs. Willie B. Hawkins to C. C. Spaulding, October 25, 1941, Spaulding Papers.

71. See, for example, Betty Claiborne to C. C. Spaulding, April 1, 1931; Geneva M. Jones to Spaulding, March 14, 1933, Spaulding Papers.

72. Estelle Mitchell to C. C. Spaulding, November 21; Spaulding to Mitchell, November 28, 1939, Spaulding Papers.

73. C. C. Spaulding to Adelle Smith, April 13, 1931, Spaulding Papers.

74. Mrs. Frank Gottlieb to C. C. Spaulding, July 8, 1943, Spaulding Papers.

75. Walter P. Evans to C. C. Spaulding, November 18; Spaulding to Evans, November 23, 1931, Spaulding Papers.

76. For such an example, see Beatrice M. Suitt to C. C. Spaulding, April 3, 1931, Spaulding Papers.

Social Security Act in 1935 hundreds of letters from policyholders and non-policyholders alike poured into the Company asking
for assistance in the verification of ages for prospective black
pensioners. Spaulding complied and went a step further with
releases to the black press instructing the race on eligibility and
application procedures for the government benefits—an interesting gesture, considering that many insurance companies saw
Social Security as a threat to their existence.[77]

Beyond requests for advice and information, blacks looked to
Spaulding as the rich uncle of the race and the Mutual as his
bankroll. Financial appeals from a burgeoning number of ostensible relatives amounted to more than enough to bankrupt the
president, and these family requests were multiplied by literally
thousands of others from unknown Negroes throughout the nation, the West Indies, and Africa. Despite Spaulding's protests
the myth of the black millionaire followed him to his grave. For
an impoverished race the myth was functional; for whites, en-
chantment with the Mutual story was motivation to reinforce
the myth.[78] Whatever his means, Spaulding gave small sums of
money to an amazing number of requests, some of them rather
eccentric, including five dollars to a bankrupt French interpreter
he had hired on his tour of Europe and twenty-five dollars to a

77. See, for example, Lena Haynes to W. J. Kennedy, Jr., March 2, 1939,
Kennedy Papers; letters from C. C. Spaulding to Mrs. Julia Ross, May 31; to
whom it may concern, November 30, 1937; to Louis E. Austin, July 10, 1946,
Spaulding Papers.

78. I estimate that from 1930 to 1952 the Company received an average of
fifty letters per week requesting gifts and loans, quite apart from policy and
business loans. In its April, 1949, issue *Ebony* magazine referred to Spaulding as
a millionaire and generally pictured him in the overdrawn black bourgeois
rhetoric that he detested. "Mr. Johnson and his group will never realize how
much damage this article has done me," he lamented to Claude A. Barnett of
the Associated Negro Press (March 23, 1949, Spaulding Papers). Also see
Spaulding to Carl Goerch, editor of a North Carolina magazine, the *State*, to
whom Spaulding complained of a "gross error as to my alleged wealth. . . . I
have never felt that I could afford a Lincoln, and such cars as I have been able
to buy have been paid for on the usual 12 or 18 month plan" (Spaulding to
Goerch, September 29, 1943, Spaulding Papers). It would appear from Spaulding's tax returns and financial statements that his complaints were justified.
During the last twenty years of his presidency, his annual salary averaged less
than $15,000. When he died in 1952 he owned a small bank account, insignifi-
cant securities, $66,000 in real estate, and $76,000 in life insurance.

black aviator who proposed to inspire an Afro-American aviation industry.[79]

Indeed, there must have been a thousand ways in which Spaulding could "pay his dues." Would he like to speak at a commencement; at celebrations of Emancipation Day or Negro History Week; at Robert Smalls Day in South Carolina; at a Jersey Cattle Show in North Carolina? Would he give a hundred dollars toward the publication of Edgar Thompson's *Race and Region*; a similar amount to sponsor J. A. Rogers's research in Negro history; purchase band uniforms for a Negro high school; buy a bedpan sterilizer for Lincoln Hospital; deliver a "pep talk" to the staff of the *Carolina Times*; send "100 words of holiday cheer" to the subscribers of the *Baltimore Afro-American*; organize North Carolina for the Association of Negro Life and History; give Gunnar Myrdal entry to the black community of Durham; supply Guy Johnson with Negro speakers for his sociology classes; finance an exposition of Afro-American songs and poetry at the New York World's Fair? Would he participate in a Washington ceremony unveiling the portraits of the Negro Recorders of Deeds; attend a tea in honor of Channing Tobias at the New York apartment of Dr. William Jay Schieffelin; serve as escort for Mary McCleod Bethune in a Shaw University pageant honoring her as "Queen of the Negro Race?"[80] If the burden of race had limits of logic and geography, perhaps they were strained to full extension when in 1952 a Japanese social worker

79. James Franklyn to C. C. Spaulding, August 25; Spaulding to Franklyn, September 12, 1934; Spaulding to Jessie L. Boland, February 19, 1931, Spaulding Papers.

80. W. Kent Alston to C. C. Spaulding, January 23; Spaulding to Alston, March 21, 1941; R. L. Hannon to Spaulding, August 30, 1946; John H. Jones to Spaulding, January 5, 1942; N. C. Newbold to Spaulding, July 28, 1938; Spaulding to Carl Murphy, June 23, 1931; Spaulding to W. M. Rich, September 6, 1945; James A. B. Hubbard to Spaulding, October 14, 1940; Louis E. Austin to Spaulding, January 26, 1939; Carl Murphy to Spaulding, December 14, 1937; Carter G. Woodson to Spaulding, January 25; Guy B. Johnson to Spaulding, October 17; Gunnar Myrdal to Spaulding, November 24; Spaulding to Myrdal and Richard Sterner, November 29; W. A. Morgan to Spaulding, April 21, 1938; William J. Thompkins to Spaulding, November 21, 1936; Spaulding to William Jay Schieffelin, December 10, 1937; Spaulding to Sarah M. Eason, December 8, 1938. Spaulding spoke at so many commencements that he occasionally lost track of his cap and gown (Spaulding to Frederick D. Patterson, March 24, 1938; May 11, 1943, all material in Spaulding Papers).

wrote the Company asking if it did not want to share the responsibility for supporting the orphaned offspring of Japanese women and black American soldiers.[81]

The most insistent requests for aid, however, came from Africa, primarily from Nigerian students who revealed a naïveté about America and a contrived approach to the "black millionaire." Their appeals introduced an ironic twist to economic pan-Africanism; namely, that Spaulding as a black man was obligated to redeem Africa, not by returning or by investing in the homeland, but by bringing Africans to America, where (following his example) they could lift themselves out of poverty. Since "local philanthropists do not lend a help," one student wrote, "why should I not look across the seas to 'God's land' where the success and freedom of the Negro race depend on self-help. . . . Won't you help me 'my blood.' "[82] Many of the students thought Spaulding might send for them, pay their way through Howard University, and then provide them employment at the Mutual. Their view of racial solidarity nearly reversed the notion of African repatriation: "As much as I know that I am writing to a Negro, I present my request [to come to America] as a son asking for an obligation from his father."[83]

West Indian blacks had a more realistic view of the Mutual. More often than not they invited the Company to finance a business venture in the islands, to establish an agency in Nassau before "another American insurance company comes down here," or to invest in Cuban sugar and build "a rum factory in Miami."[84] As a rule the Mutual rejected the myriad proposals

81. Chuzo Nagano to C. C. Spaulding, June 29, 1952, Spaulding Papers.

82. S. Udoh to C. C. Spaulding, October 6, 1950, Spaulding Papers.

83. Mosobalaje Oyawoye to C. C. Spaulding, June 15, 1950, Spaulding Papers. Spaulding received a great number of letters from Nigeria in the summer of 1950 because the *West African Pilot* reprinted the piece from *Ebony* and another from the *Reader's Digest*. To the editor of the *Pilot* Spaulding wrote, "I am the salaried officer of a mutual company which is itself limited in its gifts, and neither I nor the North Carolina Mutual are financially able to accommodate them [requests for money]" (C. C. Spaulding to editor of *West African Pilot*, August 25, 1950, Spaulding Papers).

84. L. W. Duvalier to C. C. Spaulding, August 25, 1931; Alonzo G. Morón to Spaulding, February 21, 1934; Jose Garcia to Spaulding, September 8, 1937, Spaulding Papers.

asking that it support efforts in black capitalism on an international scale, particularly in the African or Afro-Caribbean export trade.[85]

On one occasion Spaulding did join R. R. Wright, Sr., the prominent black banker and educator in Philadelphia, to sponsor the import and sale of Haitian coffee to black communities in the eastern United States. The coffee trade (reminiscent of Garveyism) followed a trip to Haiti in 1937 by Spaulding, Wright, Elder Lightfoot Michaux, and other black leaders who claimed to be on a "good-will mission" for President Roosevelt, as well as examining the possibilities for Afro-American economic cooperation with the "sovereign black republic."[86]

Most of Spaulding's energy in economic cooperation continued to be spent on behalf of the National Negro Business League. He had helped the League survive a time of uncertainty after Washington's death in 1915, and now during the Depression he saw it facing a far greater crisis. Just as the panic began, the League launched what was probably its most ambitious project, the Colored Merchants Association, a grocers' cooperative based in Harlem which marketed its own CMA brands and promised to bring an important retail business in the black community under black control. But hard times and dissension killed the CMA and nearly brought down the NNBL as well.[87]

In 1933 the League succeeded in holding its traditional convention only because the Mutual brought the meeting to Durham and provided the necessary money and facilities. In 1934, for the first time in its long history, the League held no annual con-

85. See for example, L. A. Champon to C. C. Spaulding, September 30; Spaulding to Champon, October 4, 1938, Spaulding Papers. Champon addressed his letter to "C. C. Spaulding, American Millionaire" and asked him to invest $50,000 in a Nigerian export business that would cut out the European middleman.

86. Letters from C. C. Spaulding to A. L. Lewis, February 6; to Floyd J. Calvin, April 7; to O. H. Lennon, April 27; to Elder Lightfoot Michaux, May 4; to M. S. Stuart, July 9; letters to C. C. Spaulding from Ira F. Lewis, February 22; from R. R. Wright, Sr., July 2, 1937, Spaulding Papers; *Durham Sun*, April 26; *Whetstone*, May, 1937.

87. Gunnar Myrdal, *An American Dilemma* (New York: Harper and Row, 1944), II, 802, 815, 816; Albon L. Holsey, "The CMA Stores Face the Chains," *Opportunity*, VII (July, 1929), 210–213; Albon L. Holsey to C. C. Spaulding, October 29, 31; Spaulding to Holsey, November 21, 1934, Spaulding Papers.

vention, nor could it finance another until Spaulding reorganized the League in 1938. In the meantime many leaders considered the NNBL defunct, and Spaulding protested that "the Negro seemingly believes more in individualism than in cooperation."[88] Spaulding grieved over the demise of the League much as if it were the Mutual that was dying. In his view both institutions expressed the legacy of Booker T. Washington, and he was thoroughly hostile to any suggestion that the League could not be saved. After persistent but futile efforts to raise funds, including petitions to New Deal agencies, Spaulding in 1937 managed at least an ad hoc convention in Atlanta, where the delegates made him president in place of the ailing R. R. Moton and gave him a mandate to resuscitate the League. With characteristic vigor he carried his campaign for cooperation to twenty major cities ranging from Chicago and New York in the North to Charleston and New Orleans in the South. He awakened old loyalties and at the same time served notice that the NNBL needed new blood. He took the 1938 convention to a fresh site (Houston, Texas), and with the success of that convention and the apparent rescue of the League he handed the reins to younger men and consented to serve after 1938 only as "President Emeritus."[89]

That the Mutual assisted the League in surviving to the present time as one of the oldest Afro-American institutions is a point worth making here, but more important is the illustration

88. C. C. Spaulding to Harrison S. Jackson, September 1, 1934, Spaulding Papers.

89. Letters from C. C. Spaulding to Albon L. Holsey, October 3, November 22, December 14, 1933; January 12, November 21, 1934; January 14, April 21, 30, June 11, 1936; January 29, 1938; Holsey to Spaulding, September 30, October 7, November 13, 23, December 13, 21, 1933; February 12, 1934; January 10, April 14, 23, May 15, December 14, 1936; February 25, 1938; letters from C. C. Spaulding to R. R. Moton, January 12; to Harrison S. Jackson, September 1; to Eugene Kinckle Jones, November 10, 1934; to John P. Davis, May 7; to Robert Weaver, May 7, 1935; to F. B. Ransom, July 17, 1936; to Fred R. Moore, July 2; to J. B. Blayton, August 13, 1937; to R. R. Moton, February 24, 1938; letters to C. C. Spaulding from Clark Foreman, December 12, 1933; from Harrison S. Jackson, August 23, 1934; from Eugene Kinckle Jones, April 18, 1935; from Fred R. Moore, August 11; from Monroe Work, September 24; from J. C. Napier, October 14, 1937. Also see minutes of NNBL executive committee held at Tuskegee Institute, November 25, 1935; Albon L. Holsey, typescript report of NNBL meeting in Atlanta, Ga., August 18–20; and *Whetstone*, August, 1937. All above materials in Spaulding Papers.

of how black statesmen played out their lives in a restricted, subterranean world of ethnic trade associations when a truly democratic society could have enriched itself with their talents at the highest levels of national life. For the subculture itself, the point is that the Mutual stood as a salient institution which attracted a heavy burden of responsibility to that culture. This burden was the additional price of success paid by black leaders and their institutions, as well as by certain other ethnic groups in America. In theory, of course, the burden meant much more. It meant opportunity—the opportunity to secure at one and the same time cultural integrity and cultural accommodation in what often seemed an alien land.

8

The Company
and the Community:
Politics and
Race Relations

If the Company attracted more attention than its size and economic function would dictate, it did so not only because of the burden of race but because of C. C. Spaulding's remarkable flair for public relations. His close friend and traveling companion A. E. Spears remembers how Spaulding, with an air of mystery and drama, would ride through the rural South in his chauffeur-driven Buick, tossing literature from his window to black folks congregated at intersections and country stores.[1] In any case, by the 1930's the Company appeared conspicuously as a sphere of influence that might act in some small way to enrich the poor, to empower the powerless; it might act, Spaulding acknowledged, "as a service station to the race."[2] Inevitably part of that service and much of its function within the black community became political.

It has been argued earlier that the very existence of the Mutual was a political fact, albeit a negative one, that arose out of the denial of positive political alternatives at the turn of the century. One could argue, moreover, that the question of race relations made every black institution a political institution. The Mutual's survival in the white South was based in no small part on the carefully cultivated politics of John Merrick—the politics

1. A. E. Spears, Sr., Founders Day speech, "C. C. Spaulding as I Knew Him," October 20, 1967.
2. C. C. Spaulding to J. K. Doughton, February 13, 1933, Spaulding Papers.

of no politics. Such, of course, was the style of Booker T. Washington, possibly the greatest politician in Afro-American history. C. C. Spaulding inherited the style, and even when buried in the depths of political intrigue he intuitively protested, "I am a businessman, not a politician."

The political life of the Company, however, has never been altogether traditional or static. Instead there has been a pattern of evolution which appears to be reciprocally linked to what has been referred to here as the burden of race. The positions of racial ombudsman and politician formed inseparable sides of the same coin—that is, a token of black power that could be used to purchase favors in the white domain. Insofar as the Mutual could deliver these favors frequently enough to reinforce its image of influence, it acquired political power in its own right. The demands for philanthrophy assumed that the Company possessed power, and the Company possessed power because it could on occasion meet the demands. Obviously the same could be said about patronage. Unlike Negro principals or college presidents whose existence depended directly on white legislatures, Mutual leaders, with their all-black constituency, were relatively invulnerable to white economic sanctions. Spaulding also had genuine respect in both the black and white communities, quite different from the much-maligned "Uncle Tom" figures who surfaced in the political life of many southern cities as the white man's idea of a black leader. Spaulding successfully sought the middle ground in the no-man's land of race politics at a time when generally no such position existed in the South.[3]

That he found and occupied this slender territory is not only a tribute to his inimitable skill as race diplomat but an indication that he worked from a strong institutional base, also quite the exception for a black community leader in the South. He had so

3. Everett Carll Ladd, Jr., *Negro Political Leadership in the South* (Ithaca: Cornell University Press, 1966), p. 198, for example, describes Negro politics in the period before World War II as so completely constrained by the rigidity of race relations, with each side believing, "All those who are not for us are against us," that a middle ground was impossible to find. Also see Gunnar Myrdal, *An American Dilemma*, 2 vols. (New York: Harper and Row, 1944), II, 720; and Guy B. Johnson, "Negro Racial Movements and Leadership in the United States," *The American Journal of Sociology*, XLIII (July, 1937), 71.

elevated the image of the Mutual that it served as much more than an errand boy between the races; conversely, the Mutual had done the same for him. Like Washington, he still believed successful black businesses held the key to the future of Negro politics in the sense that a self-help organization like the North Carolina Mutual could better unlock the doors to political freedom than could a protest organization like the NAACP. He would not rule out protest, however, and he pragmatically counseled a variety of tactics. As it turned out, he and other Company leaders, especially the younger and more militant officers of the subordinate enterprises on Parrish Street, came to play an important role in the decline of the classic conservative model of Negro politics in the South. They provided a transition between the old politics and the new, between the timid politics of indirection and the undisguised use and organization of the electoral process.

Prerequisite to its politics, but generally without political motivation, the North Carolina Mutual by World War II had built itself into a clearinghouse for Negro philanthropy in the upper South. First, there were the literally thousands of appeals for personal aid. For the most part these requests were without political significance, except those in Durham, where President Spaulding might in turn expect individual loyalty on political issues. Second, and more important, were the constant appeals from Negro institutions. At the close of the Depression and increasingly throughout the 1940's the Mutual gave thousands of dollars annually to black institutions. Negro colleges and churches received the lion's share, but sizable amounts went to the Urban League, the NAACP, the YMCA, and countless lesser organizations, including $125 to the allegedly communist National Negro Congress.[4]

4. Letters from John P. Davis to C. C. Spaulding, January 29, September 10, 1937; April 27, 1939; letters from Spaulding to Davis, February 3, September 30, 1937; March 30, October 16, 1939, Spaulding Papers. It is not always easy to distinguish contributions which came out of Company funds from those that were simply collections taken up among officers and employees. In many cases it was clearly the latter, as the Company was limited in its contributions by state

But the Mutual's own philanthropy was much less important than the promise of what it might stimulate from others. The legendary relationship between the Duke family and the Mutual led some to believe that C. C. Spaulding held a blank check from the Duke Endowment. Beyond this vital connection, Spaulding in 1931 became the first Negro ever elected to the board of the Slater Fund, and in the meantime he had built the early contacts between Dr. Moore and the Rosenwald Fund into a close, working institutional relationship in which the Company served as a regional broker for Rosenwald money, scholarships, and employment.[5] With this in mind, virtually every black institution at one time or another offered Spaulding a position on its board and accorded him and the Company uncommon deference. "I hope you can tap the 'big sources,'" a black college president wrote to Spaulding. "In fact I know you can do that better than anyone else," he praised, perhaps even so well that the college could build a new "C. C. Spaulding Library."[6] In the words of Mary McCleod Bethune, Spaulding was the man who could "set in

---

laws governing mutual insurance firms. In either case the Company provided the financial base for the philanthropy, and in the mind of the black public a gift from C. C. Spaulding and a gift from the Company were indistinguishable. During the Depression, Spaulding parlayed up to $500 per month for Shaw University by leading a joint drive within the Mutual and the White Rock Church. Spaulding himself gave $50 per month for a time. See letters from Spaulding to O. S. Bullock, December 23; to C. S. Brown, November 30; to Vernon Johns, March 17, 1931, Spaulding Papers. During the prosperous 1940's the Company increased its contributions: $1,000 in 1944 to the United Negro College Fund, for example, and the next year Spaulding personally gave $1,000 to Shaw University. The typical $25 gift to the NAACP in the 1930's became a $100 gift in the 1940's. See letters from Spaulding to Rufus E. Clement, July 1, 1944; to Milton Starr, February 27, 1945; to Harry Emerson Fosdick, November 19, 1947; to Walter White, November 27, 1931; October 9, 1933; April 12, 1948; White to Spaulding, October 13, 1938; April 30, 1948; W. E. B. Du Bois to Spaulding, April 1, 1934, Spaulding Papers. A good many of the Company's smaller gifts were clearly directed toward public relations: "We find," Kennedy advised the Raleigh district, "that contributions, however small the amount, to [Negro] churches, colleges and orphanages do more good than a much larger sum spent in newspaper advertising" (W. J. Kennedy to H. C. Brower, March 29, 1938, Kennedy Papers).

5. Letters to C. C. Spaulding from Edwin R. Embree, April 16; from J. H. Dillard, June 22; from Caledonia Simpson, August 10; from J. J. Starks, October 28, 1931, Spaulding Papers.

6. I. M. A. Myers to C. C. Spaulding, September 16, 1937, Spaulding Papers.

motion a rescue campaign" for financially imperiled black colleges, as he did for Bethune-Cookman in 1937.[7]

Shaw University, North Carolina College, and Howard University, the three institutions which Spaulding served simultaneously as trustee, claimed much of his time and energy. He and other Mutual officers made many of the business decisions for Shaw, and when it came time to make formal application for grants from the northern foundations, Spaulding rather than the college president often handled the requests.[8] From within the Slater Fund and the white liberal establishment in general he could direct pressure on every source of philanthropy for Negroes—the General Education Board, for example, when he felt that Shaw had been slighted in the distribution of the Rockefeller funds.[9] Spaulding's greatest asset in these matters was his credibility. He had few enemies and enjoyed almost universal trust. If he said an institution needed funds, nobody questioned his judgment; thus he was a powerful liaison man between the black community and its white benefactors. If he did not write the Rosenwald directors with suggestions for the best placement of their northern-educated Negro physicians and scholars, they wrote him. Moreover, they solicited him for the names of "exceptionally talented Negroes" who might be brought North on Rosenwald Fellowships to keep the cycle going.[10]

He played a less direct role in the affairs of Howard than he did in the affairs of the two North Carolina schools, but even at Howard, where he served on the building committee and the executive committee, he found himself holding more power and responsibility than he cared for. He could influence the choice of contractors and realtors in the building and development pro-

7. C. C. Spaulding to Emmett J. Scott, June 17; Mary McCleod Bethune to Spaulding, September 25, 1937; December 28, 1938, Spaulding Papers.

8. See, for example, Robert P. Daniel, president of Shaw, to C. C. Spaulding, October 7, 1938; C. C. Spaulding to Arthur D. Wright, president of the Slater Fund, March 9; Wright to Spaulding, March 17, 1937, Spaulding Papers.

9. C. C. Spaulding to Arthur D. Wright, March 9, 1937, Spaulding Papers.

10. Letters from C. C. Spaulding to M. O. Bousfield, December 29, 1934; February 4, 7, 1935; January 16, 1939; Bousfield to Spaulding, January 29, 1935; June 4, 1937; George M. Reynolds to Spaulding, July 12, 1939, Spaulding Papers.

gram of Howard, and thus he was inundated with requests to serve as a friend in court, including one urgent appeal from Millard E. Tydings, the powerful senator from Maryland. Tydings asked that Spaulding give favorable consideration to a Maryland architect in the planning of new buildings for Howard.[11]

Through the Mutual Spaulding extended himself into the affairs of the black college as he did in the black church, sometimes more so. Church, school, and business were one in his version of race cooperation. He knew the presidents of the major Negro colleges on a personal basis and viewed them as colleagues, much as he viewed W. J. Kennedy or Asa Spaulding, and he recruited money and personnel for them, as he did for the Mutual.[12] With his wide contacts he became a key figure on the search committees of black colleges. He could reach across institutions. What, for example, did John Hope, president of Morehouse, think of black historian Benjamin Brawley as a candidate for the presidency of Shaw; or how did T. Arnold Hill of the Urban League assess the administrative abilities of theology professor Benjamin Mays for that same position? Did Albon Holsey, secretary of Tuskegee and the NNBL, consider it wise for Spaulding to suggest a successor to Tuskegee President R. R. Moton, as he had been asked to do? A more subtle but nonetheless enviable power was Spaulding's chairmanship of Howard's committee on degrees, from which he could virtually name the annual recipients of honorary degrees from Howard.[13]

Inevitably his activities in college administration led to politics. Because of his reputation for fairness he was sought out as mediator in the internecine warfare of university politics. Perse-

11. James E. Scott to C. C. Spaulding, November 15; Spaulding to V. D. Johnston, November 23; Johnston to Spaulding, November 25; telegram from Millard E. Tydings to C. C. Spaulding, May 12, 1938, Spaulding Papers.

12. Letters from C. C. Spaulding to J. H. Dillard, February 4, 12, 1931; to Benjamin Mays, June 4, 1938; August 5, 1940; to Bibb Graves, governor of Alabama, June 3, 1938; to A. W. Dent, August 27; to Frederick D. Patterson, August 27; to Rufus E. Clement, August 30, 1946; letters to Spaulding from J. H. Dillard, January 30, February 5, 1931; from Bibb Graves, June 6; from Benjamin Mays, July 11, 1938; July 31, 1940, Spaulding Papers.

13. Letters from C. C. Spaulding to John Hope, January 26, 1931; to T. Arnold Hill, April 16, 1936; to A. L. Holsey, December 14, 1934, Spaulding Papers.

cuted professors and deans appealed to him over the heads of college presidents, asserting that only he could bring them justice.[14] Of his own volition Spaulding once tried to patch over the differences between W. E. B. Du Bois and Rufus Clement, president of Atlanta University. He saw no reason why Clement could not simply "talk with Dr. Du Bois and have an understanding."[15] This was the kind of gentle role that he wished to play in campus quarrels. Certainly he was not prepared for the administrative battleground that unfolded at Howard in 1938, when the faculty and administration divided over their loyalty between President Mordecai Johnson and Secretary Emmett J. Scott. Spaulding found himself in the thick of a dispute too large and too distant to yield before his personal negotiations, which had proved effective in the smaller southern schools.[16]

If the Mutual served as a base to introduce Spaulding into the private sector of white money and influence with its attendant politics, it did the same in the public sector, where, through minor appointments and a network of contacts, he became a small power to reckon with. At the onset of the Depression Governor O. Max Gardner appointed him to the North Carolina Council on Unemployment and Relief, or at least to its "Negro Advisory Committee."[17] He held a similar post on President Hoover's Federal Relief Committee; thus his informal private role in Negro welfare took on official public sanction, and his image as community patriarch grew to greater proportions in the minds of destitute black citizens who carried little notes bearing his signature to the relief office.[18]

14. Benjamin Quarles to C. C. Spaulding, September 8, 1935; Charles H. Wesley to Spaulding, June 25, 1938, Spaulding Papers.
15. C. C. Spaulding to Rufus E. Clement, March 29; Clement to Spaulding, April 1, 1944, Spaulding Papers.
16. See letters from C. C. Spaulding to Carl Murphy, April 15, 27; to P. B. Young, April 15, 22; letters to Spaulding from Carl Murphy, April 14, 18; from P. B. Young, April 19; from Raymond Pace Alexander, April 9; clipping, *Chicago Defender*, March 19, 1938, Spaulding Papers.
17. L. A. Oxley to C. C. Spaulding, September 19, 1931, Spaulding Papers.
18. Letters from C. C. Spaulding to R. B. Eleazer, January 4; to A. E. Langston, January 17, December 17, 1933, Spaulding Papers; *Whetstone*, January, 1933.

However, it was President Roosevelt and the New Deal that captured Spaulding's energy and gave him political standing. The Urban League, in coordination with the federal government, appointed Spaulding national chairman of its Emergency Advisory Council, a body organized to "enlist the support of Negroes for the NRA [National Recovery Administration]; to receive complaints of violations affecting Negroes; and to acquaint Negroes with the laws respecting the codes, relief, re-employment, Federal Home Mortgage Loans. . . ."[19] Spaulding took to the New Deal like a worker rather than a businessman, and he sold FDR's program to Negroes as if he were selling insurance. Indeed, in the euphoric days of the first New Deal he was much too enthusiastic a supporter to provide the critical oversight that was as necessary as his salesmanship. He saw Roosevelt administering the nation as he administered the Mutual, pulling people together around the sacred ideas of faith and cooperation, asking that men "obey the Golden Rule and 'reason together.'" He interpreted the NRA as more a national catechism than an economic program, and he urged black teachers to drill their pupils in the codes as part of their citizenship classes. He shamed those who sinned against the codes, lamenting that "some businessmen have blue eagles on the door and black hearts behind the desk." The New Deal tested Spaulding's identity and found a conscious underdog—a black man—rather than a comfortable business executive. He desperately wanted to believe that "President Roosevelt's New Deal marks the beginning of a new era for the Negro." "I thank God," he wrote to a friend, "that the day has come when the spirit of fairness seems to prevail."[20]

While Spaulding was primarily a front man for the New Deal, without commensurate power to oversee or to influence its policies, he did have indirect access to the inner circles of government through FDR's famed black cabinet, several members of which he had recommended for their posts. Robert C. Weaver,

19. *Whetstone*, October, 1933; August, 1934.
20. C. C. Spaulding, typescripts of speeches on the New Deal, see in particular notes dated October 17, 1933; telegram from Spaulding to Franklin D. Roosevelt, June, 1933 (exact date illegible); Spaulding to Pauli Murray, December 12, 1933, Spaulding Papers.

Negro adviser in the Department of the Interior, had once worked for the Mutual. Lawrence Oxley, in the Department of Labor, had gone to Washington from the North Carolina Department of Welfare with Spaulding as his sponsor. Eugene Kinckle Jones, in the Department of Commerce with Spaulding's blessing, had been in contact with the Mutual for years through the Urban League. Similarly, Mary McCleod Bethune, Negro adviser in the National Youth Administration, had a long-standing friendship with Spaulding. Beyond these contacts Spaulding on occasion had the ear of Eleanor Roosevelt, honored guest of the Mutual in 1934, who generally stood well in advance of her husband on racial matters.[21]

With his foot in the door Spaulding maintained a persistent pressure on his black colleagues in Washington. "If Mr. Jones is unable to find a place for you, I shall take up the matter with Mr. Robert Weaver," he assured a black applicant for a federal job.[22] He instructed Negroes on how to save their property through federal assistance from the Home Owner's Loan Corporation, and he worked with Weaver to employ the machinery of the federal government as a delaying tactic against farm foreclosures. To stave off mortgage sales Spaulding spread the word that every black farmer so threatened should apply for a Federal Farm Loan. "Conditions are such now that any firm trying to foreclose property for which federal aid has been applied will meet with resistance," he advised, and he asked Negro ministers to be his couriers. "See to it," he ordered, "that no [Negro] home or farm is sold until the Government has refused to make the loan."[23] Weaver's office, in turn, suggested

21. Letters from C. C. Spaulding to Daniel Roper, Secretary of Commerce, March 7, 1934; to Senator Josiah W. Bailey, January 30, 1933; to Eleanor Roosevelt, December 6, 1934; Mary McCleod Bethune to C. C. Spaulding, December 4, 1936, Spaulding Papers.

22. C. C. Spaulding to Maggie Rivera, March 8, 1934, Spaulding Papers.

23. Letters from C. C. Spaulding to William N. Cooper, August 13; to J. S. Shaw, July 24; to William H. Murray, January 26; to A. L. Holsey, March 6; to Robert Weaver, October 26, 1934; November 27, 1935; Weaver to Spaulding, November 12; William H. Murray to W. J. Kennedy, Jr., January 31, 1934. Spaulding emerged as a liaison man with Washington for other black leaders in the South. His colleague, J. E. Walker, president of Universal Life in Memphis, informed him that "the whole Negro population of Memphis" was counting

that President Spaulding use his network of agents in the South to quietly "gather information" on violations of the NRA.[24] The Company had long experience in collecting intelligence this way. Documenting injustice, however, was one thing; doing something about it was quite another, as Spaulding learned when the euphoria of the "hundred days" wore thin.

His front line of attack had centered on securing employment for blacks on New Deal projects in the South, initially in the Civilian Conservation Corps and the Tennessee Valley Authority, later in the Works Progress Administration. But increasingly he found himself thoroughly frustrated by unwieldy layers of racist bureaucracy and a southern intractability that would not bend before his style of personal politics. To cultivate the good will of one white liberal or even an entire bureau was not enough in such situations.[25] The federal government consistently disappointed Spaulding with its impotence in face of the violations he uncovered. In Durham he found that, under temporary compliance with NRA codes, white hotels had been paying Negro bellhops $6.75 per week, but when the owners discovered the codes were without sanctions, they lowered the wage to $3.50 per week, part of which went to a protection racket. Weaver heard Spaulding's protest and admitted the government's weakness: "After substantiating the evidence presented, it is very doubtful

on him to put Walker "in touch with the proper person on our Black Cabinet. . . ." Walker's cause was the release of federal funds for a PWA Negro school construction project in Memphis. Spaulding wrote directly to Secretary of the Interior Harold Ickes; two weeks later Memphis had the money (J. E. Walker to C. C. Spaulding, September 2; Spaulding to Ickes, September 4; Walker to Spaulding, September 18, 1937). Whites, too, considered Spaulding a man of influence. The president of Durham radio station WDNC, for example, asked Spaulding to speak to the "federal men" on behalf of the station's request to the FCC for an increase in power (C. C. Council to C. C. Spaulding, June 9, 1937, Spaulding Papers).

24. Mabel J. Byrd to C. C. Spaulding, November 17; Spaulding to J. A. Cotton, December 2; Cotton to Spaulding, December 7, 1933, Spaulding Papers.

25. Letters from C. C. Spaulding to A. E. Langston, April 20; to Luther H. Barbour, November 18, 1933; to Mrs. J. W. Holmes, August 8, 1935; to J. B. Blandford, November 15, 1937; letters to C. C. Spaulding from Mrs. J. W. Holmes, August 6, 1935; from W. J. Trent, Jr., November 10; from J. B. Blandford, December 6, 1937, Spaulding Papers.

if the Compliance Director would recommend more than the removal of the Blue Eagles from the offending hotels."[26]

His hopes battered, Spaulding began to share the cynicism of his more critical colleagues, who quipped that the NRA stood for "Negro Removal Administration" and that the trouble with the New Deal was that there were too many "white color" jobs.[27] "Tell me what to say," he challenged Weaver, "and I shall make use of it through the press. Sometimes it helps to smoke them out." Two days after the National Youth Administration was established, Spaulding suggested to Harry L. Hopkins that the NYA might endeavor to be more "democratic" than had the other federal programs.[28]

If Spaulding's dream of a moral and economic renaissance on behalf of blacks in a New South under a New Deal met with constant frustration, he took some consolation in the less important and more symbolic matter of sending hand-picked southern Negroes north to Washington for a token number of federal jobs. At least he could see direct returns, diminishing as they were, from his appeals to Postmaster General James A. Farley, FDR's overseer of patronage; to Secretary of the Interior Harold Ickes; or to Senator Josiah W. Bailey, powerful Democrat from North Carolina. He pushed as hard for an elevator operator's position in the Library of Congress as he did for a federal judgeship in the District of Columbia. Whether or not his influence proved decisive in any single case remains an open question. But it is clear that he did not write national leaders simply because he held an exaggerated view of his own importance. Such an attitude would have been entirely out of character. He never had the time nor the inclination to indulge in idle activity. More-

26. C. C. Spaulding to Robert C. Weaver, August 7; Weaver to Spaulding, September 3; also see copy of Paul R. Hutchings to Weaver, August 27, 1934, Spaulding Papers.

27. C. C. Spaulding, undated speech, Spaulding Papers.

28. C. C. Spaulding to Robert Weaver, June 29; Spaulding to Harry L. Hopkins, June 28, 1935. Spaulding later became a participant in high-level conferences of the NYA (Mary McCleod Bethune to C. C. Spaulding, December 4, 1936; December 22, 1938; Aubrey Williams to Spaulding, January 19, 1939, Spaulding Papers).

over, his acknowledged role as interpreter of the New Deal to the Negro gave him license to lobby white officials in high places who otherwise might have considered him presumptuous. By the end of the 1930's the White House and Congress recognized Spaulding as the key black figure, however restrained, in the North Carolina Democratic party, a recognition which in the 1940's would bring him, among other things, invitations to the presidential inaugurations of 1941 and 1945, as well as offers for a position on the Fair Employment Practices Committee and the post of Minister to Liberia. Obviously the Mutual profited more from Spaulding's debut in national politics than did the black citizens of North Carolina. Nonetheless, it is fair to say that the motivation, insofar as it was conscious, ran the other way. Spaulding believed that the entire race stood to rise or fall on the personal achievements of each of its members. He had long since construed his every success as an indivisible racial success.[29]

The most that can be said about Spaulding and the New Deal is that he expended a tremendous amount of energy, as was his style, for very meager results, an unusual and sobering experi-

29. Letters from C. C. Spaulding to James A. Farley, November 25, 1933; April 24, 1940; to Josiah W. Bailey, March 13, July 3, October 17; to Lester A. Walton, December 6; to Eleanor Roosevelt, December 6; to Franklin D. Roosevelt, November 1, 1934; to Harold D. Cooley, March 5; to Armond W. Scott, May 7, 1935; to Harold Ickes, June 8, 1937; to Frances Perkins, April 28, 1938; letters to Spaulding from Josiah W. Bailey, March 15, 1934; from Harold D. Cooley, March 9; from Armond W. Scott, May 1, 1935; from James Roosevelt, September 27, 1937; from Lawrence A. Oxley, May 7, 1938; from Mary McCleod Bethune, December 1, 1941; from James A. Farley, July 2, 24, 1940; from Charles A. Ray, July 21, 1945. Spaulding's correspondence to the White House brought at least one direct personal reply from FDR; see Spaulding to Franklin D. Roosevelt, June 20; Roosevelt to Spaulding, July 5, 1935, concerning the special problems of Negro unemployment and the plight of the South; also see Spaulding to Roosevelt, August 26; M. A. McIntyre (Roosevelt's secretary) to Spaulding, September 4, 1935. Spaulding may have had some indirect effect on white appointments for federal positions: in 1938 Thurgood Marshall, representing the NAACP, wrote Spaulding asking if in his opinion the NAACP should fight the nomination of Texas Governor James V. Allred for federal judge (Marshall to Spaulding, September 17; Spaulding to Marshall, September 30, 1938); also see letters on behalf of a white Durham judge, Walter Bass, seeking a position as deputy collector of internal revenue (Spaulding to Josiah W. Bailey, November 29; to C. H. Robertson, November 29, 1937, Spaulding Papers).

ence for him. On the other hand, in local affairs his influence and that of the Mutual carried considerable weight. The politics of philanthropy in black Durham had run through the good offices of the Mutual since at least 1903, when Merrick and Moore joined forces to build Lincoln Hospital. They had raised $25,000 in the black community and $100,000 in the white community—$75,000 from the Duke family alone. The white contribution carried with it the notion that southern whites owed southern blacks something for their "fidelity and faithfulness . . . to the Mothers and Daughters of the Confederacy. . . ."[30]

Spaulding, a generation later, knew exactly how to keep the money flowing. He appealed to tradition, to the "memory of fathers and grandfathers" for "yet another monument in the name of the Dukes," and he effectively recounted the story of the Mutual, a testament of black-white cooperation in the economic progress of the New South. White industrialists viewed the Parrish Street experience as a satisfying mirror image of their own experience, a reflection in minature of heroic initiative and enterprise overwhelming all adversity, including the Great Depression. This romance of the New South proved as evocative as had the romance of the Old South in Merrick's day. Spaulding recognized that, and, like many black leaders in the South, he became a master of applied psychology. That he understood the importance of symbol is perhaps best revealed by his celebrated fund-raising drive in the black community for the construction of the great Gothic chapel at segregated Duke University. He collected a mere pittance among the black citizens, but surely in this case it was the spirit that counted—the Durham spirit—out of which he and others could skillfully bargain in turn for a new Colored Library, a college auditorium, a nursing home, or an instant $6,000 to replace a ruptured boiler at the hospital. In the meantime he used the Duke philanthropy as a stalking horse from which he could spur contributions from Liggett and

30. These words, inscribed on the marble facade of the hospital, seemed at the time a small and necessary price to pay for the white largess. See Robert Andrews, *John Merrick: A Biographical Sketch* (Durham: Seeman Printery, 1920), p. 50; also see C. C. Spaulding to "The Citizens of Durham," October 18, 1935, Spaulding Papers.

Myers, banker James Sprunt Hill, and others. They might not be able to keep up with the Dukes, but Spaulding urged them to try, lest they desert the town tradition.[31]

If it seemed that the Mutual, directly or indirectly, often paid the piper in supporting Durham's black institutions, there can be no question that it often called the tune. Lincoln Hospital, as much as White Rock Church, fell under its administrative influence. A Lincoln director, like a White Rock pastor, could scarcely secure his position without Company consent. The charter of the hospital required that at least two of its trustees come from the North Carolina Mutual, and of course Spaulding, as chairman of Lincoln's board of trustees and its finance committee, wielded power far beyond his single vote. To complete the circle the Company appointed William M. Rich, nominal head of the hospital, to the board of directors of the Mutual.[32]

Spaulding at times must have appeared sovereign to those looking up through the institutional pyramid. For example, from his office at the Mutual he could write a letter as president of the Mechanics and Farmers Bank to Lincoln Hospital, where in his capacity as trustee he could act unilaterally to attach the salary of a resident physician who neglected his note at the bank.[33] Or when evidence surfaced that a Lincoln official had accepted kickbacks for every corpse delivered to a certain undertaker, the hospital looked to Spaulding for discipline, not so much as trustee, but as the respected community leader, the moral chief-

31. C. C. Spaulding to W. S. Ranking, July 8, 1933; to W. B. Stiles, November 8; to Mary Duke Biddle, December 4; to R. L. Flowers, January 8; to C. H. Livengood, September 9; to J. S. Hill, August 14; to C. C. Council, October 18; to George Watts Hill, October 31; to W. F. Carr, October 19; to "The Citizens of Durham," October 18; J. S. Hill to Spaulding, August 16; A. H. Carr to Spaulding, August 16, 1935; Thomas H. Houck, "A Newspaper History of Race Relations in Durham, North Carolina" (Master's thesis, Duke University, 1941), p. 152; folder on "Duke Memorial Fund," 1929, Spaulding Papers.

32. William M. Rich to W. J. Kennedy, Jr., November 3, 1936. From other letters and receipts in the Kennedy Papers, it appears that the Mutual, quite apart from the personal gifts of its executives, gave from $500 to $1,000 annually to Lincoln Hospital; also see W. J. Kennedy, Jr., *The North Carolina Mutual Story* (North Carolina Mutual Life Insurance Co., 1970), p. 188.

33. C. C. Spaulding to Mary E. Kennedy, April 22, 1931, Spaulding Papers. Spaulding in this case simply instructed the hospital treasurer to divert $80 per month from the doctor's salary to the Mechanics and Farmers Bank.

tain entrusted to rule over an extended family within an informal system of subcommunity justice designed to seclude black errors from public view and to avoid the uncertainties of the larger system.[34]

The Negro press in Durham met the Mutual on something closer to equal terms than did the hospital. Like Lincoln, the *Carolina Times* was often indebted to the Company, but the singular character of its editor, Louis Austin, made it a relatively independent institution. Austin, along with black attorneys Robert McCants Andrews, Conrad O. Pearson, and later Floyd J. McKissick, proudly wore the label of town radical. Austin wrote so candidly as to more than uphold the motto of his paper, "the truth unbridled," and in the process he won recognition in the white community as "that nigger communist from Massachusetts." Despite the difference in their political styles, or perhaps because of it, Spaulding and Austin had great respect for one another. Indeed, they functioned well as a team, one rocking the boat, the other stabilizing it, their reciprocal actions maintaining movement without upheaval. Together they pressured the city government to hire black policemen; they registered black voters; battled against vice and the numbers racket; campaigned for sanitation, parks, and paved streets; petitioned the school board to adopt Carter G. Woodson's textbook in Negro history; boosted National Negro History Week along with National Negro Health Week; and generally cooperated to organize the community. When Austin ran for public office, which he often did, Spaulding supported him, at least with private finances if not with public avowal.[35] With ill-concealed admiration

34. C. C. Spaulding to William M. Rich, November 21, 1934, Spaulding Papers. Spaulding ordered Rich in this instance to reprimand and threaten those responsible with dismissal. The Colored Library in Durham was also tied to the Mutual. Dr. Moore had founded the library, and Mutual officials always served on its board. The Company successfully lobbied county officials for public funds and white philanthropists for private donations; in addition, the Company in 1940 held a $25,000 mortgage on the library (see report of NCM Executive Committee, June 5, 1940, Spaulding Papers).

35. Interviews, Louis E. Austin, January 15; Conrad O. Pearson, February 13; W. J. Kennedy, Jr., January 22, 1968; John H. Wheeler, April 3, 1972; Harry J. Walker, "Changes in Race Accommodation in a Southern Community" (Ph.D. dissertation, University of Chicago, 1945), pp. 305–310; Hugh P. Brinton, "The

Spaulding spoke of Austin as the "fearless editor" who "says anything." "He calls white people big apes and fools. . . . That's the kind of nerve he's got . . . and white people are scared to death of him."[36] But Spaulding always worried that fear would reap violence, a massacre of blacks; thus he urged Austin to be "more discreet," to use "a little more diplomacy," to "stop when you have said enough."[37] More conservative heads saw the *Times* as "a menace to Negro progress" and asked Spaulding to muzzle Austin. This Spaulding would not do, assuming that he could have, but he was not averse to playing on the financial strings that ran between the Mutual and the newspaper in an effort to tone down the editorials. On at least three occasions the Company advanced the *Times* advertising money or loans to bail it out of insolvency, and in part Spaulding justified this assistance to his board of directors as necessary in order to "have a paper we can controll, [*sic*] so to speak."[38] But outright control of the press never really fit Spaulding's purposes. Instead, he needed a conspicuous radical front to afford him greater mobility and safety in exploring a moderate position behind the lines; like Booker T. Washington, he needed a forum to his left, where he could anonymously present information for the purpose of pro-

Negro in Durham: A Study of Adjustment to Town Life" (Ph.D. dissertation, University of North Carolina, 1930), p. 395; Louis E. Austin to W. J. Kennedy, Jr., August 25, 1930, Kennedy Papers; Austin to C. C. Spaulding, July 12, 1937; May 22, 1939; October 21, 1941; May 17, 1945; C. C. Spaulding to Austin, July 13, 1937; October 23, 1941; to R. W. Flack, Durham City Manager, July 6, 1934; March 21, June 20, 1935; to J. H. Epperson, August 8, 1934; to H. A. Yancey, Durham City Manager, October 7, 1935; letters to C. C. Spaulding from J. H. Epperson, August 9; from Martha V. Spaulding, March 22, 1934; from Clara B. Hamilton, April 15, 1932; clipping, *Carolina Times*, October 31, Spaulding Papers. George W. Cox of the Mutual also played a key role in the hiring of black policemen. R. McCants Andrews was a product of Harvard law school and the Mutual attorney until his untimely death in the 1920's; Conrad Pearson was the nephew of W. G. Pearson; Floyd McKissick is of course better known as a director of CORE in the 1960's.

36. C. C. Spaulding to Louis E. Austin, November 8, 1933, Spaulding Papers; Walker, "Changes in Race Accommodation," p. 306.

37. *Ibid.*; C. C. Spaulding to Louis E. Austin, May 10, 1937, Spaulding Papers.

38. C. C. Spaulding to North Carolina Mutual Board of Directors, September, 1937 (no exact date); C. M. Eppes to C. C. Spaulding, January 8, 16; Spaulding to Eppes, January 12, 24, 1940. Also see Report of Reorganizing Committee for the *Carolina Times*, July 13, 1940, in Spaulding Papers.

test. Moreover, as the owner of a black institution Austin saw eye to eye with the Mutual on racial solidarity in support of black business. He praised the Mutual as "this great company" which "we must support for our future well-being," and thus lent the firm invaluable legitimacy with the masses.[39]

If the relationship between Parrish Street and the press was more complementary than competitive, the relationship between the Company and the North Carolina College was a close institutional partnership involving a level of collaboration in the politics of Negro education that is little known or appreciated. It should be remembered that James E. Shepard, who founded the college in 1910, also served as an organizer of the North Carolina Mutual in 1898. Spaulding and Shepard shared the poignant consciousness of race pioneers building their black institutions from the ground up against great odds on the dangerous frontiers of the New South. In retrospect, Shepard's achievement was probably more difficult. He established the first publicly supported black liberal arts college in the South— a nearly impossible task, considering the white legislative resistance to higher education for Negroes, except in the poorly funded industrial or normal schools.[40] That the college survived

39. Clipping, *Carolina Times*, November 7, 1929, North Carolina Mutual clipping file; Brinton, "The Negro in Durham," p. 185. Particularly on the matter of injustice in education did Spaulding provide grist for Austin. Spaulding's position in the Commission on Interracial Cooperation and the Urban League, among a variety of other sources, gave him access to information not readily available to the editor (see undated typescript analyzing expenditures of southern legislatures on Negro education, in Spaulding Papers, 1934); interview, Louis E. Austin, January 15, 1968. Myrdal in *An American Dilemma* has several chapters on Negro leadership in the South which place Spaulding's role and his relationship with Austin in a larger context, see esp. vol. II, 709–780.

40. Shepard, too, formed a network of contacts with influential whites and their foundations, and he was probably as close to the Dukes as were the Mutual leaders. In part it was the argument that the private white investment in North Carolina College was already so substantial (but still inadequate) that the legislature was persuaded to assume support of the institution in 1925. Yet it took another kind of appeal to persuade the state legislature: "They [Negroes] stayed at home and protected the hearthstones of our fathers, while they were away . . . fighting," one Durham assemblyman reminded his colleagues. Durham's other representative clinched the argument: "Most of us have been fondled as children by black mammies. I was on a trip to New York. As I stepped off the train . . . there emerged from the crowd my old black mammy. Throwing her arms around me and kissing me, she exclaimed, 'Bless God, here's my boy.

and later opened graduate and law schools is a further tribute to Shepard's political adroitness—some would say his Machiavellian wile—but another part of the credit belongs to Spaulding and the Mutual.[41]

Philosophically, the two institutions provided vindication for one another: the college turned out students trained in business; the Company employed them, or at least some of them, thus giving substance to the theory of the "double-duty dollar."[42] However, Shepard's preoccupation was less that of finding jobs for his graduates than it was that of finding funds to keep his college open, and in this effort the Mutual also lent direct assistance. For virtually every letter that Shepard wrote to philanthropists and politicians, Spaulding wrote one, too. He could pose as an objective third person, verifying the plight of the college and making Shepard seem less the ubiquitous supplicant. "Dr. Shepard is undergoing quite a struggle . . . and cannot succeed without the aid of friends," Spaulding wrote to Mary Duke Biddle. "You might be interested to know that . . . one white institution . . . in Greenville, North Carolina receives more support from the state than all five of the Negro state schools. A few years ago, I joined with a number of citizens in Durham in making it possible for the school to receive $10,000. At this time, it is in need of a similar amount."[43] At the depth of the Depression, Shepard confessed to Spaulding, "We do not know how we are

---

Gentlemen of the house, I hope you will vote for this bill. It is right. It is just' " (*Durham Morning Herald*, February 18, 1925, quoted in Houck, "Race Relations in Durham, p. 53).

41. The old-guard black radicals, who stood at the polar extreme politically from Shepard, refused to call him a conservative or an "Uncle Tom" without considerable qualification and ambivalent admiration for his cleverness in dealing with white political leaders.

42. In 1937 the Mutual and its affiliates employed about one hundred men and women who had attended North Carolina College (C. C. Spaulding, dedicatory address for a new building at North Carolina College, December 5, 1937, Spaulding Papers). The company also tried to stimulate interest in business education by awarding an annual cash prize to the business student with the highest average, and by giving students practical experience in business through a summer employment program (W. J. Kennedy, Jr., to Ester L. Smith, May 4, 1931, Kennedy Papers; James E. Shepard to C. C. Spaulding, May 31, 1934, Spaulding Papers).

43. C. C. Spaulding to Mary Duke Biddle, November 20, 1931, Spaulding Papers.

going to pay salaries," unless, as he suggested, Spaulding could wring something out of the Slater Fund and the other foundations. "Write them," Shepard appealed, "you know exactly what to say."[44] At the same time Shepard launched a desperate campaign among alumni and friends, but he found that he could not send out the letters until the Mutual donated some 5,000 postage stamps.[45]

In Shepard's view he and Spaulding working as a team, "standing each for the other," could be well nigh "invincible," especially at appropriation time.[46] Ostensibly detached from the college and independent of white money, Spaulding operated as the front man of the team, Shepard's star witness at the appropriation hearings. In white circles Spaulding's name added respect to any Negro cause, and he never failed to make a commanding appearance. Trim and poised, impeccable in his banker's clothing, his rich brown skin set off with gold-trimmed spectacles and a crown of snow-white hair, "he looked like he ought to be the president of something."[47] Always businesslike, never emotional, and well armed with facts and figures, he knew precisely how far to point up injustice without appearing to be on the attack, and yet never retreating to sycophancy. Shepard spoke more truth than flattery when he told Spaulding, "It would be a great asset to our Institution if you could . . . be present [at the legislature] and add a word in our behalf."[48]

Although Spaulding took lessons from the dexterous Shepard,

44. James E. Shepard to C. C. Spaulding, June 13, 1933, Spaulding Papers.
45. See James E. Shepard to C. C. Spaulding, November 23, 1933, in which Shepard thanked Spaulding for the stamps. At a later date Spaulding also served as chairman of a committee appealing for contributions from alumni of North Carolina College; see "Petition for Money from the Alumni Association of North Carolina College in Cooperation with the Durham Committee on Negro Affairs," July 22, 1937, Spaulding Papers.
46. James E. Shepard to C. C. Spaulding, December 24, 1943, Spaulding Papers.
47. Interview, Conrad O. Pearson, February 22, 1968. Every person interviewed for this study agreed that Spaulding's imposing appearance accounted for much of his effectiveness in public relations and politics.
48. James E. Shepard to C. C. Spaulding, October 14, 1938. Eight years later Shepard still thought it necessary for Spaulding to represent the college in the state assembly: "A word from you would mean very much to us," he pleaded (Shepard to Spaulding, September 17, 1946, Spaulding Papers).

the Mutual gave him certain political advantages that may have
made him the senior partner in the relationship—even to the
extent of selecting Shepard's successor.[49] The New South was
full of Negro college presidents, but not world-famous black
business executives. Thus Spaulding could command a larger
hearing, especially in a land where business enterprise had displaced cotton as king. From his favored entrepreneurial position
Spaulding had carried on a regular correspondence with four
North Carolina governors on a wide variety of subjects. He considered himself a "personal friend" of Governor J. Melville
Broughton, and, within the limits of southern race relations,
the correspondence suggests that he was.[50] Also, while Shepard
had remained a Republican, Spaulding had become at least a
token figure in the Democratic party; thus, if Shepard had any
patronage to dispense, it came down through Spaulding from
the governor.[51] Similarly, the college turned to the Company for
favors from the federal government. "I wonder if it would be
possible for you . . . to secure a personal interview for you and
me with Secretary Ickes," Shepard asked Spaulding. "I am very
anxious to go there and see if we can get a PWA grant for the
new buildings."[52]

Because Spaulding usually lobbied for institutions other than
his own, he established a valuable credibility in speaking for the

49. Claude Barnett to C. C. Spaulding, January 31; Charlotte Hawkins Brown
to Alonzo Elder, September 9; Brown to Spaulding, September 9; Spaulding to
Brown, September 16, 1948, Spaulding Papers.

50. The correspondence between the two men continued after Broughton
left public office; see Broughton to Spaulding, August 7, 1945, congratulating
Spaulding on his seventy-first birthday. While Spaulding described Broughton as
his "personal friend" (Spaulding to Frederick D. Patterson, February 5, 1945,
Spaulding Papers), this is indeed a relative term, and Spaulding probably allowed the "personal" relationship to delude him as to the strength of Broughton's
friendship for the race.

51. For example, see James E. Shepard to C. C. Spaulding, May 14, 1937, in
which Shepard on behalf of a friend asked Spaulding to recommend the man
to the governor for a position on the board of the Morrison Training School.
For Spaulding's position in the Democratic party, see letters to Spaulding from
Senator Frank Hancock, November 23, 1937; from Governor R. Gregg Cherry,
September 30, 1938; from Governor Clyde R. Hoey, April 6, 1939; from Frank
Porter Graham, December 16, 1944; June 13, 1950, Spaulding Papers.

52. James E. Shepard to C. C. Spaulding, November 11, 1936, Spaulding
Papers.

interests of others. Shepard astutely perceived this and skillfully displayed Spaulding as emissary to do what the college president would have found very difficult as a black Republican working against the grain of industrial education.[53] Shepard also knew that the Mutual, during the 1930's and 1940's, had a direct voice in the state government that was almost too good to be true. Spaulding actually had in his employ an influential white legislator from Durham, Victor S. Bryant, Sr., who served as the Company attorney for more than a generation. Bryant represented his client in political affairs with as much interest as he did in legal affairs—but not without profound ulterior motives. "Before going to Raleigh," he announced to Spaulding, "I wanted you to let me have the benefit of any advice or suggestions . . . on matters coming before the Legislature."[54] As Spaulding soon discovered, Bryant was offering a quid pro quo: legislative influence for the moderation of black demands. Shepard was more than alive to the possibilities of this political connection; indeed, he cultivated it and carefully coordinated his own appeals to Bryant with letters of reinforcement from Spaulding.[55]

Surely the Spaulding-Shepard strategy that flowered in the 1930's could not in itself explain the larger state appropriations for North Carolina College; economic recovery from the Depression accounted for part of the increase, as did outside pres-

53. However, Spaulding did not always agree with Shepard's strategy: "As I have told you from time to time, the Governor is expecting *you* [emphasis mine] to attend some of these meetings" (C. C. Spaulding to James E. Shepard, May 19, 1938, Spaulding Papers).

54. Victor S. Bryant to C. C. Spaulding, January 6, 1941; Spaulding in turn gave Bryant instructions on the North Carolina College and Greensboro A&T College appropriations, and asked him to push for more Negroes on their boards of trustees (Spaulding to Bryant, January 18, 1941, Spaulding Papers).

55. James E. Shepard to C. C. Spaulding, November 11, October 14, December 8, 1937; June 28, 1939; Spaulding to Governor Clyde R. Hoey, February 6, 1937; August 5, 1938; Shepard to Victor S. Bryant, February 26; Spaulding to Governor J. Melville Broughton, telegram, February 27; Spaulding to Shepard, February 28; Bryant to Spaulding, March 4, 1941; Spaulding to Broughton, January 30, 1943, Spaulding Papers; interview, John H. Wheeler, April 3, 1972. In later years Spaulding and Shepard found it effective to retire behind the more aggressive political efforts of other men from the Mutual; see Shepard to Spaulding, May 15, 1946, suggesting that John Hervey Wheeler, head of the Mechanics and Farmers Bank, be used to make demands out of which the elder statesmen could negotiate a compromise.

sure from the NAACP and the threat of integration from the Supreme Court in *Gaines* v. *Missouri*.[56] Nonetheless, in the restricted arena of Negro politics Spaulding's involvement in education advanced him, and hence the Mutual, an important and irretrievable step toward direct politics. In the meantime he put on display, for later scholars at least, a political style that pragmatically coupled accommodation with protest and represented in microcosm the fitful efforts that built the bridge between the age of Booker T. Washington and the "civil rights revolution."

Nowhere was Spaulding's style more in evidence than in his attempt to play off the threat of integration against the recalcitrance of the state to correct the gross inequities of the Jim Crow school system. In February, 1933, in a bold move backed by the national office of the NAACP, Louis Austin and attorneys Conrad Pearson and Cecil A. McCoy selected a very black and highly qualified student from North Carolina College, Thomas R. Hocutt, who wanted a degree in pharmacy—a degree not offered by any Negro college in the state. They personally escorted him to the admissions office of the University of North Carolina at Chapel Hill, where Austin announced to a thunderstruck registrar, "This is Mr. Hocutt, a new student . . . who needs his class schedule and dormitory assignment."[57]

Within a matter of hours Austin, Pearson, and McCoy found themselves in the sixth-floor offices of the North Carolina Mutual before C. C. Spaulding, who remonstrated their actions as quixotic and painted terrifying pictures of the Wilmington race riot. Spaulding remembered the "Red Shirts," and his fear was genuine; but his argument betrayed the influence of Victor Bryant, and other evidence confuses his role. Just two weeks earlier, in his capacity as president of the North Carolina Mutual, he had

56. The appropriation for the college increased from a little over $20,000 in 1933 to $128,000 in 1940; Augustus Merrimon Burns III, "North Carolina and the Negro Dilemma" (Ph.D. dissertation, University of North Carolina, 1968), pp. 130–131. In *Gaines* v. *Missouri*, 1938, the Court held that Missouri had to provide a law school for blacks within the state rather than providing out-of-state tuition.

57. Interviews, Louis E. Austin, January 29; Conrad O. Pearson, February 22, 1968; John H. Wheeler, April 3, 1972; Burns, "North Carolina and the Negro Dilemma," pp. 117–120.

sent out an "Appeal to the General Assembly and the White People of North Carolina" which lamented the pathetic legislative appropriations that placed North Carolina near the bottom among southern states in support of Negro higher education. Pointing to the example of West Virginia and Missouri, he asked that North Carolina provide out-of-state tuition for black students like Hocutt who sought professional and graduate training not available within the state's Negro colleges. He further protested the unequal teachers' salaries, an injustice common to the South.[58] As the Hocutt suit proceeded, accompanied by sensational reporting and an avowal by the NAACP to establish a test case for integration, Spaulding realized that black "radicals" had excited a fear among whites at least as great as his own, which, if properly channeled, might produce an area of compromise. In fact, up to a point, the whole affair played into his hands as if he had planned it. It is tempting to argue that he did, for the files of the NAACP disclose that it was none other than Spaulding who in a letter to NAACP Secretary Walter White apprised the national office of the dramatic plans for the suit and vouched for Pearson and McCoy as "two of our active and progressive young attorneys [who] are approaching you with a matter that I feel is of vital importance to Negroes." Spaulding also held out the promise of funds for the NAACP. This letter, which stands as the first official act in the stream of events that led to the confrontation at Chapel Hill and the ensuing test case, suggests a highly contrived and clever collaboration between Spaulding and his ostensible adversaries.[59]

58. Interviews, Louis E. Austin, January 29; Conrad O. Pearson, February 22, 1968; John H. Wheeler, April 3, 1972; Burns, "North Carolina and the Negro Dilemma," pp. 62, 115–116. Several copies of Spaulding's "Appeal" are in his papers, 1933; also see Spaulding to A. L. Stockton, editor of *Greensboro Daily News*, January 20; *Greensboro Daily News*, January 23; *Durham Morning Herald*, January 24, 26, 1933. There is no evidence to suggest that Spaulding's letter was a public relations ploy, but one of his managers instantly saw such a possibility for the letter, and he ordered a thousand copies for distribution to the teachers in his district (R. A. Cheek to Spaulding, January 23, 1933, Spaulding Papers).

59. C. C. Spaulding to Walter White, February 6, 1933. Conrad Pearson and Cecil McCoy were using Spaulding's name as a means of introduction to White. His letter served in effect as a cover letter for theirs, which was mailed on the

Unfortunately for the sake of intrigue, the story does not unfold so neatly. If Spaulding contemplated any such strategy, he kept it entirely private, for Pearson, McCoy, and NAACP officials believed they had been betrayed. Walter White lamented to his chief legal counsel, Charles H. Houston, that Spaulding had "promptly run to cover." In Durham McCoy concluded bitterly that because of the "pressure of a few white politicians upon our so-called Negro leaders . . . those upon whom we had counted for our staunchest moral support have been found leading the attack against us." Pearson and John H. Wheeler agreed that powerful whites sometimes caused Spaulding to have "bad dreams." The Hocutt case provided one of Spaulding's early lessons in big-time politics; he simply got caught in the middle and then tried to extricate himself and play the astute role that he wished he had conceived from the outset.[60]

He soon understood that, with his "Appeal" circulating and the Hocutt case pending, he could play on the apprehension of state officials like Nathaniel Carter Newbold, white superintendent of Negro education, who petitioned Spaulding to interdict "an unseen hand stretched out from afar guiding and directing the activities" of the Durham radicals.[61] Spaulding assured New-

same day and gave more details on the prospective suit (Conrad O. Pearson and Cecil A. McCoy to Walter White, February 6, 1933). White considered, however, that it was Spaulding who had made the first contact with the NAACP; see White to Charles H. Houston, March 20, 1933, NAACP Papers, Legal File, box D 96, Manuscript Division, Library of Congress.

60. Walter White to Charles H. Houston, March 20; Cecil A. McCoy to White, March 23, 1933; interviews, Conrad O. Pearson, February 13, 1968; John H. Wheeler, August 4, 1970; April 3, 1972. Between early February and late March, one can see Spaulding's support for the case falling away. On February 11, McCoy wrote White that he and Pearson had selected Hocutt, a student with "an excellent record . . . and a hue approaching ebony . . . [and] Mr. Spaulding is very enthusiastic about the matter." By February 22, McCoy felt compelled to write White, "Mr. Spaulding feels that he will be better able to render aid to our . . . present fight by standing in the background with no mention of himself at all." Spaulding had not counted on the tremendous publicity the case would receive. Indeed, publicity to spark a membership drive was part of the NAACP's motivation in the case. White sent special news releases to hundreds of newspapers, and when the hearings actually began, William H. Hastie wired White: "Getting moneys worth. Town agog. Incalculable good done whatever the outcome" (White to McCoy and Pearson, March 22; Hastie to White, telegram, March 25, 1933, NAACP Papers, Legal File, box D 96).

61. N. C. Newbold to Spaulding, March 14, 1933. For similar entreaties, see

bold that he was trying to "work quietly on the [Hocutt] situation," but "now the NAACP has charge . . . and I am afraid our good state . . . is going to be embarrassed." "If only the state authorities had acted," he chastised.[62] He then fell back on what he considered his ace: "I have just had another conference with the attorneys prosecuting this suit, and they are willing to drop the suit if some arrangements are made . . . to take care of the [out-of-state] tuition. On the other hand if nothing is done within the next sixty days, they are determined to carry it to the Supreme Court."[63] In the meantime Spaulding hoped to regain his respectability as he labored frantically to bring a tuition bill before the General Assembly. He wrote Newbold's counterpart in West Virginia for a model of such a statute, which he quickly passed on to Victor Bryant with instructions to draft and present a similar bill to the legislature. But Spaulding spent his energy and raised his hopes only to suffer defeat. The assembly rejected the measure.[64]

Spaulding emerged from the Hocutt affair badly burned, his image a little tarnished. Not only had the tuition bill failed (and it would fail again in 1935), but he and Shepard also had to share the blame for the subsequent failure of the court case. As part of an alleged "bargain," Shepard, with Spaulding's support, had effectively sabotaged the suit by refusing Hocutt an official transcript, thus allowing the state to dismiss the case on the ludicrous technicality that Hocutt had never *officially* applied for admission to the University of North Carolina. In exchange, Shepard was to get a graduate school and a law school for North Carolina College. However, the state did not deliver on the agreement until 1940, and even then one strongly suspects that

L. P. McLendon to Spaulding, March 20, in which McLendon adjured Spaulding, "You could render no greater service to your community and the interest of your race than to use your influence to stop this suit"; also see S. D. McPherson to Spaulding, March 20, 1933, Spaulding Papers.

62. C. C. Spaulding to N. C. Newbold, March 27, 1933, Spaulding Papers.
63. C. C. Spaulding to N. C. Newbold, March 31, April 4, 1933, Spaulding Papers.
64. C. C. Spaulding to William W. Sanders, March 8; Sanders to Spaulding, March 14, 1933, Spaulding Papers; *Durham Morning Herald*, March 30, 1933; Burns, "North Carolina and the Negro Dilemma," pp. 117–120.

the fulfillment came more out of fear from the *Gaines* case than out of good faith from the bargain.[65]

The political consciousness of the Company and its president took on a new sophistication after the Hocutt case. This chastening experience came less than eighteen months after Spaulding had been beaten in the Raleigh drugstore, and at a time when his optimism was being tested by the plight of the Scottsboro boys. Spaulding never lost his innocence because he lived in a relatively protected world, hedged about by his own success and its supportive Americanism, but events of the 1930's did adulterate his innocence. The participation of the NAACP in the Hocutt case, particularly of the Association's distinguished attorney, William H. Hastie, heightened his respect for "radicalism," and this overt presence of the NAACP in Durham gave him what he thought was a more powerful lever to move the legislature on the less complicated question of equal teacher's salaries.

In the summer of 1933, with a clearer sense of the *realpolitik*, he set his office to work with Walter White to organize the NAACP throughout the state and to fight for equal salaries for black teachers. "I have presented the matter to the State Education Commission although nothing was done about it," he advised White. "They must not expect the Negro to remain silent very much longer. . . . You may count on my cooperation."[66] He sent White "generous contributions" and asked him to use the money to dispatch NAACP organizers to North Carolina. Simultaneously he went into his "frightening act" and alerted New-

65. C. C. Spaulding to Governor J. Melville Broughton, March 6; Victor S. Bryant to Spaulding, March 4, 1941; interviews, Louis E. Austin, January 29; Conrad O. Pearson, February 13, 1968; John H. Wheeler, August 4, 1970; Burns, "North Carolina and the Negro Dilemma," pp. 117–120. Spaulding and Shepard apparently worked at cross purposes on the tuition matter. Shepard obviously would not favor the out-of-state tuition because it would preclude the addition of professional schools to his college, but Spaulding continued to work for the tuition bill at least through 1935, even collaborating with radical Conrad Pearson, who drafted an appeal that went out over Spaulding's name: see Spaulding to John Sprunt Hill, Victor S. Bryant, Howard Odum, and Frank Porter Graham, January 23, 1935, Spaulding Papers.

66. Walter White to C. C. Spaulding, September 18; Spaulding to White, September 27, 1933, Spaulding Papers.

bold that "serious threats are being made to organize an active branch of the NAACP in this state . . . and nobody wants that!"[67]

Spaulding knew what he was doing this time. He lay in the background, stroking the big whites, while his lieutenants, notably George W. Cox and R. L. McDougald, marshaled the resources of the Mutual and the Mechanics and Farmers Bank on behalf of the NAACP and the equal salary bill. Once before, through the leadership of John Avery in the 1920's, the Company had been identified as an organizer of the NAACP. Cox, McDougald, and R. McCants Andrews had assisted Avery, but generally his efforts as president of the Durham branch had met with a cool reception. A 1927 fund drive within the Mutual netted no more than thirty-one dollars; C. C. Spaulding gave but a dollar.[68] Now, however, the glaring injustice of unequal pay for black teachers and the recognized need for a statewide pressure group became a single issue. Moreover, this was an issue which the Mutual could easily afford to join and one which its administrative structure was eminently well suited to support. Unlike the Hocutt case, the demand for equal salaries posed no threat to segregation. Separate and equal was no radical slogan that could cost the Company its white friends, and, more important, the movement could enhance the image of the Mutual among prospective black policyholders, especially teachers.

Walter White knew that no other Negro institution in North Carolina could match the Mutual's resources for organization. On paper its agency system looked like a vast political machine, and White also knew that few people could match George Cox

67. *Ibid.*; C. C. Spaulding to N. C. Newbold, September 23; Walter White to Spaulding, October 30, 1933, Spaulding Papers. John H. Wheeler uses the term "frightening act" to describe Spaulding's adeptness at playing roles in race politics.

68. John Avery to Charles N. Hunter, May 24, May 31, June 15, July 7; C. C. Spaulding to Charles N. Hunter, May 21, 1921, Hunter Papers; Durham NAACP Membership Report, December 9, 1925; NAACP contribution reports, January 21, April 13, 25, 1927; Robert W. Bagnall to Eula L. Wade, August 28, 1928, Kennedy Papers; Walter White to John Avery, February 1, 1921; R. McCants Andrews to Walter White, July 1, 18, 1922; Andrews to James Weldon Johnson, June 29, July 26, 1922; clipping, *Carolina Times,* November 23, 1929; C. C. Spaulding to James Weldon Johnson, May 16; John Avery to Walter White, June 20, 1930, NAACP Papers, branch file, box G 147.

as an organizer. "I do hope," White inquired of Cox, "you are going to . . . let us count on . . . that fine energy and organizing ability of yours."[69] Cox thrived on such challenges and immediately established himself as a liaison man for White, and the Mutual as an administrative adjunct of the NAACP. Spaulding more than approved of his agency director's activities, and in an effort to mend fences he suggested to White that Cox and Conrad Pearson work together to organize the NAACP.[70] Acting out of contrition, perhaps, he asked to be counted among the vanguard and wondered if White would address him on a first-name basis, as he did Cox and McDougald. "I want you to feel free to call on me at any time," he reassured White. "If I can't do what you want, I shall try to get it done." To certify his good faith, he pledged $250 to the NAACP, explaining to White, "I believe I can better serve you in a quiet way."[71]

Cox was far from quiet. He sent scores of letters to local leaders across the state, asking them to organize their communities. "Frankly speaking," the black businessman advised, "I know no better way of investing a dollar than . . . in the NAACP."[72] He instructed his agents and managers to prepare the way for NAACP organizers and to build enthusiasm for the climactic state conference, scheduled for the state capital in Raleigh that October. But most important, he used his agency network to gather for the NAACP the names of virtually every black teacher in North Carolina. "My set up of . . . agents places me in a peculiar position to get this information . . . and I am going to get it," he promised White.[73] Without Cox and the Mutual, the logistics of

69. Walter White to George W. Cox, September 6, 1933, NAACP Papers, brach file, box G 146.

70. Letters from Walter White to George W. Cox, June 3, 23, September 21; Cox to White, June 14; Lucile Black to Cox, June 5; Cox to Black, June 14; White to Mrs. Julia Delany, September 20; C. C. Spaulding to White, May 31; White to Spaulding, June 9, 1933, NAACP Papers, branch file, boxes G 146–147.

71. C. C. Spaulding to Walter White, May 31, October 24; White to Spaulding, October 30, 1933, NAACP Papers, branch file, boxes G 146–147.

72. See, for example, George W. Cox to J. K. Wells, W. S. Chambers, A. T. Watson, June 14; Cox to Walter White, June 14; White to Cox, June 23, 1933, NAACP Papers, branch file, box G 146.

73. *Ibid*.; Conrad O. Pearson to Walter White, October 4; White to E. R.

the NAACP state conference, which hinged on the attendance of black teachers and their mass protest rally, would have proved nearly impossible for the NAACP national office. The Mutual supplied much of the labor and material support for the conference, including automobiles and lodging for NAACP officials; R. L. McDougald, ideologue and strategist throughout the effort, emerged as a major speaker at the rally.[74] A sycophantic Negro principal who had worked against the NAACP and the struggle for equal salaries later maligned the whole affair as the work of "outsiders, lawyers . . . a few West Indian Negroes . . . and agents of the North Carolina Mutual."[75]

In one sense the unctuous principal was correct. This movement, despite its skillful organization, did not embrace the interests of the masses—who could not vote anyway. It was the politics of petition without the benefit of power. The state legislature ignored the protest and once again moved no faster than the Supreme Court; not until 1944, after the Court found Virginia's dual salary schedule unconstitutional, did North Carolina redress the injustice.[76] In the meantime Spaulding began to express his grievances to Newbold in more cynical tones: "I wonder how the State Department of Education and those in charge . . . feel, [Newbold was in charge] seeing Negro children walking in the rain for miles to school, while white children are transported in buses." With obvious introspection, he added, "and usually when Negroes contend for better treatment . . . he is considered radical."[77]

Merrick, October 9; George W. Cox to White, October 10, 20; White to Cox, October 24; NAACP to Negro Teachers of North Carolina, October 17, 1933, NAACP Papers, branch file, box G 146, administrative file, box C 281.

74. Walter White to Mrs. Julia Delany, September 20; White to H. C. Miller, September 5; White to George W. Cox, September 21; Cox to White, October 20; White to E. R. Merrick, October 14; Merrick to White, October 16; White to R. L. McDougald, June 8, 22, September 18, October 5; McDougald to White, July 21, September 20; William H. Hastie to White, September 22, 1933, NAACP Papers, branch file, boxes G 146–147, administrative file, box C 281.

75. Typescript of editorial from *Rocky Mount* (N.C.) *Evening Telegram*, November 9, 1933, NAACP Papers, branch file, box G 146.

76. Burns, "North Carolina and the Negro Dilemma," p. 79; Governor J. Melville Broughton to C. C. Spaulding, June 9, 1944, Spaulding Papers.

77. C. C. Spaulding to N. C. Newbold, September 12, 1934, Spaulding Papers.

Spaulding had no choice but to recognize the limitations of his political style, but he was spared the dilemma of choosing between conservatism and radicalism. The political ground beneath him shifted during the 1930's, and he merely shifted with it, shielded by a growing body of white liberals and his more aggressive black colleagues. He ran to catch his people, shouting, "A voteless people is a hopeless people"—a potentially suicidal slogan in Merrick's day—and not to be outdistanced, he took his place at the head of the most significant political movement in the history of black Durham: the Durham Committee on Negro Affairs.

The DCNA, born in 1935 at the Algonquin Tennis Club with the Mutual as midwife, openly asserted that it planned to put political power in the hands of black people. While its success in this enterprise has been steady but not spectacular, the Committee remains today the most important political force in the Durham black community, and as an Afro-American institution it anticipated by as much as twenty-five years the pattern of Negro politics and community organization in the New South. The Committee became, according to political scientist Everett Carll Ladd, Jr., the South's most effective "peak organization"— that is, a single organization which embraced what often stood as three separate movements: economic welfare, civil rights, and electoral politics. A kind of Urban League, NAACP, and nonpartisan voters' league all rolled into one, it reminds the historian of a diminutive Freedman's Bureau.[78]

78. William Alexander Mabry, *The Negro in North Carolina Politics since Reconstruction* (Durham: Duke University Press, 1940), p. 80; Ladd, *Negro Political Leadership in the South*, pp. 41, 99, 143, 234, 237; Donald R. Matthews and James W. Prothro, *Negroes and the New Southern Politics* (New York: Harcourt Brace and World, 1966), pp. 145–146; Robert Louis Bowman, "Negro Politics in Four Southern Counties" (Ph.D. dissertation, University of North Carolina, 1964), pp. 227–241, 253–261. For the best analysis of the DCNA, see William R. Keech, "The Negro Vote as a Political Resource: The Case of Durham" (Ph.D. dissertation, University of Wisconsin, 1966), along with his published work, *The Impact of Negro Voting* (Chicago: Rand McNally and Company, 1968). As a primary source on the DCNA, Harry J. Walker, "Changes in Race Accommodation," is invaluable. Walker, a black sociologist, worked as a participant-observer in the DCNA during its early years, and his lengthy quotations from the all-black meetings reveal that the Committee provided an im-

Parrish Street easily dominated the DCNA, commanding a majority on an executive committee that had Spaulding as its chairman. The intent, however, was to build a coalition; thus Louis Austin was named to the executive committee, as were James E. Shepard and a professor from North Carolina College. Moreover, the DCNA, in theory, was to be a "people's organization," something like the New England town meeting. Occasionally citizens did come to bare their complaints, to offer testimony on police brutality and other municipal shortcomings, or to break open an intraracial dispute—to pillory the Parrish Street Gang. "You can't get Negroes . . . to carry on a boycott," announced one critic, "all of these girls up at the Mutual keep on buying. . . ."[79] The upper-class leaders in turn used the meetings to assuage class feelings, to preach unity and a hard line against injustice. Behind closed doors in Hayti, Spaulding could afford the luxury of praising his revolutionary ancestor, Henry Berry Lowry, who carried out guerrilla warfare against the Ku Klux Klan in Columbus County. "Lowry was different," Spaulding acclaimed. "He wasn't afraid. I think we need some Negroes like that. We got to fight . . . to get justice."[80] Someone might have asked the chairman to speak for himself. But in the appeal for solidarity, another businessman reminded the audience, "We have to forget all of this class feeling. When it comes to white people we are all in same boat. All of you know Mr. Spaulding went down to Raleigh and . . . what happened to him when he bought a drink in a white drugstore. A little old ignorant peckerwood paid five dollars and cost for the pleasure of slapping him down. The only way we can get white people to respect us is by getting power."[81]

---

portant community outlet for the political energy and seldom-seen anger of Durham's black businessmen, Spaulding included.

79. Walker, "Changes in Race Accommodation," p. 215.

80. *Ibid.*, p. 213. C. C. Spaulding's relationship to the legendary Lowry family cannot be firmly established. For the most part the Lowrys were Lumbee Indians, but they did intermarry with mulattoes in the community. Asa T. Spaulding's mother, for example, was a Lowry. For a fascinating account of the Lowry gang, see William McKee Evans, *To Die Game: The Story of the Lowry Band, Indian Guerrillas of Reconstruction* (Baton Rouge: Louisiana State Press, 1971).

81. Walker, "Changes in Race Accommodation," pp. 219–220. The meeting

In practice, however, the DCNA proved to be less a people's organization than a benevolent oligarchy. That the Committee had its origins and held its subsequent meetings at the Algonquin Tennis Club, a social subsidiary of the Mutual, was neither accidental nor ironical. In contrast to the pathological playhouses of E. Franklin Frazier's "black bourgeoisie," the Algonquin Club had a membership that more closely resembled W. E. B. Du Bois's "talented tenth." They were a new aristocracy with old values, a black gentry whose impulse for reform came less from the bitter anguish of the man farthest down than from a sense of racial duty and *noblesse oblige* that saddled the men of the Mutual. In fact, a leading motivation in founding the DCNA was the fear that the masses would be corrupted by a grant of suffrage without responsible instruction for its exercise. Neither the Mutual nor the DCNA initiated the drive to register Negro voters in Durham; that distinction belongs to Louis Austin and R. McCants Andrews, who began such a movement in the mid-1920's. Their militant thrusts opened the way for the Durham Independent Voters' League, precursor of the DCNA, in which Mutual executives (most notably George W. Cox)[82] did play a leading role. In the meantime, however, the Democratic party began periodically to encourage Negro voting. So close was the 1928 Senate race between Furnifold Simmons and Josiah W. Bailey that North Carolina Democrats, who had never rigidly invoked the "white primary" and had outlawed the poll tax in 1920, began openly to buy black votes, particularly in cities like Durham, where large white majorities offset the fear of "Negro rule." For a righteous Spaulding and a radical Austin, a corrupt white-owned black vote was worse than no vote at all, and on this common ground they could build a coalition to salvage and to extend the gains in registration, and at the same time to purge the likes of infamous "black Annie," a millworker for the Carr family who boasted that for a price she "went around and got all the niggers

that Walker quoted from took place in the late 1930's, probably 1938. The incident at the drugstore took place in 1931.

82. Independent Voters' League to W. J. Kennedy, Jr., July 7; Kennedy to Independent Voters' League, July 18; Kennedy to W. J. Thompson, August 4, 1932; Walker, "Changes in Race Accommodation," pp. 188–190, 206–208.

to register . . . hauled them to the polls," and then "went over to Mr. Carr's home [where] Mrs. Carr fried me a T-bone steak . . . and . . . told me to go upstairs and take a bath in her bath tub."[83]

In the judgment of Spaulding and his colleagues these black wardheelers were reprehensible "Uncle Toms" who merely reinforced the point that "somehow we have to teach our people to use the ballot intelligently." DCNA leaders remembered too well that the cry of corruption historically had been used by whites as an effective justification for Negro disfranchisement.[84] Endorsement of candidates and voter registration became the principal activities of the DCNA in its overall effort to educate the community and to build an independent political force— a force that never threatened to turn the tables, but one that might provide the margin of victory in close elections and thus influence public policy and lay claim to part of the spoils. Endorsement often amounted to an edict of the executive committee distributed to the black community on election eve or printed in the *Carolina Times*. White candidates took the endorsement seriously, appealing in person before the Committee, because they knew that the DCNA could deliver the Negro vote with "extraordinary efficiency."[85] Doubtless the key function of the Mutual leadership in the endorsement process was to lend such amorphous respectability to the DCNA so as neither to plant the kiss of death on white candidates nor to lose the trust and discipline of black voters. Obviously white Democrats would never bargain with the DCNA if its endorsement cost them white votes, and blacks would never support the DCNA if its leadership appeared too conservative.

But first, of course, the DCNA had to apply its talents to voter registration. In 1928, despite the efforts of Austin and others, there were but 50 black voters in Durham. At the end of 1935,

83. Paul Lewinson, *Race, Class, and Party* (New York: Oxford University Press, 1932), pp. 153–155; V. O. Key, *Southern Politics in State and Nation* (New York: Alfred A. Knopf, 1950), pp. 227, 578; Walker, "Changes in Race Accommodation," pp. 188–191.

84. Walker, "Changes in Race Accommodation," pp. 210, 223, 224, 226.

85. Keech, *The Impact of Negro Voting*, pp. 17, 24. Indeed, says Keech, "Durham Negroes . . . reached a technical efficiency in mobilizing a moderately sized electorate that would be the envy of interest group leaders anywhere."

the Committee's first year of operation, the registration count stood at 1,000. By 1939 over 3,000 blacks could vote; this number made up 13 percent of the total registration for the county. By 1960 the DCNA had enrolled a bloc of 13,200 voters, or 22 percent of the total registration, and nearly 68 percent of those Negroes eligible to register were actually registered, an unusually high figure which contrasted with 38 percent for the rest of North Carolina, 23 percent for Virginia, and 6 percent for Mississippi.[86] Winston-Salem, North Carolina, a New South industrial city in many ways identical to Durham, provides a more meaningful contrast. Without the institutional resources to organize a pressure group like the DCNA, the Winston black community, somewhat larger than Durham's, had only 300 registered voters as late as 1944, Not until after World War II, and with outside assistance from labor unions, would Winston equal the Negro registration of Durham a decade earlier.[87]

Beyond its success in voter registration, it was the Committee's influence over the turnout, cohesion, and maneuverability of the black vote that made it a recognized power in local politics. Consistently in Durham the black registration has yielded a higher percentage of turnout than the white registration, a remarkable exception to the rule.[88] Moreover, once in the polling booth, black voters have adhered to DCNA instructions: between 1937 and 1967 DCNA endorsees received on the average more than 80 percent of the black vote. Even when opposing candidates were black, cohesion did not break down. In a 1957 city council election James Taylor, dean of North Carolina College, received only 25 percent of the black vote when he challenged Parrish Street's John S. Stewart, DCNA endorsee and president of the Mutual Savings and Loan Association.[89] One

86. *Ibid.*, pp. 27–29; Walker, "Changes in Race Accommodation," p. 189. Over the years blacks have constituted a steady 30 to 35 percent of the total population of Durham County.

87. Ladd, *Negro Political Leadership in the South*, pp. 60–61.

88. Keech, *The Impact of Negro Voting*, pp. 28–29. Keech concludes that the historically "higher turnout in Negro precincts can without much doubt be attributed to the superior political organization of the Negro community, and to the efforts of the DCNA to get voters to the polls on election day."

89. *Ibid.*, pp. 30–32; Bowman, "Negro Politics in Four Southern Counties,"

can further calculate that between 1937 and 1967 the black vote as delivered by the DCNA spelled the difference between defeat and victory in approximately 40 percent of all contested city council ward elections. In at-large elections the Committee obviously could not command such a clear balance of power. In bond elections, however, available data (1947–66) reveal that the DCNA marshaled such a relatively large and singleminded turnout as to determine the outcome in over 50 percent of the bond issue questions.[90]

None of this is to say that the DCNA transformed a caste community into a political democracy. Even if it had, a minority of the electorate, no matter how well organized, could not have won concessions from an unwilling majority. The DCNA influenced the outcome of elections and was instrumental in securing

pp. 287–288; *Durham Morning Herald*, May 17, 1957. Significantly, most of the elected or appointed black public officials in Durham have come from Parrish Street, and of course with DCNA support. In 1953 Rencher N. Harris, vice-president of Bankers Fire Insurance Company, became the city's first Negro councilman. He was succeeded in 1957 by John S. Stewart, who has been re-elected ever since. Stewart also served as de facto chairman of the DCNA while C. C. Spaulding held the official title. From 1940 to the present, executives from the Mutual and its allied enterprises have served in the following city and county positions: C. C. Spaulding and W. J. Kennedy, Jr., Durham County Selective Service Board; Rencher N. Harris, Durham City Board of Education; J. J. Henderson (vice-president–treasurer of the North Carolina Mutual), Durham Housing Authority; John H. Wheeler (president of Mechanics and Farmers Bank), Urban Redevelopment Commission and Durham Committee on Community Relations; Aaron Day, Jr., Durham County Zoning Board; Noah H. Bennett, Jr. (vice-president–actuary of the North Carolina Mutual), Durham Good Neighbor Council; W. J. Walker, (secretary-treasurer of Bankers Fire Insurance Company), Durham City Planning Commission; W. J. Kennedy III (financial vice-president of the North Carolina Mutual), Durham Recreation Advisory Committee and Durham County Board of Social Services; Asa T. Spaulding, Durham County Board of Adjustment and Durham Committee on Community Relations. In 1951 C. C. Spaulding was appointed to the Durham City Board of Education, but he declined the appointment when he learned that the all-white City Council had refused to appoint aggressive John H. Wheeler, thus implying that Spaulding was the more manageable white man's Negro. North Carolina Mutual executives, of course, have always served on the boards of Lincoln Hospital and the Stanford L. Warren Colored Library. In 1968 Asa T. Spaulding was elected as Durham County Commissioner, reelected in 1970, and in May, 1971, was narrowly defeated in the Democratic primary run-off election for mayor of Durham, after having led all candidates in the first-round election.

90. Keech, *The Impact of Negro Voting*, pp. 33, 38, 39, 45, 61, 62. The DCNA realized that bond elections, while unexciting, were probably more important to the black community than other elections, for here the issues were relatively clear-cut involving the equal distribution of public funds and services.

for the black community a new library, better segregated school facilities, a park, a playground, a swimming pool, a fire station, black policemen, and a black manager for the state liquor store. The Committee also deserves credit for the employment of a few blacks in white businesses, the appointment of blacks to city boards and commissions, and the election of a small number of blacks to public office. But despite its postwar legal victories the electoral power of the DCNA could scarcely make a dent in issues like open housing, equal employment, or the integration of schools and public accommodations.[91]

The argument here is not that the DCNA was or was not the answer to the black man's problems in Durham—a corrupt machine might have produced as many benefits—but that whatever it accomplished, that it existed at all, that it began as early as it did, and that it came into being with a minimum of conflict was largely because of the North Carolina Mutual. Behind this assumption one acknowledges the important hypothesis that, if whites make up 70 percent or more of a local population, they will not rise up in terror and crush the fetal signs of black political development; nonetheless, among the dozens of communities in the upper South demographically similar to Durham, none gave birth to anything like the DCNA.[92]

Working within this golden mean of permissible black power, the Mutual and its leaders functioned as the catalyst in the conversion from the old politics of abstinence to the new politics of reenfranchisement. At a very practical level the Company supplied the men and the means to organize the electorate and to keep it organized. John H. Wheeler, gifted young summa cum laude of Morehouse and son of the Mutual's John L. Wheeler, came up from Atlanta in 1929 to work in the Mechanics and Farmers Bank. If Wheeler seemed too aggressive for the DCNA

91. Walker, "Changes in Race Accommodation," p. 212; Keech, *The Impact of Negro Voting*, p. 94; Frank H. White, "The Economic and Social Development of Negroes in North Carolina since 1900" (Ph.D. dissertation, New York University, 1960), p. 233; letters from C. C. Spaulding to L. R. Reynolds, March 5, 1938; to Ben E. Douglass, July 25; to J. S. Ross, July 30, 1941; to Benjamin Mays, August 21, 1946, Spaulding Papers.

92. Keech, *The Impact of Negro Voting*, pp. 26, 100–101; Bowman, "Negro Politics in Four Southern Counties," pp. 188–192.

to put forward as a candidate for public office, especially after securing his law degree and filing suits to integrate the public schools of Durham and the law school of the University of North Carolina, he perhaps better served the Committee as dean of its brain trust, its ablest tactician and toughest negotiator. His immediate superior at the bank for many years, R. L. McDougald, was no less vital to the DCNA. In fact, the bank rather than the Mutual served as the working headquarters for the Committee. An expert in finance, McDougald scrutinized bond issues for their value to the black community and provided general oversight of municipal policies. He prevailed upon the city to rezone undeveloped areas of the Negro quarter, to cut streets, and to extend public services so that he and Wheeler could finance new housing for Negroes through low-cost FHA loans. Criticism leveled at Parrish Street seldom extended to McDougald. Black people spoke proudly of him as "our banker," and after his early death they gave his name to a housing development in Hayti.[93]

Easily the most combative political figure at the Mutual itself was Davis Buchanan Martin, an ex-English professor who came to the Company in the late 1920's and soon worked himself up to agency supervisor. Serving as understudy to the forceful George Cox merely heightened his own dynamism, and he applied the lessons of organization from the business world of the Mutual to the political world of the DCNA. Among his many activities, he chaired the DCNA subcommittee on precinct organization and built an important coalition with the Negro tobacco workers' union. Corporate oral history alleges that C. C. Spaulding once sent Martin on a distant mission in order to remove him from a volatile political situation. Martin drove all night, completed his business, and then drove back to Durham the next night, arriving in time to lead the action on the follow-

93. Interviews, Conrad O. Pearson, February 13; Louis E. Austin, January 29; Mrs. Viola G. Turner, July 13; Asa T. Spaulding, July 18, 1968; John H. Wheeler, August 4, 1970. Wheeler has been chairman of the DCNA since 1957 and is currently president of the Southern Regional Council. In Wheeler's estimation the most important economic legacy of the Mutual, the Mechanics and Farmers Bank, and the Mutual Savings and Loan was the granting of large long-term loans to blacks, the success of which eventually persuaded white banks to do the same.

ing day.[94] Other Parrish Street political leaders included the respective vice-presidents of Bankers Fire Insurance Company and Mutual Savings and Loan Association, Rencher N. Harris and John S. Stewart. Neither of them matched the aggressiveness of Martin, but when the time came they proved to have the most "availability" as the DCNA's candidates for the city council.

These men and others from the Mutual family, along with the resources of their enterprises, constituted a pool of expertise greater than that of the city government itself. Not only did the Company have its accountants, its tax and real estate experts; it should also be reemphasized that, for the first fifty years of its history, the Mutual and its offspring drew their executives from the ranks of the economically frustrated "talented tenth." Thus among the administrators one could find professional organizers, writers, orators, musicians, lawyers, college presidents, professors, physicians, and preachers—creative talent for community organization. One of Spaulding's skills was to surround himself with able young men who often stood to his left and could bring moderate change under his aegis. And they had at their disposal the indispensable sinews of modern politics: offices, meeting rooms, typewriters, duplicating machines, clerks, secretaries, telephones, plus the Company tradition of racial cooperation and C. C. Spaulding's good will in Raleigh and Washington.

The North Carolina Mutual, then, provided the DCNA with a strong institutional base: an independent black base relatively immune from white economic reprisals, an indigenous base having local legitimacy (even sanctity) quite unlike the northern labor unions, NAACP chapters, or Communist party movements that attempted to organize other southern Negro communities during the 1930's. Simultaneously the Mutual sustained the old politics and the new—C. C. Spaulding and D. B. Martin—and therein lies part of the explanation for the ease of reenfranchisement. C. C. Spaulding had been registering "his people" for years; now "his organization" was doing the same, and from outside black Durham the status quo seemed undisturbed as

94. *Whetstone*, first quarter, 1946; interviews, Murray J. Marvin, July 10, 1970; John H. Wheeler, April 3, 1972.

long as he continued to preface his public remarks with a disa-
vowal of "social equality."

Spaulding's role, both in act and in symbol, was intrinsic to
the passage between two political eras in Durham and is sugges-
tive of similar roles played in the South at large. As one of Guy
Johnson's "neo-Washingtonians" who combined "the philosophy
of Booker Washington with as much dignified militancy as . . .
[was] compatible with the increase in white liberalism,"[95]
Spaulding moved amphibian-like between two environments—
advancing with dexterity in the new land of direct politics and
black protest, then retreating with grace to the ancestral home
of personal politics and white patrons. Implicit in the acceptance of the new was the inevitable rejection of the old; thus in
the transitional short run, Spaulding's function was to exploit
the advantages of both, that is, to preserve the benefits of patron-client relationships while at the same time representing a
suffrage movement designed to replace those whimsical relationships.

He easily mastered the dilemma. Change in Durham bore his
stamp of gradualism, and under his influence the two systems
comfortably overlapped. Being chairman of the DCNA did not
mean that he gave up his personal pleading with the governor to
stay executions, to commute sentences, to spend more money
on Negro schools, and to hire more blacks in the state government. Nor did it mean that he stopped flattering the city manager and the fire and police chiefs of Durham whenever a new
street light appeared in Hayti, whenever the fire department
promptly answered an alarm in a black neighborhood, and whenever a policeman showed discretion in dealing with black citizens; or that he no longer felt it necessary to send turkeys, hams,
pocket knives, and other personal gifts to city and state officials
at Christmas time.[96] On the contrary, Spaulding expanded his

95. Johnson, "Negro Racial Movements and Leadership in the United States,"
p. 68; Horace Mann Bond, "Negro Leadership since Washington," *South Atlantic
Quarterly*, XXIV (April, 1925), 115–130.

96. In the case of a fifteen-year-old black youth sentenced to die for raping a
white girl, Spaulding used his personal approach to buy time for further investigation: "I am willing to rest the case in your hands," he wrote Governor Clyde

personal politics and neatly complemented the operation of the DCNA with what might have been a southern version of Martin Kilson's "neoclientage."[97] The black community easily identified the old patron-client politics at work within the DCNA, Spaulding's position intact, and thus the Committee inherited an important traditional sanction in its quest for voter loyalty. Yet as seen from the white side Spaulding was no machine politician, nor was the DCNA precisely a political machine. Chairman Spaulding did not promise to deliver the black vote indiscriminately to patrons in the Democratic party. Rather, in a long-standing institutionalized relationship with the white community, he and the Mutual promised, symbolically, at least, to deliver something far more important: *social control.*

On the night of June 22, 1937, Joe Louis knocked out James Braddock to become the first Negro heavyweight boxing champion since the controversial demise of Jack Johnson. The black citizens of Durham, like others across the nation, poured spontaneously onto the streets, expressing a mixed mood of jubilation and hostility. For a fleeting moment every black man stood invincible. Symbolically black America had whipped white America, and the euphoria was enough to transfer temporarily the sym-

R. Hoey, for "you are possessed with a big soul." Hoey commuted the sentence; see Spaulding to Hoey, April 9, June 3; Hoey to Spaulding, April 11, 1938. For an almost identical case with another governor, see Spaulding to R. Gregg Cherry, April 27, 1945; also see letters from Spaulding to R. W. Flack, June 20, 1935; to Robert L. Thompson, May 19, 1937; to Hoey, December 13, 1938; November 25, 1940; to W. J. Croom, November 28, 1939; to W. R. Johnson, December 10, 1940; to J. J. Burney, June 19; to W. H. Murdock, June 21, 1941; to Theodore Johnson, April 18; to H. E. King, July 25, 1944; to Charles R. Frazier, November 17, 1950; letters to Spaulding from Hoey, June 19, August 3, 1937; December 14, 1938; November 29, 1940; from M. F. Spaulding, June 17; from Charles R. Frazier, November 29, 1937; from D. L. Cox, December 28, 1949; from E. J. Evans, December 26, 1951, Spaulding Papers.

97. See Martin Kilson, "Political Change in the Negro Ghetto, 1900–1940's," in Nathan I. Huggins, Martin Kilson, and Daniel M. Fox, eds., *Key Issues in the Afro-American Experience*, 2 vols. (New York: Harcourt Brace Jovanovich, Inc., 1971), II, 182–185. Here Kilson sees the old-style clientage politics merging with machine politics in the northern ghetto. Spaulding and the DCNA represent a composite of Kilson's southern model based on personal contacts and clientage, and his northern model based on "specialization, modernization and differentiation of black leadership." The Mutual helped to synthesize all of this into a unique form—the DCNA.

bol into the reality. Whites driving through Hayti at that historic instant were stunned beyond belief to see metamorphosed black men racing alongside their autos, hurling rocks and shouting insults. When white firemen answered false alarms throughout the black community, they too met a hail of stones. Within minutes the chief of police had C. C. Spaulding on the telephone, warning him to get "your people" off the streets. Spaulding mounted a running board and moved down Fayetteville Street, commanding the clusters of celebrants to return to their homes lest they invite the holocaust. Realism returned as quickly as it had departed; black folks obeyed, and the "race riot" fizzled.[98]

Ever since 1898, when John Merrick denounced black political agitators as partly responsible for the Wilmington race riot, the leaders of the Mutual had been considered "shock absorbers" between the races. C. C. Spaulding reinforced the image when, during the national outbreak of race riots in 1919, he admonished his employees to preserve the Durham spirit, to do nothing to disturb the "delicate issues of our economic and civic life . . . and to counsel sanely with each other and with liberal white business men and friends of the race . . . that we might pass safely thru this perplexing hour. . . ."[99] The men of the Mutual were portrayed as the literal "connecting links" in Durham's race relations, and it would seem that the Company resided on Parrish Street as a psychological safeguard between the white and the black communities. White leaders walked Main Street shoulder to shoulder with Spaulding, discussing interest rates, investments, and the state of the economy. They saw black businessmen who talked, behaved, and in a few cases even looked like themselves. And these were the men who went home to Hayti each night—black envoys whose soothing presence assuaged white fear and guilt. After business hours Parrish Street retired to Fayetteville Street, which in the minds of whites meant that no savage netherworld lurked across the tracks. Parrish Street proved somehow that there was no race problem, but even if

98. Walker, "Changes in Race Accommodation," pp. 302–305; *Durham Morning Herald*, June 23, 24, 1937; Houck, "Race Relations in Durham," p. 141.
99. Quoted in Andrews, *John Merrick*, pp. 132–133, 216.

there was, Parrish Street could solve it. Following the distur-
bance in 1937 Durham's city manager, who had kept the police
out of black neighborhoods, explained how Spaulding's inter-
vention vindicated the "understanding" between the two communities: "The Negro leaders [who gave assurances through the
DCNA that nothing like this would happen again] worked out
the whole thing themselves. We . . . work with their leaders,
for the Negroes trust them and fall in line with what they say;
that's the way for us to have peace. . . ."[100]

It cannot be overemphasized that the meaning of the Mutual
for the Durham community was rooted in the bedrock of race.
Not only was the Company's pattern of political behavior intrinsic to the pattern of race relations (one of Gunnar Myrdal's
axioms), but its every action, indeed its stated *raison d'etre*, was
tied to "finding a way out." Its very existence was taken to mean
that race relations in Durham were good; its continued existence
would only make them better. New South Negroes and their
white patrons believed that economic progress and better race
relations went hand in hand (one of Booker T. Washington's
axioms), and by assuming an active role in interracial politics
the Mutual believed that it could double up on the race problem:
its efforts in business would improve the chances for successful
race relations; its efforts in race relations would improve the
chances for successful business—a cycle that would surely produce a triumphant New South.

The Company realized, however, that too great an official
concern with race might jeopardize existing white friendships.
To tackle race relations through the NAACP was too direct and
dangerous, but to work through the NNBL was too indirect and
ineffectual. The DCNA partially resolved the dilemma, but the
organization which best expressed the political position of the
Company and the personal temperament of its president was
the Commission on Interracial Cooperation, an Atlanta-based
human relations group founded during the violence of 1919 by
a white Methodist minister, Will W. Alexander, to promote "in-

100. Quoted in Walker, "Changes in Race Accommodation," p. 304.

terracial peace through interracial communication."[101] In 1928 Spaulding accompanied Alexander to an interracial conference in Washington D.C., where he met a stellar gathering of black intellectuals including W. E. B. Du Bois, Alain Locke, Kelly Miller, and James Weldon Johnson. Shortly thereafter he became treasurer of the North Carolina branch of the Commission (NCCIC), a position he held until 1942 when the larger Commission evolved into the Southern Regional Council. It is noteworthy that the transition in 1942 from the Commission to the more ambitious Council took place at a meeting in Durham and that John H. Wheeler later became president of the new organization.[102]

Spaulding was easily the most important black figure in the NCCIC, and he played a conspicuous role in the regional Commission as a member of its executive committee. Charles S. Johnson remarked that he and Spaulding were on one occasion the only *gens d'couleur* sitting on the high council at Atlanta.[103] Indeed, most of Spaulding's contacts in the Commission were with white southern liberals, men like Howard Washington Odum, president of the NCCIC, and Guy Benton Johnson, both distinguished sociologists at the University of North Carolina. Spaulding now had two white constituencies: conservative businessmen in Durham and liberal professors in Chapel Hill. Conflict never developed, because the NCCIC posed no direct threat to social and economic arrangements in the South. When Chapel Hill playwright Paul Eliot Green sent ten dollars to the NCCIC he wished Odum well, but doubted that "shackles would be loosed" by a "crowd that meets . . . and talks sanctimoni-

101. For the best short summaries of the Commission, see George B. Tindall, *Emergence of the New South 1913–1945* (Baton Rouge: Louisiana State University Press, 1966), pp. 177–183; and Myrdal, *An American Dilemma*, II, 847–849.

102. Report of the National Interracial Conference, December 16–19, 1928, Washington, D.C., copy in Spaulding Papers; Burns, "North Carolina and the Negro Dilemma," pp. 23–28; Southern Regional Council, "The Southern Regional Council: Its Origin and Purpose" (Atlanta: Southern Regional Council, 1944), pp. 3, 4, 7, 21.

103. Charles S. Johnson to C. C. Spaulding, January 10, 1938, Spaulding Papers.

ously."[104] Louis Austin was less kind and denounced the NCCIC as the "North Carolina *Circus* on Interracial Cooperation."[105]

Whatever the influence on race relations, the Company's involvement with the NCCIC reaffirmed a basic concern for social issues. Certainly the professor-leaders of the NCCIC thought of the Mutual as a social institution, an instrument of reform, and an element of Afro-American culture, and on this basis an intriguing relationship grew up between the black insurance enterprise and the white department of sociology—two institutions otherwise separated by race and purpose.[106] Even the radical students of the liberal professors in Chapel Hill saw Spaulding as something other than a capitalist, and they expected him to support their leftist journal, *Contempo*, which featured articles by Lincoln Steffens, Max Eastman, Upton Sinclair, and Norman Thomas. "The South hates it," the editor wrote Spaulding; sufficient reason, he thought, for a black leader to support it.[107]

Spaulding's association with white liberals in the NCCIC assisted him in his search for a tenable political position. Surely he could move as fast as respectable southern white men. Under the aegis of their particular liberalism he could embrace what Washington had renounced—overt politics—and still stand as an honored heir-apparent to the Tuskegeean. His steady absorption of the politics to his immediate left is perhaps a test case for what Washington himself might have done. The hundreds of interracial meetings which Spaulding attended taught him to

104. Paul E. Green to Howard W. Odum, December 18, 1934, Spaulding Papers.

105. Clipping, *Carolina Times*, November 3, 1934, North Carolina Mutual clipping file; emphasis mine.

106. Odum and Johnson, in addition to being in frequent contact with the Mutual on matters of interracial cooperation, were interested in the Company as a subject for research. They invited Spaulding and other executives to speak to their classes in Chapel Hill, and at one point they proposed a major study of Negro business in Durham. Interview, Guy Benton Johnson, February 9, 1968; Guy B. Johnson to C. C. Spaulding, June 29, July 4, 1931; Howard W. Odum to Spaulding, December 6, 9, 13; Spaulding to Odum, December 8, 11, 1937; January 12, 1938; May 20, 1943, Spaulding Papers.

107. A. J. Buttitta to C. C. Spaulding, October 28, 1931, Spaulding Papers. Langston Hughes, who contributed to *Contempo*, wrote an interesting vignette on Buttitta and the radical scene in Chapel Hill at this time in his *I Wonder as I Wander* (New York: Rinehart, 1956), pp. 44–47.

speak more directly, to take bolder positions, to avoid the sancti-
monious talk, and "to keep the white folks honest."[108] Through
his work on the Commission he became overtly sensitive to
subtleties of racism that he had previously taken for granted.
"Durham has always maintained an amicable feeling between
the races," he wrote the publisher of the *Durham Herald-Sun*
newspapers, "but your emphasis on Negro crime to the exclusion
of all other Negro news tends to give the public a distorted conception of the Negro population." Moreover, Spaulding wanted
to know why it was that the *Herald's* contest for the first baby
born each year was limited to whites. With surprising contrite-
ness the newspaper sent Spaulding a check for the NCCIC and
admitted that "discrimination has gone on for several years, and
we have recognized our error." Spaulding in turn sent the publisher information for a Sunday feature article on the John Avery
Boys Club.[109]

On the more serious issue of police brutality Spaulding found
that he could no longer temper his protest. When the police
beat a black youth for whistling at them, he warned that such
brutality committed with impunity was "breeding feeling," and
that it was asking too much to expect "the [black] citizens . . . to
be sane about the matter."[110] He charged homicide when a white
officer killed a black man who resisted an illegal search of his
home. He successfully demanded the suspension of an off-duty
policeman who attacked a black man for allegedly violating the
Jim Crow arrangement on the city bus. And when a plainclothes-
man shot and killed a Negro soldier "suspected of having a
knife," Spaulding erupted: "There has been a long series of out-
breaks in Durham caused mostly by officers of the law . . . who
have mistreated people they are sworn to protect. Why was this

108. C. C. Spaulding, "Notes on the Proceedings of the Southeastern Regional
Advisory Committee of the Commission on Interracial Cooperation," n.d.,
Spaulding Papers; interview, John H. Wheeler, August 4, 1970.

109. C. C. Spaulding to C. C. Council, January 3, June 17; Council to Spaulding, January 4; Spaulding to Charles Hudson, December 10, 1941, Spaulding
Papers.

110. Letters from C. C. Spaulding to R. W. Flack, August 3, 1933; to E. G.
Belvin, December 28; to G. W. Proctor, December 28, 1934; to H. A. Yancey,
October 7, 1935, Spaulding Papers.

officer kept in Hayti when he had a history of brutality against Negroes? Why aren't there Negro police in Hayti?"[111] In each instance Spaulding raised the specter of racial warfare. After the affray of 1937 he issued the threat with greater credibility, advising that officials assent to his moderate demands or run the risk of a race riot.

Ironically, the reputedly conservative Commission on Interracial Cooperation moved Spaulding closer to the protest tradition. As an official of the NCCIC he collaborated more rather than less with the NAACP, consenting on one occasion to lend his agency system to Walter White's investigation of a lynching. He threw the resources of the Company into the lobby effort for the federal anti-lynching bill, and later he joined White in signing a telegram from the NAACP to President Roosevelt, protesting segregation in the armed forces. He also endorsed a similar and more militant statement from the black Communist leader Max Yergan.[112] But none of this is to say that Spaulding ever became more than a neo-Washingtonian. He might sign letters of protest, but he studiously avoided placing himself or the Company in a position of public approval for direct action. He refused, for example, to support Asa Philip Randolph's March on Washington Movement.[113]

If the NCCIC gave Spaulding and the Mutual a formalized positive role in race relations, thus strengthening their joint reputation, they in turn did not come to the NCCIC empty-

111. Houck, "Race Relations in Durham," pp. 107, 140; Walker, "Changes in Race Accommodation," p. 283; *Durham Morning Herald*, May 30, June 1, 1937; letters from C. C. Spaulding to Judge R. H. Sykes, April 8; to H. A. Yancey, Durham City Manager, April 6; to F. W. Kurfees, April 30; to R. L. Lindsey, June 3, 1943, Spaulding Papers.
112. Walter White to C. C. Spaulding, July 31; Spaulding to White, August 3; L. R. Reynolds to Spaulding, August 5; Spaulding to Reynolds, August 6; Spaulding to Eleanor Roosevelt, April 29; Spaulding to Josiah W. Bailey, August 16, 1935; June 17, 1936; Bailey to Spaulding, August 19, 1935; Spaulding to White, August 24, 1938; White to Spaulding, October 24; Spaulding to White, October 25; White to Franklin D. Roosevelt, telegram, 1941, exact date illegible; Max Yergan to Spaulding, March 6; Spaulding to Yergan, April 5, 1941, Spaulding Papers.
113. Clipping, *Durham Morning Herald*, June 22, 1941, Kennedy Scrapbook; C. C. Spaulding to A. Philip Randolph, June 21; to Eleanor Roosevelt, June 21, 1941, Spaulding Papers.

handed. Spaulding's position as treasurer was neither pro forma nor a matter of tokenism. Odum and other leaders in the Commission knew him as one of the most productive fund-raisers in the state; moreover, his black business probably had more legitimacy among the wealthy patrons of racial causes than did the white university. It was unspoken but understood that Spaulding could simultaneously evoke paternalism and genuine respect from white donors; thus it was he who sent out "S.O.S. Letters" to a "few white friends," and he upon whom the regional director prevailed to convince "a prominent white person to speak over the radio on behalf of the NCCIC."[114] Like the Negro church in other southern towns, the Mutual served as the institutional base for interracial meetings and strategy sessions, providing much the same logistical support and managerial expertise that it did for the DCNA.[115]

Whether or not the Mutual's efforts in interracial cooperation measurably improved the race relations of Durham remains a moot question. Certainly black and white leaders thought so, but they had such a profound stake in the spirit of the New South that they may have succumbed to the myth of idyllic Durham. As early as the 1920's romance about "the friendly city" had mounted to such proportions that it generated its own mythography. John Merrick and Washington Duke, the muses of racial amity, had a relatively easy task, the rationale ran, because "Durham Station" marked the "neutral ground" where Johnston surrendered to Sherman—where Yankees and Rebels threw down their arms and fraternized over their cooperatively purloined tobacco. Somehow this spirit carried over to the relations between blacks and whites, insuring that the "two great races would grow and develop side by side on terms of good

114. L. R. Reynolds to C. C. Spaulding, May 23; Spaulding to Reynolds, May 28, 1934; Reynolds to Spaulding, December 31, 1938, Spaulding Papers.

115. The "Mutual Spirit" sometimes invaded these meetings with entertainment from the Mutual's "Treble Clef Club" or the Company's soprano, Nell Hunter. The Company also contributed on an average of $500 each year to the Commission; C. C. Spaulding, Minutes of NCCIC Meeting, December 16, 1936; NCCIC Treasurers Report on Contributions, 1937; C. C. Spaulding to L. R. Reynolds, December 27, 1937; also see various manuscript reports in the NCCIC file, Spaulding Papers.

feeling."[116] The city historian and the white town fathers believed, moreover, that Durham attracted Negroes of "an exceptionally high order, progressive, wide awake, with ability, character, and a strong drive"—"splendid Negro citizens, the best in the nation"—who through their "efforts in uplift built the best model of negrodom to be found in North Carolina or in any section of the country. . . ."[117]

The two sets of racial spokesmen came close to creating a delusory world of mutual admiration dependent more on ingratiating rhetoric than on indisputable reality. To speak of interracial harmony was to create it, and too frequently black leaders viewed the effects of caste through the filter of their own favorable experience. Others, however, painted a more sober picture. Pauli Murray, black author, attorney, and civil rights advocate, remembered the black Durham of her childhood as the "Bottoms" where

> shacks for factory workers mushroomed in the lowlands . . . on washed out gullies. It was as if the town had swallowed more than it could hold and had regurgitated, for the Bottoms was an odorous conglomeration of trash piles, garbage dumps, cow stalls, pigpens, and crowded humanity. You could tell it at night by the straggling lights from oil lamps glimmering along the hollows and the smell of putrefaction, pig swill, cow dung and frying foods.[118]

In 1936 the North Carolina State Board of Health conducted a study of the Negro community in Durham and deplored the social conditions it found, including significant malnutrition and fourteen homicides in the space of six months. The Urban League concurred that Hayti was "overcrowded and unsanitary," filled with "crime and immorality." A Works Progress Administration survey expressed alarm at Durham's "slum conditions."[119] The

116. Andrews, *John Merrick*, p. 30.
117. William K. Boyd, *The Story of Durham: The City of the New South* (Durham: Duke University Press, 1927), pp. viii, 278–279; Houck, "Race Relations in Durham," pp. 55, 56, 159, 190; *Durham Morning Herald*, November 8, 1922; December 15, 16, 1929; August 1, 1931.
118. Pauli Murray, *Proud Shoes: The Story of an American Family* (New York: Harper and Brothers, 1956), p. 27.
119. Houck, "Race Relations in Durham," pp. 97–148, 166–168.

Baltimore Afro-American affirmed "that the heart of more than one great financial body beats steadily and surely under the tutelage of the powerful North Carolina Mutual. But many things that have been said about Durham are false. . . . Durham has been advertised to death."[120] The *Cleveland Call and Post* believed that "Negroes have piled up millions . . . in Durham," but doubted that "interracial conditions in the city are . . . better than they are elsewhere in the South."[121] And on the streets of Hayti a black tobacco worker showed little patience with upper-class Negroes who argued that "race relations are good in this city" simply "because we haven't had a lynching. . . . I guess things are pretty good for them."[122]

Yet as with most myths the spirit of Durham was not without substance and never without function, the latter point being one which obscured the distinction between myth and reality. A scholar no less critical than W. E. B. Du Bois felt that Durham possessed a special quality, and Dr. Moore, usually taciturn and unwilling to issue saccharine statements to please whites, praised Durham as "the greatest city in the country [where] . . . white people and colored people are too busy to have racial differences."[123] Nor was the black lower class consistently critical. A black worker testified that Durham at least did not operate on the "Mississippi plan": "This about the last town going South where the white people ain't so 'rebish' [rebel-like] but from here on down they are mean as hell. The reason this town is so good . . . is because the town was built up by the Dukes and the Merricks. . . . They just started out right and its been that way ever since."[124]

120. Undated clipping, *Baltimore Afro-American*, Kennedy Scrapbook.
121. Clipping, *Cleveland Call and Post*, April 14, 1938, Kennedy Scrapbook.
122. Quoted in Walker, "Changes in Race Accommodation," p. 95. For a full description of conditions among the lower classes of Durham, particularly the migrant tobacco workers, see Brinton, "The Negro in Durham," pp. 141–150, 202–242.
123. *Durham Morning Herald*, June 20, 1919, quoted in Houck, "Race Relations in Durham," p. 157.
124. Quoted in Walker, "Changes in Race Accommodation," p. 82. Margaret Elaine Burgess in her community study of Durham, *Negro Leadership in a Southern City* (Chapel Hill: University of North Carolina Press, 1960), pp. 151, 161, 167, 174, 192, believes that there is a grain of truth in the myth of Durham,

The conflicting images coexisted, but the positive generally prevailed over the negative. Hylan Lewis in his classic *Blackways of Kent* found that his respondents constantly found fault with their community and at the same time exhibited a need to praise it. "The overall design which gives meaning to [Negro] life in Kent would probably collapse without the sentiment that Kent is a good—and in some ways, a superior—place to live," Lewis observed.[125] Durham Negroes rationalized their existence in much the same way, and the Mutual functioned as the pivotal point for their ambivalence. A black woman who one week remarked derisively of her neighbor, "'Don't she think she's something, working up at the Mutual,'" took a job herself at the Company the next week and was overheard to boast, "'Guess where I'm working.'"[126] The Mutual served as a sociological baseline for sorting out the layers of social stratification in the black community. The same could be said for every other city in which the Company had a district office. Insurance agents, not to mention their managers, enjoyed upper-class status in southern black society; thus the man of the Mutual, like the teacher and the minister, affected the sociology, and hence the culture, of every town in which he lived.[127]

It hardly need be repeated that the Company influenced the community in countless intangible ways. Blacks, of course, could not help identifying in one way or another with the outstanding enterprise of the race when it was located in their own city. In a material sense the Company could not uplift the masses, nor could it serve them as a primary institution, as had the mutual

---

and that the North Carolina Mutual provided a level of black leadership not generally found in other southern cities.

125. Lewis, *Blackways of Kent*, p. 34.

126. Interviews, W. J. Kennedy, Jr., January 26; Miles Mark Fisher, March 10, 1968.

127. Hortense Powdermaker, in *After Freedom*, pp. 65, 122, found in Mississippi that Negro insurance agents commanded at least as much prestige as teachers and perhaps more than principals. E. A. Shils, "The Bases of Social Stratification in Negro Society" (Memoranda from the Carnegie-Myrdal Study, 1940), p. 12, observed that throughout the South the black insurance agent enjoyed a "higher deference than his occupation alone would entitle him to."

benefit society; yet nobody denied that in *abstraction* it functioned as a monument to the race, the centerpiece of the community, a semi-autonomous institution which offered an unusually visible black counterpoise to the psychologically corrosive pattern of success and status for whites only. Even if the pride was ambivalent, it was on balance a positive force in bolstering a battered self-image. To the black middle class, especially to those who found a position on Parrish Street, the Mutual was obviously Zion—the "honey hole," as they affectionately called it—where one could burrow in and live the good life shielded from white hostility.

But in theory the retreat was temporary, "an economic detour," as Negro insurance executive M. S. Stuart described it.[128] Booker T. Washington's ideal remained intact: business was the black man's frontier, the cutting edge of the Afro-American effort to carve out a permanent and respectable place in the larger society. Black businessmen lived under the spell of the New South and the American dream, believing that their own example predicted imminent fulfillment, when in fact they existed only as an aberration of a dream that was never meant to include them.

Their obsession with progress, an essential psychological defense, had produced a generation or more of uncritical optimism. Under the promise of a New South the disciples of Washington hoped to harvest democracy out of industry, and in Durham the organic union between the North Carolina Mutual and the DCNA seemed to suggest such a possibility. But the plan was at best naïve, at worst cynical, for it made no move to disturb the basic divisions of caste and class. It is interesting to speculate as to what might have happened in the 1930's had the DCNA sponsored a political alliance with white workers and labor unions.[129]

128. M. S. Stuart, *An Economic Detour: A History of Insurance in the Lives of American Negroes* (New York: Wendell Malliet and Co., 1940).

129. It is only fair to note that John H. Wheeler, among others, championed such an alliance after World War II, and a working coalition existed during the period 1947–54. The movement split, however, when white conservatives aroused the white workers' fear of "social equality" in the wake of the 1954 Supreme Court decision. Bowman, "Negro Politics in Four Southern Counties," pp. 160–165, 234–235; interview, John H. Wheeler, April 3, 1972.

However, the escape hatch was not political insurgency but individual mobility, the legendary opportunity for every man to work his way to the top, even though he would find two distinct and temporarily unequal summits. If anyone doubted the genius of the system, he needed only to look to the example of Washington Duke, who began with nothing, and to John Merrick, the ex-slave, who began with less than nothing. Racial segregation in this arrangement was at least irrelevant, at most functional. Separate and equal was an ideal whose time would come, and black Durham impressed wistful whites as a satisfying proto-type—the harbinger of utopian apartheid. "If Negro Durham . . . were moved to some great clearing in some distant forest," mused a state official in Raleigh, "we would have one of the best towns in . . . the country."[130]

But more than serving as useful symbols of the New South, the Mutual and its leaders symbolized an era of Afro-American history. They represented a middle range of leadership—bishops, editors, college presidents, government functionaries, and fellow businessmen—who quietly dominated the interregnum between Booker T. Washington and Martin Luther King. With the notable exception of Marcus Garvey, American society for more than a generation effectively stifled popular black political leadership, thus partly explaining the uncommon appeal of black athletes, entertainers, and messianic cultists like Father Divine and Sweet Daddy Grace. Between the Randolphs, the Robesons, and the Du Boises on the one hand, and the small-town tyrants on the other hand, stood the Weavers, the Bethunes, and the Spauldings, men and women who believed that faith and work along with patience and protest could carry the victory. As Oliver C. Cox put it, they "protested within the status quo," believing that America, despite the gravity of its sins, was capable of redemption.[131]

As heir to Washington's legacy, C. C. Spaulding saw himself

130. Clipping, *Norfolk Journal and Guide*, April 16, 1938, quoting Gurney Hood, North Carolina Banking Commissioner, Kennedy Scrapbook.
131. Oliver C. Cox, "Leadership among Negroes," *Studies in Leadership*, ed. Alvin W. Gouldner (New York: Harper and Brothers, 1950), p. 270.

practicing "the art of the possible" and believed fundamentally that his moderation staved off genocide. Within tightly restricted alternatives he steered what he perceived as a precarious course between complacency and cataclysm as he and others fastened themselves to the Washingtonian dialectic in which Negro entrepreneurs represented the advance guard of a rising bourgeoisie—black Algers—breaking out ahead of an oppressed peasantry in the process of accommodating to industrialism, capitalism, and racism. Guided by the Tuskegeean's theory and their own success, they often mistook the absence of racial warfare as evidence of progress and the smallest example of racial uplift as a precursor of liberation. They sometimes saw themselves as American immigrants following a familiar pattern of mobility; yet they knew the analogue had limitations. Denied an equal footing with the European, they found it difficult to tread in his steps; moreover, they met internal restraints within their own culture. The call for black solidarity, unlike the call for white—Irish or Italian—solidarity, could be interpreted as a selfish ruse to maximize individual profit at the expense of the group, or as a shortsighted move serving to sabotage integration and civil rights.

Yet much of what the North Carolina Mutual did as an institution was done apart from conscious theory, out of a social compulsion little different from the pragmatism of immigrant organization or perhaps linked to what E. J. Hobsbawm has described as pre-capitalist social movements.[132] Although middle class and tending toward modernization, the Mutual retained the earmarks of preindustrial associations, reflecting the inertia of an ongoing folk history and the proscriptions of caste that at certain base points it shared with the folk. Stretched between worlds that were both modern and premodern, both black and white, the Mutual acted as institutional mediator between disparate segments of time and culture thrown together in a setting that simultaneously encouraged and denied assimilation.

132. E. J. Hobsbawm, *Primitive Rebels: Studies in Archaic Forms of Social Movement in the 19th and 20th Centuries* (New York: W. W. Norton and Co., 1959).

At a lower level of abstraction, it expressed kinship—familial, racial, and spiritual—not unlike countless other groups ranging from the Mennonites to the Mafia who constructed around their members protective subsocieties sponsoring individual mobility while promoting the interests of the group through community organization. As the institutional strong point, with pockets of community power clustered around it, the Company imposed sanctions, extended services, and generally formed the matrix of subordinate institutional development embracing everything from libraries, hospitals, and boys' clubs to civil rights organizations and political pressure groups.

To a large extent this was the meaning of the Mutual as it directed the political economy of black Durham. By the end of the 1930's, however, it seemed that the Company had made its point as a racial institution, and that for the future it could rest its case merely by perfecting its business. America had promised as much, and the fulfillment of that promise appeared deceptively real under the stimulus of World War II and a new era of optimism.

Epilogue

The Dividends
of War

April 2, 1966, began damp and chill in Durham, the kind of spring day that held the scent of shredded tobacco close to the ground. Above the pungent factories, on a hill overlooking the American Tobacco empire, intense activity on the site of the old Benjamin Duke estate captured the town's attention that morning. This day, in fact, would provide the climax to an intrigue that had begun early in the decade when the North Carolina Mutual secretly purchased the Duke property and embarked on the remarkable transformation of the baronial estate. Gone now was the Victorian mansion; and in its place stood a twelve-story pillar of glass and concrete, a daring architectural sentinel of the New South announcing that Durham was still the "Magic City." And magical the setting must have seemed to those who understood that this new structure usurping a landmark of white authority was a building owned and occupied by black men. It was the new home office of the North Carolina Mutual.

Surely all this symbolized "progress." Some thought it a singular phenomenon of the Durham spirit. Of course, that could not account for the "K K K" scrawled on the stone facade the night before, but such a response gave reassurance that one epoch, however stubbornly, was retreating before another and that this was indeed a historic occasion. Thus the Mutual family could scrub the letters in good humor as they made ready for the arrival of Vice-President Hubert Horatio Humphrey, who had come to town to christen the edifice and to herald a changing South.

Change in the American South has become a cliché, as has the term "New South," but perhaps nowhere else in the nation is change so measurable and its resulting ambiguity so poignant. Behind "Mutual Plaza" the remains of Ben Duke's fruit orchards, where black gardeners once toiled, were in full bloom that April morning. Directly across Duke Street to the west, the five-story home office of an insurance firm owned by a first family of Durham, the descendants of slave-holders, stood in the shadow of what the despised race had built. In the hollows that lay between the new office building and the old tobacco factories, freeway construction and urban renewal intruded on slums where democracy worked best in this segregated city. Here poor whites and poor blacks sat integrated on their sagging porches. Back yards with chopping blocks and kindling piles rested within easy view of gleaming modernity, air-conditioned offices, electric-eye elevators, and glassed-in computer rooms. The panorama from the twelfth story displayed a mixture of worlds pastoral and industrial, urban and rural, modern and traditional, black and white, rich and poor. And this was the mixed identity of the black executives as they looked out from their top-floor suites, vainly trying to measure the meaning of the distance from the hill to the heart of the business district where Parrish Street faded into a montage of dirty brick, or further still to the heart of the black community from which they and their fathers came.

Mostly that distance was measured in history. Much had happened since the eve of World War II which tended both to clarify and to obscure the identity of the Mutual and its leaders.[1] The war formed a threshold for the Company, as it did for black Americans in general. Afro-Americans who remembered World War I pledged that never again would they fight for democracy abroad and surrender to tyranny at home. The Mutual made no

---

1. Any detailed scholarly treatment of the Company in the postwar period will have to await sources not yet available, particularly the Asa T. Spaulding Papers.

militant pledge, but the war and the civil rights movement which followed brought economic gains and a sense of momentum that pushed the enterprise into a steady drift toward the mainstream, toward what some saw as assimilation—a prophecy filled with mixed blessings for an institution built on ethnocentrism. Yet the mainstream had always been a magnet, and the next thirty years would introduce new pressures to old tendencies, to the old dualism that pitted the vision of assimilation and secularization—color-blind capitalism—against the reality of segregation and racial solidarity.

Ultimately the issue was a cultural one: could the North Carolina Mutual become an integral part of the modern American business community without forsaking a spiritual tradition born out of exclusion from that community? Unprecedented prosperity, expanding investment opportunities, the declaration of dividends, technological advances, specialization of management, unionization of agents, heightened class feeling, accelerated migration to the North, the death of C. C. Spaulding in 1952, the succession of three new presidents by 1968, the rising number of white policyholders, white tenants, even white employees—the dilemma of desegregation—all of this, plus increasing competition from white firms, led the Mutual toward secularization, away from the cultural distinctiveness which had characterized the Company for half a century. In the 1960's the Mutual found itself driven toward a critical intersection of economic assimilation and ethnic identification. The call for black power in 1966 presented the crisis in full relief against a backdrop of the black man's institution resting atop the white man's turf, far removed from the segregated black community. One elderly black citizen later complained, "I bet a colored man can't even get a loan up there anymore."[2]

The long train of events pulling the Mutual toward secularization began at an optimistic moment between the economic recuperation of the late 1930's and the economic renaissance of World War II. In the fall of 1938 the Company expanded into Pennsylvania, thus ending an era of retrenchment and a mood

2. Interview, Conrad O. Pearson, February 13, 1968.

of stoicism. The keen sense of adversity and the race consciousness it produced gave way to an unaffected optimism that made the opening of Pennsylvania a pragmatic business decision. In contrast to the spirited overexpansion of the 1920's, this addition of new territory was methodical and conservative. George Cox had lost none of his zeal. He spent the early fall inducing Philadelphia ministers "to cultivate and fertilize the soil," and he inspired such enthusiasm in the black press that the *Philadelphia Tribune* made the "Invasion of the North Carolina Mutual" a major news event of the season. But Cox knew he had a sure thing before he began his campaign. Several generations of Negro migration had established a large and relatively flush market in Pennsylvania, and the bulk of that migration came from Mutual territory to the south. Indeed, each year hundreds of migrating policyholders chose to service their policies by mail rather than allow them to lapse. The infrastructure was already there; the Mutual quite literally followed its clientele north to Philadelphia and Pittsburgh.[3]

The move to Pennsylvania proved to be a smart one. The state's steel mills and shipyards provided the Mutual a northern industrial base which served as a vanguard in reaping wartime profits. Philadelphia quickly distinguished itself as the perennial district leader in sales production, and its new crop of agents, particularly an indomitable corps of women, goaded the older districts to the south. The Philadelphia district was first to collect over $1,000,000 in annual premium income, and it was a woman from Philadelphia, Essie Thomas, who led all agents in sales during the 1940's; in fact, three of the top five Mutual agents during the war were women from Philadelphia. In addition to its impressive premium collections, the Philadelphia

3. C. C. Spaulding to George W. Cox, September 29; Cox to C. C. Spaulding, October 3; Cox to Asa T. Spaulding, November 8; C. C. Spaulding to Dan C. Boney, June 2, 25; C. C. Spaulding to Raymond Pace Alexander, August 1, 1938, Spaulding Papers; *Philadelphia Tribune*, October 20, 1938; *Whetstone*, fourth quarter, 1938. In acquiring its Pennsylvania license the Mutual received important assistance from North Carolina Insurance Commissioner Dan C. Boney, and from the black Philadelphia lawyer and politician Raymond Pace Alexander. Alexander was the husband of ex-Mutual executive Dr. Sadie T. Mossell.

agency also provided a new source of impressive executives, some of whom found their way to Durham after the war.[4]

Pennsylvania represented the best of a good situation. The boom there reverberated along the Atlantic seaboard into the southeastern stronghold of the Mutual. Asa Philip Randolph's militant March on Washington Movement in the summer of 1941 and the Fair Employment Practices Commission which followed generated thousands of jobs for Negroes in steel mills, shipyards, and war-related industries. Washington, D.C., Baltimore, Norfolk, Wilmington, Charleston, Savannah—always key districts for the Mutual—profited enormously from the rising black employment, as did the inland districts of Birmingham and Atlanta. Tobacco factories in Virginia and North Carolina ran at a record pace, and black farmers throughout the South generally witnessed more prosperity than at any time since World War I.[5]

This relative abundance redounded in a succession of glowing annual reports from the home office (see Table 9), and as the directors celebrated their success, they began to entertain seriously the old secular challenge of becoming the black man's Metropolitan. Since the 1920's the Mutual had skirted a vexing question: how much longer, the black critics wanted to know, would Afro-Americans have to wait for their leading company to compete with leading white companies like the Metropolitan that periodically invaded the Negro market and offered better policies, lower rates, and annual dividends besides? A typical complaint taunted W. J. Kennedy: "Members of my family have insurance with the Metropolitan. They pay interest [dividends] without sidestepping." A policyholder who discovered that other companies paid dividends demanded a "refund" from the Mutual. "That is my money and you know it," she scolded Kennedy. Even a friend of the Mutual family admitted to C. C. Spaulding, "I should be taking more insurance . . . with your company, but

4. *Whetstone*, fourth quarter, 1941; first quarter, 1942; first quarter, 1945; first quarter, 1952.
5. In 1943 the Company estimated that over 90 percent of its new business was "directly connected with the war effort" (*Whetstone*, second quarter, 1943).

TABLE 9. NORTH CAROLINA MUTUAL LIFE INSURANCE COMPANY
ASSETS AND LIFE INSURANCE IN FORCE, 1940–49

Year	Assets	Insurance in force
1940	$ 6,415,786	$19,461,957 (O)* 31,766,233 (I)* 51,228,190
1941	7,222,193	21,969,386 35,671,304 57,640,690
1942	8,273,734	24,669,738 39,775,129 64,444,867
1943	9,878,560	29,275,267 46,752,619 76,027,886
1944	11,880,685	34,162,809 55,503,032 89,665,841
1945	14,430,145	39,483,832 61,063,578 100,547,410
1946	17,176,604	46,024,351 71,106,636 117,130,987
1947	19,902,805	51,067,203 79,720,755 130,787,958
1948	23,011,329	54,641,593 85,226,643 139,868,236
1949	26,250,001	58,250,840 87,990,302 146,241,142

* O = Ordinary
  I = Industrial

SOURCE: *Best's Life Insurance Reports*, 1941, p. 693; 1942, pp. 676, 678; 1943, pp. 575, 578; 1944, p. 580; 1945, pp. 600, 602; 1946, p. 634; 1947, p. 646; 1948, p. 678; 1949, p. 709; 1950, pp. 719, 721.

it is most discouraging to pay the full premium . . . without one cent dividend."[6]

Vindication came finally in January, 1944, when the board of directors, resting securely on a financial cushion of $1,000,000 in surplus funds and 50 percent mortality ratios, announced that the first dividend checks would be mailed that April to coincide with the Company's forty-fifth anniversary. For C. C. Spaulding it was a "day of triumph, a year of jubilee, a new era . . . dispelling any lingering doubts about the business ability of Negroes." The Metropolitan, he pointed out, had been in business fifty-five years before it paid dividends.[7]

Spaulding, like most of his black contemporaries, labored under the preoccupation of proving that blacks were not inferior to whites, and to do that he directed the Mutual toward the expectations of the industry, in effect, toward "whiteness." Just as the firm had shed its identity as a Negro assessment association during the prosperous years of World War I, it had begun to attenuate its identity as a Negro institution during the prosperous years of World War II. These were tiny stepping stones into the mainstream, barely perceptible suggestions of assimilation. One could argue that the pursuit of objective business performance had little to do with the pursuit of "whiteness," for surely there were neutral standards that any enterprise must obey in order to survive. But the standards could never be seen apart from race. If the Mutual provided a model for smaller black firms, all of its models in turn were white. What it meant for the Mutual to measure up to the white business world, President Spaulding concluded, was that "color is only skin deep." This statement became his slogan as he suggested that inside every black businessman there existed the potential of a white

6. Nellie Lee Elmore to W. J. Kennedy, Jr., November 9, 1932; Ella Todd to Kennedy, September 13, 1938, Kennedy Papers; James H. Murphy to C. C. Spaulding, January 7, 1944, Spaulding Papers.

7. Board of Directors Dividend Resolution, December 15, 1943; C. C. Spaulding to James H. Murphy, January 12; Asa T. Spaulding to Board of Directors, February 16, 1944, Spaulding Papers; clippings, *Carolina Times*, January 22; *Atlanta World*, January 26; *Pittsburgh Courier*, February 5; *The State*, March 11, 1944, Kennedy Scrapbook; *Whetstone*, first quarter, 1944.

businessman; paraphrasing Booker T. Washington, he counseled his colleagues "to conduct yourselves so that no one could guess the color of your skin by the character of your work." The ultimate implication of Washington's philosophy—assimilation through economic uplift—took on renewed significance with the unprecedented success of the Mutual, a success which measured itself now against white business rather than black business, and one which quickened the American dream and hence the latent assimilationism within the outlook of the enterprise.

There was much to encourage such an outlook. How could the Company be very far from the mainstream when Merrill, Lynch, Pierce, Fenner, and Beane solicited its investment account; when Hollywood inquired about filming its history; when its president sat on the Selective Service Board, turned down appointments on the FEPC and as Minister to Liberia, and received national acclaim in the *Saturday Evening Post*, the *Reader's Digest*, and *American Magazine*; when Arthur Godfrey confided in his radio audience that no American should miss seeing the North Carolina Mutual; or when the U.S. Navy commissioned a merchant ship out of the Wilmington yards as the S.S. *John Merrick*?[8]

The good ol' Mutual spirit so prominent during the 1930's found itself subsumed by patriotism and prosperity during the 1940's. The Forum gave way from a weekly family affair to a monthly meeting more formal and perfunctory in tone. C. C. Spaulding, sounding a little like Calvin Coolidge, epitomized this tone in a piece he wrote for the *Negro Digest* entitled, "My Business Is Business."[9] And he eagerly lined up with America's

8. Letters from C. C. Spaulding to A. L. Fletcher, May 27, 1941; to Lewis B. Hershey, February 23; to E. M. Butler, July 2; to Archibald Rutledge, June 18, 1943; to F. W. Kurfees, July 7, 1945; letters to C. C. Spaulding from Murray C. Shoun, July 7; from Archibald Rutledge, June 15, 1943; from Joseph H. Harris, January 18, 1949, Spaulding Papers; *Whetstone*, third quarter, 1943; first quarter, 1945; *Saturday Evening Post*, CXV (March 27, 1943), 215ff.; *American Magazine*, CXLVI (December 1948), 21ff.; *Reader's Digest*, LIV (March, 1949), 22–25; *Durham Sun*, July 12, 1943. The S.S. *John Merrick* was launched July 11, 1943. The interested Hollywood studio, Twentieth Century Fox, bought the film rights to the *Saturday Evening Post* article; see Archibald Rutledge to C. C. Spaulding, April 2, 1944, Spaulding Papers.

9. *Negro Digest*, I (February, 1943), 32–33.

leading industrialists as a celebrated "dollar-a-year man," selling the war, especially its bonds, to sometimes skeptical black citizens. To those who remembered the ill-fated optimism of W. E. B. Du Bois in 1918, Spaulding seemed to be one war behind in his call to "close ranks." But proving that Negroes were loyal, like proving they were mentally competent, was another essential element of his special burden. "This is not a time for splitting hairs," he warned. "We must work together against our common enemy, the Japs, Italians, and Germans."[10] And he made sure the Mutual set a good example. A large red V dominated each sheet of company stationery; the *Whetstone* published an honor roll of "Mutualities in Service"; the directors waived the war clause and paid all war casualty claims; and by 1945 the Company had purchased a much-publicized $4,450,000 of war bonds. All this, of course, made good business sense. The bond purchase was a wise investment for a firm expecting a postwar depression; the free publicity was a valuable bonus; and one could hardly expect Spaulding to neglect the interests of the Mutual in his travel and speeches as associate administrator of the War Savings Staff, nor was he averse to using his federal post as a lever to secure deferments for his key executives.[11]

For all its influence, the war did less to transform the Company's character than it did to accelerate changes already under way. The *Whetstone*, like the Forum, for example, became a more businesslike production during the war years—a slick quarterly full of reprints from trade journals, technical news, and business forecasts, along with advice from Dale Carnegie and the lore of successful salesmanship. But these changes began in the 1930's. The *Whetstone* converted from the old in-house monthly to the commercially printed quarterly in 1938. Its technical emphasis began even earlier in the decade under the guid-

10. Undated clipping, *Norfolk Journal and Guide*; C. C. Spaulding to Marcus H. Boulware, September 7, 1943, Spaulding Papers.
11. J. L. Wheeler to C. C. Spaulding, December 26, 1941; letters from Spaulding to J. F. Lane, September 28, 1943; to Gurney P. Hood, November 17, 1944; to Selective Service Board no. 15, Charleston, S.C., December 4, 1943, Spaulding Papers; *Whetstone*, first and second quarters, 1943; first and fourth quarters, 1944; first and fourth quarters, 1945.

ing hand of Asa T. Spaulding. The new *Whetstone* of the 1930's signaled the young actuary's more substantial innovations, which prepared the Company for the opportunities of the 1940's; these secular reforms, in turn, were but part of a larger although unsteady process that dated back to the founding of the Mutual, partly a secular act in itself designed to direct the business of Negro life insurance away from lodges and churches. World War II, then, brought little that was brand new to the Mutual, but acted instead as the single most important event in reinforcing an evolutionary pattern. In this turn of events Asa Spaulding was more than an accessory technician. He stood as a transitional figure between the race-burdened "talented tenth" whose memories stretched back to the nineteenth century and a new breed of administrators whose consciousness came less from a sense of tradition than from specialized business training financed by the G.I. Bill.

The decline of the old order, beginning in 1944 with the death of R. L. McDougald and continuing into the late 1950's, removed virtually everyone who could remember the days of the triumvirate.[12] Unavoidably much of the Mutual's élan passed with these leaders. The spirit of race pioneering declined with the pioneers and with their sense of fulfillment. After the Depression the unifying feeling of being "up against it" never returned. As early as 1937 a perceptive district manager lamented the loss of the "old do or die spirit." For years, he explained to President Spaulding, "this spirit idea was the only thing I knew. . . . Now we have swung to the technical side at the expense of the spirit side."[13]

C. C. Spaulding never abandoned the missionary spirit, but he preached with less fire after the war—not because he was well over seventy years old, but because there was good reason

12. John Avery, of course, had died in 1931. Among those who passed on after McDougald were: W. D. Hill, 1945; C. C. Spaulding, 1952; M. A. Goins, 1953; George W. Cox and A. J. Clement, 1956; John L. Wheeler, 1957; Bessie A. J. Whitted, 1959. W. J. Kennedy, A. E. Spears, and E. R. Merrick all retired in 1959; Dr. Donnell, in 1960.

13. C. V. Kelley to C. C. Spaulding, June 29, 1937, Spaulding Papers.

to believe he had completed his mission. For a while he worried about the postwar probability of "the greatest depression the world has ever seen," and he grew anxious over keeping peace in the Mutual family if scores of ex-agents returned from the war to claim their jobs from women, often wives and sisters, who had recast themselves from substitutes into proud professionals and multiplied many times over the prewar volume they inherited. But these crises that might have absorbed his energy and talent never came. The hypothetical panic became an extended boom, and the Mutual's major problem became an accumulation of more money than it could invest. Conditions were almost too good to maintain the morale of an institution that drew its spiritual strength out of adversity.[14]

Spaulding bragged that he still worked ten hours a day, but he found increasingly less to do. Moreover, since 1939, when he realized that the Company was out of danger and that he had nearly lost his health in the strenuous effort to save the National Negro Business League, he had cut back on his work load. He remained the perennial "PR" man, but he combined that with more leisure. He carried along his portable pool cue on business trips, arranged winter sojourns to Hot Springs, Arkansas, and summer retreats to the Negro beaches in Virginia and the Carolinas, and generally assumed responsibility for keeping up the camaraderie among a disappearing generation of race men. He and Fred R. Moore, editor of the *New York Age* and an intimate contemporary of Booker T. Washington, exchanged health tips and their latest discoveries in good cigars as they reminisced about the early days—the frontiers they had crossed. Spaulding mailed George Washington Carver "an interesting article on strawberries," and to another aging Tuskegeean, R. R. Moton, he sent get-well cards and promises of a fishing trip to Capahosic. Spaulding admitted to his comrades that, after "becoming grey from worry," he had "learned to relax" at the Algonquin Club in

14. Letters from C. C. Spaulding to O. H. Lennon, July 21, 1941; to P. B. Young, November 24; to D. C. Deans, December 8, 1943, Spaulding Papers; *Whetstone*, second and third quarters, 1944; first quarter, 1945.

Durham, where he "beat all the young men" at pool and chinese checkers.[15]

The old war horse had begun to put himself out to pasture. If he had worries after the war, they reflected those of the stereo- typed American businessman: labor unions, communism, and perhaps Mrs. Spaulding's account at Bonwit Teller. In the 1930's he had cheered the CIO for organizing black workers; now he took offense at "outside forces" infiltrating his agencies in Phila- delphia and Pittsburgh. He questioned the loyalty of those who joined the union—what had happened to the Mutual spirit? He stood too close to history to understand that the spirit had neces- sarily suffered from big money and modernization. For a new generation he was no longer "Papa," nor was the Mutual the only opportunity in sight. Spaulding wanted it both ways—per- haps the impossible—a tightly knit family and an imitation of the Met.[16]

In his last years there was less and less to separate "Mr. Negro Business" from the business world at large. "What we want," he told *Time* magazine, "is not Negro businesses but businesses [run] by Negroes."[17] But "all businesses will fail," he warned, unless "we combat godless communism."[18] The emerging black Cold Warrior may have seen the specter of communism as a hostage held by Negroes to demand full democracy, but increas-

15. Ethel S. Berry to Dr. Roscoe C. Brown, October 9; letters from C. C. Spaulding to George Washington Carver, June 21; to Carl Murphy, January 17; to F. L. McCoy, August 19, 1939; to Fred R. Moore, January 19, 1940, January 23, 1941; to R. R. Moton, April 2; to Joseph Jenkins, January 23, 1940; to T. E. McCurdy, May 15, 1945; to Elbert K. Fretwell, February 5, 1947; to L. A. Alexander, July 29, 1948; Fred R. Moore to Spaulding, January 11, October 17, 1940; January 15, 1941, Spaulding Papers; interview, George Wayne Cox, Jr., April 4, 1968.
16. Ethel Berry to C. C. Spaulding, January 18, 1945; T. O. Spaulding to C. C. Spaulding, April 12, 1950; Report to the Owners of the North Carolina Mutual Life Insurance Company, *Philadelphia Tribune*, July 24, 1951; Robert Lipton to Directors of North Carolina Mutual, August 6, 1941; G. W. Cox to Asa T. Spaulding, August 29; C. C. Spaulding, Summary Statement to the Un- ion, October 5; C. C. Spaulding to Policyholders, October 22, 1951; C. C. Spauld- ing to Agents, form letter, n.d., Spaulding Papers.
17. *Time*, LVI (September 11, 1950), 95–96.
18. C. C. Spaulding, typescript of speech given in Atlanta, Ga., 1951 (no exact date); also see Spaulding, "The Negro in the Next 50 Years," *Chicago Defender*, October 14, 1950.

ingly he was taken in by his own rhetoric, by his own success and sentimental reflections on "what America means to me."[19]

More significant, however, was what Spaulding meant to America. If the South needed him as an example to refute indictments from the North, the nation needed him even more to serve as counterpropaganda to the communists. His article in *American Magazine* was reprinted in a variety of languages for consumption in Europe, India, and Africa; a senator read the story into the *Congressional Record*; and Harcourt Brace publishers purchased the same piece for a high school literature text, which introduced the selection as evidence to still "the voices . . . some of them no doubt following the Party Line, [that] have been clamoring, 'America is no longer a land of opportunity.' "[20]

The saga of C. C. Spaulding and the North Carolina Mutual lay very close to the heart of the American value system. Even Hollywood, with its hand ever near the nation's pulse, agreed that here was the stuff of an American fantasy. The Mutual Story permitted America to pass through the looking-glass and invert fantasy into reality, to hide the unhappiness of its history behind the illusion of one bright moment. The much-heralded example caught America in one of its many contradictions regarding race. Pointing to Spaulding, the nation denied its racism, but it did so in the incriminating context of suggesting that if he, a Negro, could make it in America, anybody could make it. Spaulding was the ordinary and the oddity all at once: 100 percent American, typecast from the most familiar script, and cultural anomaly, held in great fascination because as a black man he acted out of character. If his achievement was the predictable outcome of opportunity under free enterprise, why all the uncommon celebration? It was not without meaning when the old man's heart

19. C. C. Spaulding, "What America Means to Me," *American Magazine*, CXLVI (December, 1948), 21ff.

20. *Raleigh News and Observer*, April 23, 1950; clipping from the *Congressional Record*, U.S. Senate, March 2, 1949, p. 1765; W. H. Cunningham to C. C. Spaulding, August 10, 1949. Cunningham was editor of the literature text; Spaulding approved the draft of his introduction (Spaulding to Cunningham, August 12, 1949, Spaulding Papers).

failed in the summer of 1952 that Durham held the largest funeral in its history, and that the mayor of the city, in "an unprecedented action," set aside an official "day of respect to the
memory and works of C. C. Spaulding."[21]

The death of C. C. Spaulding ended an era, but only in a
personal sense. The process of secularization and its attendant
prosperity continued without interruption. (See Table 10.) The
Mutual never missed a stride when W. J. Kennedy, Spaulding's
brother-in-law, assumed the presidency; indeed, Kennedy had
been managing most of the day-to-day affairs of the Company
for a quarter of a century anyway.

Shortly before Spaulding's death the Mutual secured a license
to operate in New Jersey. Early in 1953 it opened an agency in
Newark, thus continuing a methodical trend of territorial expansion that pursued the endless black migration to the ghettoes
in the North and West. By 1961 the Mutual had journeyed all
the way to California—to Watts; the next year to Illinois through
the absorption of Unity Mutual Life, a black firm in Chicago;
and in 1969 to Michigan and Ohio through a similar arrangement with Great Lakes Mutual, a black company in Detroit.
This expansion, like the black migration itself, placed new strains
on cultural unity. Increasing heterogeneity among employees
and policyholders, the logistical demands of distance, keener
competition from northern white firms, and the general growth
of an enterprise toward a stature both modern and national in
scope inevitably produced a management more technical and
specialized, more impersonal and secular than ever before.

The mood of the Mutual during the 1950's was quiet, steady,
and optimistic—much like the man who ran the Company. The
optimism flowed in part from continued business success and in
larger part from the surrounding euphoria of the civil rights
movement. W. J. Kennedy was only one of thousands of Negro
leaders who saw the nation becoming more democratic because
the Supreme Court in 1954 said it should be so. These were tran-

21. *Durham Morning Herald,* August 2; *Durham Sun,* August 2; *Carolina
Times,* August 9, 1952.

TABLE 10. NORTH CAROLINA MUTUAL LIFE INSURANCE COMPANY
ASSETS AND LIFE INSURANCE IN FORCE, 1950–70

Year	Assets	Insurance in force
1950	$ 29,541,387	$ 63,002,404 (O)*
		89,946,432 (I)*
		152,948,836
1952	37,694,297	74,935,491
		104,231,311
		179,166,802
1954	45,751,269	90,185,303
		115,287,384
		205,472,687
1956	54,001,033	109,736,742
		123,376,563
		233,113,305
1958	61,104,149	124,583,395
		130,243,244
		254,826,639
1960	67,600,990	140,180,119
		137,006,539
		277,186,658
1962	76,762,506	158,993,000
		178,050,000
		337,043,000
1964	85,376,436	178,949,000
		176,767,000
		355,716,000
1966	89,800,177	266,394,000
		179,392,000
		445,786,000
1968	98,313,816	294,719,000
		188,494,000
		483,213,000
1970	118,048,833	512,247,000
		236,608,000
		748,855,000

* O = Ordinary
  I = Industrial

SOURCE: *Best's Life Insurance Reports*, 1951, p. 709; 1953, p. 767; 1955, p. 911; 1957, p. 1124; 1959, pp. 1244–1245; 1961, p. 1367; 1963, p. 852; 1965, p. 987; 1967, p. 1034; 1969, p. 1083; 1971, p. 1078. Best's rounds off figures after 1960. Ordinary figures since 1960 include all group insurance; the 1970 ordinary total, for example, includes $158,473,000 of group insurance.

sitional years in which the black leadership worked and waited
for integration. Black businessmen provided no exception. They
hailed *Brown* v. *Board of Education,* and they talked about a
"unified national economy" and access to the "larger market."
They could not predict precisely how this would happen or how
soon; in the meantime they understandably experienced ambivalence. After decades of sustenance from a market protected
by segregation, the black entrepreneur looked to integration as
the warrior looked to peace. Nonetheless integration appeared
as an inevitable good, and hence racial solidarity as a device
whose days were numbered. It was no coincidence that 1954
was also the year that the National Negro Insurance Association
changed its name to the National Insurance Association, or
that shortly thereafter the National Negro Business League
became simply the National Business League and its *Journal of
Negro Business,* very appropriately, the *Mainstream.*[22]

The Mutual too deemphasized race. It soft-pedaled the old
slogans of solidarity and modeled its advertisements after the
industry. Alongside the mood of integration, more tangible signs
of an open society attracted the Company toward the assimila-
tionist view. In 1955 Governor Luther Hodges appointed Kennedy to the North Carolina State Board of Higher Education
and sent him to a White House conference on education hosted
by Vice-President Richard M. Nixon. In 1956 the United States
included Asa T. Spaulding in its five-member delegation to a
United Nations conference at New Delhi, India. By the early
1960's Congress had admitted the Mutual into the select pool of
life insurance companies underwriting group life coverage for
federal employees and military personnel; and more significantly, the American Life Convention and the Life Insurance
Association of America, the lofty and lily-white sovereigns of the
life insurance trade associations, lowered their race barriers and
made the Mutual their first black member.[23]

22. National Insurance Association, *Proceedings,* Thirty-fourth Annual Meet-
ing, 1954; National Business League, mimeographed minutes, Fifty-seventh
Annual Meeting, Washington, D.C., 1956; other information on file at NBL
Headquarters, Washington, D.C., kindly made available by David Rice.
    23. W. J. Kennedy, Jr., *The North Carolina Mutual Story* (Durham: North

White competition as much as anything else compelled the Company to think of itself as a part of the larger industry. In 1940 the vast majority of white underwriters still refused to insure Negroes at all, and of the 55 firms that did solicit Negro risks, only 5 did so at standard rates. By 1957 over 100 white companies competed for black policyholders, often at standard rates, and added to this competition was a steady increase in the number of black companies: from 15 in 1930 to 46 in 1960. If the Mutual was to maintain its share of this limited market and to keep its best agents out of the hands of white recruiters, it would indeed have to emulate at least the technical characteristics of the Metropolitan. In the long run it would have to do more than that. At one and the same time it would have to strengthen its social bonds with the black community and begin a courtship with the white market.[24]

Black businessmen could continue to live in a relatively comfortable half-way house between the two worlds, but Kennedy and Asa Spaulding, who succeeded him in 1959, sensed that such a choice admitted ultimate extinction. With this in mind the Company in 1961 founded its Department of Corporate Planning and hired an innovative outsider to direct it. Much of the burden, then, for finding the way between the worlds fell on the shoulders of a gifted young M.B.A. from the University of Chicago, Murray J. Marvin. As director of planning, Marvin spent much of the next five years expressing plans for the future of the Mutual through the construction of its new home office building. To some it seemed that he was intent on bringing Chicago to Durham. He proposed a twenty-two story office tower—"Mutual Plaza"—with space four times beyond the immediate needs of

Carolina Mutual Life Insurance Company, 1970), pp. 180–183, 186–187, 217, 254; *Whetstone*, fourth quarter, 1956; interview, Asa T. Spaulding, July 18, 1968.

24. Winfred O. Bryson, Jr., "Negro Life Insurance Companies" (Ph.D. dissertation, University of Pennsylvania, 1948), pp. 8–9; Robert C. Puth, "Supreme Life: The History of a Negro Life Insurance Company" (Ph.D. dissertation, Northwestern University, 1967), pp. 147, 170; David Abner III, "Some Aspects of Negro Legal Reserve Insurance Companies, 1930–1960" (Ph.D. dissertation, Indiana University, 1962), pp. 56, 230. The increase in the number of black insurance firms refers here only to legal reserve companies.

Parrish Street and specifications that purposely exceeded those of the General Services Administration. Although the structure was scaled down by one-half, Marvin's concept remained: Mutual Plaza would lease several of its floors to the federal government as planned through the Washington contacts of Viola Turner, Asa Spaulding, and John H. Wheeler, and this in turn would act as another entering wedge to the political economy of the nation. Socially, the Mutual saw itself striking down Jim Crow, and only the naïve could miss the satisfying irony of white public officials residing as tenants in a black-owned high rise.[25]

Was the Mutual moving toward the mainstream or the mainstream toward the Mutual? To many black observers it made no difference—the Mutual was "turning white." Louis Austin, never one to pin his hopes on white people, grew angry when he learned that the Mutual's expensive rates tied the black firm to powerful white tenants and, in effect, excluded local black lawyers, doctors, and dentists. The dedication of the new building also elicited a mixed response from the black community. This was no common ceremony, but rather a five-day "Dedication Festival" with a formal banquet in the Gothic "Great Hall" at Duke University and formal seminars on every likely topic from "The Negro in Business" to "The Negro in Sports." A galaxy of black professionals participated, including Robert Weaver, Andrew Brimmer, Benjamin Mays, J. Saunders Redding, Arna Bontemps, and Claude "Buddy" Young. But white dignitaries dominated the scene. In addition to Vice-President Humphrey, Secretary of Commerce John T. Connor, and North Carolina Governor Dan K. Moore, there were in attendance a number of congressmen and senators, a selection of representatives from foreign embassies, the vice-president of Bank of America, and in general "more federal officials in one place," jested Humphrey, than at any time "since the last Cabinet meeting." The Mutual had not meant to appear "dicty," but neither had it presented a folk event.[26]

25. *Whetstone*, fourth quarter, 1963; Kennedy, *The North Carolina Mutual Story*, pp. 217, 253; interview, Murray J. Marvin, April 3, 1972.
26. *Whetstone*, second quarter, 1966; North Carolina Mutual program,

Parrish Street had no more than moved itself up to Duke Street when Stokely Carmichael, in the summer of 1966, announced a new era of black pride and "Black Power." The mood of black power caught the Mutual in what some perceived as full flight toward whiteness, and thus vulnerable to the fire of its black critics. The importance of this conflict must be viewed in the light of the long-standing black ambivalence over the Mutual's location in the white community, just as it must be viewed in the larger context of more than a century of tension in the national Afro-American community over questions of class and culture. Everyone agreed that no economic institution in the community held more "black power" than did the Mutual, but the criticism centered on the cultural legitimacy of the institution—its "blackness," its class values.

The post-1966 revolution brought generations of discord before a telescope, and to older heads things appeared badly out of focus. Slogans of racial solidarity they had grown up on, many of them from the repertoire of Booker T. Washington, now came from the mouths of their militant critics. What had once brought the Ku Klux Klan to Parrish Street—whites working in the Mutual building—now brought radical blacks to Duke Street. After fifty years of defending themselves against the charge of self-segregation, and after only recently passing through the "revolutionary" sit-in movement, old Mutualites now encountered young nationalists, sometimes the same persons who had their heads beaten at Woolworths, demanding to know, "Why all the white people in *our* cafeteria?"

If black power amplified the confusion of voices from the Afro-American past, it also made it easier to hear the harmony beneath the dissonance. Differences in class and culture were real and important, yet the common heritage counted for something. Those who searched the past for the institutional precedents of black power unavoidably came face to face with the Mutual. In many cases, mostly style and status separated a man like W. J. Kennedy from the nationalist proponents of "black

---

"Dedication Festival, March 28–April 2, 1966"; interviews, Louis Austin, January 15; Conrad O. Pearson, February 13; Mrs. Viola G. Turner, June 13, 1968.

capitalism." He had practiced many of their proposals, and he had heard their every idea, often more eloquently spoken, from Booker T. Washington, Marcus Garvey, W. E. B. Du Bois, Elijah Muhammad, and C. C. Spaulding. Moreover, the Mutual could point to its recent past as evidence that it had by no means isolated itself from the struggle of its people. Had it not celebrated the independence of Ghana, hosted Pan-African theorist George Padmore as well as the militant African socialist Sékou Touré; posted bonds for those arrested in the Durham sit-ins; contributed $25,000 to the United Negro College Fund; invested the maximum of its portfolio in mortgage loans for black homeowners, including a black housing development in Lawndale, New Jersey; and demanded that the architect and contractors for its new building be either black or have a high quota of black workers? But one might have expected at least that much. Now, under the aegis of an aroused black consciousness, the Company found itself free to think about doing much more. It could once again think of itself as a black institution, and advertise itself as such, without fear of counteracting the civil rights movement or exploiting a captive clientele.

By 1968, the year Joseph Goodloe succeeded Asa Spaulding as president, the Company could begin to have it both ways—like other ethnic groups. It spoke confidently of its "stake in the future of America," and at the same time it reclaimed its black past: "Mutualized" its employees, revitalized the Forum and Founders Day, and initiated the Merrick-Moore-Spaulding Achievement Award. It successfully developed its "black pride" advertising theme at the same time it launched its "Operation Big Push," a strategy designed to secure group policies from large white corporations. In the judgment of agency director W. A. Clement, the phenomenon of black power promoted sales with the black masses and attracted the black bourgeoisie back from the Metropolitan. More importantly the new intensity of black protest, highlighted by the holocaust of urban rebellion, pressured white business to support black business. From the beginning of 1969 to the end of 1971 the Mutual experienced almost incredible growth in its life insurance in force: from

$483,212,705 to $1,035,074,118, thus becoming the first black company to pass the important billion-dollar mark.

Most of that increase, over $400,000,000, came from group insurance contracts with the likes of General Motors and IBM. General Motors, stimulated by the troubled times and the astute salesmanship of Murray J. Marvin, W. A. Clement, and home office director Maceo A. Sloan, gave the Mutual $125,000,000 of its group business. Marvin had only to suggest that for GM to "count NCM in" was an opportunity for the industrial giant to express its "social concern" and its commitment to "minority progress through minority enterprise," a means to complement its black hiring program, and obviously a chance to gain greater "identification" with the Negro market. What appealed to General Motors also appealed to Chrysler, Procter and Gamble, Sun Oil, Atlantic Richfield, and a host of others.

This dramatic growth through group insurance came as the most significant event in the recent history of the Company—as much for social as for economic reasons. In effect, the Mutual now possessed a large number of white policyholders, and conversely, they now owned a part of the Mutual. No longer could the Company identify itself as black-owned, but rather as "black-managed," and it also felt constrained to declare itself an "equal opportunity employer"—to hire whites as a complement to its new policyholders. There is a nice irony in all of this: white industrial workers dependent in time of distress on payments from a black institution, or a half-dozen token whites working for the big Negro enterprise. But what if white society should ever take seriously this gesture of reciprocity? Should not the Mutual employ whites in direct proportion to the source of its income? Should not there be white managers, officers, and directors? If the Reverend Leon H. Sullivan is a board member of both General Motors and the Mutual, should not the Mutual someday soon invite a GM executive to join its directors? And if none of this happens, should not whites then proclaim, "Don't buy where you can't work"?

The justifiable answer to these and similar questions might be no, but in any event the Company has reached a critical juncture.

It could lose its ethnic identity overnight in an intermarriage with white corporations; yet if it does not pursue such relationships, it stands to lose its newfound economic strength. For the first time in its history, and well ahead of the rest of black society, the Mutual is free to exercise meaningful choices; it is in a position to oversee its own integration. This is a new experience for Afro-Americans. For C. C. Spaulding, who could not join the Durham Chamber of Commerce, integration was an academic question; for W. J. Kennedy III,[27] it is a palpable alternative. To the extent that the Mutual moves uncritically into the American mainstream, or to the extent that it conceives its alternatives as limited to either separation or integration and interprets both alternatives through the bias of business opportunity, it risks the loss of that critical sense so necessary to secure its own identity, as well as the opportunity to make a fresh statement on black economic development, the institutional relationship between blacks and whites, and the social behavior of all American business institutions.

There need not be a dilemma at all—so long as the Company maintains a conscious distinction between integration and ethnic pluralism. Unconsciously, its home office building represents a model of this distinction. Mutual Plaza is often advertised as integrated; whites do indeed outnumber blacks four to three, but there is little integration. The floors occupied by the Mutual are virtually black; those occupied by tenants, predominantly white. The building is more layer cake than marble cake, and thus it poses as an analogue to the multi-ethnic nation around it. Unwittingly the Company has prepared its own lesson in pluralism.

Booker T. Washington's hope, as well as that of the Mutual leadership and the U.S. government, was that the example of the North Carolina Mutual would foster an entrepreneurial tradition sufficiently powerful to purge the legacy of slavery and caste. The Company can point with pride to over seventy years

27. In October, 1972 (after this book had gone to press), W. J. Kennedy III, son of W. J. Kennedy, Jr., succeeded Joseph W. Goodloe as seventh president of the North Carolina Mutual.

of economic activity that has paid its black policyholders over $180,000,000 in benefits and $18,000,000 in dividends; provided black homeowners and black institutions nearly $30,000,000 in mortgage loans; and pumped into the community well over $100,000,000 in wages and salaries to its thousands of black employees. Yet in the context of uplift, this is a drop in the ocean. "Black capitalism" has reemerged, however, as a highly touted theory of liberation. Such an idea may yet bear fruit, but not simply in emulation of the Mutual, which remains in many respects *sui generis*, and not without massive assistance from both public and private sources, which raises again the unsettling question of autonomy.

The emergence of the Mutual as another triumph of American capitalism ought not to obscure the half-century or more that it lived as a creature of caste in the backwaters of that system, where through sheer will it learned to adapt and to survive in the margins of economic opportunity. In retrospect, its history appears less a dramatic episode of American business success than an enduring social process deeply enmeshed in the whole of Afro-American life and thought. To be mindful of the process is not to dim the celebration of the success, but only to ask that the exception not be taken as the rule and that there remain a capacity to criticize an economic system which kept the black man on the mudsill.

The North Carolina Mutual may not prove to be a model for liberation, but if it remembers its history it will never forsake its people nor the stern advice of Dr. Moore, who fifty years ago hoped his comrades would never "so forget their responsibility to the race as to measure their efforts by dollars and cents." "If the company cannot live on [that] truth," the black doctor added, "then let her go."

Sources

No effort is made here to account for all sources consulted in this study; rather, the emphasis is on what I found to be the most useful and in some cases the most obscure. There is little point in listing recent secondary materials easily found in standard bibliographies, but there is some value, I think, in listing fugitive and esoteric items, both primary and secondary, that are pertinent to black business and that the interested scholar might not otherwise find in one place.

The Charles Clinton Spaulding Papers made this study possible, or at least its scope and direction. These voluminous, uncatalogued papers, along with the smaller collection of William Jesse Kennedy, Jr., are in possession of the North Carolina Mutual Life Insurance Company and are not open to scholars on a general basis. Together, the two collections contain material dating roughly from 1920 to 1958, including approximately 100,000 manuscript items along with other thousands of receipts, reports, speeches, clippings, and a vast store of miscellany. The papers are thin until 1930, but very full thereafter, although they are less valuable after World War II, in my opinion. In addition to this main body of largely unsorted material, W. J. Kennedy has established an unofficial Company archive which contains biographical sketches, photographs, clippings, pamphlets, reports, and North Carolina Mutual printed literature of both antiquarian and scholarly interest.

Obviously, other manuscript sources related to this topic are fugitive at best. The Julian Shakespeare Carr Papers at the University of North Carolina's Southern Historical Collection are largely a mass of speeches which vividly portray white supremacy in politics and the character of race relations in early twentieth-century Durham. The Duke Family Papers at Duke University yielded a small number of letters to North Carolina Mutual officials and other early leaders of the Durham black community, usually in regard to the philanthropy administered by Benjamin Newton Duke. The Charles N. Hunter and Rencher N. Harris Papers, both also at Duke University, are two of a scant number of black manuscript collections. Hunter, ex-slave, educator, editor, businessman, Republican politician, and North Carolina Mutual manager of the Raleigh district, 1907–8, carried on correspondence with Mutual executives during and after his employment. His papers, of course, are more valuable for other topics of research. Rencher Harris spent most of his life working in the Mutual circle, eventually emerging as head of Bankers Fire Insurance Company and then becoming better known as Durham's first Negro city councilman. His papers have a perfunctory quality and are of limited value before the 1950's. There are few topics in Afro-American history that would not be enriched by research in the Booker T. Washington Papers at the Library of Congress. Although Washington corresponded very little with the North Carolina Mutual, this massive collection is a vital source for understanding the scope and character of the early Negro business movement. Washington's secretary, Emmett J. Scott, also left a large and valuable collection of papers—at Morgan State College—and it likewise is an important source for the history of Negro business. Scott corresponded with Dr. Moore and C. C. Spaulding, but there is little of real significance on the Mutual. However, the collection appears to be full of information on the Standard Life Insurance Company. The United States Archives, Department of Foreign and Domestic Commerce, record group 151, folder 402.10, holds interesting correspondence (1927–29) between C. C. Spaulding and government officials concerning the formation of federally sponsored programs to encourage black business. The NAACP Papers at the Library of Congress produced a surprising amount of significant correspondence revealing the involvement of Mutual leaders in the Hocutt case, the fight in North Carolina for equal teachers' salaries, and the recurring efforts to organize a chapter of the NAACP in Durham. The Urban League Papers at the Library of Congress, on the other hand, disclosed nothing not already seen in the Spaulding Papers. Similarly, the Howard W. Odum and Commission on Interracial Cooperation Papers at the Southern Historical Collection added little, because the Spaulding Papers supplied both sides of that correspondence.

Newspaper research for this study could have been prohibitive, had not the Company maintained a newspaper morgue—in addition to the clippings filed away in the Spaulding Papers. Moreover, John Avery and W. J. Kennedy kept private scrapbooks, and it was Kennedy who saved the priceless issues of the very early black newspapers in Durham: the *North Carolina Mutual*, the *Durham Negro Observer*, and the *Durham Reformer*. A newspaper clipping collection of immense size and value is the five-hundred-volume mine of information at Hampton Institute, which helped to fill gaps on the early history of the Company and beyond this is an invaluable source for Afro-American history, 1900–1920. This select base of clippings made it possible to pursue leads into the major Negro newspapers themselves, particularly the *New York Age, Baltimore Afro-American, Chicago Defender, Pittsburgh Courier, Norfolk Journal and Guide, Atlanta Independent*, and of course the *Carolina Times*, which began in the early 1920's but unfortunately was not saved, except as clippings, until 1938, when Duke University began its collection. The Duke Library also has most of the early white newspapers of Durham: the *Morning Herald, Daily Sun, Recorder*, and *Tobacco Plant*.

Out of necessity interviews became an indispensable source. It was often out of the two dozen or more interviews that went into this study that I discovered what to ask of the documentary materials and that I recovered information otherwise lost forever. If oral sources are sometimes unreliable, so are written sources, and pluralism operates here just as it does with documents. By testing one interview against another as well as against documentation and by interviewing persons both inside and outside the Company, both friends and foes of the Company, and both blacks and whites, I hope to have established what will pass for "historical truth."

There is no recent general history of black life insurance or of black business. William J. Trent's master's thesis, "Development of Negro Life Insurance Enterprises," written in 1932 at the University of Pennsylvania, and M. S. Stuart's *Economic Detour: A History of Insurance in the Lives of American Negroes* (1940) are the best sources available on insurance. The relevant chapters in August Meier's *Negro Thought in America* (1963) offer the best historical analysis of black business in the era of Booker T. Washington, and Abram Harris's *The Negro as Capitalist* (1936) is a good older study of black

business by a black economist. Harris concentrates on Negro banking, but his first chapter provides the best published summary of
Negro business before the Civil War, most of it taken from Eugene
M. Boykin's "Enterprise and Accumulation of Negroes Prior to 1860,"
a master's thesis done at Columbia University in 1934. Indeed, most
other monographs on black business and its institutions are unpublished theses and dissertations. These and other titles, along with full
citations of short titles mentioned here, are listed below. There is
valuable material on black business practices and institutions in the
literature of sociology-anthropology, particularly in the unpublished
memoranda of the Carnegie-Myrdal Study of the Negro in America
and of course in Myrdal's *An American Dilemma* (1944), and in the
works of E. Franklin Frazier, Horace Cayton, St. Clair Drake, and
Hortense Powdermaker (see below). One could advance a long way
toward a general study of black business using the resources, many
of them virtually untapped, of Howard University, Hampton Institute, Atlanta University, and Tuskegee Institute: the Hampton and
Tuskegee Annual Negro Conference Reports, Atlanta University Publications, Howard University Studies in Social Studies, and Howard
University Commercial College Studies of Negroes in Business, for
example, along with other special studies, reports, proceedings,
pamphlets, and clippings. These institutions, together with the Library of Congress and the New York Public Library Schomburg Collection, offer a complete run of the *Proceedings* of the National Negro
Business League and other Negro trade association publications. The
Southern Workman published by Hampton, the *Crisis* by the NAACP,
Opportunity by the Urban League, and a host of lesser-known Negro
periodicals like *Alexanders Magazine*, many of them recently reprinted or made available on microfilm, are key sources on the subject. And of course, in addition to the North Carolina Mutual, other
long-established black businesses may have valuable collections. Universal Life Insurance Company in Memphis, Tennessee, for example,
is rumored to be such a storehouse.

The resurgence of interest in black capitalism since 1966 has produced a large new body of secondary literature. No attempt is made
to treat that here since most of it is not historical, but an excellent
summary of both the old and the new arguments on black economic
development is found in Ron Bailey, ed., *Black Business Enterprise:
Historical and Contemporary Perspectives* (New York: Basic Books,
1972).

SELECT LIST OF INDIVIDUAL TITLES

DOCUMENTS, REPORTS, AND PROCEEDINGS

Best's Life Insurance Reports, 1918–71. New York: Alfred M. Best and Company.

Brown, W. H. *The Education and Economic Development of the Negro in Virginia*. Publications of the University of Virginia Phelps-Stokes Fellowship Papers, no. 6. Charlottesville: University of Virginia, 1923.

Burrell, William Patrick. "The Negro in Insurance." *Proceedings* of the Hampton Negro Conference, VIII, July, 1904. Hampton, Virginia: Hampton Institute Press, 1904.

Du Bois, William Edward Burghardt, ed. *Economic Cooperation among Negro Americans*. Atlanta University Publication no. 12. Atlanta: Atlanta University Press, 1907.

———. *Efforts for Social Betterment among Negro Americans*. Atlanta University Publication no. 14. Atlanta: Atlanta University Press, 1910.

———. *The Negro in Business*. Atlanta University Publication no. 4. Atlanta: Atlanta University Press, 1899.

———. *Some Efforts of American Negroes for Their Own Social Betterment*. Atlanta University Publication no. 3. Atlanta: Atlanta University Press, 1898.

Gilpin, C. B., ed. *Biographies of Presidents and Secretaries of the National Negro Insurance Association*, 1921–49.

Gover, Mary. *Mortality among Negroes in the United States*. Public Health Bulletin, no. 174. Washington, D.C.: U.S. Government Printing Office, 1928.

Hines, George W., and Cook, George W. *Negro Insurance*. Howard University Commercial College Studies of Negroes in Business, no. 11. Washington, D.C.: Howard University Press, 1939.

Houchins, Joseph R. *Causes of Negro Insurance Company Failures*. Bulletin no. 15, April, 1937. Washington, D.C.: U.S. Department of Commerce, 1937.

———. *The Negro Trade Association*. Washington, D.C.: Negro Affairs Division, Bureau of Foreign and Domestic Commerce, November, 1936.

Jones, Eugene Kinckle. "The Negro in Business, 1936: A Bibliography" (mimeographed). Washington, D.C.: Negro Affairs Division, Bureau of Foreign and Domestic Commerce, September, 1936.

Larkins, John R. *The Negro Population of North Carolina.* Special Bulletin no. 23. Raleigh, N.C.: State Board of Charities and Public Welfare, 1944.

Mitchell, James B. *The Collapse of the National Benefit Life Insurance Company: A Study of High Finance among Negroes.* Washington, D.C.: Howard University Press, 1939.

Pace, Harry Herbert. "Organizing the First Old Line Negro Insurance Company." National Negro Business League Fourteenth Annual *Report.* Philadelphia, 1913.

Tandy, Elizabeth C. *Infant and Maternal Mortality among Negroes.* Publication no. 243. Washington, D.C.: Department of Labor, Children's Bureau, 1937.

Thom, William Taylor. *The True Reformers.* Department of Labor Bulletin no. 41, July, 1902. Washington, D.C.: U.S. Government Printing Office, 1902.

United States Bureau of the Census. *Negroes in the United States.* Bulletin no. 8. Washington, D.C.: U.S. Government Printing Office, 1904.

———. *Negro Population 1790–1915.* Washington, D.C.: U.S. Government Printing Office, 1918.

———. *Negroes in the United States 1920–1932.* Washington, D.C.: U.S. Government Printing Office, 1935.

BOOKS

American Academy of Political and Social Science. *The Negro's Progress in Fifty Years.* Philadelphia: American Academy of Political and Social Science, 1913.

Andrews, Robert McCants. *John Merrick: A Biographical Sketch.* Durham: Seeman Printery, 1920.

Boyd, William Kenneth. *The Story of Durham: The City of the New South.* Durham: Duke University Press, 1927.

Brawley, Benjamin Griffith. *Negro Builders and Heroes.* Chapel Hill: University of North Carolina Press, 1946.

Burgess, Margaret Elaine. *Negro Leadership in a Southern City.* Chapel Hill: University of North Carolina Press, 1960.

Burrell, William Patrick. *Twenty-five Years History of the United Order of True Reformers.* Richmond: Privately printed, 1909.

Caldwell, Arthur Bunyan, ed. *History of the American Negro and His Institutions.* 7 vols. Atlanta: A. B. Caldwell, 1917.

Cayton, Horace Roscoe, and Drake, St. Clair. *Black Metropolis: A Study of Negro Life in a Northern City.* 2 vols. Revised edition. New York: Harper and Row, 1962.

Cox, Oliver C. "Leadership among Negroes." In Alvin W. Gouldner, ed., *Studies in Leadership.* New York: Harper and Brothers, 1950.

Cromwell, John Wesley. *The Negro in American History: Men and Women Eminent in the Evolution of the American of African Descent.* Washington, D.C.: American Negro Academy, 1914.

Dabney, Wendell Phillips. *Maggie Lena Walker and the Independent Order of St. Luke: The Woman and Her Work.* Cincinnati: Dabney Publishing Company, 1927.

Davis, Daniel Webster. *The Life and Public Services of Reverend William Washington Browne.* Richmond: Mrs. M. A. Browne Smith, 1910.

Dublin, Louis Israel. *The Effect of Health Education on Negro Mortality.* Toronto: National Council of Social Workers, 1924.

———. *Mortality Statistics of Insured Wage Earners.* New York: Metropolitan Life Insurance Company, 1919.

———. *Twenty-five Years of Health Progress.* New York: Metropolitan Life Insurance Company, 1937.

Du Bois, William Edward Burghardt. *Dusk of Dawn.* New York: Harcourt Brace, 1940.

———. *The Philadelphia Negro: A Social Study.* Philadelphia: University of Pennsylvania, 1899.

———. *Souls of Black Folk.* Chicago: A. C. McClurg, 1903.

Dula, William C. *Durham and Her People.* Durham: Citizens Press, 1951.

Edmonds, Helen Grey. *The Negro and Fusion Politics in North Carolina, 1894–1901.* Chapel Hill: University of North Carolina Press, 1951.

Frazier, Edward Franklin. *Black Bourgeoisie.* Glencoe, Ill.: The Free Press, 1957.

———. *The Negro Family in the United States.* Revised ed. Chicago: University of Chicago Press, 1966.

———. *The Negro in the United States.* Revised ed. New York: Macmillan Company, 1957.

———. "Durham, Capital of the Black Middle Class." In Alain

Locke, ed., *The New Negro: An Interpretation*. New York: Albert and Charles Boni, 1925. Pp. 333–340.

Fuller, Thomas Oscar. *Twenty Years in Public Life*. Memphis: T. O. Fuller, 1913.

Gay, Joseph R. *Life Lines of Success: A Practical Manual of Self Help for the Future Development of the Ambitious Colored American*. Chicago: W. R. Vansant and Company, 1913.

Grimshaw, William H. *Official History of Free Masonry among the Colored People of North America*. Montreal: Broadway Publishing Company, 1903.

Harlan, Louis R. "Booker T. Washington and the National Negro Business League." In William G. Shade and Roy C. Herrenkohl, eds., *Seven on Black: Reflections on the Negro Experience in America*. New York: J. B. Lippincott Company, 1969.

Harmon, John Henry, Jr.; Lindsey, Arnett G.; and Woodson, Carter G. *The Negro as a Business Man*. Washington, D.C.: Association for the Study of Negro Life and History, 1929.

Harris, Abram Lincoln. *The Negro as Capitalist: A Study of Banking and Business among American Negroes*. Philadelphia: American Academy of Political and Social Science, 1936.

Hartshorn, William Newton. *An Era of Progress and Promise, 1863–1910: The Religious, Moral, and Educational Development of the American Negro since His Emancipation*. Boston: Priscilla Publishing Company, 1910.

Hill, Timothy Arnold. *The Negro and Economic Reconstruction*. Washington, D.C.: Associates in Negro Folk Education, 1937.

Hoffman, Frederick Ludwig. *History of the Prudential Insurance Company of America, 1875–1900*. New York: Prudential Press, 1900.

———. *Race Traits and Tendencies of the American Negro*. New York: Macmillan Company, 1896.

Hunter, Charles N. *Negro Life in North Carolina with My Recollections*. No imprint, 1928.

Jackson, Giles B. *The Industrial History of the Negro Race of the United States*. Richmond: Virginia Press, 1908.

Keech, William R. *The Impact of Negro Voting*. Chicago: Rand McNally and Co., 1968.

Kennedy, William Jesse, Jr. *The North Carolina Mutual Story*. Durham: North Carolina Mutual Life Insurance Company, 1970.

Kinzer, Robert H., and Sargarin, Edward. *The Negro in American*

Business: The Conflict between Separatism and Integration. New York: Greenburg, 1950.

Kip, Richard DeRaimes. *Fraternal Life Insurance in America.* Philadelphia: College Offset Press, 1953.

Ladd, Everett Carll, Jr. *Negro Political Leadership in the South.* Ithaca, N.Y.: Cornell University Press, 1966.

Mabry, William Alexander. *The Negro in North Carolina Politics since Reconstruction.* Durham: Duke University Press, 1940.

Meier, August. *Negro Thought in America, 1880–1915.* Ann Arbor: University of Michigan Press, 1963.

Murray, Pauli. *Proud Shoes: The Story of an American Family.* New York: Harper and Brothers, 1956.

Myrdal, Gunnar. *An American Dilemma.* 2 vols. New York: Harper and Row, 1944.

Nichols, J. L., and Crogman, William Henry, eds. *Progress of a Race: The Remarkable Advancement of the Afro-American.* Naperville, Ill.: J. L. Nichols and Company, 1920.

Oak, Vishnu Vitthal. *The Negro's Adventure in General Business.* Yellow Springs, Ohio: Antioch Press, 1949.

Odum, Howard Washington. *Social and Mental Traits of the Negro.* New York: Columbia University Press, 1910.

Paul, Hiram Voss. *History of the Town of Durham, North Carolina.* Raleigh: Edwards, Broughton and Company, 1884.

Pierce, Joseph Alphonse. *Negro Business and Business Education.* New York: Harper and Brothers, 1947.

Pitts, Nathan Alvin. *The Cooperative Movement in Negro Communities of North Carolina.* Washington, D.C.: Catholic University of America Press, 1950.

Powdermaker, Hortense. *After Freedom: A Cultural Study in the Deep South.* New York: Viking Press, 1939.

Richardson, Clement, ed. *The National Cyclopedia of the Colored Race.* Montgomery, Ala.: National Publishing Company, 1919.

Richings, G. F. *Evidences of Progress among Colored People.* Philadelphia: G. S. Ferguson Company, 1902.

Rogers, Joel A. *World's Great Men of Color.* 2 vols. New York: J. A. Rogers, 1947.

Simms, James N. *Blue Book and National Negro Business and Professional Directory.* Chicago: James N. Simms, 1923.

Washington, Booker Taliaferro. *The Negro in Business.* Boston: Hertel, Jenkins and Company, 1907.

————. *The Story of the Negro.* 2 vols. New York: Doubleday, Page and Company, 1909.

————. *Up from Slavery.* Cambridge: Riverside Press, 1900.

————, and W. E. B. Du Bois. *The Negro in the South: His Economic Progress in Relation to His Moral and Religious Development.* Philadelphia: George W. Jacobs and Company, 1907.

Weatherford, Willis Duke. *Negro Life in the South: Present Conditions and Needs.* New York: Young Men's Christian Association, 1910.

Woodson, Carter Godwin. *The Negro Professional Man and the Community.* Washington, D.C.: Association for the Study of Negro Life and History, 1934.

Wright, Richard Robert, Jr. *The Negro in Pennsylvania: A Study in Economic History.* Philadelphia: A.M.E. Book Concern Printers, 1912.

ARTICLES

Aery, William Anthony. "Business Is Life: A Survey of Negro Progress." *Survey,* XXX (September 13, 1913), 709–710.

————. "The Negro in Business." *Southern Workman,* XLII (October, 1913), 522.

Allen, Isabel Dangaix. "Negro Enterprise: An Institutional Church." *Outlook,* LXXXVIII (September 17, 1904), 179–183.

————. "The Savings Bank Militant." *Outlook,* LXXVII (May 14, 1904), 118–122.

Barnhart, W. L. "How Barbers' Tips Started Flourishing Negro Life Insurance Companies." *Insurance Field,* LIV (August 6, 1926), 6.

Blayton, Jesse B. "The Negro in Banking." *Banker's Magazine,* CXXXIII (December, 1936), 511–514.

Bond, Horace Mann. "Negro Leadership since Washington." *South Atlantic Quarterly,* XXIV (April, 1925), 115–130.

Browning, James Blackwell. "The Beginning of Insurance Enterprise among Negroes." *Journal of Negro History,* XXII (October, 1937), 417–432.

Calloway, T. J. "Negro as a Business Man." *World's Work,* XVI (June, 1908), 10348–10351.

Carter, Elmer A. "Negro Business in Transition." *Opportunity,* VII (August, 1929), 236.

Clements, Forrest. "Racial Differences in Mortality and Morbidity." *Human Biology,* III (September, 1931), 397–419.

Cohn, David Lewis. "Durham: The New South." *Atlantic Monthly,* CLXV (May, 1940), 614–619.

Dublin, Louis I. "The Health of the Negro." *Annals of the American Academy of Political and Social Science,* CXL (November, 1928), 77–85.

———. "Life, Death and the Negro." *American Mercury,* XII (September, 1927), 37–45.

Du Bois, William Edward Burghardt. "The Upbuilding of Black Durham." *World's Work,* XXIII (January, 1912), 334–338.

Edwards, Paul K. "Negro Business and Economic Advancement." *Opportunity,* XII (March, 1934), 80–82.

Fitchett, Elijah Horace. "The Traditions of the Free Negro in Charleston, South Carolina." *Journal of Negro History,* XXV (April, 1940), 139–152.

Frazier, E. Franklin. "The American Negro's New Leaders." *Current History,* XXVIII (April, 1928), 56–59.

———. "Some Aspects of Negro Business." *Opportunity,* II (October, 1924), 293–297.

"Growth of Negro Business." *Literary Digest,* LXXXI (October 25, 1924), 62.

Hamilton, Joseph Gregoire de Roulhac. "The Sons and Daughters of I Will Arise." *Scribners Magazine,* LXXX (September, 1926), 325–331.

Harmon, John Henry. "The Negro as a Local Business Man." *Journal of Negro History,* XIV (April, 1929), 116–155.

Holland, Thomas W. "Negro Capitalists." *Southern Workman,* LV (December, 1926), 536–540.

Holsey, Albon L. "Business Points the Way." *Crisis,* XXXVIII (July, 1931), 225–226.

———. "The CMA Stores Face the Chains." *Opportunity,* VII (July, 1929), 210–213.

———. "The National Negro Business League—Forty Years in Review." *Crisis,* XLVIII (April, 1941), 104–105.

———. "Negro Business." *Messenger,* IX (November, 1927), 321.

———. "Pearson: The Brown Duke of Durham." *Opportunity,* VI (April, 1923), 116–117.

———. "The RFC and the Negro." *Opportunity,* XII (March, 1934), 87–90.

———. "Seventy-five Years of Negro Business." *Crisis,* XLV (July, 1938), 201.

Johnson, Charles Spurgeon. "Negro Business and Public Confidence." *Opportunity*, III (March, 1925), 66.

———. "Notes on a Trip with the Business Men's Party." *Opportunity*, II (June, 1924), 186–188.

———. "A Sound Negro Business Institution." *Opportunity*, II (August, 1924), 247.

———. "A Task for the National Negro Business League." *Opportunity*, IV (August, 1926), 241.

Johnson, Guy Benton. "Negro Racial Movements and Leadership in the United States." *The American Journal of Sociology*, XLIII (July, 1937), 56–72.

———. "A Stock Taking Conference on the Negro." *Social Forces*, VI (March, 1928), 445–447.

Johnson, James A. "Where Negro Insurance Falls Down." *Opportunity*, XVII (August, 1939), 239–240.

Keyes, J. B. "Big Business for Negroes." *Southern Workman*, XLIV (April, 1915), 239.

Meier, August. "Negro Class Structure and Ideology in the Age of Booker T. Washington." *Phylon*, XXIII (Fall, 1962), 258–266.

———, and Lewis, David. "History of the Negro Upper Class in Atlanta, Georgia, 1890–1958." *Journal of Negro Education*, XXVIII (Spring, 1959), 128–139.

"Aaron McDuffie Moore, M.D." *Journal of the National Medical Association*, XVI (January–March, 1924), 72–74.

Moton, Robert Russa. "Business Progress." *Southern Workman*, LIV (October, 1925), 443.

———. "Business Prosperity of the Negro." *Southern Workman*, LIII (October, 1924), 469.

———. "A Definite Business Program." *Southern Workman*, LI (October, 1922), 453.

———. "National Negro Business League: Business Progress of the Negro." *Southern Workman*, LII (November, 1923), 531.

———. "National Negro Business League: New Business Program." *Southern Workman*, LI (October, 1922), 453–457.

———. "The Significance of Mr. Washington's Lecture Trip in Mississippi." *Southern Workman*, XXXVII (December, 1908), 691–695.

———. "Signs of Growing Cooperation." *Southern Workman*, XLIII (October, 1914), 552.

"North Carolina Mutual." *Opportunity*, II (August, 1924), 247.

Pace, Harry H. "The Attitude of Life Insurance Companies toward Negroes." *Southern Workman*, LVII (January, 1928), 3–7.

———. "The Business of Insurance among Negroes." *Crisis*, XXXII (September, 1926), 219–224.

———. "The Possibilities of Negro Insurance." *Opportunity*, VIII (September, 1930), 266–269.

Palmer, Edward Nelson. "Negro Secret Societies." *Social Forces*, XXIII (October, 1944), 207–212.

Pettiford, W. R. "How to Help the Negro to Help Himself." *Southern Workman*, XXX (November, 1901), 586–589.

Reid, Ira DeAugustine. "Social Problems of Negro Business." *Crisis*, XLIII (June, 1936), 166–167.

Richardson, Clement. "What Are Negroes Doing in Durham?" *Southern Workman*, XLII (July, 1913), 385.

Rutledge, Archibald. "They Call Him Mr. Cooperation: World's Biggest Negro Business and Its Founder." *Saturday Evening Post*, CXV (March 27, 1943), 215.

Spaulding, Asa Timothy. "Negro Insurance." *Best's Insurance News*, Life ed. (December, 1943), 17, 36–37, 40–44.

Spaulding, Charles Clinton. "Business in Negro Durham." *Southern Workman*, LXVI (December, 1937), 364–368.

———. "Business Is My Business." *Negro Digest*, I (February, 1943), 32–33.

———. "Is the Negro Meeting the Test in Business?" *Journal of Negro History*, XVIII (January, 1933), 66–70.

Tucker, David M. "Black Pride and Negro Business in the 1920's: George Washington Lee of Memphis." *Business History Review*, XLIII (Winter, 1969), 435–451.

Washington, Booker Taliaferro. "Durham, North Carolina: A City of Negro Enterprise." *Independent*, LXX (March 30, 1911), 642–650.

———. "Fifty Years of Negro Progress." *Forum*, LV (March, 1916), 269–279.

———. "The National Negro Business League." *World's Work*, IV (October, 1902), 2671–2675.

Wheelcock, Fred D. "A Successful Negro Building and Loan Association." *Southern Workman*, LIII (December, 1923), 600.

Woodson, Carter Godwin. "Insurance Business among Negroes." *Journal of Negro History*, XIV (April, 1929), 202–226.

Work, Monroe N. "Fifty Years of Negro Progress." *Southern Workman*, XLII (January, 1913), 9.

————. "The Negro in Business and the Professions." *Annals of the American Academy of Political and Social Science,* CXL (November, 1928), 138–144.

————. "A Survey of Negro Business, 1863–1923." *Messenger,* V (November, 1923), 868–869.

UNPUBLISHED MATERIALS

Abner, David, III. "Some Aspects of the Growth of Negro Legal Reserve Life Insurance Companies, 1930–1960." Ph.D. dissertation, Indiana University, 1962.

Arnold, Adam S., Jr. "The Investment of Seven Negro Life Insurance Companies." Ph.D. dissertation, University of Wisconsin, 1951.

Bowman, Robert Louis. "Negro Politics in Four Southern Counties." Ph.D. dissertation, University of North Carolina, 1964.

Boyd, Harold Kent. "Louis Austin and the *Carolina Times.*" Master's thesis, North Carolina College, 1966.

Boykin, Eugene M. "Enterprise and Accumulation of Negroes prior to 1860." Master's thesis, Columbia University, 1934.

Brinton, Hugh Penn. "The Negro in Durham: A Study of Adjustment to Town Life." Ph.D. dissertation, University of North Carolina, 1930.

Brown, Lawrence N. "Insurance on American Negro Lives." Master's thesis, University of Pennsylvania, 1930.

Bryson, Winfred Octavus, Jr. "Negro Life Insurance Companies: A Comparative Analysis of the Operating and Financial Experience of Negro Legal Reserve Life Insurance Companies." Ph.D. dissertation, University of Pennsylvania, 1948.

Burns, Augustus Merrimon. "North Carolina and the Negro Dilemma, 1930–1950." Ph.D. dissertation, University of North Carolina, 1968.

Cole, Olivia W. "Rencher Nicholas Harris: A Quarter Century of Negro Leadership." Master's thesis, North Carolina College, 1967.

Gardner, Thomas J. "Problems in the Development of Financial Institutions among Negroes: Historical Development, Current Trends, and the Future in Business." Ph.D. dissertation, New York University, 1958.

Gloster, Jesse Edward. "North Carolina Mutual Life Insurance Company: Its Historical Development and Current Operations." Ph.D. dissertation, University of Pittsburgh, 1955.

Goldston, Maude Perkins. "An Analysis of Life Insurance Programs of Selected Families in Durham, North Carolina." Master's thesis, North Carolina College, 1962.

Houck, Thomas H. "A Newspaper History of Race Relations in Durham, North Carolina." Master's thesis, Duke University, 1941.

Hypps, Irene C. "Changes in Business Attitudes and Activities of the Negro in the United States since 1619." Ph.D. dissertation, New York University, 1943.

Keech, William R. "The Negro Vote as a Political Resource: The Case of Durham." Ph.D. dissertation, University of Wisconsin, 1966.

Kennedy, William Jesse, Jr. "North Carolina Mutual Life Insurance Company: A Symbol of Progress, 1898–1966." Manuscript in possession of William Jesse Kennedy, Jr., Durham, N.C., 1966.

Kiser, Vernon Benjamin. "Occupational Changes among Negroes in Durham, North Carolina." Master's thesis, Duke University, 1942.

McConnell, Roland Calhoun. "Negro in North Carolina since Reconstruction." Ph.D. dissertation, New York University, 1945.

Muraskin, William. "Black Masons: The Role of Fraternal Orders in the Creation of a Middle Class Black Community." Ph.D. dissertation, University of California, Berkeley, 1970.

Page, Benjamin F. "Social Stratification among Negroes in a Southern Town." Master's thesis, North Carolina College, 1952.

Puth, Robert C. "Supreme Life: The History of a Negro Life Insurance Company." Ph.D. dissertation, Northwestern University, 1967.

Reid, Ira DeAugustine. "The Negro in the American Economic System." Memorandum for the Carnegie-Myrdal Study of the Negro in America, 1940.

Rice, John Donald. "The Negro Tobacco Worker and His Union in Durham, N.C." Master's thesis, University of North Carolina, 1941.

Shils, Edward Albert. "The Bases of Social Stratification in Negro Society." Memorandum for the Carnegie-Myrdal Study of the Negro in America, 1940.

Sproggins, Linsley L. "The History of Negro Business prior to 1860." Master's thesis, Howard University, 1935.

Trent, William Johnson, Jr. "Development of Negro Life Insurance Enterprises." Master's thesis, University of Pennsylvania, 1932.

Waite, E. Emerson, Jr. "Social Factors in Negro Business Enterprise." Master's thesis, Duke University, 1940.

Walker, Harry Joseph. "Changes in Race Accommodation in a South-

ern Community." Ph.D. dissertation, University of Chicago, 1945.
White, Frank Hallowell. "The Economic and Social Development of
Negroes in North Carolina since 1900." Ph.D. dissertation, New
York University, 1960.

Index